Microsoft® Office 2007
for Independent Contractors and Freelancers

Studio Visual Steps

Microsoft® Office 2007 for Independent Contractors and Freelancers

Visual Steps™
www.visualsteps.com

This book is written using the Visual Steps™ method.

© 2008 Visual Steps B.V.

In cooperation with Henk Mol.

Cover design by Studio Willemien Haagsma bNO.

Edited by Ria Beentjes, Rilana Groot and Jolanda Ligthart.

Translated by Yvette Huijsman and Chris Holingsworth.

First printing: December 2008
ISBN 978 90 5905 295 6

Would you like more information?
www.visualsteps.com

Do you have questions or suggestions?
E-mail: info@visualsteps.com

Website for this book:
www.visualsteps.com/office2007freelance

Would you like to subscribe to the free Visual Steps Newsletter?
www.visualsteps.com/newsletter

Table of Contents

Appendices

Foreword

Office programs such as *Outlook, Word, PowerPoint, Publisher* and *Excel* have become the standard tools for the independent professional.

There are many tasks you can quickly and easily perform using *Office 2007*. For example drafting letters, estimates, quotes and invoices, doing project accounting, managing contacts with customers as well as sending and receiving e-mail.

This book provides a large number of complete business forms, documents and accounting models that you can use for your own company. You will learn how to adapt these sample documents to fit your own business. Each procedure is explained in a simple step by step manner. You will be able to quickly create a convenient set of standard documents such as letters, estimates and quotes that will help you save time when you perform your administrative tasks. You will notice that there are many similarities in the controls of the various *Office* programs and that these programs work very well together.

We hope this book will be very useful to you.

The Studio Visual Steps Authors

P.S.
Your comments and suggestions are most welcome.
Our e-mail address is: mail@visualsteps.com

Visual Steps Newsletter

All Visual Steps books follow the same methodology: clear and concise step by step instructions with screenshots to demonstrate each task.
A complete list of all our books can be found on **www.visualsteps.com**
You can also sign up to receive our **free Visual Steps Newsletter**.

In this Newsletter you will receive periodic information by e-mail regarding:
- the latest titles and previously released books;
- special offers, supplemental chapters, tips and free informative booklets.
Also our Newsletter subscribers may download any of the documents listed on the webpages **www.visualsteps.com/info_downloads** and **www.visualsteps.com/tips**

If you subscribe to our newsletter, be assured that we will never use your e-mail address for any purpose other than sending you the information as previously described. We will not share this address with any third-party. Each newsletter also contains a one-click link to unsubscribe.

Introduction to Visual Steps™

The Visual Steps handbooks and manuals are the best instructional materials available for learning how to work with computers. Nowhere else can you find better support for getting to know the computer, the Internet, *Windows* and related software programs.

Properties of the Visual Steps books:
- **Comprehensible contents**
  Addresses the needs of the beginner or intermediate computer user for a manual written in simple, straight-forward language.
- **Clear structure**
  Precise, easy to follow instructions. The material is broken down into small enough segments to allow for easy absorption.
- **Screenshots of every step**
  Quickly compare what you see on your screen with the screenshots in the book. Pointers and tips guide you when new windows are opened so you always know what to do next.
- **Get started right away**
  All you have to do is turn on your computer, place the book next to your keyboard, and begin at once.

In short, I believe these manuals will be excellent guides for you.

dr. H. van der Meij

Faculty of Applied Education, Department of Instruction Technology, University of Twente, the Netherlands

What You Will Need .

In order to work through this book, you will need a number of things on your computer:

- Microsoft Office Word 2007
- Microsoft Office Excel 2007
- Microsoft Office Outlook 2007
- Microsoft Office PowerPoint 2007
- Microsoft Office Publisher 2007

The primary requirement for working with this book is having the right version of **Microsoft Office 2007** on your computer. The *Office* suite is available in various editions that contain different programs.
In this book the following programs are used: *Excel 2007, PowerPoint 2007, Word 2007, Publisher 2007* and *Outlook 2007* with *Business Contact Manager*.

In *Chapter 1 Preparation* you can read more about the different editions of the *Microsoft Office 2007* suite.

Furthermore, you need to have a computer with **Windows Vista** or **Windows XP**.
The screenshots in this book were made on a computer running *Windows Vista*. If you use *Windows XP* the screenshots of *Windows* panes and windows may look a bit different. This makes no difference however in performing the necessary actions.

Internet
Internet Explorer

You also need a functioning **Internet connection** and an e-mail account that is already setup in *Outlook*.

A printer is recommended for some exercises. If you do not have a printer, you can skip the print exercises.

How to Use This Book

This book has been written using the Visual Steps™ method. You can work through this book independently at your own pace.

In this Visual Steps™ book, you will see various icons. This is what they mean:

Techniques
These icons indicate an action to be carried out:

⊕	The mouse icon means you should do something with the mouse.
▦	The keyboard icon means you should type something on the keyboard.
☞	The hand icon means you should do something else, for example insert a CD-ROM in the computer. It is also used to remind you of something you learned before.

Help
These icons indicate that extra help is available:

⇨	The arrow icon warns you about something.
✖	The bandage icon will help you if something has gone wrong.
👣1	Have you forgotten how to do something? The number next to the footsteps tells you where to look it up at the end of the book in the appendix *How Do I Do That Again?*

In separate boxes you find tips or additional, background information.

Extra information
Information boxes are denoted by these icons:

📖	The book icon gives you extra background information that you can read at your convenience. This extra information is not necessary for working through the book.
💡	The light bulb icon indicates an extra tip for using the program.

In the chapter headers a clock is displayed.

🕐 20 min.	The clock in the chapter header indicates the approximate number of minutes you will need to work through that chapter. The indicated time is an estimate. You may be able to work through the chapter slower or faster. The actual time you need depends on your prior knowledge and computer skills.

Prior Computer Experience

This book has been written for people that already have some experience with *Windows*. In order to work through this book successfully, you should be able to perform the following tasks on your computer:

Windows:
- Click, right-click, double-click and drag;
- Use a scroll bar;
- Use tabs.

File management:
- Create a new folder;
- Save something in a folder;
- Copy and delete files;
- Change a file name.

You also need to have some basic knowledge of working with *Office* programs. You should be able to perform the following tasks:

Basic tasks Word:
- Type text, move the cursor, correct typing errors, select text.

Basic tasks Outlook:
- Create e-mail messages, send and receive messages, send an attachment, open and save an attachment.

Basic tasks PowerPoint:
- Open, play and save a presentation, add slides with text, image or music.

Basic tasks Excel:
- Work with cells, rows, columns, select, copy formulas.

If you do not yet have enough basic *Excel* skills you can work through the guide **Basic Excel tasks** located on the website with this book.

How This Book Is Organized

The subjects of this book are grouped by chapter. You can work through these chapters at your own pace and in the order you want. You can also decide to work through just the chapters that are of interest to you. It is advisable to work through a complete chapter from beginning to end. The approximate time it will take to perform the necessary tasks is indicated in each chapter.

This book is created using examples based on rules and laws in the United States and United Kingdom. If you live in another country, please check the rules and laws in your own country. And even when you live in the US or UK, please check the rules and laws from time to time, to be sure they haven't changed.

The Website That Accompanies This Book

This book is accompanied by a website with current information. Any possible changes or errata that are important to you when working though this book can be found on this website:

The web address is:
www.visualsteps.com/office2007freelance

On the website you can also find several additional material, such as the practice files used in this book and several PDF files. You can find the material on the button *Extra material*. You can only access this page using the authorized code: **18231**.

The component *Practice files Office 2007* contains many different files that can be used with the exercises listed in the chapters of this book. There are also several standard business forms, templates and accounting models that can act as basis for your own business administration. You can use this forms and models as many times as you like. This is a zipped folder that you will have to download and upzip to use the files.

The component *Practice files for PDFs* contains the practice files that go with the **PDF guide Writing Data CDs**. This is a zipped folder that you will have to download and upzip to use the files.

The component *PDF files* contains a number of PDF files that serve as additions or replacements of the chapters in this book for *Windows XP* users. You will be pointed to these files as needed in the text of the book. You can open these PDF files with an authorized code: **18231**.
You can print these PDF files using the program *Adobe Reader*. You will then be able to do the exercises, just like you do in the chapters of this book.

The component *Sample logos* contains some examples of business logos created with the program *Paint*. *Paint* is a simple drawing program that comes with *Windows*. Even though *Paint* has limited possibilities, it is suitable to design a fitting logo for your company using your own creativity. The example logos are meant to provide inspiration for your own designs. You can also use the example logos and customize them yourself. The designs are not copyrighted.
This is a zipped folder that you will have to download and upzip to use the files.

Some examples of logos created in *Paint*:

Your Suggestions for the Next Volumes in This Series

Visual Steps is developing a series of books for independent contractors and freelancers that will cover computer applications suitable for business use. The idea is to offer efficient solutions that can be used in your business with only minor adjustments.

Do you like the Visual Steps method and the way the subjects are tackled in this book? Would you like to buy more of these books?
Then send us your suggestions for subjects you would like to see covered. Your comments about this first volume of the series are also more than welcome.

On the website that accompanies this book, **www.visualsteps.com/office2007freelance**, you can find a special survey page where you can enter your opinion about this book and your suggestions for the next volumes. You can send your reaction with just one mouse click.

Every quarter of a year, participants in this survey have the chance to win two Visual Steps books of their own choice. You can find a list of all Visual Steps titles on the website **www.visualsteps.com**

1. Preparation
⏱ 30 min.

In order to work through this book, you will need the *Microsoft Office 2007* suite. There are several different versions of this suite available.
Your *Office* suite should contain the following programs: *Microsoft Word 2007*, *Microsoft Excel 2007*, *Microsoft PowerPoint 2007*, *Microsoft Publisher 2007* and *Microsoft Outlook 2007* with *Business Contact Manager*.
In *section 1.1 Comparing the Different Microsoft Office 2007 Suites* you can read more about the different versions.

To be able to save files in the PDF format you need the free *Save as PDF or XPS add-in* created by *Microsoft*.
PDF and XPS are fixed-layout document formats that preserve document formatting and enable file sharing. For example, you can e-mail invoices or quotes to your customers in the PDF format.

If you have recently purchased your *Office* suite, you will need to install it on your computer. You can learn how to do that in this chapter.

In this chapter you will learn how to:

- install *Microsoft Office 2007*;
- install *Business Contact Manager*;
- download and install the *Save as PDF or XPS add-in*;
- copy the practice files from the website with this book.

⇨ Please note:

The *Office* suite does **not** come with this book. You can purchase the software at a computer store or buy it online, for example on the *Microsoft* website www.microsoft.com or from another online software reseller.

Would you like to try the *Office 2007* suite first before you buy it?
You can download a free 60-day trial version from the webpage
http://us20.trymicrosoftoffice.com/default.aspx
This trial version has the same functionality as the full suite. After the 60-day trial period you can still continue working but with limited functionality.
Due to the fact that there are frequent updates to the *Microsoft* website, it is possible that the webpage mentioned above is renamed or relocated. Type the search term 'trial version Office 2007' in the Search box on the website www.microsoft.com. The hyperlink to the trial version will then be displayed on your screen.

1.1 Comparing the Different Microsoft Office 2007 Suites

Microsoft Office 2007 is available in different versions. Every suite contains a series of programs. Below you see a summary:

	Microsoft Office Basic 2007	Microsoft Office Home & Student 2007[1]	Microsoft Office Standard 2007	Microsoft Office Small Business 2007	Microsoft Office Professional 2007	Microsoft Office Ultimate 2007 NEW!	Microsoft Office Professional Plus 2007	Microsoft Office Enterprise 2007 NEW!
Microsoft Office Word 2007	●	●	●	●	●	●	●	●
Microsoft Office Excel 2007	●	●	●	●	●	●	●	●
Microsoft Office PowerPoint 2007		●	●	●	●	●	●	●
Microsoft Office Outlook 2007	●		●				●	●
Microsoft Office Outlook 2007 with Business Contact Manager[2]				●	●	●		
Microsoft Office Accounting Express 2008[3]				●	●	●		
Microsoft Office Publisher 2007				●	●	●	●	●
Microsoft Office Access 2007					●	●	●	●
Microsoft Office InfoPath 2007						●	●	●
Microsoft Office Groove 2007						●		●
Microsoft Office OneNote 2007		●				●		●
Microsoft Office Communicator 2007[4]							●	●
Integrated Enterprise Content Management[5]						●	●	●
Integrated Electronic Forms[6]						●	●	●
Advanced Information Rights Management and Policy Capabilities[7]						●	●	●

In this book the *2007* editions of *Word, Excel, PowerPoint, Publisher* and *Outlook* with *Business Contact Manager* are used. The suites *Microsoft Office Small Business 2007* and *Microsoft Office Professional 2007* are fully compatible with this book. If your company has a volume license, you can also use the *Microsoft Office Professional Plus 2007* and *Microsoft Office Enterprise 2007* suites. In that case you can download *Outlook 2007 with Business Contact Manager* from the website for volume licensing services.

1.2 Installing Microsoft Office 2007

To be able to install *Office 2007* on a *Windows* computer, you need to be logged in with an administrator account. Then you will not encounter any problems installing *Office 2007*. For the installation you need your *Office* suite DVD:

☞ **Insert the *Office* DVD in your DVD drive**

In most cases, the following window should appear after a few moments:

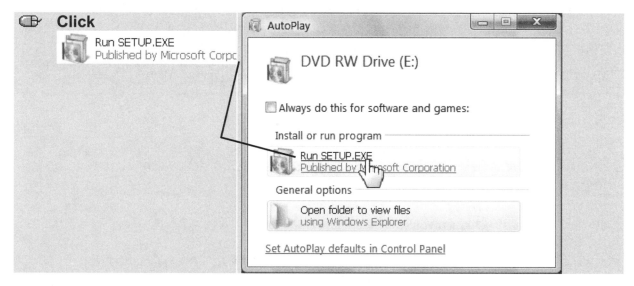

🞨 HELP! The window does not appear.

If the window shown above does not appear on your computer:
In *Windows Vista*:

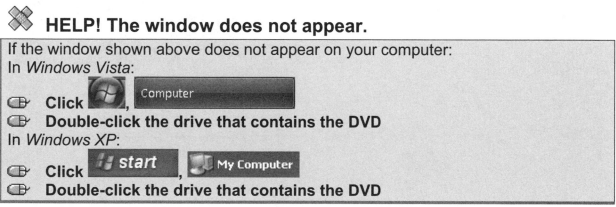

☞ **Click** ,
☞ **Double-click the drive that contains the DVD**
In *Windows XP*:

☞ **Click** ,
☞ **Double-click the drive that contains the DVD**

The installation procedure starts right away. The installation wizard will take you through this procedure in a series of consecutive windows.

☞ **Follow the instructions until the installation process is completed**

Office 2007 is installed. In the next section you can read how to install *Business Contact Manager*.

1.3 Installing Business Contact Manager

Microsoft Office Small Business 2007 and *Microsoft Office Professional 2007* come with an extra CD-ROM that contains the program *Business Contact Manager*. This add-on to *Microsoft Outlook* adds many extra features for business use.

➡ **Please note:**

Business Contact Manager comes packaged with *Microsoft Office Small Business* and *Microsoft Office Professional*.
If your company holds a volume license you can also use the *Microsoft Office Professional Plus 2007* and *Microsoft Office Enterprise 2007* suites. In that case you can download *Outlook 2007 with Business Contact Manager* from the website for volume licensing services. After downloading the software, the installation procedure will be the same as described below.

➡ **Please note:**

Business Contact Manager will not be used until *section 2.9 Business Contact Manager*. We advise you to delay installing *Business Contact Manager* until after you have worked through sections 2.1 – 2.8.

You can install the program like this:

☞ **Insert the *Business Contact Manager* CD-ROM in your DVD drive**

After a few moments this window should appear:

☞ **Click**

    Run SETUP.EXE
    Published by Microsoft Corpc

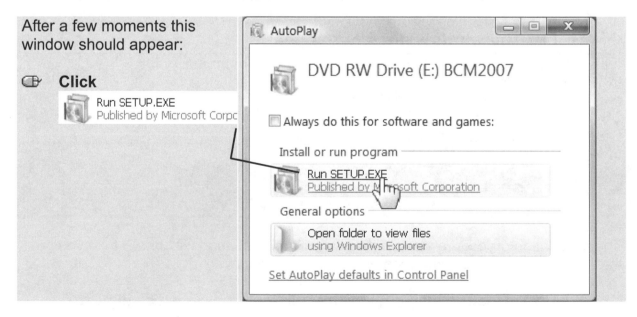

HELP! The window does not appear.

If the window shown previously does not appear on your computer:

In *Windows Vista*:

☞ **Click** ,
☞ **Double-click the drive that contains the CD-ROM**

In *Windows XP*:

☞ **Click** ,
☞ **Double-click the drive that contains the CD-ROM**

⇨ Please note:

Before you continue the installation process, make sure the program *Microsoft Outlook* is not open.

☞ **Click** Next > **in the following two windows**

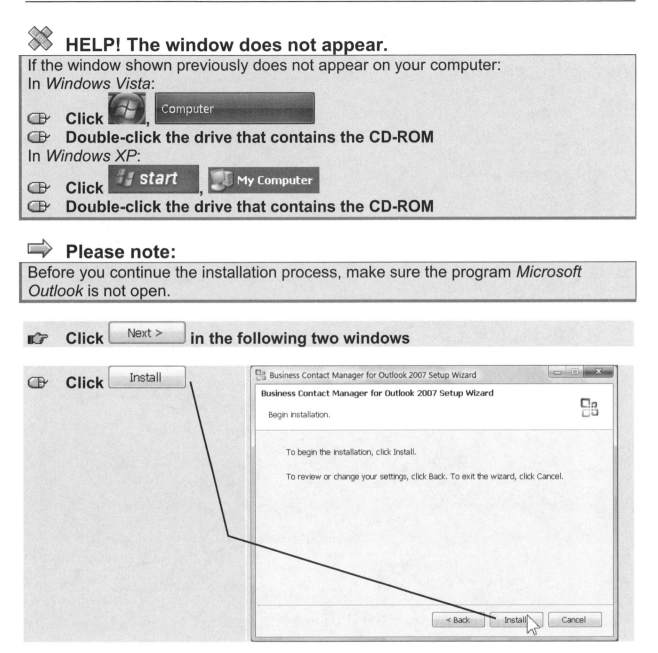

☞ **Click** Install

You can follow the progress in this window:

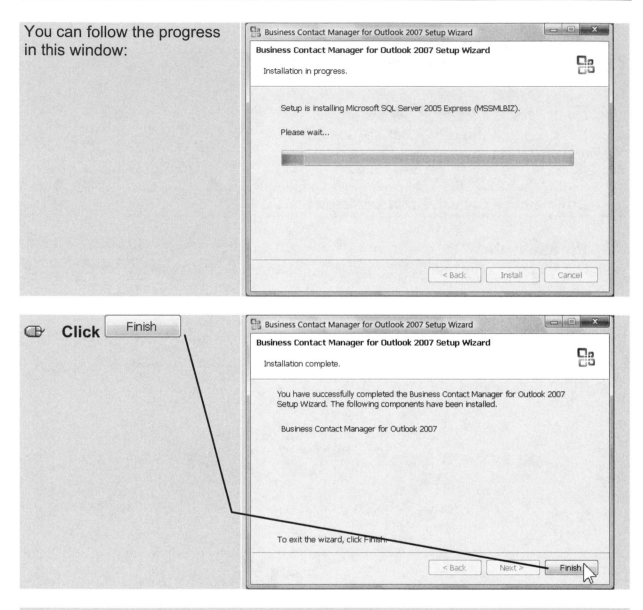

☞ **Remove the CD-ROM from the DVD drive**

☞ **Open *Microsoft Outlook*** 🐾¹

When you open *Microsoft Outlook* with *Business Contact Manager* for the first time, there are a few settings to be configured. You see the *Startup* window:

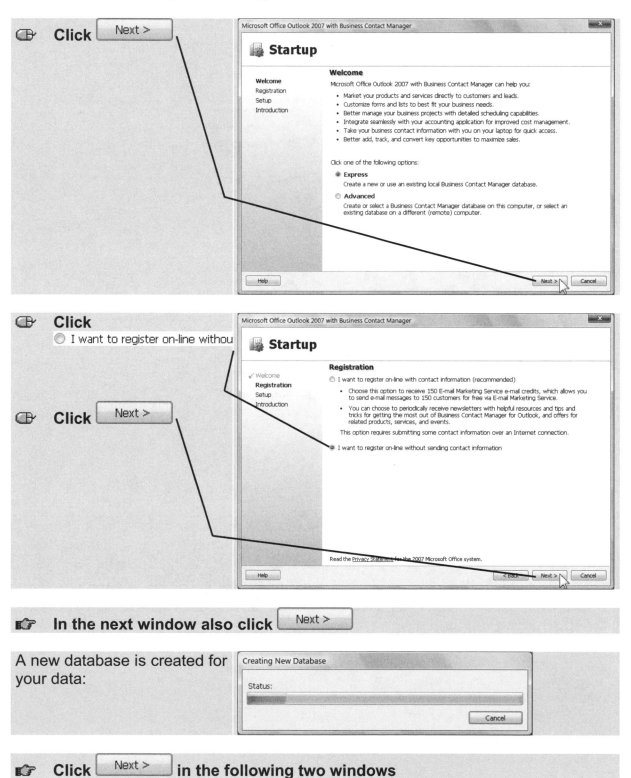

In the next window also click [Next >]

A new database is created for your data:

Click [Next >] in the following two windows

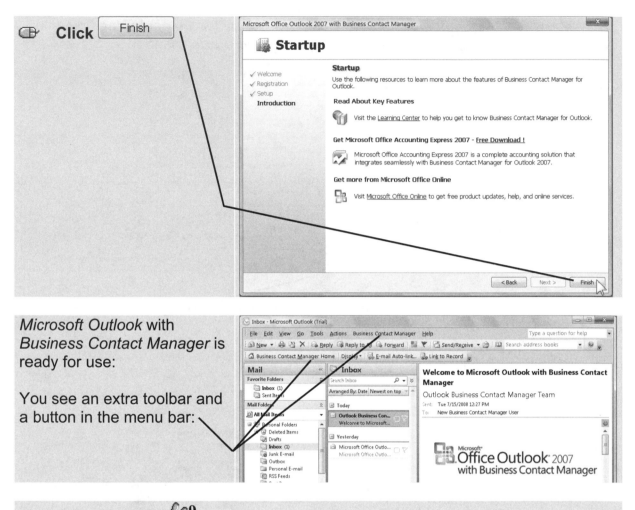

Click [Finish]

Microsoft Outlook with *Business Contact Manager* is ready for use:

You see an extra toolbar and a button in the menu bar:

☞ **Close** *Outlook*

⇨ **Please note:**

When you open other *Microsoft Office* programs you may see the message that the *Office* application version does not match. In that case most likely you will need to download the latest *Windows* and *Office* updates. After installing these updates you will be able to use the *Business Contact Manager* features available in these programs.

💡 **Tip**

A quick feature overview

You most likely will have received a message in your *Inbox* listing the new and updated features of *Business Contact Manager:*

🖱 **Click**

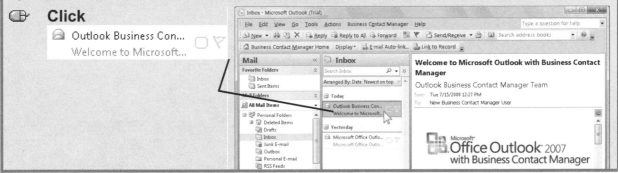

1.4 Installing the Save As PDF or XPS Add-in

You can download the free *Save as PDF or XPS add-in* from the *Microsoft* website.

👉 **Open *Internet Explorer* 🐾41**

👉 **Surf to www.microsoft.com 🐾42**

In the top right corner of the page you see a Search box:

⌨ **Type in the Search box:**
SaveAsPDFandXPS.exe

🖱 **Click** 🔍

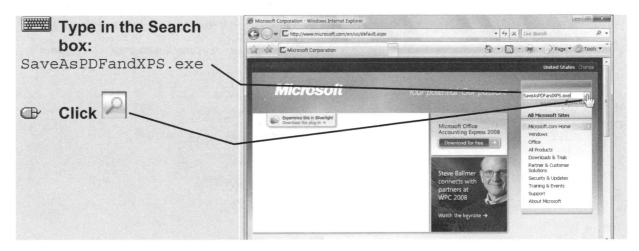

The search results page
shows a list of hyperlinks:

Click
Download details: 2007 Micro
File Name: **SaveAsPDFandPS**

Next, you will need to validate
your version of *Office*:

Click | Continue |

You may see this window
now:

Click | Close |

If you do not see this window,
continue reading on page 29.

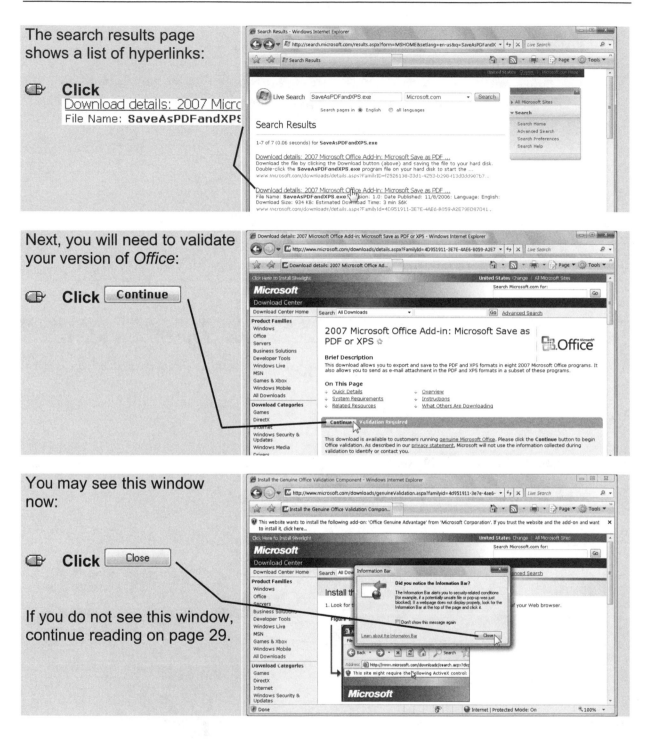

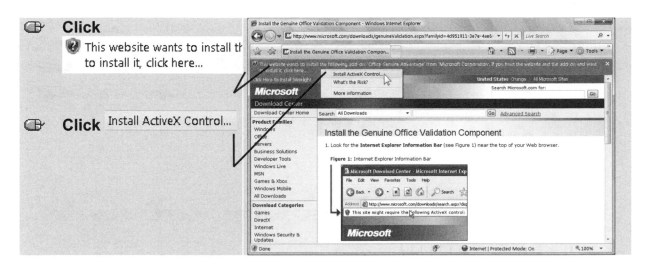

Click

🛡️ This website wants to install th
to install it, click here...

Click Install ActiveX Control...

Your screen goes dark and you need to give your permission to continue:

Click `Continue`

Click `Install`

Internet Explorer Add-on Installer - Security Warning

Do you want to install this software?

Name: Office Genuine Advantage
Publisher: Microsoft Corporation

❯❯ More options   `Install` `Don't Install`

🛡️ While files from the Internet can be useful, this file type can potentially harm your computer. Only install software from publishers you trust. What's the risk?

Click `Continue`

Genuine Office Validation - Windows Internet Explorer

http://www.microsoft.com/downloads/handoff.aspx?familyid=4d951911-3e7e-4ae6-b059-a2e7 ▾ +₊ ✕ Live Search

☆ ☆ Genuine Office Validation   🏠 ▾ 🔊 ▾ 🖶 ▾ Page ▾ Tools ▾

Click Here to Install Silverlight   United States Change | All Microsoft Sites

Microsoft   Search Microsoft.com for: Go
Download Center
Download Center Home   Search All Downloads ▾ Go Advanced Search
Product Families
Windows
Office   **Genuine Office Validation**
Servers
Business Solutions   Thank you for taking part in genuine Office validation. Validating will enable you to receive   **Why Validate?**
Developer Tools   your download now and quickly access other downloads and additional benefits in the
Windows Live   future. To complete the validation process, we need you to provide some additional   ● Greater reliability
MSN   information.
Games & Xbox   ● Faster access to
Windows Mobile   Please click **Continue** to complete the validation process.   support
All Downloads   ● A richer Office
Download Categories   `Continue`   experience
Games
DirectX   Find out more about
Internet   the Office Genuine
Windows Security &   Advantage program.
Updates
Windows Media
Drivers

handoff.aspx?familyid=4d951911-3e7e-4ae6-b059-a2e79ed87041&dis   🔘 Internet | Protected Mode: On   🔍 100% ▾

After the validation process (which checks to see if you are using genuine *Office* software), you can download the add-in:

☞ **Click** | Download |

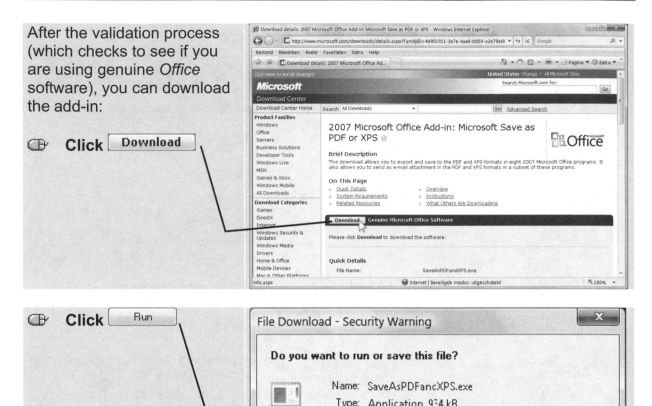

☞ **Click** | Run |

Your screen goes dark and you need to give your permission to continue:

☞ **Click** | Continue |

In this window you will need to accept the software license terms:

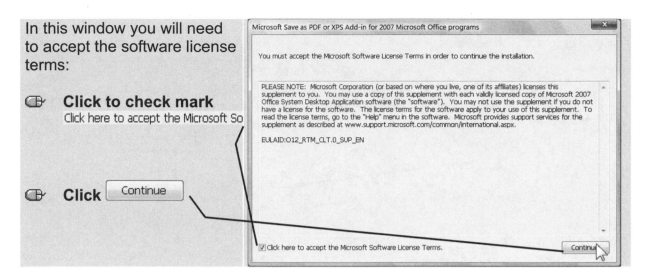

⊂⊃ **Click to check mark**
   Click here to accept the Microsoft So

⊂⊃ **Click** Continue

When the installation is complete you see this window:

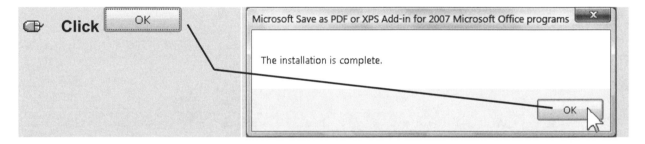

⊂⊃ **Click** OK

The *Save as PDF or XPS add-in* is installed.
In the next section you are going to copy the practice files.

1.5 Copying the Practice Files to Your Computer

To be able to work through all the chapters in this book you will need the practice files that are found on the website with this book. You can copy the folder containing the practice files to your computer like this:

☞ **Open** *Internet Explorer* 🦶⁴¹

☞ **Surf to www.visualsteps.com/office2007freelance** 🦶⁴²

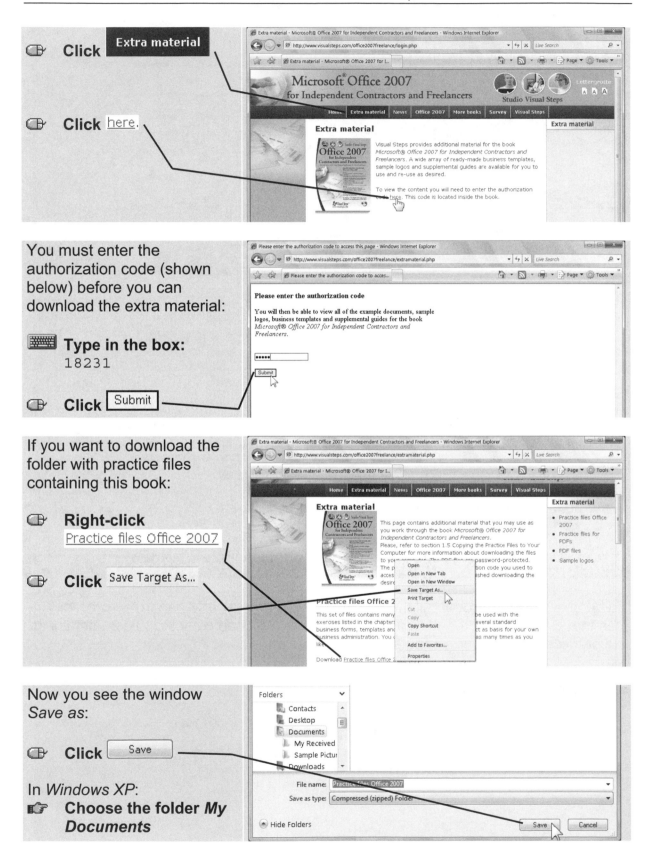

Click Extra material

Click here.

You must enter the authorization code (shown below) before you can download the extra material:

Type in the box:
18231

Click Submit

If you want to download the folder with practice files containing this book:

Right-click
Practice files Office 2007

Click Save Target As...

Now you see the window *Save as*:

Click Save

In *Windows XP*:
☞ **Choose the folder *My Documents***

When downloading is completed, you see this window:

☞ **Click** Open Folder

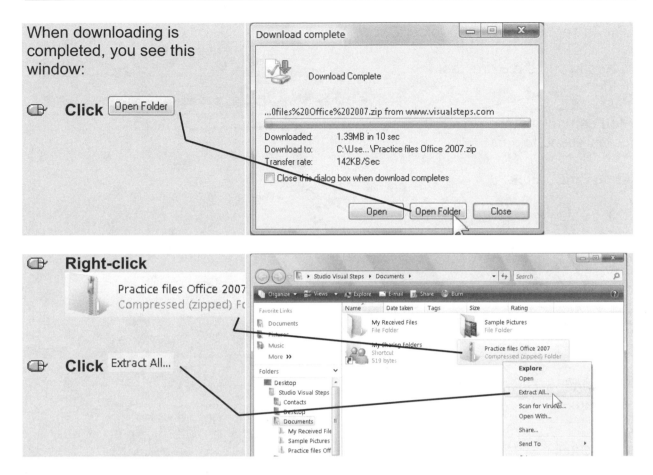

☞ **Right-click**

Practice files Office 2007
Compressed (zipped) Fo

☞ **Click** Extract All...

If you have *Windows XP* on your computer, a wizard will start. In that case, follow the steps in the windows.

The correct location is already selected:

Now you can extract the files:

☞ **Click** Extract

The files will be extracted.

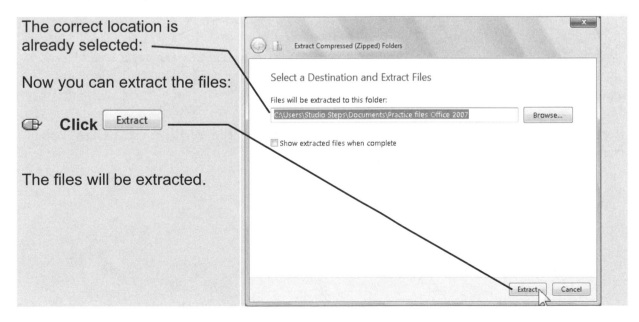

The folder is saved in the folder *Documents*:

You can see the extracted folder:

You can delete the compressed folder:

☞ **Right-click**

   Practice files Office 2007
   Compressed (zipped) Fo

☞ **Click** Delete

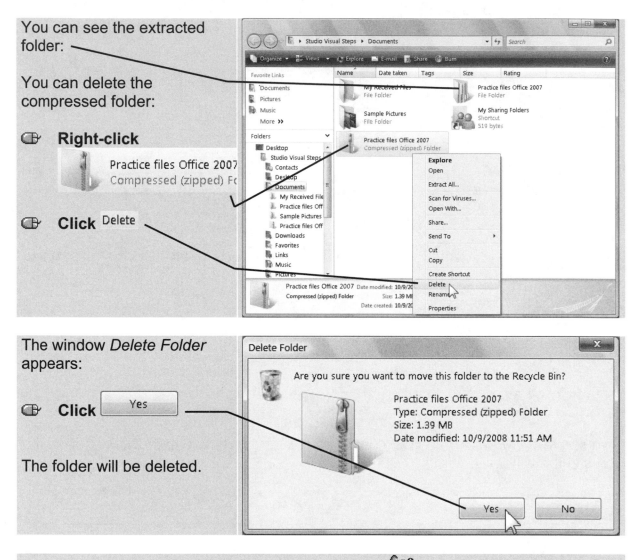

The window *Delete Folder* appears:

☞ **Click** Yes

The folder will be deleted.

☞ **Close the window of the folder *Documents*** 🐾⁹

If you want to use the practice files containing the **PDF file Writing data CDs**, you can follow the same steps as mentioned above.

1.6 Opening the PDF Files from the Website

To open the PDF files from the website, follow these steps:

In the *Internet Explorer* window:

☞ **Drag the scroll bar down**

☞ **Click a PDF file, for example**
Computer Security

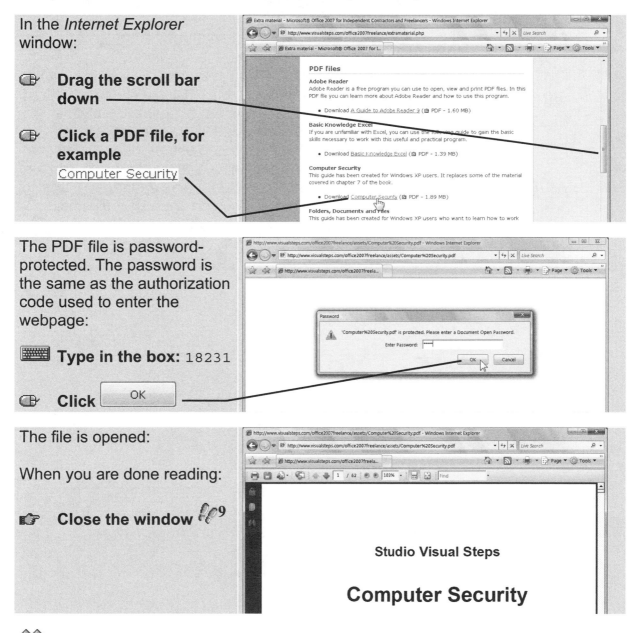

The PDF file is password-protected. The password is the same as the authorization code used to enter the webpage:

⌨ **Type in the box:** 18231

☞ **Click** OK

The file is opened:

When you are done reading:

☞ **Close the window** $\ell\ell^9$

HELP! I cannot open the file or work with the program.

If you cannot open the file, the program *Adobe Reader* might not be installed on your pc. Please refer to the webpage www.visualsteps.com/adobereader to see how you can install the program.
If you don't know how to work with the program *Adobe Reader*, you can download the **PDF file Adobe Reader** first. You can print this document using the button 🖶.

1.7 Background Information

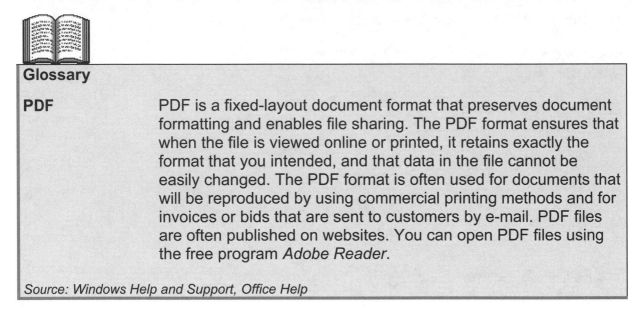

Glossary

PDF	PDF is a fixed-layout document format that preserves document formatting and enables file sharing. The PDF format ensures that when the file is viewed online or printed, it retains exactly the format that you intended, and that data in the file cannot be easily changed. The PDF format is often used for documents that will be reproduced by using commercial printing methods and for invoices or bids that are sent to customers by e-mail. PDF files are often published on websites. You can open PDF files using the free program *Adobe Reader*.

Source: Windows Help and Support, Office Help

2. Customer Relationship Management

⏰ 90 min.

One of the most important things in running a business is the management of your customer relations. By accurately keeping track of your customer data, organizing your contacts and following up on both established and prospective customers, you can quickly adapt to your customer's changing needs and deliver better service. *Microsoft Outlook* is the central program to manage your customer relations.

Business Contact Manager adds additional functionality to *Outlook*. The program enables you to set up marketing campaigns and track their effectiveness for example, or keep track of client-based projects and tasks. With just a few mouse clicks you can create reports and track the history of your accounts.

Regularly updating customer information and entering each action you have taken is essential for customer relationship management. An up to date customer relationship management system is an excellent support for your business activities.

In this chapter you are going to use *Outlook 2007* and *Business Contact Manager*. You will learn the following:

- create and use categories;
- archive documents that belong to contacts;
- create and use electronic business cards;
- organize your e-mail messages in folders;
- search for messages and set up e-mail rules;
- flag and sort messages in mailboxes;
- use search queries and find related messages;
- create accounts and contacts in *Business Contact Manager*;
- keep track of marketing campaigns and opportunities;
- enter projects and project tasks;
- view reports;
- view the history of an account.

➡ **Please note:**

You need to have some previous experience working with *Microsoft Outlook 2007* in order to be able to do the exercises in this chapter. Please refer to page 15 of this book.

⇨ **Please note:**

Starting with section *2.9 Business Contact Manager*, you need to have *Business Contact Manager* preinstalled on your computer. You also need to have copied the *Practice Files Office 2007* folder to your computer. See *Chapter 1 Preparation* for more details.

2.1 Grouping Contacts by Category

In *Outlook* you can store various amounts of information about persons and/or companies in the *Contacts* pane. You can group these contacts by category. In this way you can distinguish between personal contacts, customers and other business contacts.
Start by importing the sample contacts from the folder *Practice files Office 2007*.

☞ **Open** *Outlook* 🖑[1]

☞ **Click** File

☞ **Click** Import and Export...

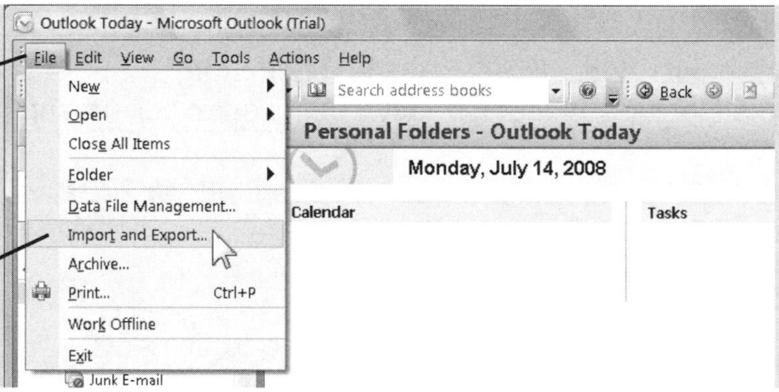

☞ **Click** Next >

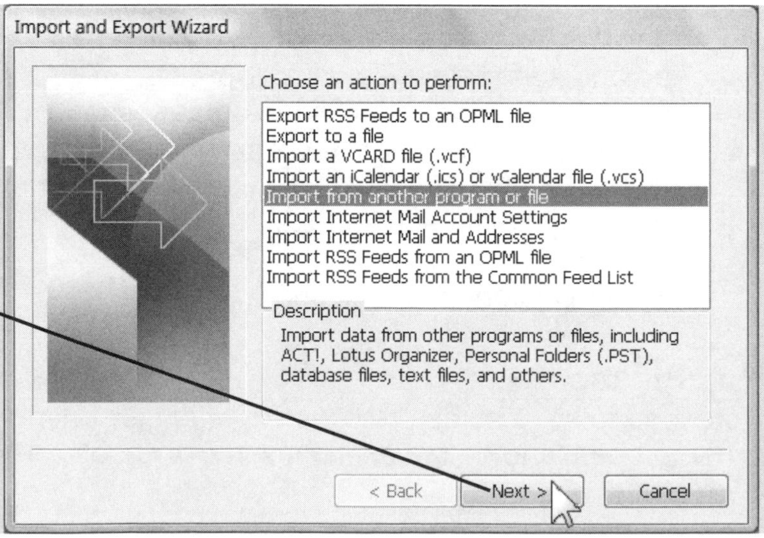

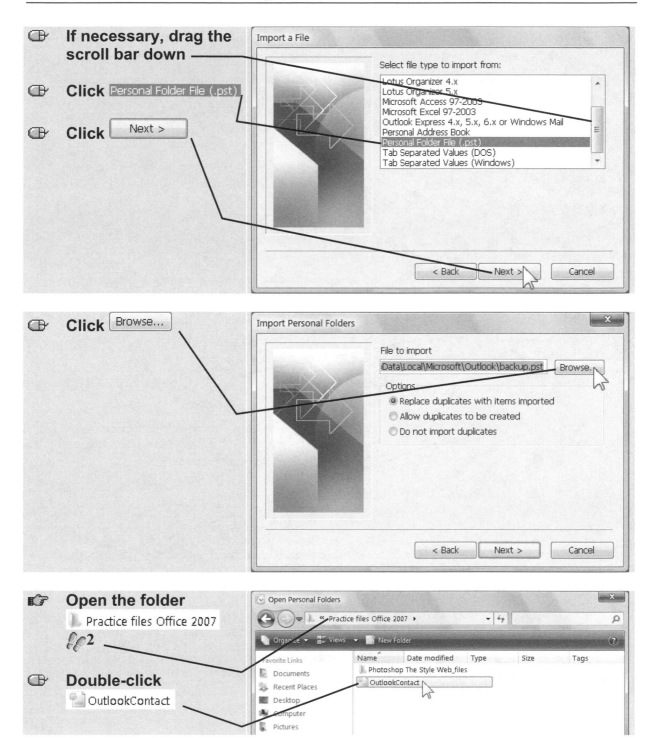

If necessary, drag the scroll bar down

Click Personal Folder File (.pst)

Click Next >

Click Browse...

Open the folder
Practice files Office 2007

Double-click
OutlookContact

Click ○ Allow duplicates to be created

Click Next >

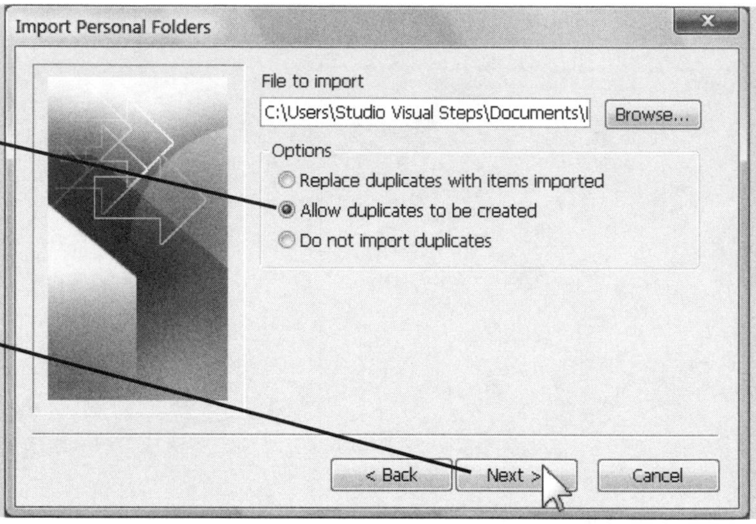

Click Contacts

Click Finish

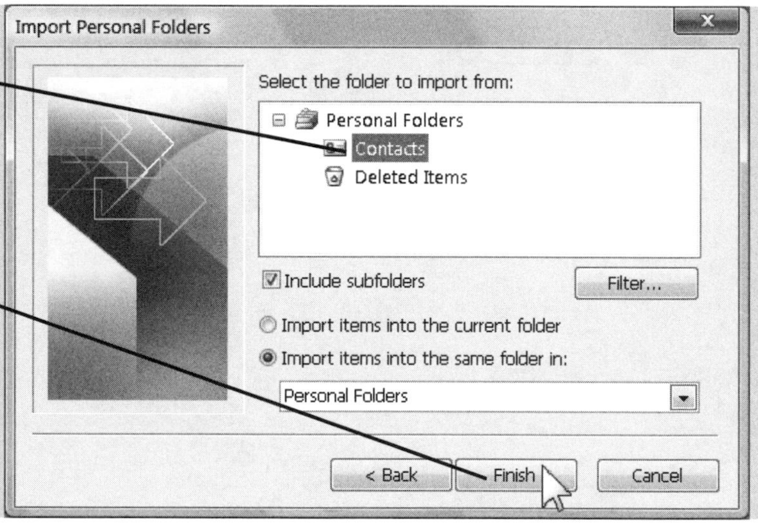

Now the sample contacts are imported.

Click Contacts

You see the contacts you just imported:

If you had previously entered contacts yourself, you will see the imported contacts listed among your own contacts.

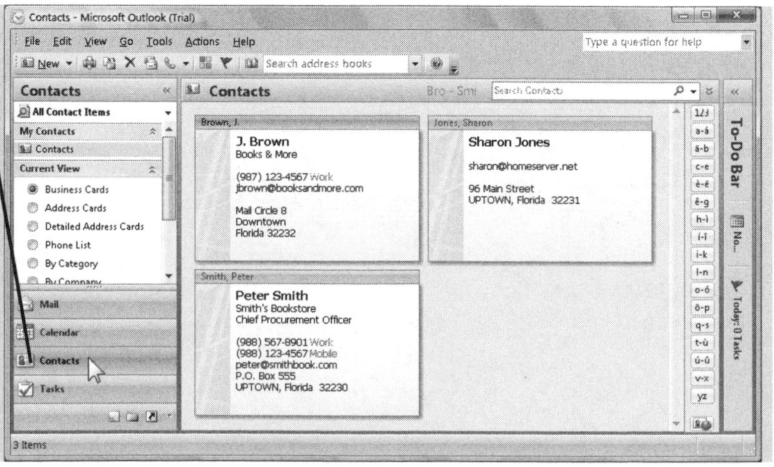

HELP! My window looks different.

To make your window appear the same as in the example shown:

☞ **Click** View , Toolbars

✔	Standard
	Advanced
	Web
	Customize...

☞ **The menu should look like this**

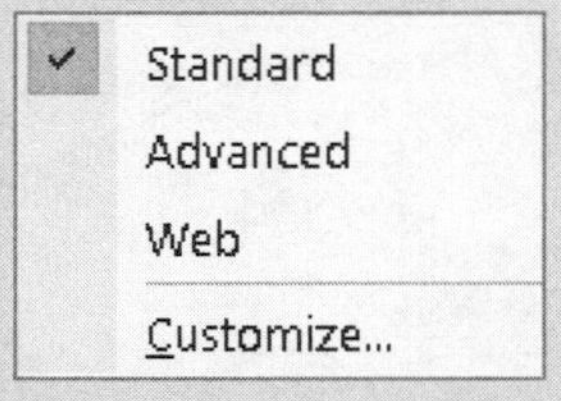

☞ **If necessary, close the** To-Do Bar » × **by clicking** ×

If your contacts are not shown in the default *Business card* view:
☞ **Continue with the next step**

You can decide how you want to view your contacts:

☞ **Click** ○ Phone List

☞ **Click** Full Name

Now the contacts are displayed in a phone list:

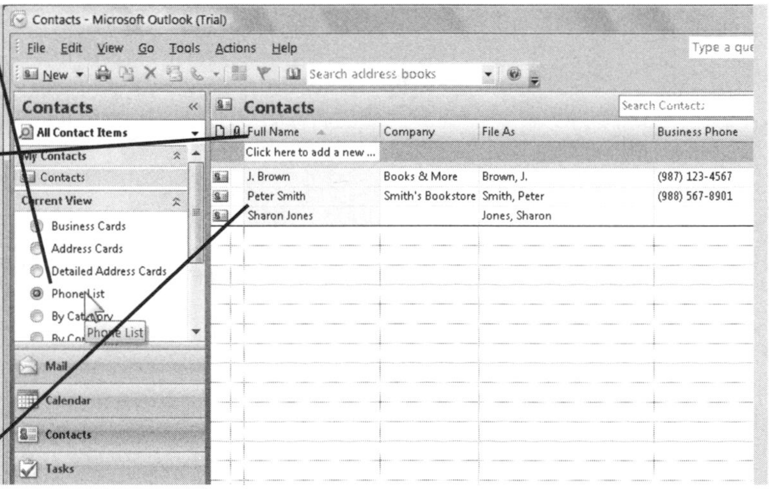

Tip

Displaying contacts
Take a look at the different contact views to determine which view you like best. You can also customize each view by right-clicking a field name, for example

Full Name ▲ and then clicking Customize Current View... . This makes it possible to group your contacts for instance by company. This is very helpful when you have more than one contact in a company.

You can also group your contacts by categories you create yourself. To create your own category:

☞ **Right-click a contact**

☞ **Click** Categorize

You see the available categories:

☞ **Click** ▦ All Categories...

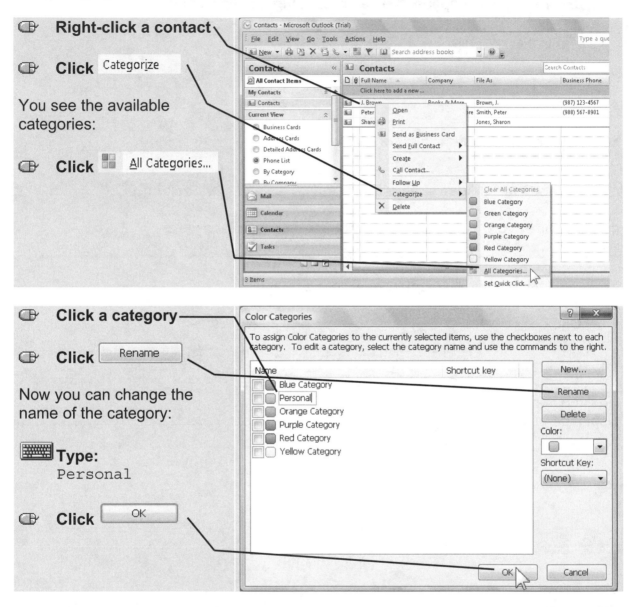

☞ **Click a category**

☞ **Click** Rename

Now you can change the name of the category:

⌨ **Type:**
Personal

☞ **Click** OK

You are going to add a contact to the new Personal category:

👆 **Right-click** Sharon Jones

👆 **Click** Categorize

You see the available categories:

👆 **Click** Personal

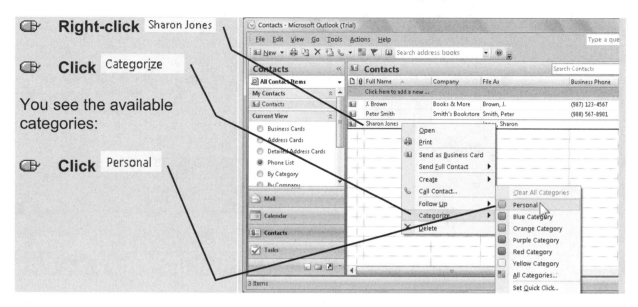

Contact Sharon Jones now belongs to the Personal category.

👉 **Create a category Customers** 📖⁴³ **and add** J. Brown **and** Peter Smith **to that category** 📖⁴⁴

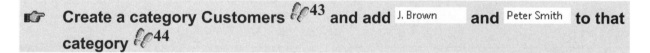

👆 **Click** ⊙ By Category

Now the contacts are displayed organized by category:

💡 **Tip**

Categories
Grouping your contacts by categories makes it easier to work with a long list of contacts. For example, you can create these categories:
- Personal
- Customers
- Suppliers
- Advisors

💡 Tip

Hide or show contacts by category
You can choose whether or not to display the corresponding contacts for each category:

By clicking 🔲 in front of the category, the contacts are hidden. By clicking 🔲, the contacts appear again:

2.2 Microsoft Outlook as a Simple Archiving System

In *Microsoft Outlook* you can archive the documents that belong to a contact in his or her contact form. This enables you to quickly access all of the e-mails, letters, sales quotes and spreadsheets for any of your contacts.

💡 Tip

More extensive customer relationship management with Business Contact Manager
If you have *Business Contact Manager* on your computer, it is better to use that program for your customer relationship management. Further on in this chapter you will learn how to work with this program.

You can link a file to a contact like this:

👉 **Double-click** Sharon Jones

2.3 Electronic Business Cards (vCards)

In *Outlook* you can use electronic business cards to send contact details. Depending on the type of e-mail client the recipient uses, the business card will either be displayed directly in the message or sent as an attached VCF file containing the contact information.
To be able to attach your contact details as a business card, you need to enter yourself as a contact first. You can decide for yourself what kind of information you want to send to the recipient. You can even add a photo if you like.

☞ **Enter your own contact details as a new contact** 🐾⁴⁵

Now your details are stored as a contact.

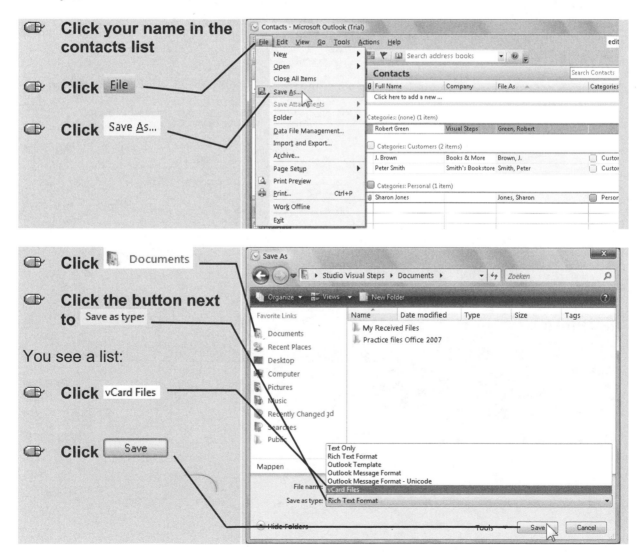

👆 **Click your name in the contacts list**

👆 **Click** File

👆 **Click** Save As...

👆 **Click** Documents

👆 **Click the button next to** Save as type:

You see a list:

👆 **Click** vCard Files

👆 **Click** Save

Now you can send your business card with every new message:

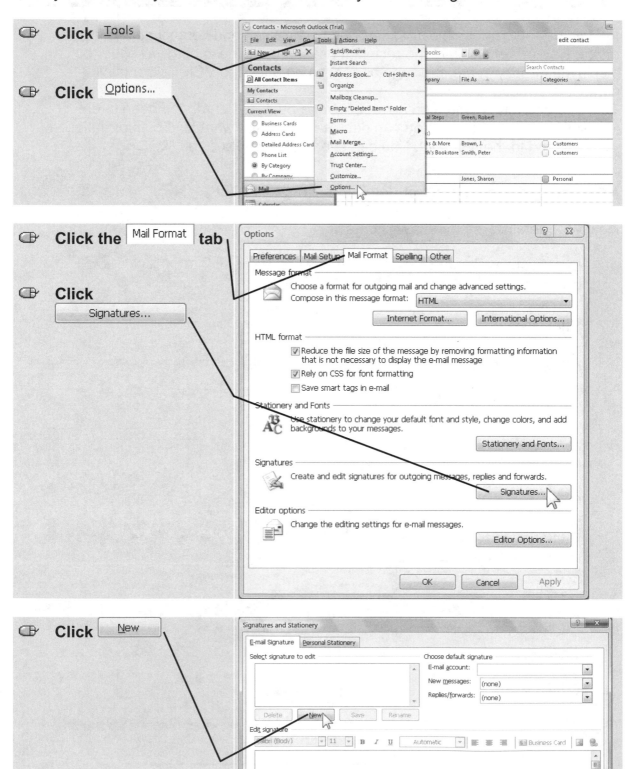

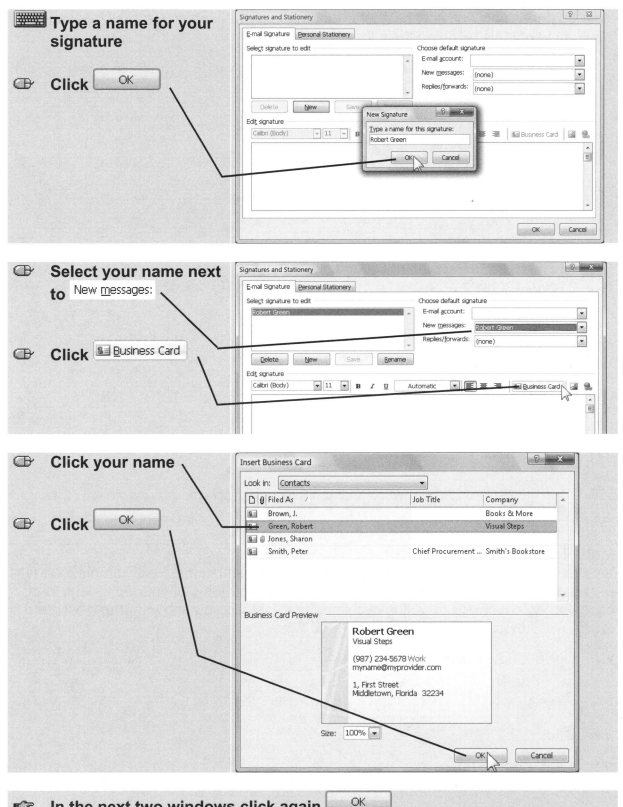

⌨ **Type a name for your signature**

🖱 **Click** OK

🖱 **Select your name next to** New messages:

🖱 **Click** 📇 Business Card

🖱 **Click your name**

🖱 **Click** OK

☞ **In the next two windows click again** OK

Your business card will now be added automatically to each new e-mail message. You can verify this by doing the following:

Click ⌄ next to 🗐 New

Click Mail Message

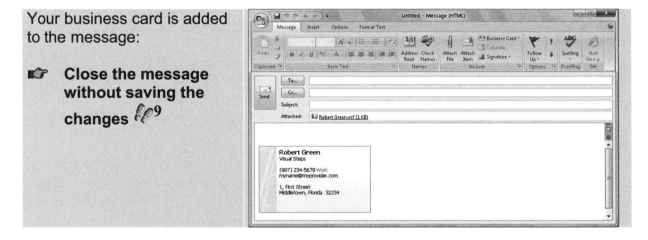

Your business card is added to the message:

☞ **Close the message without saving the changes** 👣⁹

💡 Tip

Multiple business cards

You can create different business cards for different situations. For example, one for personal or business use, and one for different departments of your company. In that case you do not create an automatic signature. Instead you add your business card to an e-mail message manually:

☞ **Open a new message**

Click the Insert tab

Click 🖼 Business Card ⌄

Click the business card you want to use

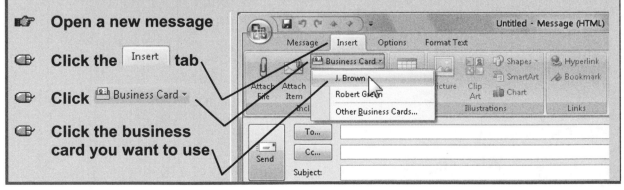

💡 Tip

Saving a business card as a contact

When you receive an e-mail message with a business card, you can easily add the sender to your contacts list.

👆 **Right-click**
   📇 J Brown.vcf (2 KB)

👆 **Click** Add to Contacts

You see the information in the *Contact* window. You can add or edit the information about this contact.

👆 **Click** Save & Close

If the contact already exists, you will see a notification.

You have seen how you can use the *Outlook* contacts list to effectively manage and organize your contacts. In the following sections you can read how to manage and organize your e-mail traffic.

2.4 Organizing Messages in Folders

To better organize your mail correspondence, you can create separate folders for different types of messages. For example, you can create a folder for personal e-mails and separate folders for your business correspondence.

💡 Tip

The Registration folder
Many programs, websites and companies will send you registration numbers and user names by e-mail. Create a separate folder to store these e-mails, so you can easily find them again. Please keep in mind that your computer may be stolen, so do not keep user names and passwords from important companies or organizations together. It is a good idea to print these e-mails and store the documents in a secure place.

☞ **Send an e-mail message with the subject *Practice message* to your own e-mail address** ✍^{5}

Depending on your *Outlook* settings the e-mail is either sent automatically, or you will need to click the button 🖼 Send/Receive .

When you receive the e-mail:

☞ **Click** 📩 Mail

☞ **If necessary, click** 📁 Inbox

You see your *Inbox*:

More than likely you will see other new messages in your inbox besides the one shown in this example.

☞ **Click the new message**

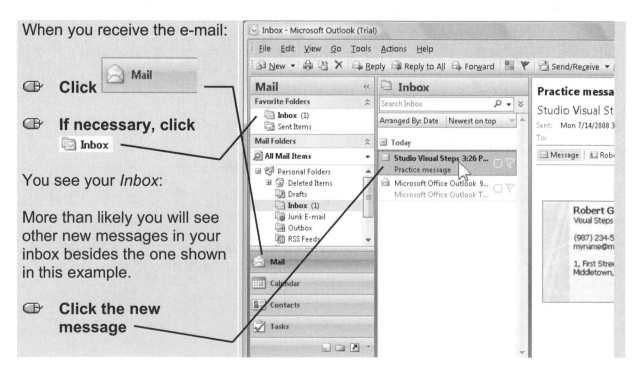

You are going to create a separate folder for your personal messages:

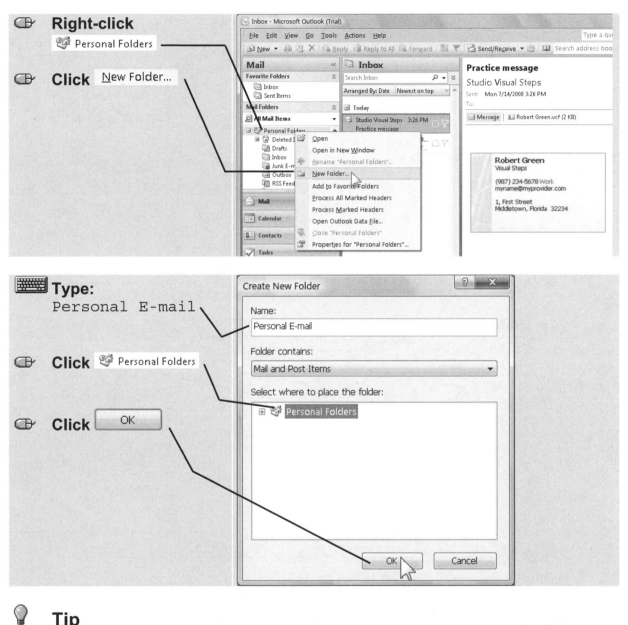

Right-click
☞ Personal Folders

Click New Folder...

⌨ **Type:**
Personal E-mail

Click 🔊 Personal Folders

Click OK

💡 **Tip**

Subfolders
Each of your folders can be divided into subfolders. For example, you can create separate folders for each customer, with subfolders for invoices, confirmations, estimates, bids, et cetera.

□ 🔊 Personal Folders
   □ 📁 Bookware Inc.
      📁 Confirmations
      📁 Invoices
   🗑 Deleted Items

Now you can move the e-mail *Practice message* to the new folder:

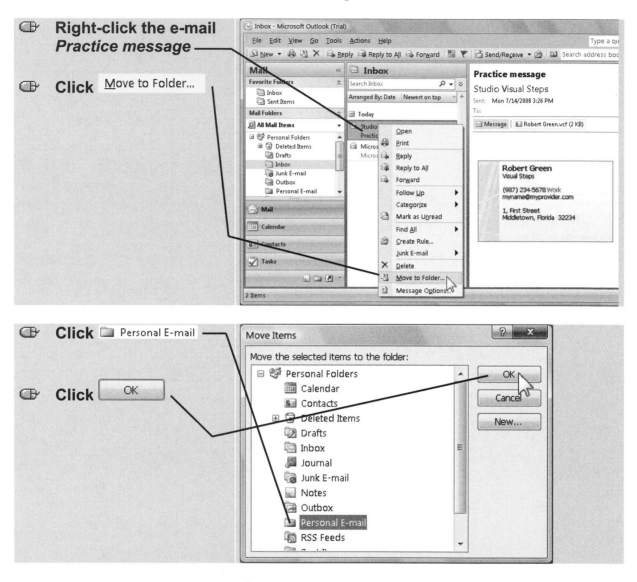

The message has been moved from the *Inbox* to the folder named *Personal E-mail.*

💡 **Tip**

Collecting messages
You can move messages from the *Sent items* folder the same way. When you store the sent and received messages in the same folder, you create a complete archive of your e-mail correspondence.
In *Business Contact Manager* messages can be collected automatically for each contact. You can read more about *Business Contact Manager* further on.

💡 **Tip**

Dragging messages
You can also move selected messages to a folder by dragging them.

2.5 Automatically Organizing Messages in Folders

Instead of organizing messages manually, you can also define e-mail rules. Using these rules, messages that match certain conditions are automatically moved to the correct folder. You can create a rule like this:

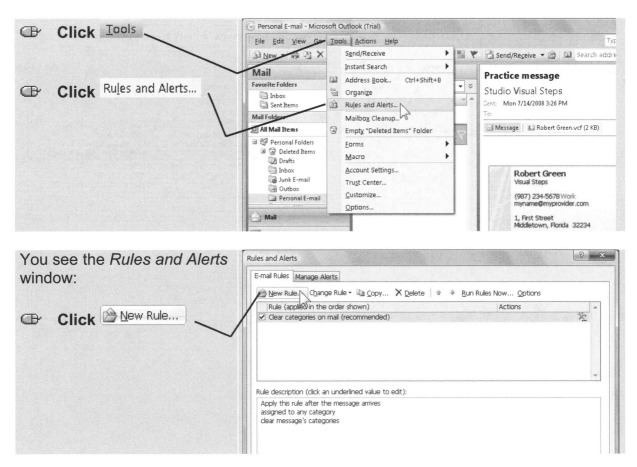

🖰 **Click** Tools

🖰 **Click** Rules and Alerts...

You see the *Rules and Alerts* window:

🖰 **Click** New Rule...

You can define the conditions that will determine whether a message is to be moved or not. For example when you receive a message from a specific sender:

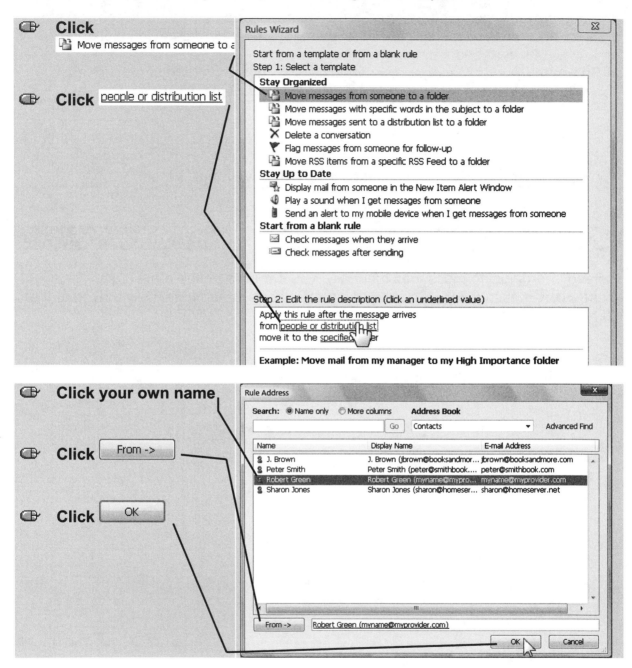

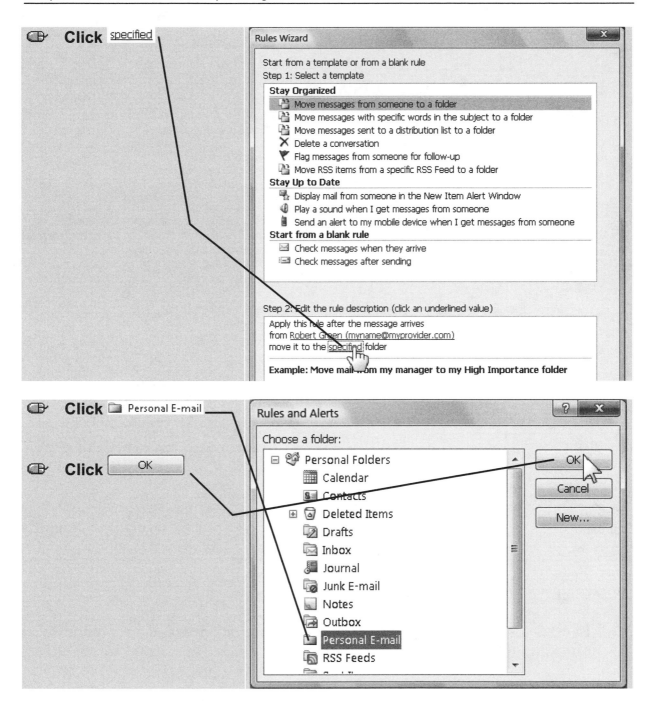

You see the rule you created:

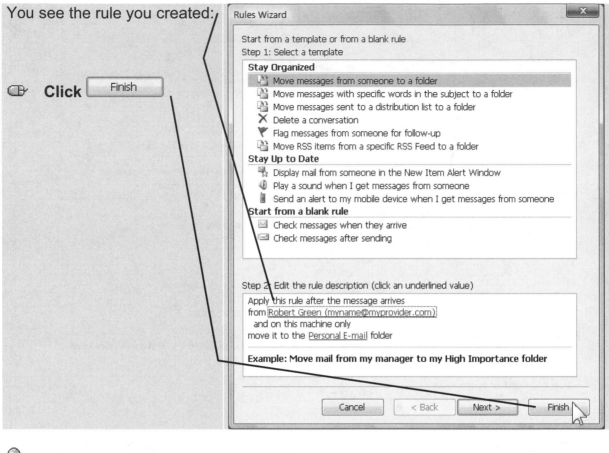

Click [Finish]

Tip

More conditions or exceptions

Click [Next >] to set some more conditions or exceptions. For example, you can have the rule search the body of the message for specific words as well.

Click [OK] in the next window

Send an e-mail message with the subject *Practice message-2* to your own e-mail address

Depending on your *Outlook* settings the e-mail is either sent automatically, or you will need to click the button ⬜ Send/Receive .

The message is delivered to the *Personal E-mail* folder:

This way you can automatically receive messages from customers and suppliers right in their own folders.

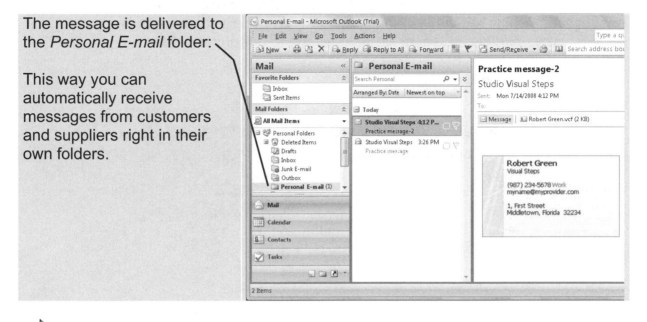

⇨ **Please note:**

As soon as you start using rules, your incoming messages are placed in the folders you specified in these rules. This means these messages are no longer received in your *Inbox*. To avoid missing important messages it is a good idea to keep a close eye on the number of unread messages indicated next to a folder: ⬜ Personal E-mail (1) You can quickly view all your unread mail by using the search folder *Unread Mail*. You can find this folder at the bottom of your list of *Personal folders*:

⊟ 🔍 Search Folders
    🔍 *Categorized Mail*
    🔍 *Large Mail*
    🔍 *Unread Mail*

You can also use the e-mail rules to move e-mails with a specific subject text to a folder. However, for incoming messages you have to rely on the subject the sender chose to specify, this may not be the same subject you indicated in the rule.

2.6 Flagging and Sorting Messages

Messages in a mailbox are usually sorted by the date they were sent or received. It is not apparent which messages require immediate action and which messages can be left until later. You can however flag a message that requires a follow up:

☞ **Right-click your first *Practice message***

That message is at the bottom of the list, because it was received before the other message.

☞ **Click** Follow Up

☞ **Click** ▼ Today

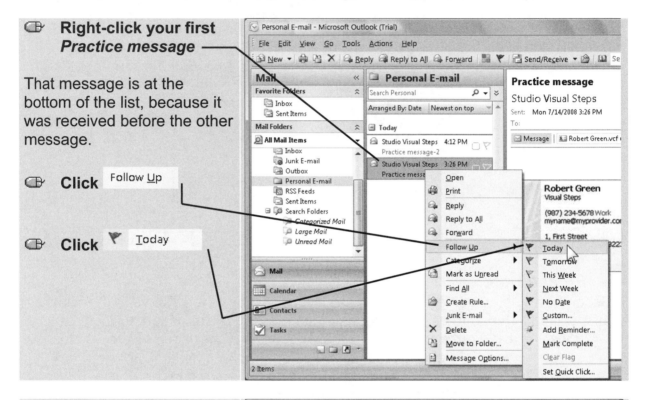

As soon as you flag a message for follow up, it is added to the *To-Do Bar* on the right side of the window:

The items listed in the *To-Do Bar* are arranged by their due date. Tasks that need to be done today are at the top of the list.

You can also sort the messages in the mailbox by their due date:

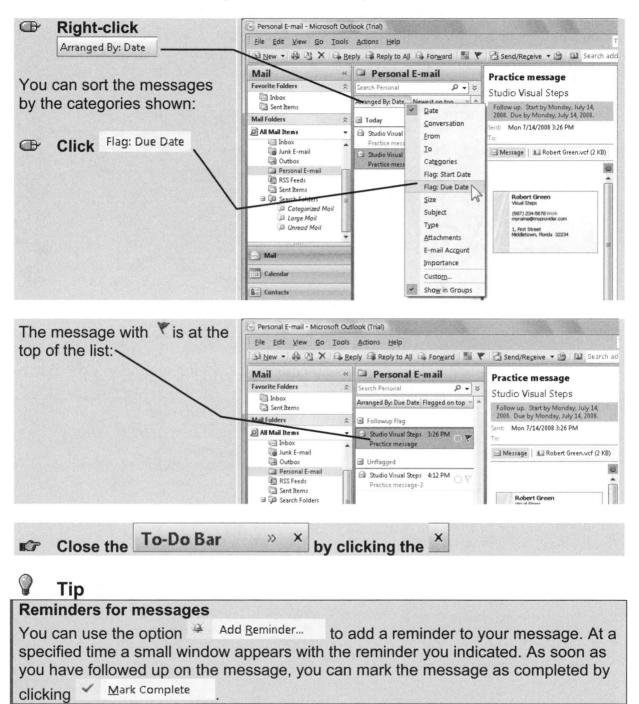

☞ **Right-click** Arranged By: Date

You can sort the messages by the categories shown:

☞ **Click** Flag: Due Date

The message with 🚩 is at the top of the list:

☞ **Close the** To-Do Bar ≫ ✕ **by clicking the** ✕

💡 **Tip**

Reminders for messages

You can use the option 🔔 Add Reminder... to add a reminder to your message. At a specified time a small window appears with the reminder you indicated. As soon as you have followed up on the message, you can mark the message as completed by clicking ✔ Mark Complete .

💡 Tip

Creating tasks from e-mail messages

If you need to follow up on an e-mail message you received, you can create a task by dragging the message to ☑ Tasks :

👉 **Point to the message**

👉 **Drag the message to**
☑ Tasks

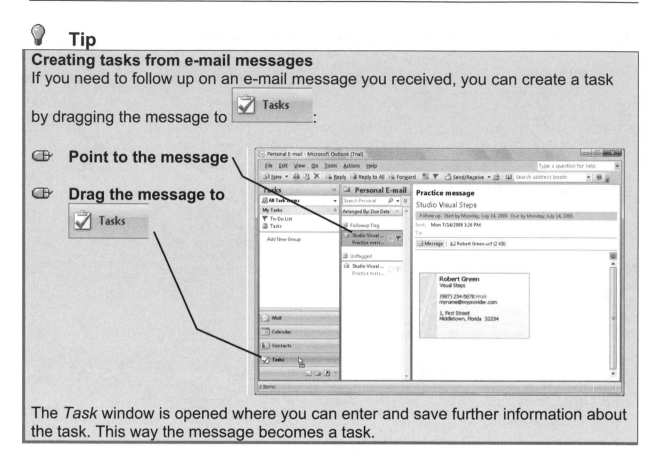

The *Task* window is opened where you can enter and save further information about the task. This way the message becomes a task.

2.7 Searching for Messages

Microsoft Outlook has different options to search for messages in mailboxes:

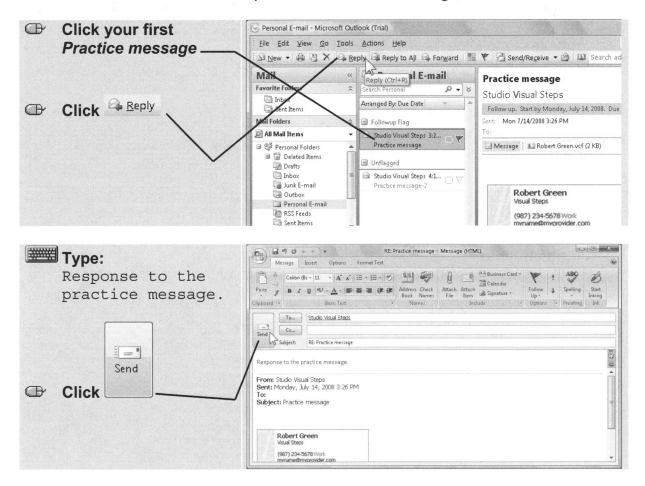

Depending on your *Outlook* settings the e-mail is either sent automatically, or you will need to click the button 🖳 Send/Receive .

You see all of the messages and the response you just sent:

🖱 **Click the Search box**

⌨ **Type:**
response

The contents of the folder are filtered as you type. Now only the message you searched for is displayed:

The search term is marked yellow in the Preview pane:

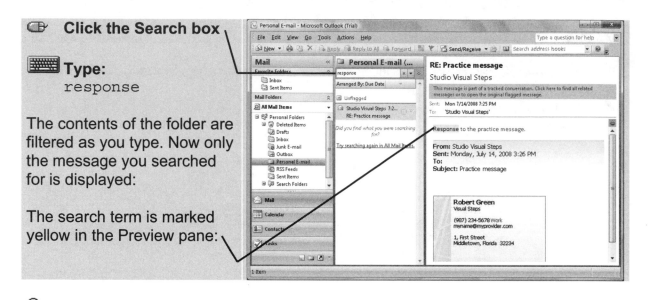

💡 **Tip**

Searching all folders
By default the search is only performed in your current folder. But when needed, you can search all of the folders in *Outlook* at once.

🖱 **Click the Search box**

⌨ **Type your search term**

🖱 **Click** ▾

🖱 **Click**
🔍 Search All Mail Items

In this example an e-mail from the *Inbox* is found, even though the search was started in the *Personal E-mail* folder:

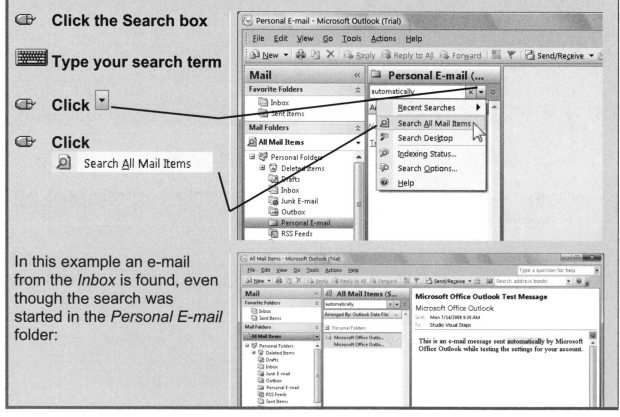

When you clear the Search box, you see all of the messages in the mailbox again:

☞ **Click** ⊠

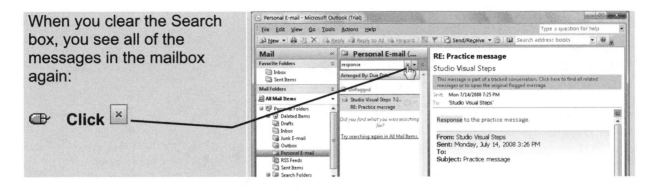

2.8 Advanced Search Functions

In addition to text, you can also search for other items, such as a date or a sender.

☞ **Click** ⮟

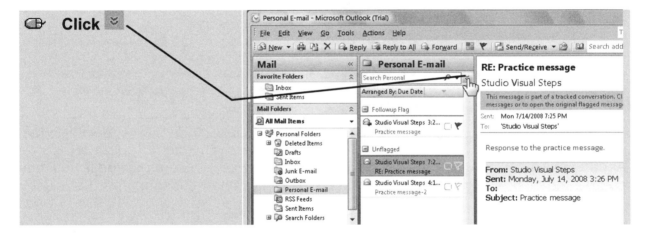

In this example you are going to search into the body of the message:

☞ **Click next to** Body

⌨ **Type:**
response

You can also add search terms to the other categories if necessary.

You see the message that was found:

☞ **Click** ⮝

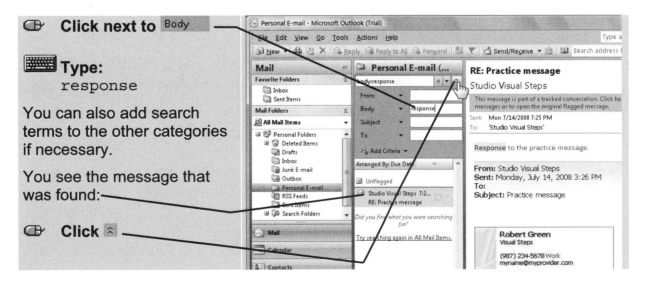

💡 **Tip**

Other search criteria

You can also add additional criteria to the search, for example the date a message was received. You can add criteria like this:

☞ **Open a received message**

🖱 **Click** 🔍 Add Criteria ▼

🖱 **Click the criteria**

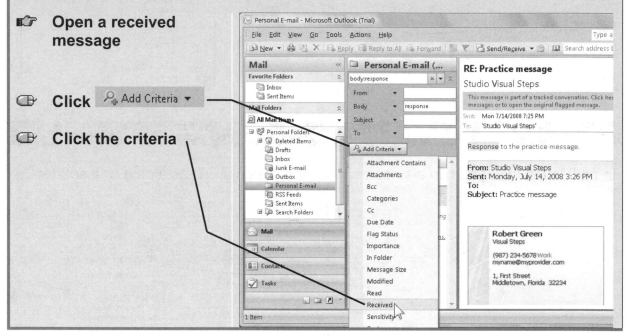

Another practical feature is the possibility to search for all related messages. You can quickly find all messages about a certain order, complaint or customer like this:

🖱 **Right-click the message with the response**

🖱 **Click** Find All

🖱 **Click** Related Messages...

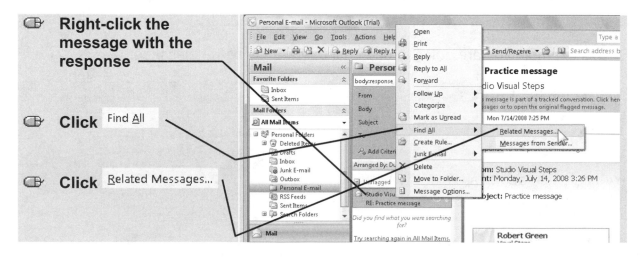

You see all related messages that were sent and received:

You have sent two messages (the practice message and the response to it) and you have also received both messages.

Click X

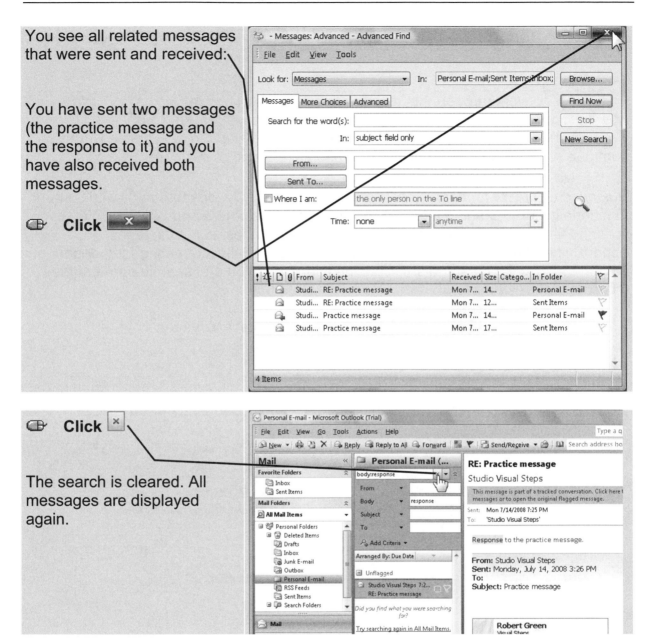

Click X

The search is cleared. All messages are displayed again.

2.9 Business Contact Manager

➡ **Please note:**

To be able to work through the following sections the program *Business Contact Manager* needs to be installed on your computer. Please refer to *Chapter 1 Preparation*. If you do not have this program, you can skip the next sections and continue reading the *Background Information* at the end of this chapter.

Business Contact Manager is an add-on for *Microsoft Outlook* that adds additional functionality for managing information about your customers and contacts. You can sort and filter data, organize and track business activities, contacts, leads, opportunities and marketing campaigns. This is especially interesting for independent contractors, freelancers and small business owners. You can sample some of the different features here.

You start by importing a practice file in *Business Contact Manager*:

➡ **Please note:**

The practice file OutlookBCM can be found on the website with this book. You need to copy it to your computer. You can read how to do that in *Chapter 1 Preparation*.

☞ **Click** File

☞ **Click** Import and Export

☞ **Click**

Business Contact Manager for Out

You are going to import a file:

👆 **Click** [Next >]

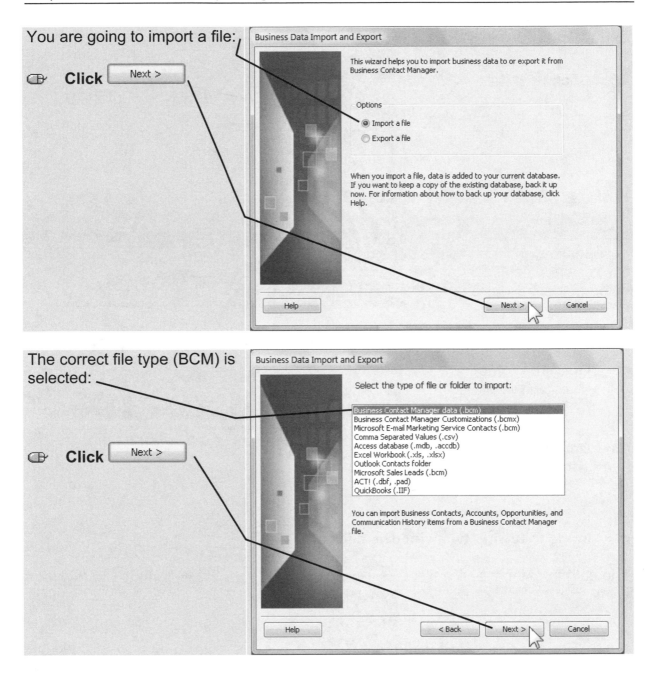

The correct file type (BCM) is selected:

👆 **Click** [Next >]

☞ **Click** ⊙ Don't import duplicates

☞ **Click** [Browse ...]

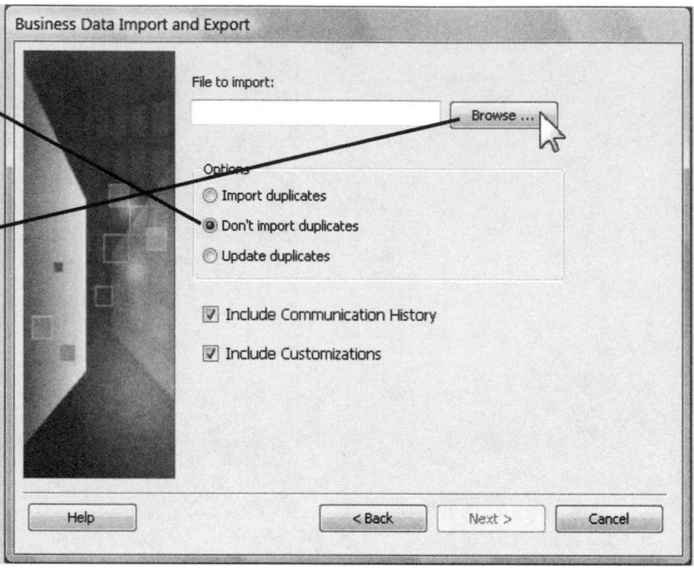

Business Data Import and Export

File to import:

[Browse ...]

Options
○ Import duplicates
⊙ Don't import duplicates
○ Update duplicates

☑ Include Communication History

☑ Include Customizations

[Help]   [< Back] [Next >]   [Cancel]

The *Open* window appears:

☞ **Open the folder**
📁 Practice files Office 2007

☞ **Double-click**
📄 OutlookBCM

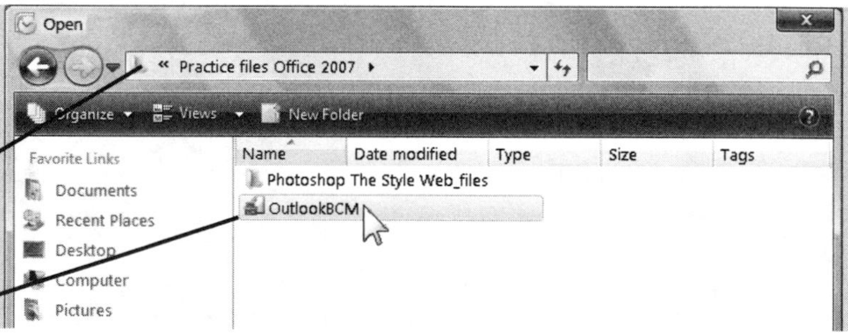

Open

« Practice files Office 2007 ▶

Organize ▾ Views ▾ New Folder

Favorite Links
Documents
Recent Places
Desktop
Computer
Pictures

Name	Date modified	Type	Size	Tags
Photoshop The Style Web_files				
OutlookBCM				

☞ **In the following two windows click** [Next >]

The data from the practice file is imported:

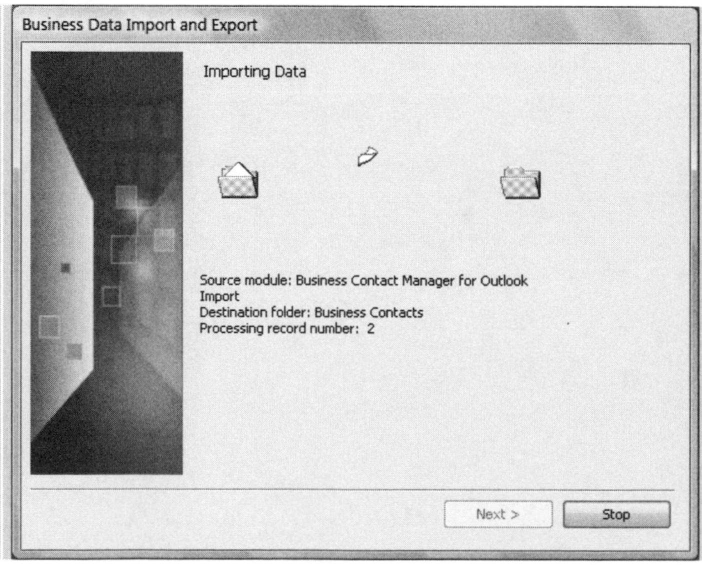

Business Data Import and Export

Importing Data

Source module: Business Contact Manager for Outlook Import
Destination folder: Business Contacts
Processing record number: 2

[Next >]   [Stop]

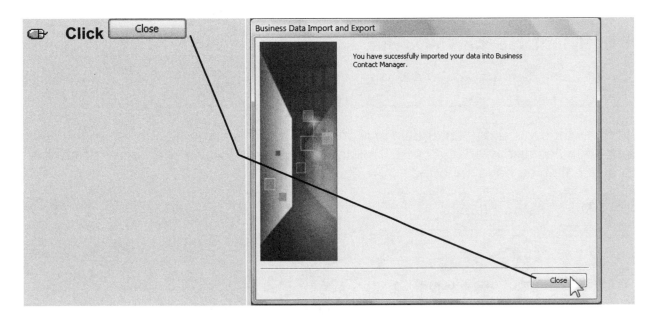

☞ **Click** [Close]

You see the *Outlook* window again:

☞ **Click**

🏠 Business Contact Manager Ho|

Now you see the *Business Contact Manager Home* page:

Here you can find information about your (business) relationships and activities:

 **Help! I see the To-Do Bar.**

☞ **Click** ⊠ **in the *To-Do Bar***
The *To-Do Bar* is closed.

In this window you can enter data and print reports. This example shows sales opportunities displayed in a chart. The data that is used for this chart comes from the practice file you have imported.

☞ **Drag the scroll bar down**

You see an opportunity funnel chart containing the expected revenue, the number of opportunities and the total value in the case that all opportunities are fully realised:

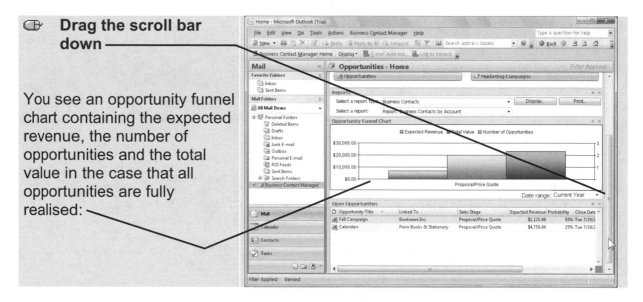

 **Help! I do not understand the chart.**

The funnel chart is created from the sales opportunities listed below the chart. In this example there are two projects:
- The project *Calendars* valued at $ 19,000. There is a 25% chance that this project will be realized. This percentage is listed below probability. The expected revenue is 25% of $ 19,000 = $ 4,750.
- The project *Fall Campaign* valued at $ 4,250. Here the probability is 50%, which creates an expected revenue of 50% of $ 4,250 = $ 2,125.

In the chart you see:
- An expected revenue of $ 4,750 + $ 2,125 = $ 6,875.
- A total number of opportunities of 2 (pay attention to the scale division on the right side of the chart).
- The total value of the opportunities is $ 19,000 + $ 4,250 = $ 23,250.

Luckily, you do not have to do these calculations yourself. The chart is created automatically when you enter the sales opportunities for your own projects. You can try that in the following sections.

2.10 Accounts and Business Contacts

All of your business activities are linked to accounts. Accounts include your current customers and also your potential customers. You can enter a new account like this:

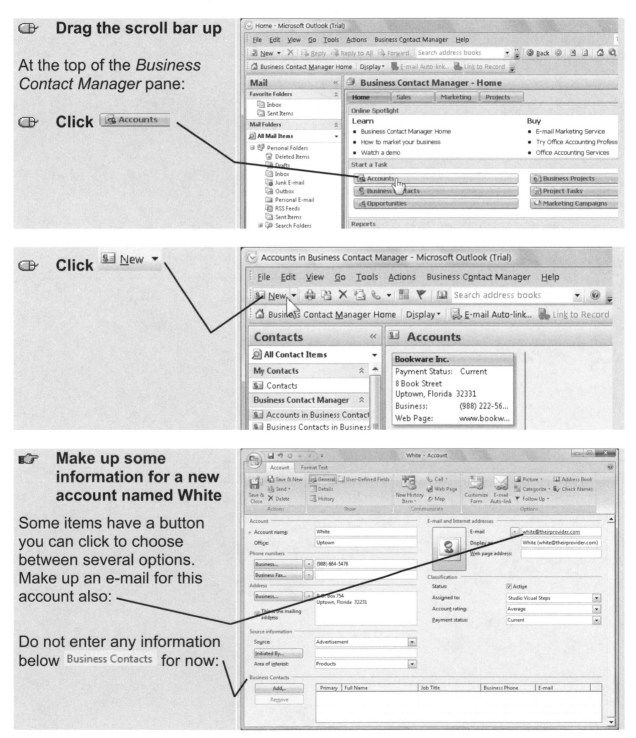

☞ **Drag the scroll bar up**

At the top of the *Business Contact Manager* pane:

☞ **Click** Accounts

☞ **Click** New ▼

☞ **Make up some information for a new account named White**

Some items have a button you can click to choose between several options. Make up an e-mail for this account also:

Do not enter any information below Business Contacts for now:

For each account *Business Contact Manager* keeps track of the projects this customer was involved in. You can also have your e-mail correspondence automatically link to the history of this account:

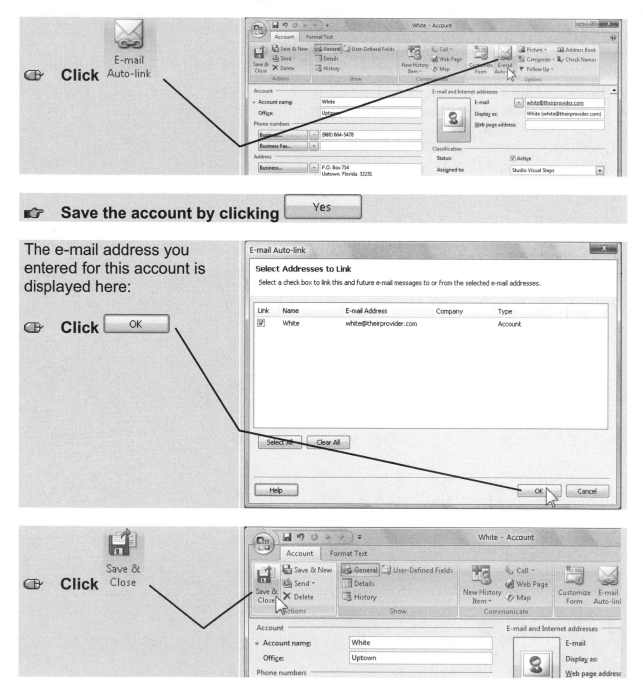

☞ **Save the account by clicking** [Yes]

The e-mail address you entered for this account is displayed here:

👆 **Click** [OK]

👆 **Click** Save & Close

You see the new account: ⟶

Click

🏠 Business Contact Manager Ho

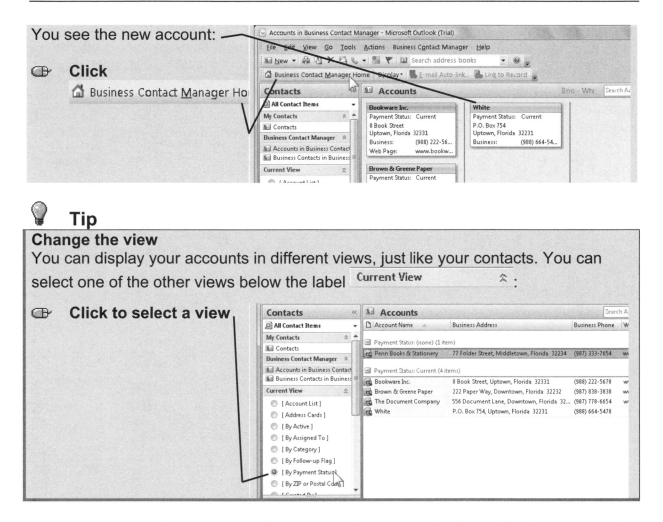

💡 **Tip**

Change the view
You can display your accounts in different views, just like your contacts. You can select one of the other views below the label Current View ⌃ :

Click to select a view

Accounts are usually customers, like companies or organizations. *Business contacts* are the people you have a business relationship with. This might include customers, banks, suppliers and the IRS. If necessary, you can add additional contacts to an account.

You can add a business contact the same way you add an account:

Click
👤 Business Contacts

You see an overview of your business contacts:

Depending on the view you selected, the list may look different on your computer.

Click 📧 New ▼

☞ **Make up some information for a new business contact named Barry Wright**

Click Account...

Click White

Click Link To ->

Click OK

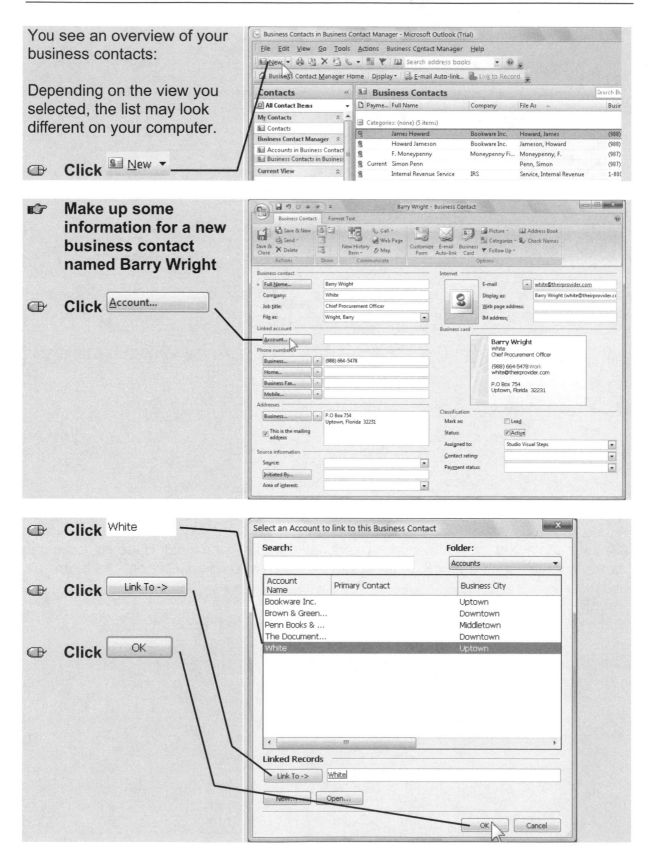

💡 **Tip**

Relevant information only

Barry Wright is the Chief Procurement Officer for account White. Some details, like Source information or Classification are not relevant in this case and do not have to be entered. Just enter the information that is relevant for your company when you enter accounts and contacts.

You can check mark the box next to ☐ Lead when the person is a potential customer.

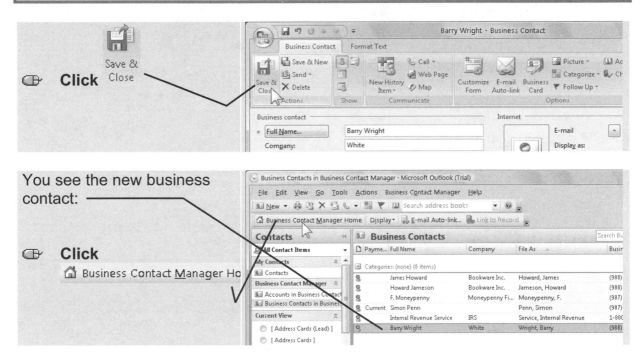

➮ **Click** Save & Close

You see the new business contact:

➮ **Click** 🏠 Business Contact Manager Ho

The *Business Contact Manager Home* page is opened again.

💡 **Tip**

Categories

You can also group your accounts and business contacts by category. This way you can make a distiction between:
- larger customers, smaller customers and private customers;
- customers, suppliers and other service providers (utilities, bank, telecommunication, shipping, storage and logistic services);
- domestic and foreign customers;
- customers divided by product group or department.

When you group your business relations in categories, it becomes a lot easier to target specific groups with mailings. You can create categories for accounts and business contacts the same way you learned earlier on in this chapter.

2.11 Marketing Campaigns

Marketing campaigns can be quite expensive, whether they consist of direct mail, telemarketing or other kinds of advertisements. This is why it is very important to keep track of their costs and their effectiveness. You can do that with the *Marketing campaign* feature of *Business Contact Manager*.

As an example you are going to enter a new marketing campaign:

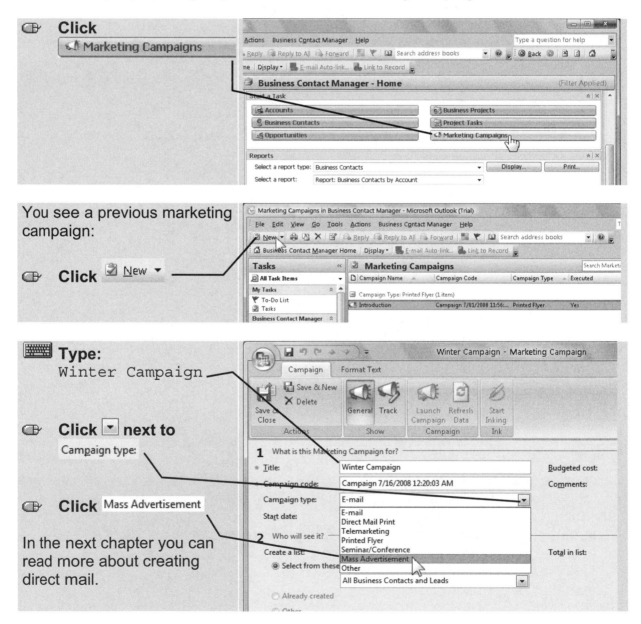

Click
 Marketing Campaigns

You see a previous marketing campaign:

Click New ▾

⌨ **Type:**
 Winter Campaign

Click ▾ **next to**
 Campaign type:

Click Mass Advertisement

In the next chapter you can read more about creating direct mail.

Click next to
Budgeted cost:

Type:
5000

The other items are not relevant for this advertisement campaign.

Click Launch

Click Yes

You see the results of this campaign. The fields are empty, because the campaign has not yet started.

Click Save & Close

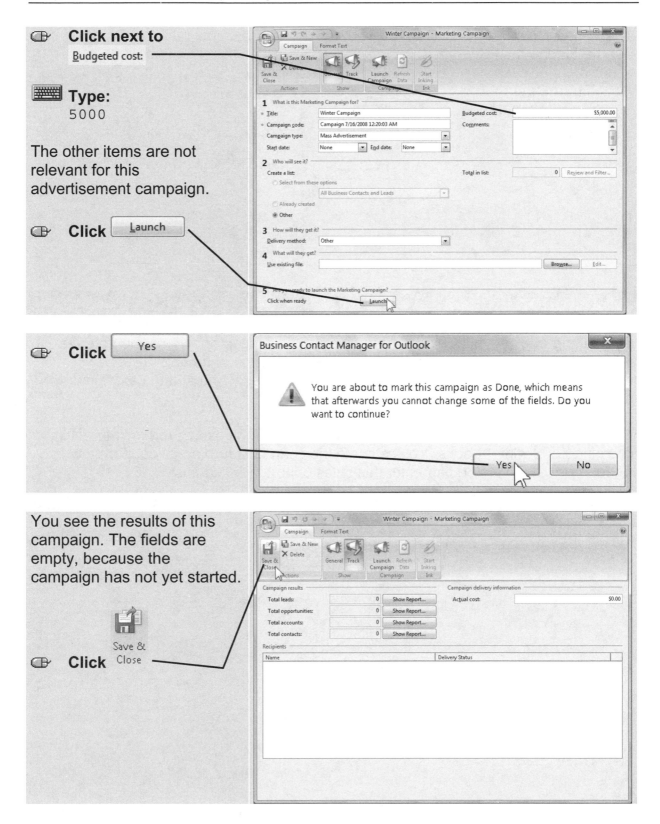

The Winter Campaign has been added to the list:

☞ **Open** *Business Contact Manager Home* 📖⁷

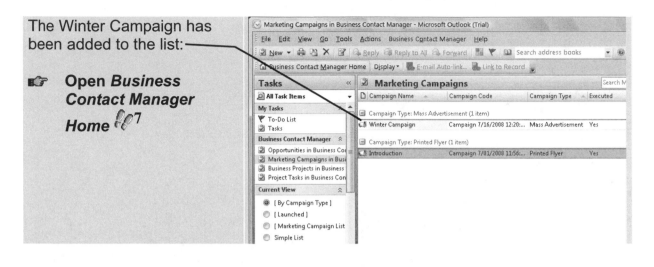

2.12 Opportunities

By keeping track of your sales opportunities you can keep an eye on the potential revenue for each customer and you increase the chance of turning these opportunities into orders. By linking these opportunities to marketing campaigns, you can also see which campaigns are succesful.

Following the Winter Campaign your customer White has expressed an interest in ordering 1500 winter books. You estimate the chance of turning this opportunity into a real order at 50%. You can enter this sales opportunity like this:

🖱 **Click**
    📇 **Opportunities**

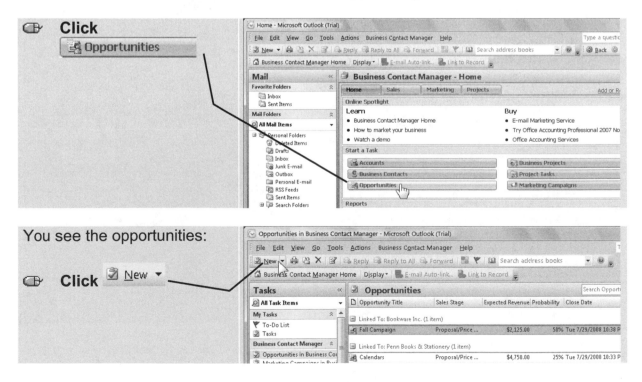

You see the opportunities:

🖱 **Click** 📄 New ▾

☞ **Enter a new opportunity titled Action White** ———

☞ **Link this opportunity to account White** 👣46

☞ **Select the option** Proposal/Price Quote **next to** Sales stage: ———

⌨ **Type next to** Probability: **:** 50%

☞ **Select the option** Advertisement **next to** Source: ———

🖱 **Click** Initiated By...

🖱 **Click** Winter Campaign ———

🖱 **Click** Link To ->

🖱 **Click** OK

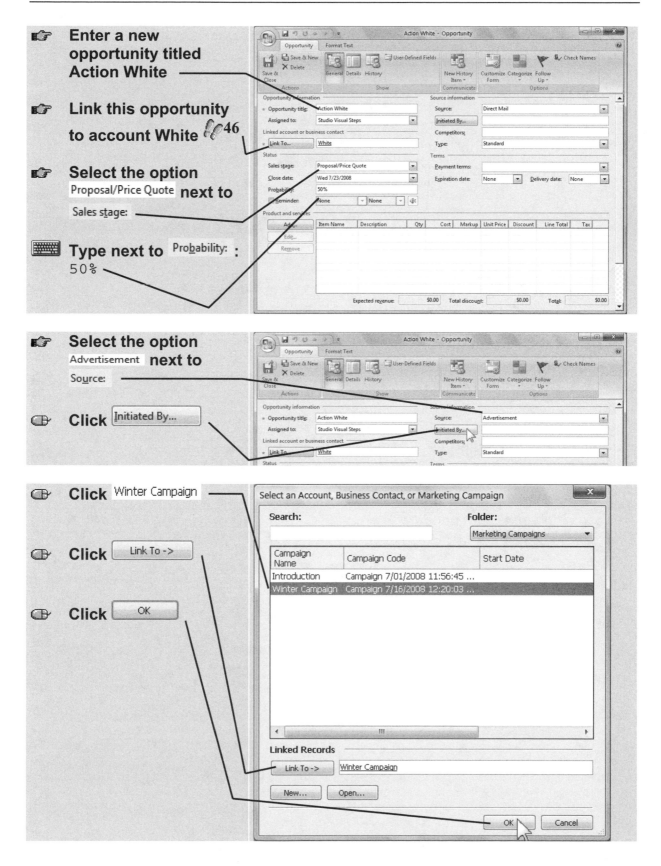

Now you enter the details of this action:

☞ **Click** `Add...` **below** `Product and services`

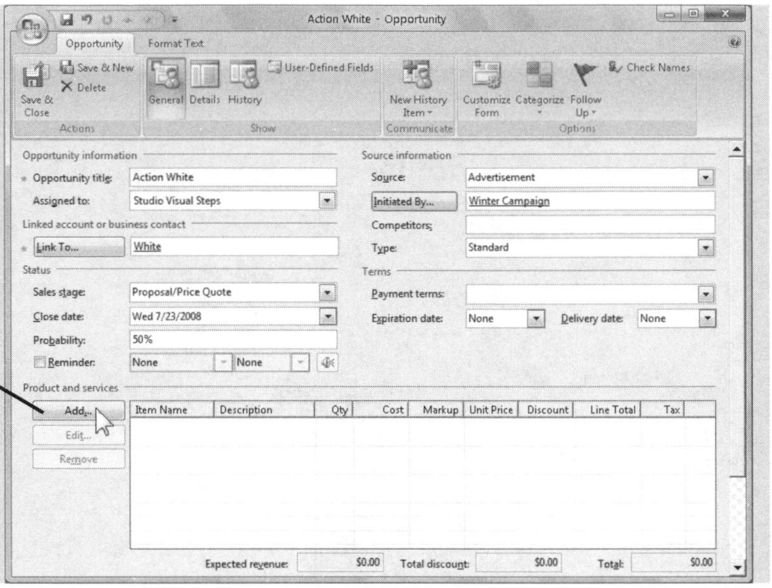

☞ **Enter the information**

Next to `Unit cost:` you enter the purchasing price or cost price.

Next to `Unit Price:` you enter the selling price.

You list the prices excluding sales tax, so you do not need to check the box ☐ `Taxable`.

☞ **Click** `OK`

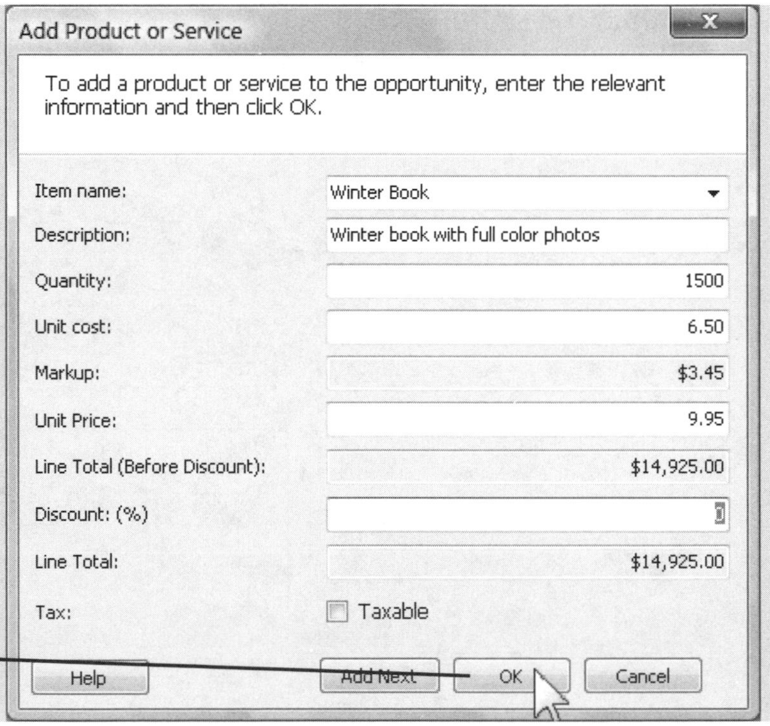

Add Product or Service

To add a product or service to the opportunity, enter the relevant information and then click OK.

Item name:	Winter Book
Description:	Winter book with full color photos
Quantity:	1500
Unit cost:	6.50
Markup:	$3.45
Unit Price:	9.95
Line Total (Before Discount):	$14,925.00
Discount: (%)	0
Line Total:	$14,925.00
Tax:	☐ Taxable

Help   Add Next   OK   Cancel

You see the data you entered for this opportunity:

When an order consists of multiple parts you can add more lines below Product and services .

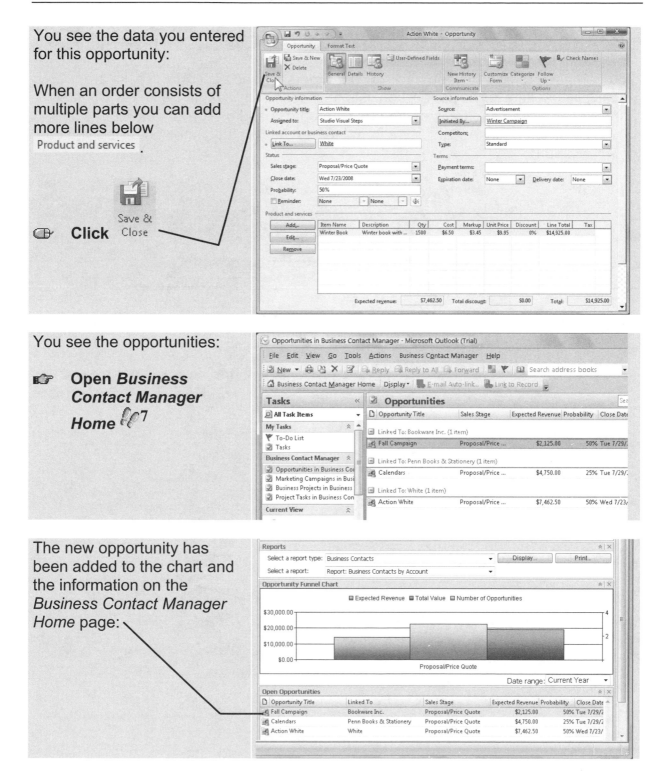

Click Save & Close

You see the opportunities:

☞ **Open *Business Contact Manager Home* &7**

The new opportunity has been added to the chart and the information on the *Business Contact Manager Home* page:

2.13 Projects and Project Tasks

You can use projects to keep track of your orders for each account. Tasks are especially useful when a project consists of various activities. In *Business Contact Manager* you can keep track of the project progress and plan your activities.
When the opportunity Action White from the next section becomes on order, you can enter it like this:

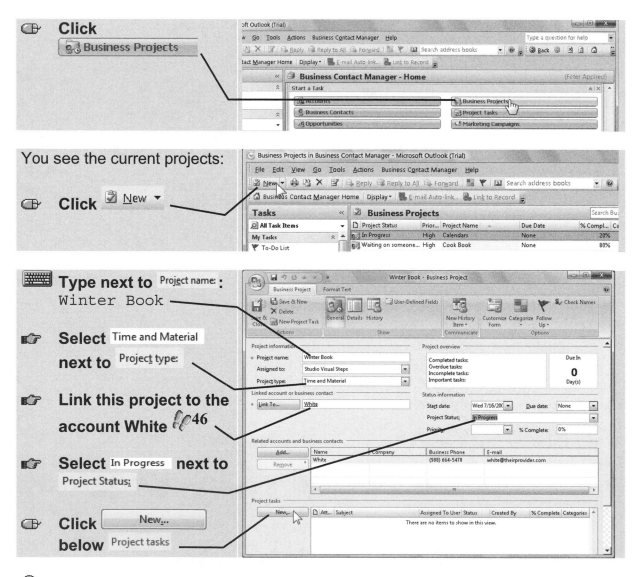

Click
   Business Projects

You see the current projects:

Click New ▾

Type next to Project name: :
Winter Book

☞ **Select** Time and Material
next to Project type:

☞ **Link this project to the**
account White 46

☞ **Select** In Progress **next to**
Project Status:

Click New...
below Project tasks

💡 **Tip**

Project with multiple parties involved

When multiple accounts are involved in a project, for example multiple customers, suppliers or a bank, you can add these below Related accounts and business contacts .

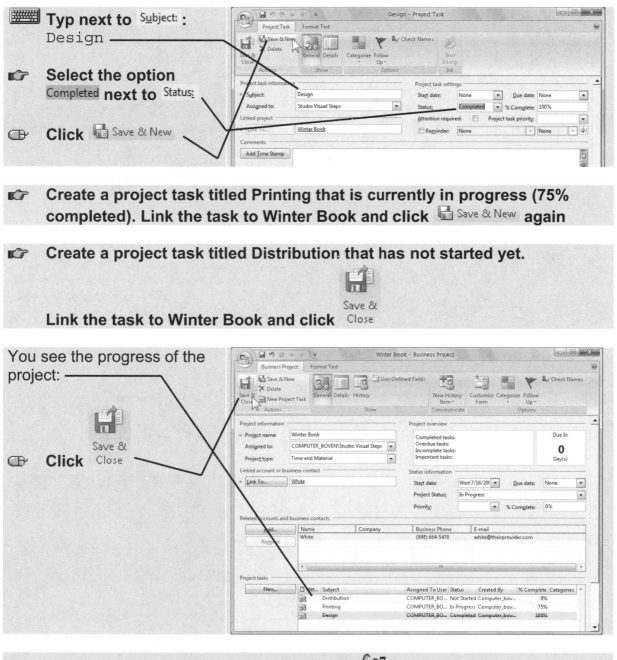

⌨ **Click** Yes **to save the project.**

Projects are divided in project tasks. You can track the progress of each task:

⌨ **Typ next to** Subject: :
Design

☞ **Select the option** Completed **next to** Status:

⌨ **Click** Save & New

☞ **Create a project task titled Printing that is currently in progress (75% completed). Link the task to Winter Book and click** Save & New **again**

☞ **Create a project task titled Distribution that has not started yet.**

Link the task to Winter Book and click Save & Close

You see the progress of the project:

⌨ **Click** Save & Close

☞ **Open** *Business Contact Manager Home* ᴳᴼ7

2.14 Reports

You have entered your campaigns, opportunities and projects. Now you can take a look at the current state of your business using reports:

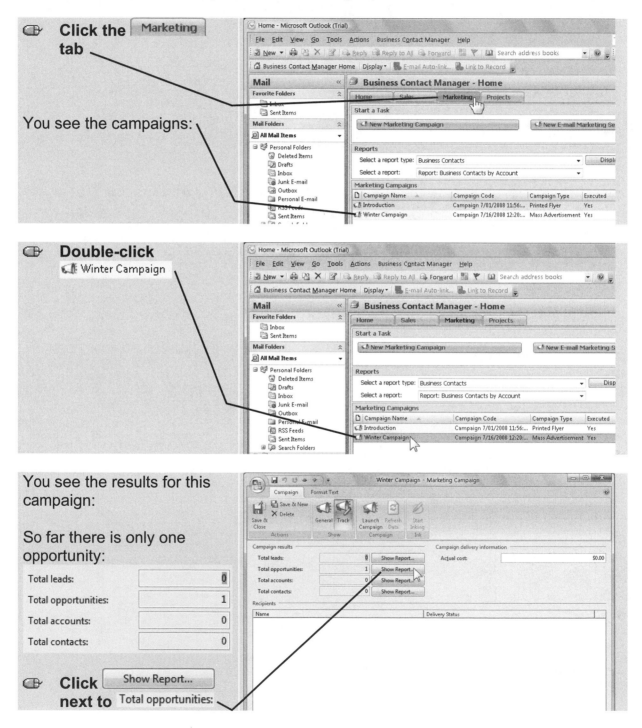

To see the full report:

☞ **Maximize the window**
   🐾8

You see the opportunity:

If necessary, you can print or save this report.

💡 **Tip**

Extra report features
In addition to printing or saving the report, you can also modify, filter or export the report:

- Sort the data in ascending or descending order using ⤓⤒ ;
- Filter the report using ▾= Filter Report ;
- Export the report to *Excel* using 🅧 ;
- Modify the report using 💥 Modify Report .

Double-clicking the title of an opportunity displays the details of this opportunity.

☞ **Close the report** 🐾9

If you made changes to the report, you will be asked if you want to save the changes. In that case you can give the report a new name.

☞ **Close the *Winter Campaign* window** 🐾9

👆 **Click the** `Projects` **tab**

You see the projects and their progress:

👆 **Double-click** `Winter Book`

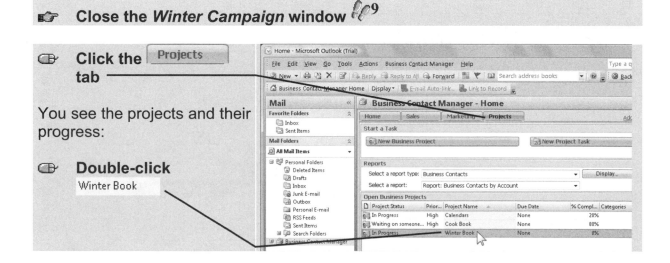

You see the information about this project. If necessary, you can make changes to this project:

You also see the progress of the project tasks:

☞ **Click** [**X**]

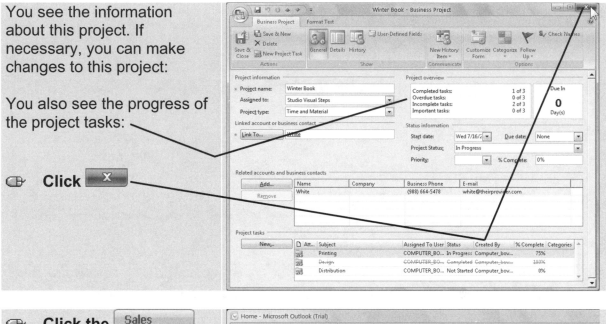

☞ **Click the** [Sales] **tab**

You see the opportunities and the projects:

When you double-click an opportunity or project the details are displayed.

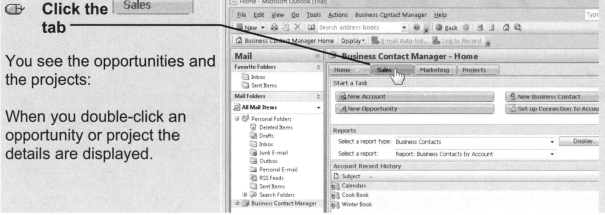

💡 Tip

More reports

On each tab you can select different types of reports below [Reports]:

☞ **Select a report type next to** [Select a report type:]

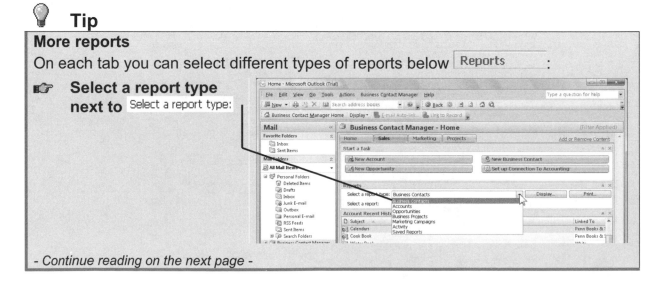

- Continue reading on the next page -

☞ **Select the report set-up next to**

To view the report:

👉 **Click** [Display...]

⇨ **Please note:**

The button [🖳 Set up Connection To Accounting] only works if you use *Microsoft Office Small Business Accounting 2006* or *Microsoft Office Accounting 2008*.
If you use another accounting system, it opens its Help feature and locates the instructions about how to integrate your accounting system with *Business Contact Manager* for *Outlook*.

2.15 History

For each account that is linked to campaigns, opportunities and projects the program keeps track of the history of your communication with this account. You can take a look at the history like this:

☞ **Open *Business Contact Manager Home*** ✍7

👉 **Click** [🖳 Accounts]

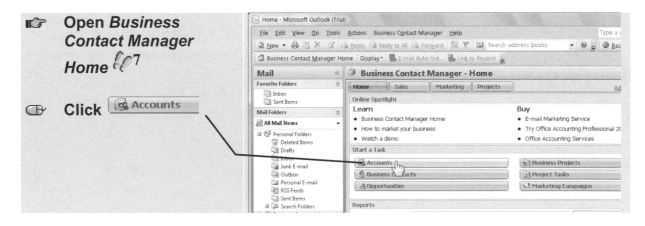

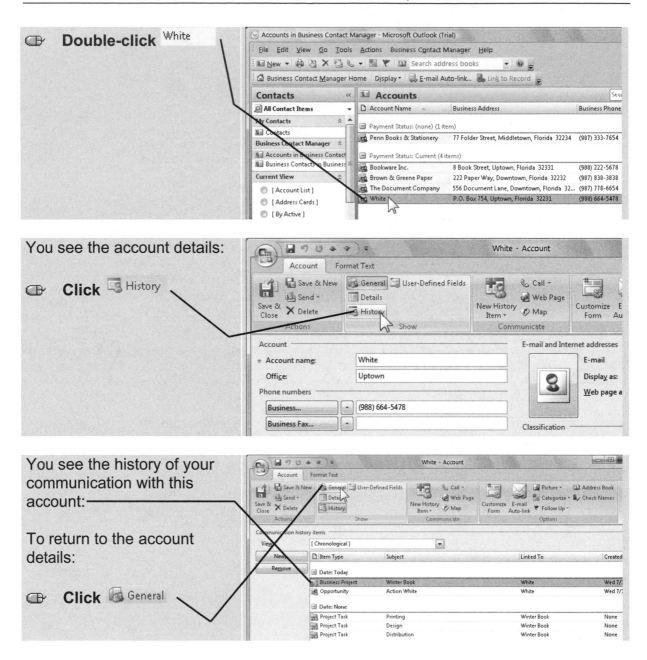

Double-click White

You see the account details:

Click History

You see the history of your communication with this account:

To return to the account details:

Click General

💡 Tip

Add to history

The communication history per account is an important overview. It tells you what an account wants, what an account means to you and what brings you success. Therefore it is very important to document your communications history. You can add information to the history like this:

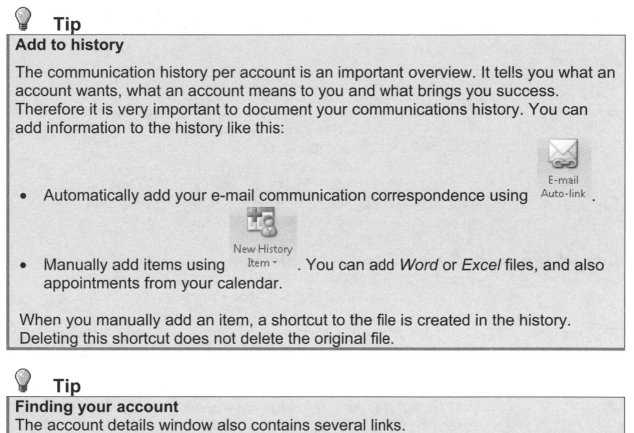

- Automatically add your e-mail communication correspondence using E-mail Auto-link.

- Manually add items using New History Item ▾ . You can add *Word* or *Excel* files, and also appointments from your calendar.

When you manually add an item, a shortcut to the file is created in the history. Deleting this shortcut does not delete the original file.

💡 Tip

Finding your account
The account details window also contains several links.

When you click 🔲 Web Page the webpage of this account is opened (only if you entered it previously).

The button 🔷 Map opens *Live Search Maps* where you can view a map of this account's address.

☞ **Close the account details window** ℓℓ⁹

☞ **Close *Outlook*** ℓℓ⁹

In this chapter you have learned about customer relationship management. Frequently updating and adding information about interactions you have had with an account and actions you have taken is essential for relationship management. A customer relationship management system that contains up-to-date information is an excellent support for your business activities.

2.16 Background Information

Glossary

Account   Company or organization you do business with.

Category   Color classification that makes it easy to identify and organize related messages, contacts and appointments. You can use the color categories to quickly find, sort, filter and group items.

Contact   Collection of data about a person or organization. Contacts are stored in the *Contacts* folder and may contain details like the name, the e-mail address, the phone number and the address.

Project   Commitment or assignment you want to document and track until it is completed. A project consists of one or more project tasks.

Rule   A rule is an action that *Outlook* takes automatically on an incoming or outgoing message that meets the conditions or exceptions that you specify in the rule.

Signature   A signature for an e-mail message consists of text and/or images. You can configure *Outlook* to add a signature automatically to outgoing messages, or you can add a signature manually when you create a new message. You can create as many signatures as you like, for example for your business and personal e-mail correspondence.

vCard   Widely used format for storing contact details. Contacts that use the vCard format are saved as VCF files.

Source: Windows Help and Microsoft Office 2007 Help

Using Business Contact Manager with mobile devices

You can take your business contacts and appointments with you by synchronizing them with a mobile device, such as a *Pocket PC*. These devices are becoming very popular. Therefore synchronizing data between these devices and the computer at the office or at your workplace at home is becoming increasingly important.

Synchronizing reconciles the differences between files on the mobile device and the computer. This is contrary to importing and exporting, where the files are overwritten.

Windows XP users need the program *Microsoft ActiveSync* to be able to synchronize data between their computer and a mobile device. You can download this tool for free from the *Microsoft* website: www.microsoft.com

In *Windows Vista* you no longer need an extra program. *Windows Vista* contains a dedicated *Sync Center* that provides synchronization with traditional PDAs, mobile phones, cameras and MP3 players.

Your mobile device needs to have the right communication software. Ask your supplier for more information. On a Pocket PC you must first install *Business Contacts for Pocket PC* before you can begin syncing. You can find more information about this on the *Microsoft* website.

Another possibility is exchanging information using a *Bluetooth* connection. These days many mobile phones are capable of *Bluetooth* communication. That is understandable, since mobile phones are used more and more for data storage. This makes communication with the PC very important. To be able to transfer the photos, videos, appointments and address details on the mobile phone with the PC, your PC also needs to be *Bluetooth* compatible. Most modern laptops are. For desktop PCs and older laptops you need to add a *Bluetooth* adapter. *Bluetooth* adapters are usually simple devices that you can connect to the USB port.

Source and more information: www.microsoft.com

2.17 Tips

☀ Tip

To-Do Bar

Instead of creating projects, you can use the *To-Do Bar* in *Microsoft Outlook* to keep track of simple tasks that need to be completed before a certain date. These tasks do not have to be performed at a specific time; they are due at a specific time. Examples of tasks are:

- Cancelling subscriptions, contracts et cetera;
- Filing (tax) reports;
- Creating sales quotes;
- Tax and other payments. If a customer needs to pay you before a certain date, you can also list that as a task in the to-do list.

You can also set a reminder for tasks in the *To-Do Bar.*

For tasks that must be completed before a specific time, you can create an appointment in *Outlook Calendar*.

☀ Tip

Exporting data

If you want to use information from *Microsoft Outlook* or *Business Contact Manager* in other programs it will sometimes be necessary to export data. You can export data in various formats. The format you choose depends on the program you are going to use. The *Excel* format and the CSV format are common formats for data exchange. CSV stands for *Comma Separated Value*.

You can export data like this:

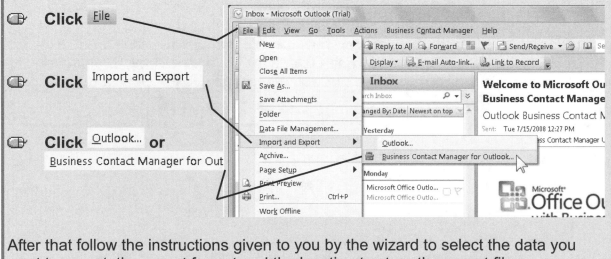

⊕ **Click** File

⊕ **Click** Import and Export

⊕ **Click** Outlook... **or** Business Contact Manager for Out

After that follow the instructions given to you by the wizard to select the data you want to export, the export format and the location to store the export file.

💡 Tip

Archiving

All messages, tasks, appointments and projects are saved. After a while, these items become less interesting and you may not need this data anymore. You should not delete the information, because in most cases it is part of your business records. You can use the archive feature in *Microsoft Outlook* to store it in a separate archive folder. Archiving is done like this:

👉 **Click** File

👉 **Click** Archive...

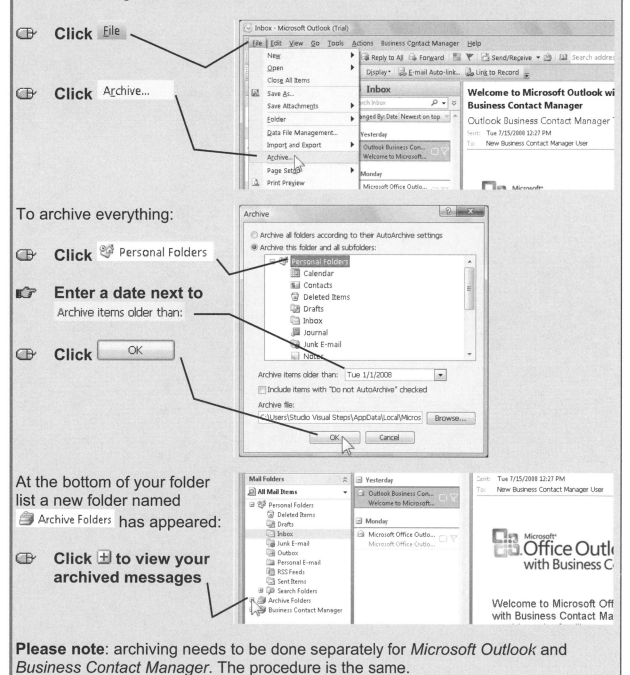

To archive everything:

👉 **Click** 🕮 Personal Folders

👉 **Enter a date next to** Archive items older than:

👉 **Click** OK

At the bottom of your folder list a new folder named 📁 Archive Folders has appeared:

👉 **Click** ⊞ **to view your archived messages**

Please note: archiving needs to be done separately for *Microsoft Outlook* and *Business Contact Manager*. The procedure is the same.

Notes

Write your notes down here.

3. Standard Documents 🕐 90 min.

Many documents that are used in a business are more or less standard documents. Sometimes the text is the same, like in a bid, purchase order, letter of introduction or confirmation letter. Or the setup is the same, like in an invoice or packing slip.

These standard documents or business forms can be created in various programs, for example *Word*, *Outlook*, *Excel* or *Publisher*.
In this chapter you will learn how to create standard documents with these programs.

You are going to use one of the excellent templates that are included with *Microsoft Office 2007*. You will also use some of the sample documents from the website of this book.

By using standard documents you save time and your business correspondence acquires a more professional allure.

In this chapter you will learn the following:

- create templates for e-mail messages;
- set up an automatic reply for incoming e-mail;
- create an e-mail mailing;
- create your own stationery;
- use and customize templates;
- create building blocks for standard texts;
- create a mailing in *Word*;
- create labels;
- customize a business card in *Publisher*;
- customize invoice templates;
- create invoices.

⇨ Please note:

To be able to work through the exercises in this chapter you need some experience working with the *Microsoft Office 2007* programs.
On page 15 of this book you can read more about the specific tasks you should be able to perform.

3.1 E-mail Templates

A large amount of correspondence these days is done by e-mail. Often these messages are standard messages like:

- confirmation receipts;
- letters of introduction;
- reminders;
- requests for information;
- terms and conditions, or terms of service.

When you create a template for these standard messages you will not have to type the same text over and over again. As an example, you are going to create a template for when you are out of the office and not able to answer your e-mail right away. Your recipients will receive an automatic reply.

☞ **Open *Microsoft Outlook*** 𝓁𝓁¹

⇨ **Please note:**

> If you did not install *Business Contact Manager*, some of the buttons shown in the screenshots are missing in the *Microsoft Outlook* toolbar on your computer. This will not interfere with any of the tasks you need to perform in the following sections.

Click 🖼 New ▼

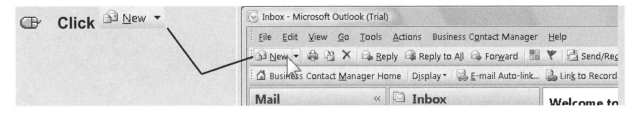

You see a new message. In this example, an electronic business card is included. This is due to settings applied in the previous chapter. If you did not set up a signature, the message will be empty.

⌨ **Type:**

Thank you for your message. I am out of the office at this time with no access to my e-mail. I will respond to your message as soon as possible.

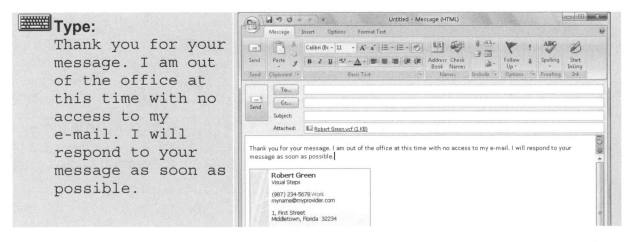

You are going to save this message as a template:

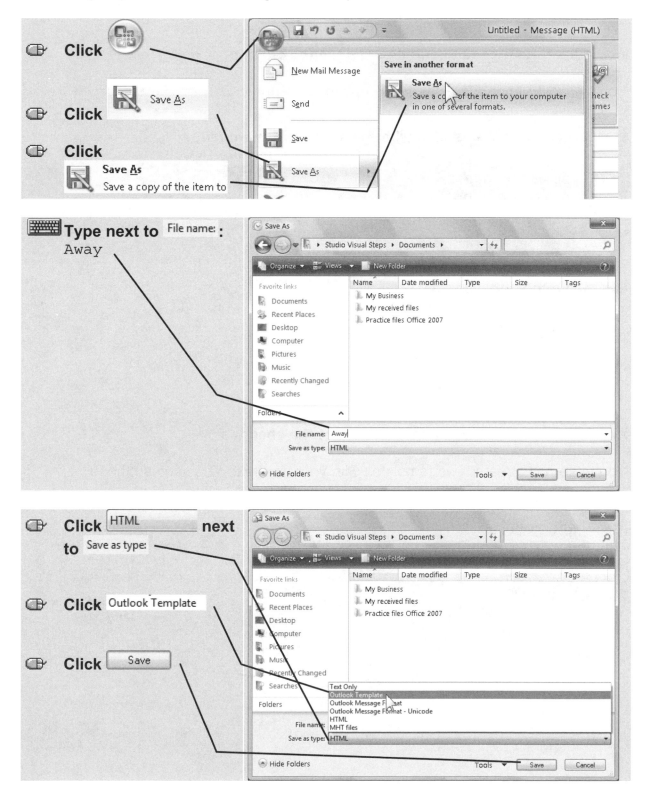

The message has been saved as a template titled *Away.* You see the message again.

☞ **Close the message and do not save the changes** 🦶⁹

You are going to create a second template:

☞ **Create a new message with the subject *New website*** 🦶⁵

⌨**Type as message:**
We have renewed our
website. Please visit
www.visualsteps.com
and take a look.

☞ **Save this message as a template titled *New website*** 🦶¹⁰

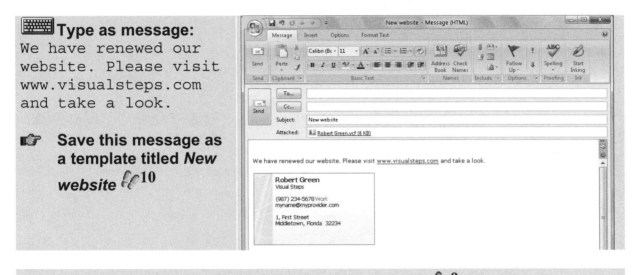

☞ **Close the message and do not save the changes** 🦶⁹

You have now created two templates with your own text. You can use these templates like this:

🖱 **Click** Tools

🖱 **Click** Forms

🖱 **Click** Choose Form...

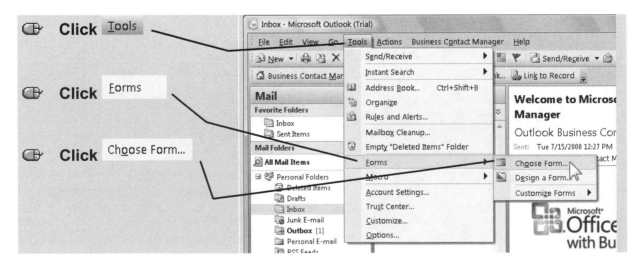

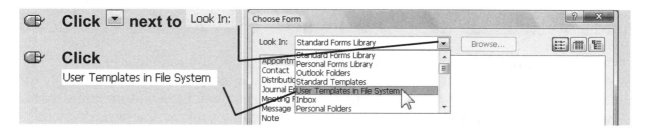

Click ⬇ next to Look In:

Click
User Templates in File System

You are going to use the *New website* template:

Click New website

Click Open

You see the message:

Now you can add an e-mail address and send the message in the usual way.

That is not necessary in this example:

☞ **Close the message and do not save the changes (if necessary)** 🦶**9**

💡 **Tip**

Templates for estimates
You can also use the *Outlook* templates to send larger documents with text that is more or less standardized. For example a confirmation or estimate. You can edit the text before sending if necessary.

3.2 Automatically Reply to Incoming E-mail

When you are out of the office it is not possible to respond immediately to every e-mail you receive. In that case you can set up *Outlook* to send an automatic reply to some or all of the people who send you messages. That way the senders know that you have received their message, even though you cannot respond to them right now.

In *Outlook* it is very easy to create a rule to automatically reply to new e-mail messages using the template *Away*:

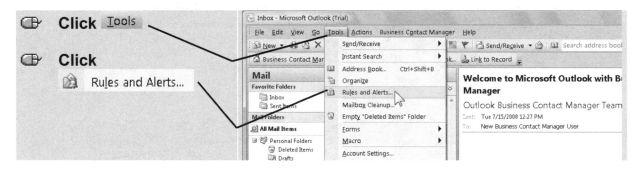

☞ **Click** Tools

☞ **Click**
    📒 Rules and Alerts...

You see the *Rules and Alerts* window:

☞ **Click** 📩 New Rule...

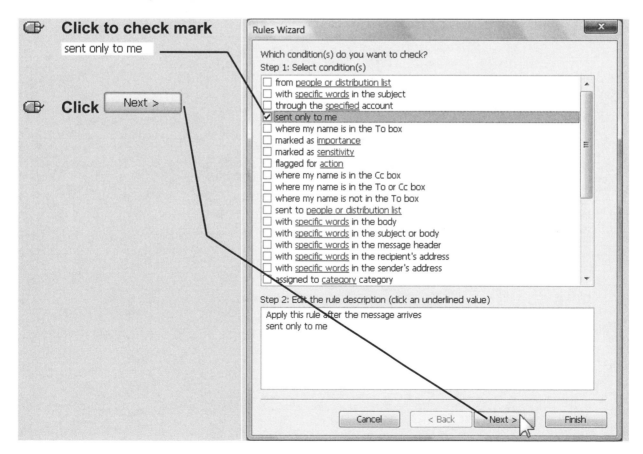

☞ **Click**

✉ Check messages when they arr

At the bottom of the window:

☞ **Click** `Next >`

You want the rule to apply to e-mails that were only sent to you, not to e-mails that were sent to multiple e-mail addresses:

☞ **Click to check mark**

sent only to me

☞ **Click** `Next >`

You are going to reply to these messages with a specific template:

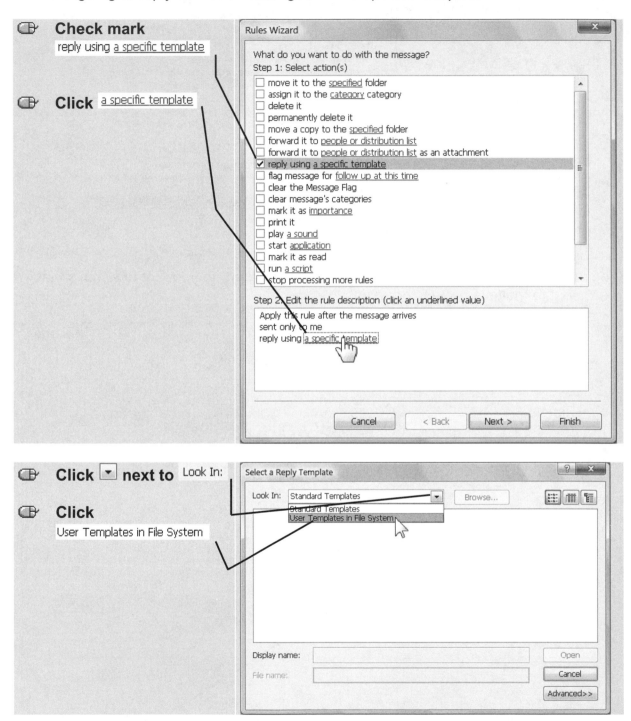

- **Check mark** reply using a specific template
- **Click** a specific template
- **Click** ▼ next to Look In:
- **Click** User Templates in File System

You see the templates you created yourself. Select the *Away* template:

Click Away

Click Open

Select a Reply Template

Look In: User Templates in File System

C:\Users\Studio Visual Steps\AppData\Roaming\Microsoft\Sjablonen*.oft

Away
New website

Display name: Away

File name: Away.oft

Open
Cancel
Advanced>>

You see the link to the *Away* template:

Click Next >

Rules Wizard

What do you want to do with the message?
Step 1: Select action(s)

☐ move it to the specified folder
☐ assign it to the category category
☐ delete it
☐ permanently delete it
☐ move a copy to the specified folder
☐ forward it to people or distribution list
☐ forward it to people or distribution list as an attachment
☑ reply using a specific template
☐ flag message for follow up at this time
☐ clear the Message Flag
☐ clear message's categories
☐ mark it as importance
☐ print it
☐ play a sound
☐ start application
☐ mark it as read
☐ run a script
☐ stop processing more rules

Step 2: Edit the rule description (click an underlined value)

Apply this rule after the message arrives
sent only to me
reply using C:\Users\Studio Visual Steps\AppData\Roaming\Microsoft\Sjablonen\Awa

Cancel   < Back   Next >   Finish

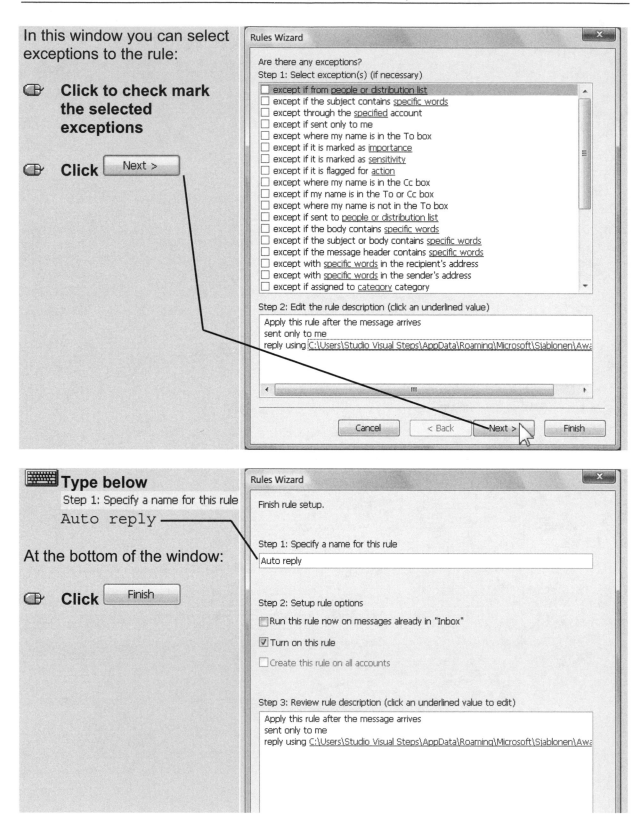

In this window you can select exceptions to the rule:

☞ **Click to check mark the selected exceptions**

☞ **Click** [Next >]

Rules Wizard

Are there any exceptions?
Step 1: Select exception(s) (if necessary)

- ☐ except if from people or distribution list
- ☐ except if the subject contains specific words
- ☐ except through the specified account
- ☐ except if sent only to me
- ☐ except where my name is in the To box
- ☐ except if it is marked as importance
- ☐ except if it is marked as sensitivity
- ☐ except if it is flagged for action
- ☐ except where my name is in the Cc box
- ☐ except if my name is in the To or Cc box
- ☐ except where my name is not in the To box
- ☐ except if sent to people or distribution list
- ☐ except if the body contains specific words
- ☐ except if the subject or body contains specific words
- ☐ except if the message header contains specific words
- ☐ except with specific words in the recipient's address
- ☐ except with specific words in the sender's address
- ☐ except if assigned to category category

Step 2: Edit the rule description (click an underlined value)

Apply this rule after the message arrives
sent only to me
reply using C:\Users\Studio Visual Steps\AppData\Roaming\Microsoft\Sjablonen\Awa

[Cancel]   [< Back]   [Next >]   [Finish]

⌨ **Type below**

Step 1: Specify a name for this rule

`Auto reply`

At the bottom of the window:

☞ **Click** [Finish]

Rules Wizard

Finish rule setup.

Step 1: Specify a name for this rule

| Auto reply |

Step 2: Setup rule options

☐ Run this rule now on messages already in "Inbox"

☑ Turn on this rule

☐ Create this rule on all accounts

Step 3: Review rule description (click an underlined value to edit)

Apply this rule after the message arrives
sent only to me
reply using C:\Users\Studio Visual Steps\AppData\Roaming\Microsoft\Sjablonen\Awa

You see your new rule:

☞ **Click** [OK]

You can see if the new e-mail rule works, by sending a message to yourself:

☞ **Send an e-mail message to your own e-mail address** ℓℓ5

You will not only receive your own message, but also the automated reply.

⇨ **Please note:**

The *reply using a specific template* rule in the *Rules Wizard* sends your automated reply only once to each sender during a single session. This rule prevents *Outlook* from sending repetitive replies to a single sender from whom you receive multiple messages. During a session, *Outlook* keeps track of the list of users to whom it has responded. If you exit *Outlook* and then restart it, however, the list of the senders who have received automated replies is reset.

⇨ **Please note:**

For the *Rules Wizard* to send a reply automatically your computer must be turned on and *Outlook* must be running. Also, *Outlook* must be configured to check periodically for new messages.

⇨ **Please note:**

Also senders of spam e-mails receive an automated reply to their messages. This may increase the amount of spam you receive! Make sure to install an updated spam filter to avoid this.

3.3 Simple Mailing by E-mail

You can also use e-mail to send a mailing to your contacts in *Business Contact Manager*.

➡️ **Please note:**

In order to work through this section *Business Contact Manager* must be installed on your computer. If you do not have *Business Contact Manager* you can skip this section.

💡 **Tip**

More elaborate mailings
In this example you create a mailing using *Microsoft Outlook*. This program is suitable for simple messages with little formatting, such as an announcement. For more elaborate mailings you can use *Microsoft Word*. You can read more about that later in this chapter.

👆 **Click**
🏠 Business Contact Manager Ho

👆 **Click the** Marketing **tab**

👆 **Click**
📧 New Marketing Campaign

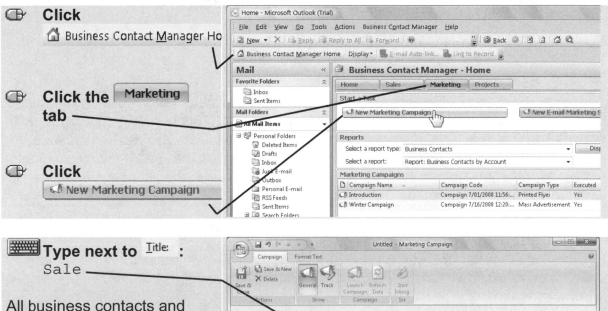

⌨️ **Type next to** Title: :
Sale

All business contacts and leads are already selected:

👆 **Click** Review and Filter...

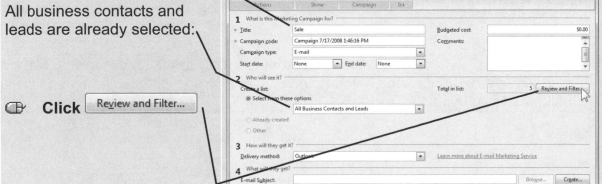

In this example you see the contacts that were added in *Chapter 2 Customer Relationship Management*:

🖰 **Click to remove the check mark by** Wright, Barry

Barry Wright will not receive a message.

🖰 **Click** OK

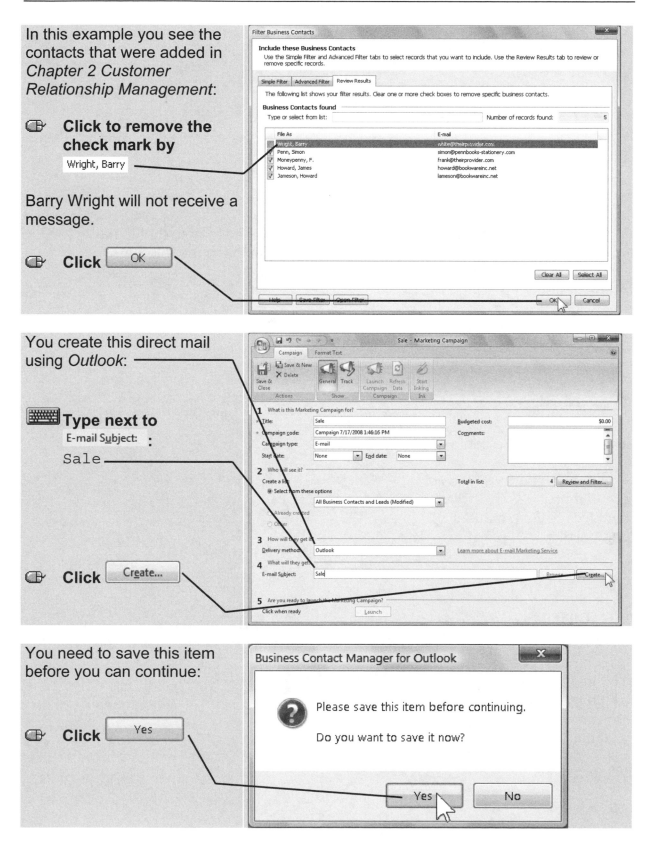

You create this direct mail using *Outlook*:

⌨ **Type next to** E-mail Subject: :
Sale

🖰 **Click** Create...

You need to save this item before you can continue:

🖰 **Click** Yes

Now you see an empty e-mail message with a signature (if you created one):

⌨ **Type your message**

🖱 **Click** Save & Close

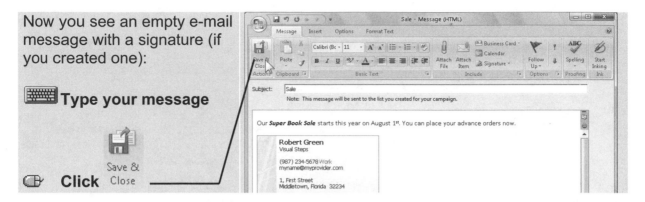

Now you can send the messages for this campaign. Please note that these messages are sent immediately when you are connected to the Internet.

At the bottom of the window:

🖱 **Click** Launch

3 How will they get it?

Delivery method: Outlook   Learn more about

4 What will they get?

E-mail Subject: Sale

5 Are you ready to launch the Marketing Campaign?

Click when ready   Launch

The messages are sent right away.

You see a report with the list of the messages that were sent for the *Sale* marketing campaign:

🖱 **Click** Save & Close

Sale - Marketing Campaign

Campaign | Format Text

Save & New · Delete

General Track | Launch Campaign Refresh Data Start Inking

Campaign results

Total leads:	0	Show Report...
Total opportunities:	0	Show Report...
Total accounts:	0	Show Report...
Total contacts:	0	Show Report...

Campaign delivery information

Actual cost: $0.00

Recipients

Name	Email	Delivery Status
Penn, Simon	simon@pennbooks-stationery.com	Sent
Moneypenny, F.	frank@theirprovider.com	Sent
Howard, James	howard@bookwareinc.net	Sent
Jameson, Howard	jameson@bookwareinc.net	Sent

The new campaign is added to the list:

You can track the results of this campaign the same way you did in *Chapter 2 Customer Relationship Management*.

Home - Microsoft Outlook (Trial)

File Edit View Go Tools Actions Business Contact Manager Help   autoreply

New · X · Reply · Reply to All · Forward · Back

Business Contact Manager Home | Display · E-mail Auto-link · Link to Record

Mail

Favorite Folders
- Inbox (1)
- Sent Items

Mail Folders
- All Mail Items
  - Personal Folders
    - Deleted Items
    - Drafts
    - Inbox (1)
    - Junk E-mail
    - Outbox
    - Personal E-mail
    - RSS Feeds
    - Sent Items
  - Search Folders
- Business Contact Manager

Marketing Campaigns - Home

Home | Sales | Marketing | Projects   Add or Remove Content

Start a Task

New Marketing Campaign   New E-mail Marketing Service Marketing Campaign

Reports

Select a report type: Business Contacts   Display... Print...

Select a report: Report: Business Contacts by Account

Marketing Campaigns

Campaign Name	Campaign Code	Campaign Type	Executed
Introduction	Campaign 7/01/2008 11:56:...	Printed Flyer	Yes
Sale	Campaign 7/17/2008 1:46:1...	E-mail	Yes
Winter Campaign	Campaign 7/16/2008 12:20:...	Mass Advertisement	Yes

💡 **Tip**

Effective mailings
Due to the increasing amount of spam received these days, more rigorous measures have been undertaken by many of the popular spam filters. For example, all messages that are sent to more than ten e-mail addresses may be filtered out. When you create a mailing the way you did in this section, it is sent as a group of separate messages. This means the mailing is not recognized as bulk mail and there is less chance of it being filtered out by spam filters.
Always make sure to enter a clear subject, otherwise there is a chance that the spam filter or the recipient deletes the message without reading it.

E-mail addresses may change sometimes. Pay attention to the *Mail System Error - Returned Mail* messages you receive. Use these returned messages to update the information about your contacts.

☞ **Close** *Outlook* 👣⁹

3.4 Creating Your Own Stationery

Most businesses have their own stationery or letterhead. Stationery that is designed with a logo and company details conveys a more professional business image. In *Word* you can quickly and easily create your own business letterhead. The practice files on the website of this book contain basic models that you can customize by adding your own details. You can give that a try:

☞ **Open** *Word* 👣¹

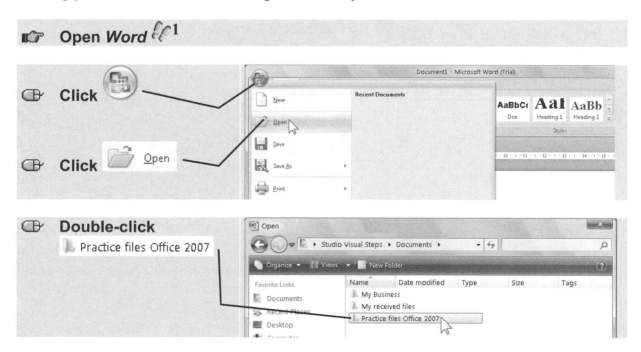

⇨ **Please note:**

You can find the folder containing the practice files on the website with this book. You can read how to copy this folder to your computer in *Chapter 1 Preparation*.

☞ **Double-click**
🗎 Simple letterhead

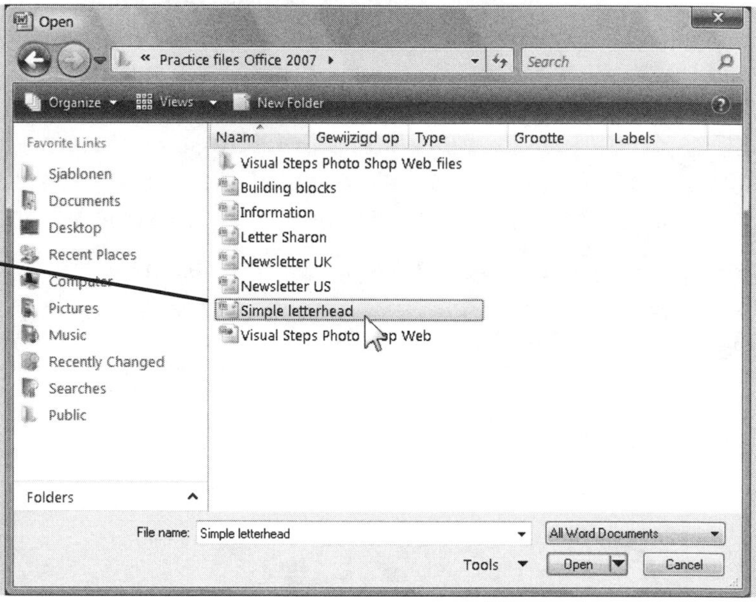

You see the layout of the letterhead. You can enter your own details in the heading, such as your company name, address and (if necessary) a logo. You do that like this:

☞ **Click**
Company information

Company information changes into
🔲 Company information .

This is the default shape of a content control that allows you to insert text at a specific location.

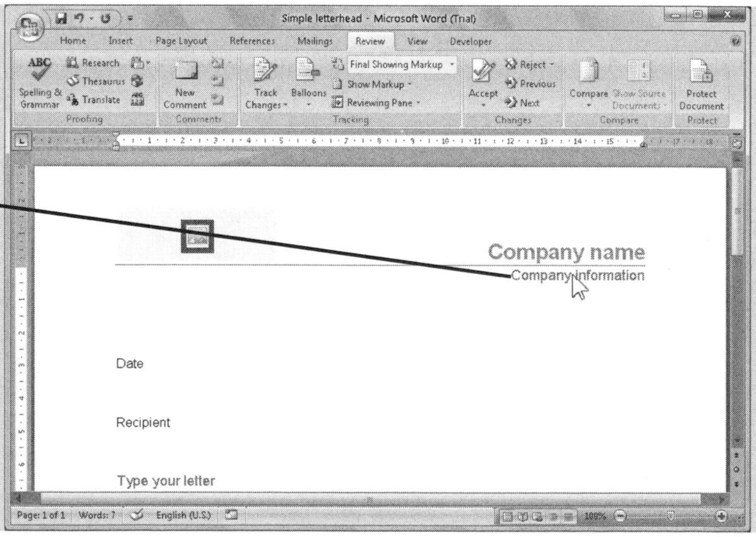

In addition to your company name and address you should also mention some other details in the heading section of the stationery. These are the most important ones: (US and UK)

- Visiting address.
- Correspondence address (in case it is different than the visiting address).
- If you work internationally, do not forget to list the country name.
- Phone number (if necessary also your mobile number) and fax number.
- E-mail address and web address.

In the UK:

- The company's full name, registered office address and registered number must appear on all business stationery. If more than one address is listed, it is recommended that you state which the registered office address is.
- If you use your stationery for invoices: your VAT registration number must be listed.
- A company does not have to state the directors' names on its business stationery. However, if the names of any of its directors appear on its letterhead, then the names of all directors must be shown.
- If the company is being wound up, every invoice, order for goods, business letter or order form (whether in hard copy, electronic or any other form) must contain a statement that the company is being wound up.

In order to enhance readability there are also some recommendations for the way addresses, phone numbers et cetera. are written in the letterhead. For the US:

- Type the city name and state abbreviation in capitals.
- Type a comma between the city and the state abbreviation.
- The traditional convention for typing phone numbers is (AAA) BBB-BBBB. AAA is the area code prefix; BBB-BBBB is the subscriber number.
- For companies that operate internationally the phone number can also be displayed like this: 1-AAA-BBB-BBBB. The number 1 is the long distance access code for the USA.
- Use lower case for e-mail addresses and web addresses.
- If you write the letter to a specific person instead of to a company as a whole, the first two lines of the recipients address must contain the name of the person and his or her formal job title. For example on the first line: Mr. John A. Smith. On the second line: Chief Executive Officer. On the third line: the company name.

- Continue reading on the next page -

For the UK the same rules apply, with these exceptions:
- Type the postal code in capitals. The format of UK postcodes is generally: A9 9AA, A99 9AA, A9A 9AA, AA9 9AA, AA99 9AA or AA9A 9AA
- Type the postal code below the city name.
- If a dependent locality (for example Bethnal Green) is mentioned in the address, type that above the city name (for example London).
- UK telephone numbers are complex due to the varying size of area codes and subscriber numbers. Phone numbers are formatted as 0AAAA BBBBBB, where 0AAAA is the STD (area) code, and BBBBBB is the subscriber number. Both have a variable length. Larger areas have shorter STD codes. The subscriber code is split into two blocks of four if it is eight digits long (e.g. 020 1234 5678).

⚲ Tip

Limit the amount of information in the heading

When you have a lot of information to list, the heading section of your stationery may become very large and unclear. Additional information such as your e-mail address, web address or bank details may be added to the footer section at the bottom of your stationery. This will make your documents look more attractive.

As soon as you have decided which details to include in the heading:

⌨ Type your company information

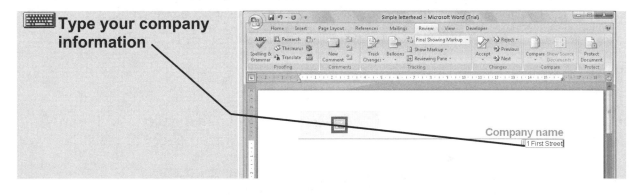

⚲ Tip

Company information on the left side?

When you enter the information you can use the regular *Word* commands. If you would rather have the company information on the left side instead of on the right side, click ▤ in the *Start* tab. Then the information is aligned on the left side.

When you type a web address or an e-mail address these are automatically turned into hyperlinks and underlined. A hyperlink is not necessary in a letterhead.

☞ **Right-click your web address**

☞ **Click** ✂ Remove Hyperlink

☞ **If necessary, also remove the hyperlink from your e-mail address**

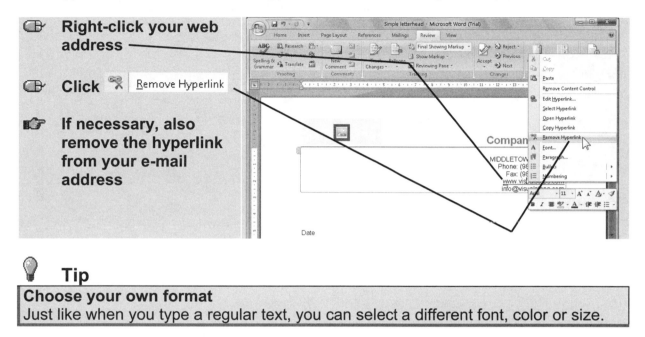

💡 **Tip**

Choose your own format
Just like when you type a regular text, you can select a different font, color or size.

In the header you can enter your company name, if necessary with a logo. All items in the header are automatically displayed on every additional page. The same thing goes for the footer. You can change the header like this:

☞ **Double-click**
Company name

On the left you see Header :

The *Design* tab appears:

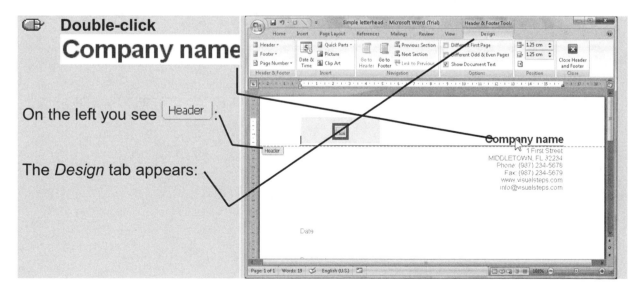

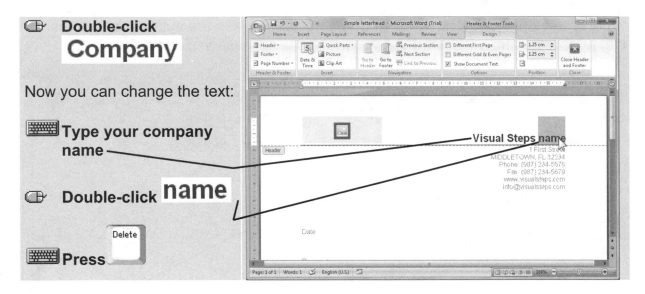

Double-click **Company**

Now you can change the text:

Type your company name

Double-click **name**

Press `Delete`

If you have an image of your company logo on your computer, you can add it to the header:

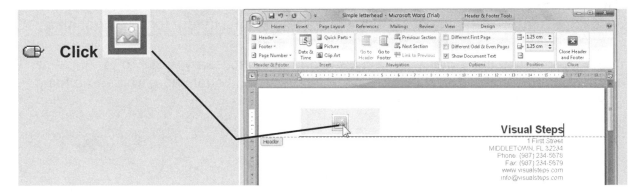

Click

If you do not have a logo, you can add a sample logo from the practice files or select an image from the image folder(s) on your computer.

Tip

No logo
If you do not want to add a logo to the header, you can remove the logo box like this:

Right-click

Click ✂ Cut

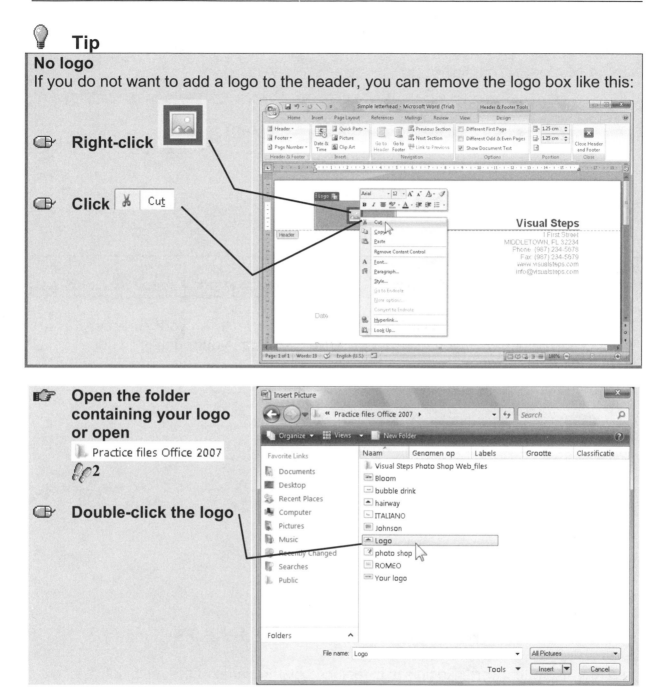

👉 **Open the folder containing your logo or open**
📁 Practice files Office 2007
👣2

Double-click the logo

The logo is inserted:

☞ **If necessary, click the**

Design **tab**

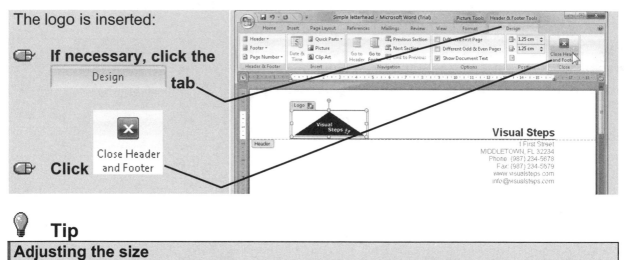

☞ **Click** ☒ Close Header and Footer

💡 **Tip**

Adjusting the size
You can adjust the size of the logo by dragging the sizing handles around the image.

The next step is to check if all items are positioned correctly on your stationery. That is especially important if you use window envelopes. Use your printer to print a sample of your stationery:

☞ **Click**

☞ **Click** 🖨 Print

☞ **Click** Quick Print

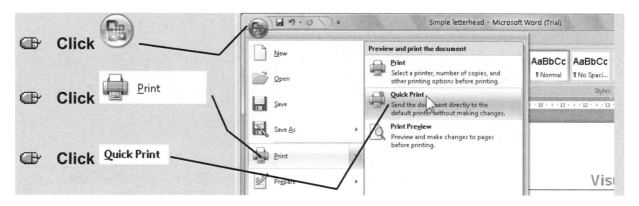

You can fold the printed letter and insert it in the envelope.

☞ **Check if the word 'Recipient' is located at the top of the window**

In a real letter, the word 'Recipient' is replaced by the name of the recipient. The other address lines are located under the name.

Help! The address is not positioned correctly.

If the address is not positioned correctly, you can move it like this:

- Click `Recipient` and click ▤ on the *Start* tab a couple of times to move the address to the right.
- To move the address down you can add a few extra blank lines above `Recipient`.
- To move the address up you can remove a few blank lines above `Recipient`.

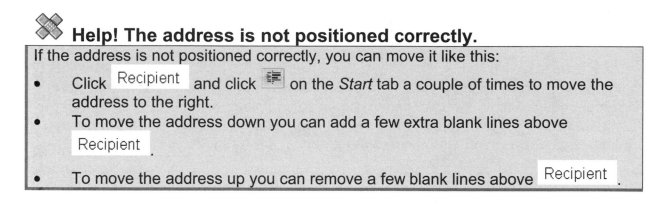

When `Recipient` is placed correctly, your letter is ready. The other details will be added when you start writing a letter.

Now you can save this letter as a template:

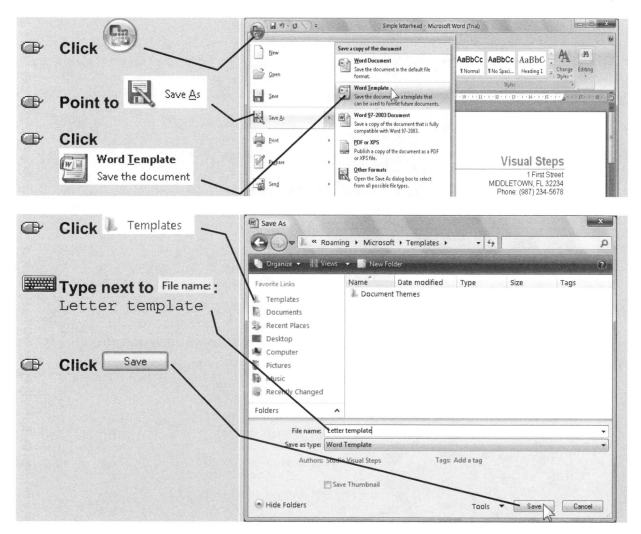

☞ **Close the document** ᶜᵉ⁹

⇨ **Please note:**

You have saved your document as a template instead of a regular document. A template is a document type that creates a copy of itself when you open it. You can use it over and over again, while the original template stays the same. There is a difference between opening a template and opening a regular *Word* document. You can try that in the next section.

3.5 Using Templates

You can quickly create a business letter using your own template:

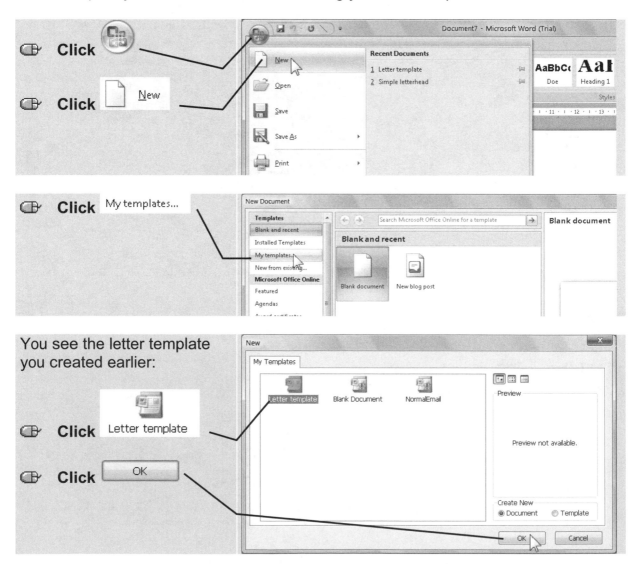

🖱 **Click** ⊞

🖱 **Click** New

🖱 **Click** My templates...

You see the letter template you created earlier:

🖱 **Click** Letter template

🖱 **Click** OK

Your company information is already listed in the heading:

👆 **Click** Recipient

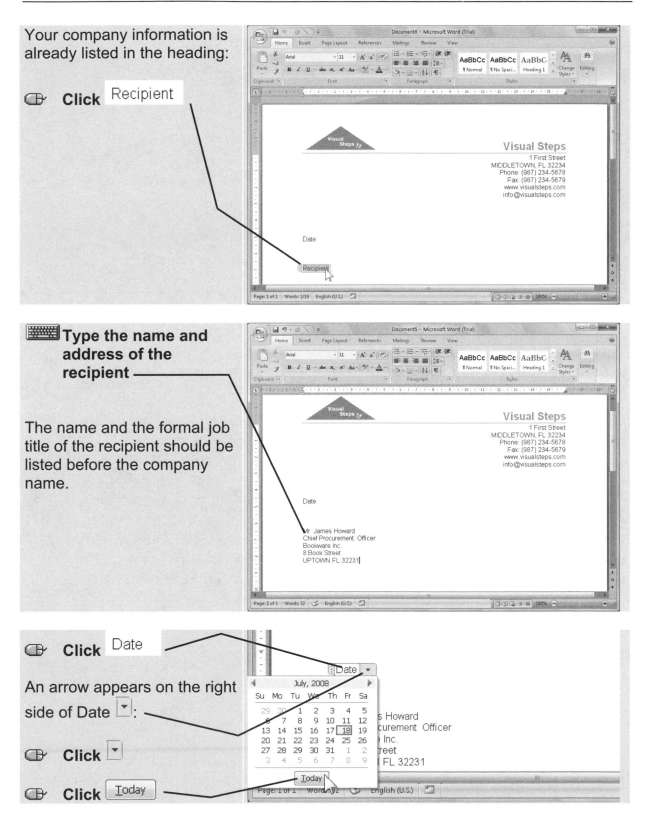

⌨ **Type the name and address of the recipient**

The name and the formal job title of the recipient should be listed before the company name.

👆 **Click** Date

An arrow appears on the right side of Date ▾ :

👆 **Click** ▾

👆 **Click** Today

The current date is added to the letter.

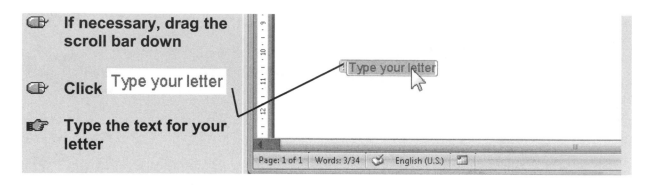

☞ **If necessary, drag the scroll bar down**

☞ **Click** Type your letter

☞ **Type the text for your letter**

💡 **Tip**

Salutation

If you know the name of the recipient, you can start the letter like this:

- in the USA: *Dear Mr. Jones:*
  Punctuation: use a colon.
- in the UK: *Dear Mr Jones* or *Dear Mr Jones,*
  Punctuation: do not use any punctuation mark or use a comma.

In American English, the abbreviations Mr, Mrs et cetera are usually written with a period at the end (Mr.). In British English the period is omitted (Mr).

In case you do not know the name of the recipient, you can choose one of these salutations:

- *Gentlemen*   for a male recipient in American English
- *Dear Sir / Dear Sirs*   for a male recipient in British English
- *Ladies*   for a female recipient in American English
- *Dear Madam*   for a female recipient in the UK
- *Ladies and Gentlemen*   gender unknown (especially in American English)
- *To whom it may concern*   gender unknown (especially in American English)
- *Dear Sir or Madam*   gender unknown (especially in British English)

Source: English Grammar 4U Online (www.ego4u.com)

You can print the letter now if you want. You can save this template as a regular *Word* document by doing the following:

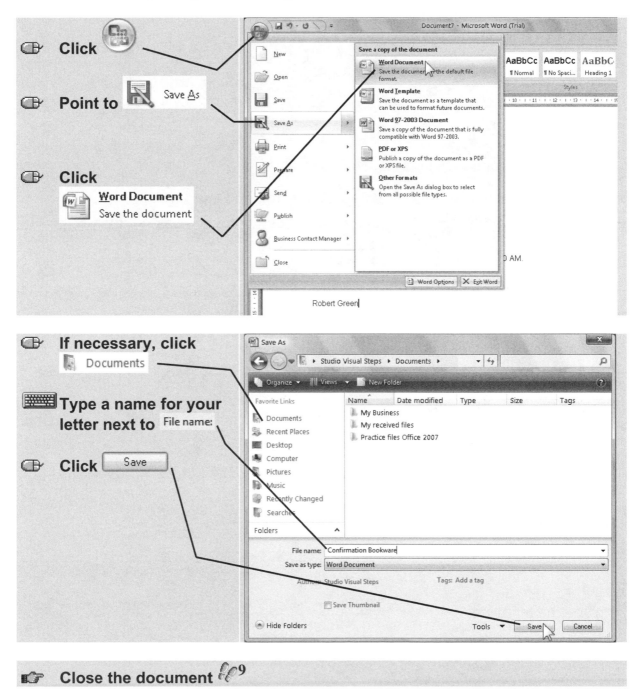

☞ **Close the document** 🐾⁹

Your letter is saved as a normal document. The template *Letter template* is still blank and can be used again later.

3.6 Customizing Templates

To be able to customize an existing template, you open it as a template first:

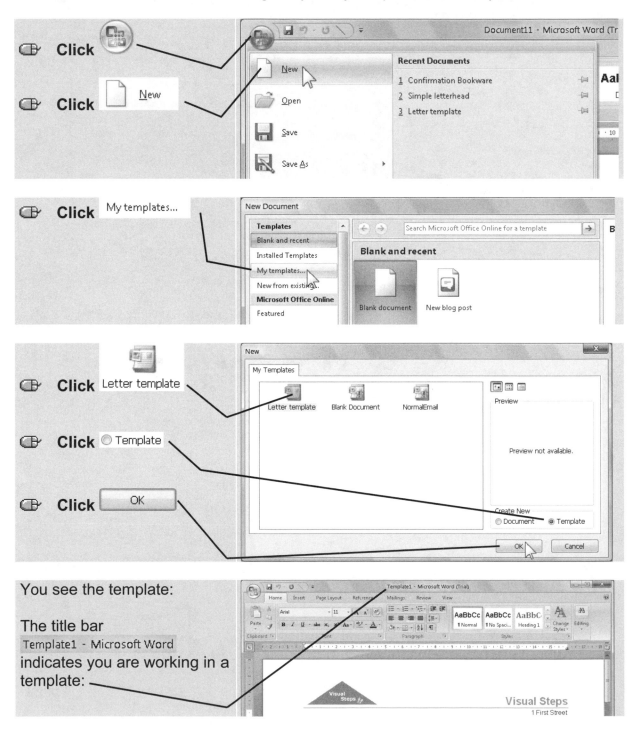

You start by entering your name at the bottom of the template *Letter*. This way you will not need to type it again with each new letter you create:

Click below Type your letter

Press Enter **three times**

Type your name

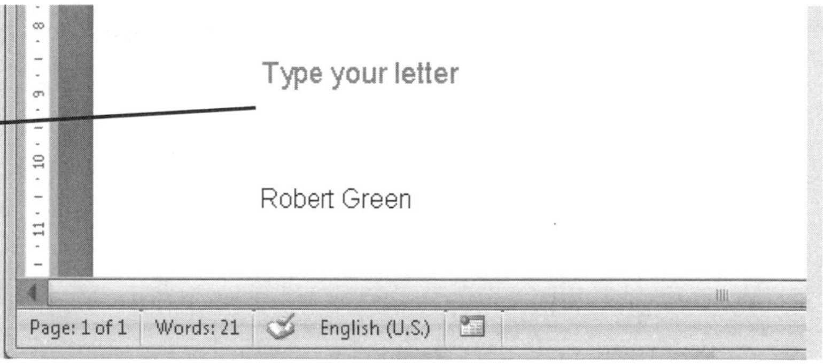

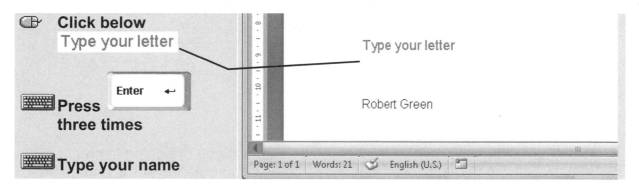

You have added a fixed text to the template.

You can also add new content controls to the template. To do this, you need to turn on the *Developer* tab:

Click

Click Word Options

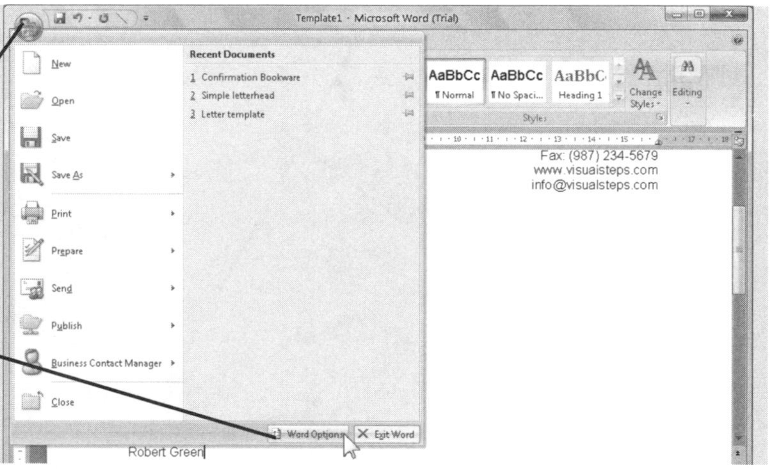

Click to check mark Show Developer tab in the Ribbon

Click OK

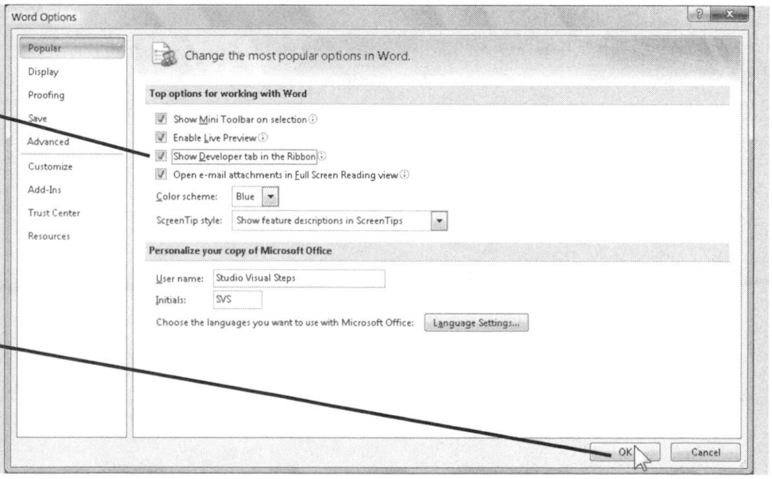

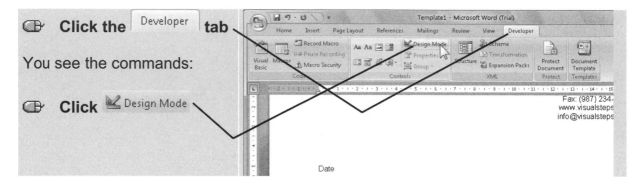

Now you can add a new content control. As an example you are going to create a drop-down list containing different options for the closing greeting at the end of the letter:

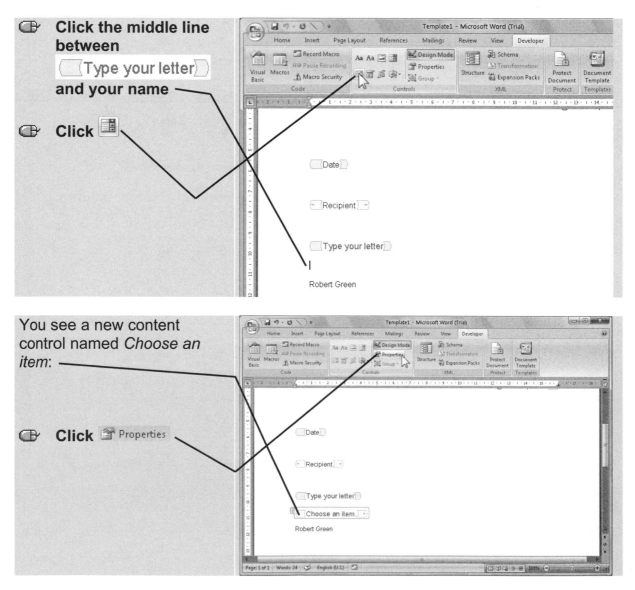

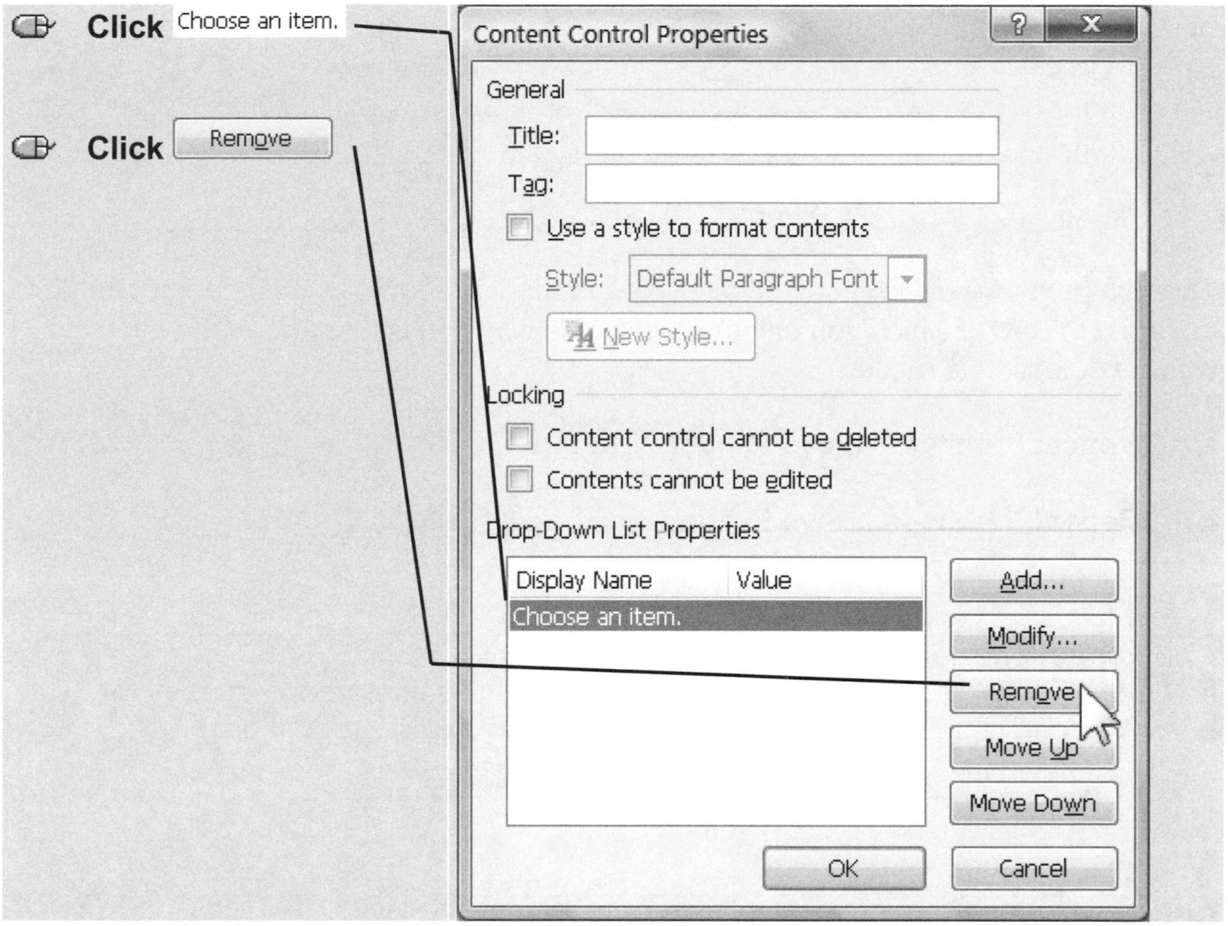

Click Choose an item.

Click Remove

Content Control Properties

General

Title:

Tag:

☐ Use a style to format contents

Style: Default Paragraph Font ▾

🔠 New Style...

Locking

☐ Content control cannot be deleted

☐ Contents cannot be edited

Drop-Down List Properties

Display Name	Value
Choose an item.	

Add...

Modify...

Remove

Move Up

Move Down

OK   Cancel

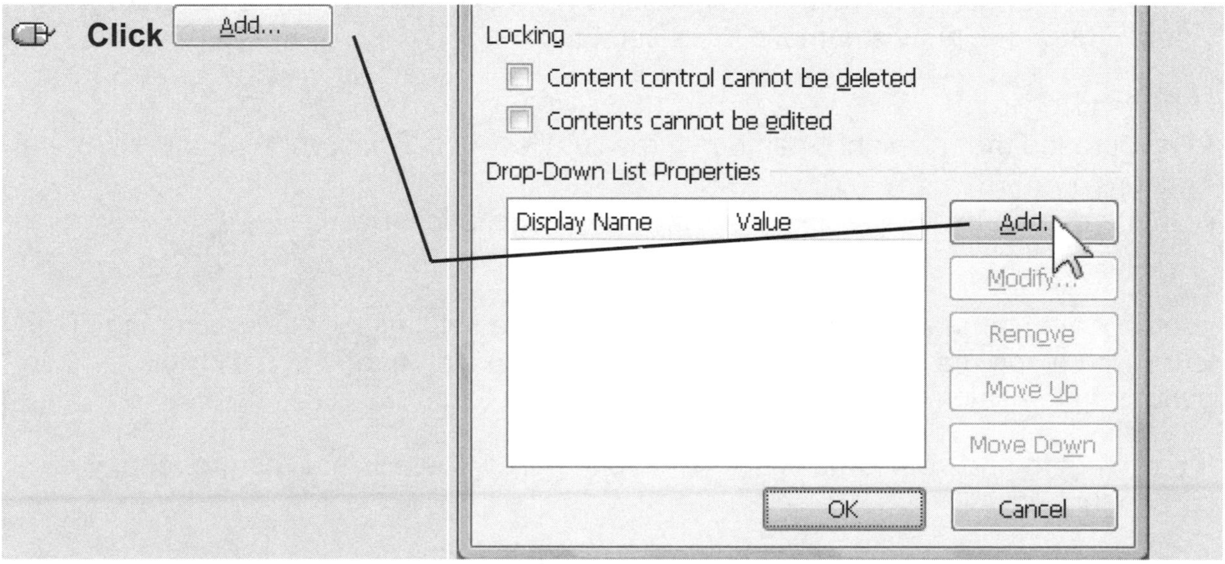

Click Add...

Locking

☐ Content control cannot be deleted

☐ Contents cannot be edited

Drop-Down List Properties

Display Name	Value

Add.

Modify...

Remove

Move Up

Move Down

OK   Cancel

⌨ Type:
Sincerely,

☞ **Click** [OK]

Add Choice [?] [X]

Display Name: | Sincerely,
Value: | Sincerely,

[OK] [Cancel]

The text next to Display Name: will be displayed in the drop-down list in the template. The text next to Value: (which you can change in this window) is inserted in the letter when a selection is made.

☞ **Repeat the steps above to add:** Sincerely yours,

☞ **Repeat the steps above to add:** Yours faithfully,

💡 **Tip**

Changing the order of the drop-down list
In the drop-down list, the options are presented in the same order they are listed here. You can change the order by clicking the display name of the option and moving it using the buttons [Move Up] or [Move Down].

💡 **Tip**

Closing greeting
In American English you can use *Sincerely* or *Sincerely yours* even if you began the letter with the recipient's name in the salutation.

In British English:
- if you used the recipient's name in the salutation, use *Sincerely* or *Sincerely yours.*
- If you did not use the recipient's name in the salutation, use *Faithfully* or *Faithfully yours.*

In both American and British English: if you end the salutation at the beginning of the letter with a comma or colon, use a comma after the greeting. If you did not punctuate the salutation, do not punctuate the greeting.

If you want to add some additional items to the drop-down list for the greeting, you can do that now.

Source: English Grammar 4U Online (www.ego4u.com)

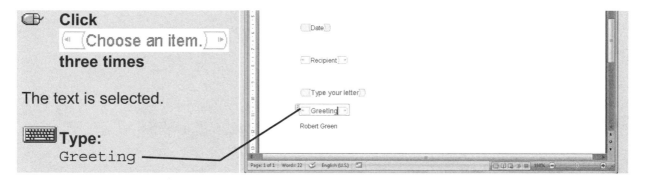

🖱 **Click** [OK]

At the location of the greeting you see the content control ◁ ⟨Choose an item.⟩ ▷ .
You can change the text of this control to clarify what it will insert in the letter:

🖱 **Click**
◁ ⟨Choose an item.⟩ ▷
three times

The text is selected.

⌨ **Type:**
Greeting

Now you make some space for your signature:

🖱 **Click below**
◁ ⟨Greeting⟩ ▷

⌨ **Press** [Enter ↵]
three times

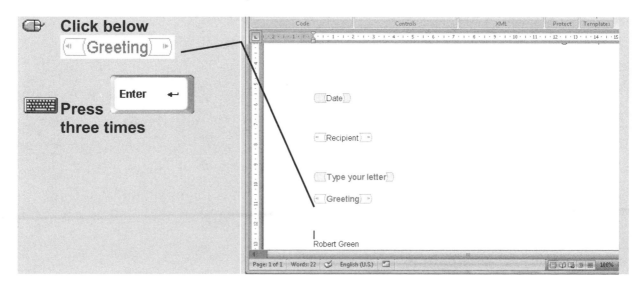

You can save the changed *Letter template* like this:

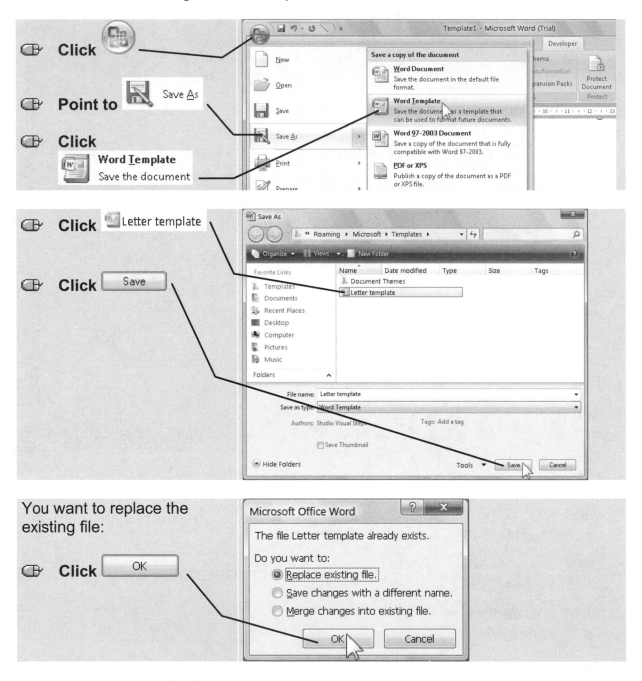

📑 **Click** [icon]

📑 **Point to** [Save As icon]

📑 **Click**
[Word Template icon] **Word Template**
Save the document

📑 **Click** [Letter template icon] Letter template

📑 **Click** [Save]

You want to replace the existing file:

📑 **Click** [OK]

You no longer need the *Developer* tab. You can close this tab the same way you opened it:

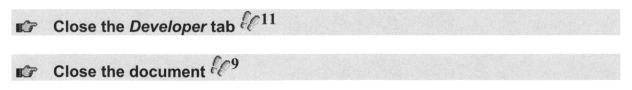

☞ **Close the *Developer* tab** ✎11

☞ **Close the document** ✎9

3.7 Creating Building Blocks

Much of the text used in many business documents, like promissory notes, bids, estimates, credit notes, invoices and purchase orders, does not need to change very often. For example, the opening sentences, company or job descriptions and payment terms can be pre-defined.

Sometimes more than one version of these blocks of text is needed, for example, one for companies and another one for private persons. You can turn these standard texts into building blocks that can be inserted into your documents as you need them. That will save you a lot of time typing.

☞ **If necessary, open** *Word* 1

☞ **Open the document** *Building blocks* **from the folder** Practice files Office 2007 12

Here you see some standard texts used by a company. As an example you are going to turn these bits of text into building blocks. In *Word* they are called *Quick Parts*:

☞ **Click the** Insert **tab**

☞ **Select the first section** 27

☞ **Click** Quick Parts ▾

☞ **Click** Save Selection to Quick Part Gallery..

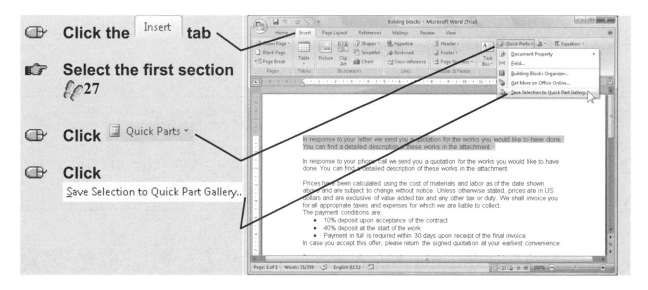

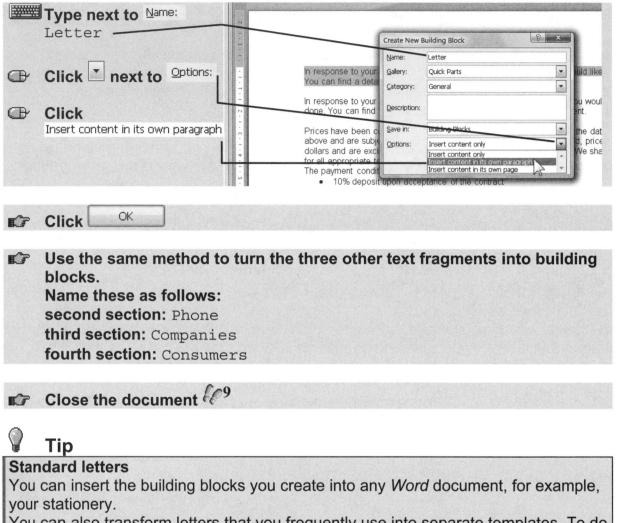

Type next to Name:
Letter

Click ▾ next to Options:

Click
Insert content in its own paragraph

☞ Click [OK]

☞ **Use the same method to turn the three other text fragments into building blocks.**
Name these as follows:
second section: Phone
third section: Companies
fourth section: Consumers

☞ **Close the document** ℓℓ⁹

💡 Tip

Standard letters
You can insert the building blocks you create into any *Word* document, for example, your stationery.
You can also transform letters that you frequently use into separate templates. To do so, type the text in the blank letter template and save the new letter as a template with a recognizable name.

3.8 Using Building Blocks

When you type a letter or other document, you can insert the building blocks wherever you want.

☞ **Open the template** *Letter template* ℓℓ¹⁴

☞ **Enter today's date** ✍16

☞ **Type the following information in the** Recipient **field:**
Mr. Alex Brown
552 Clearwater Lakes
Uptown, FL 32231

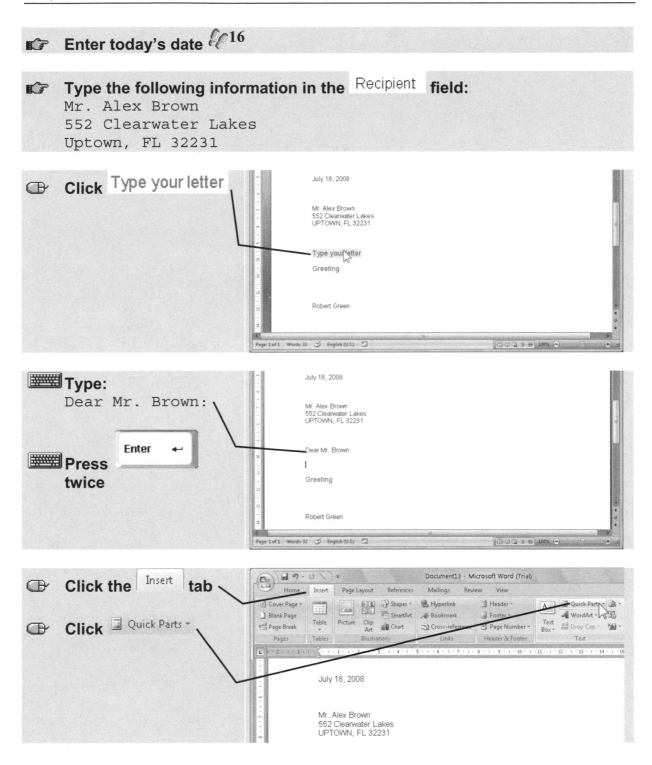

🖰 **Click** Type your letter

⌨ **Type:**
Dear Mr. Brown:

⌨ **Press** Enter ← **twice**

🖰 **Click the** Insert **tab**

🖰 **Click** Quick Parts ▾

Click **Letter**

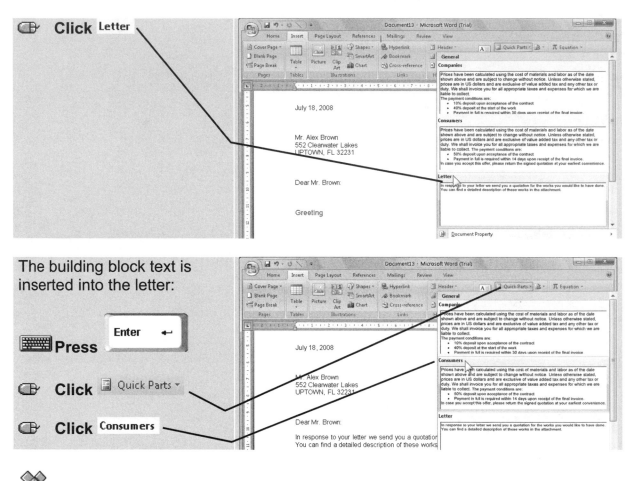

The building block text is inserted into the letter:

Press Enter ←

Click **Quick Parts ▾**

Click **Consumers**

Help! I do not see the building block **Consumers**.

If you have a long list of building blocks, you can use the scroll bar to find the right building block:

Drag the scroll bar down

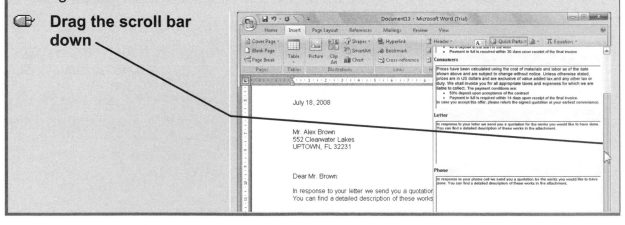

The second building block text is also inserted in the letter:

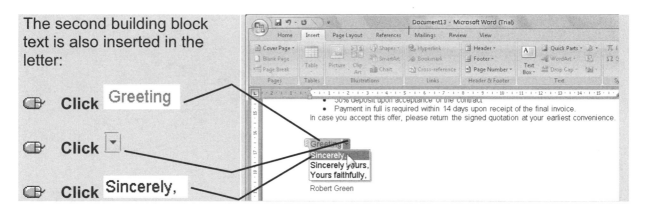

☞ **Click** Greeting

☞ **Click** ▾

☞ **Click** Sincerely,

The offer proposal is ready. You can save the document and print it if necessary.

☞ **Save it as a *Word* document named *Brown* in the *Documents* folder and close the sales quote** 🦶**17**

⇨ **Please note:**

When you add or change building blocks, you will see the following question when you close *Microsoft Word*:

☞ **Click** Yes

Microsoft Office Word

⚠ You have modified styles, building blocks (such as cover pages or headers), or other content that is stored in "Building Blocks". Do you want to save changes to "Building Blocks"?

Yes   No   Cancel

3.9 Creating a Mailing Using Microsoft Word

In *Microsoft Word* you can quickly create a mailing to address your contacts in *Microsoft Outlook* or *Business Contact Manager*. The letters are addressed using a mail merge procedure. You can print the letters and send them by regular mail.

⇨ **Please note:**

For the mailing in this section *Business Contact Manager* is used. If you do not have this program, you can only read through this section.

☞ **Open the template *Letter template*** 🦶**14**

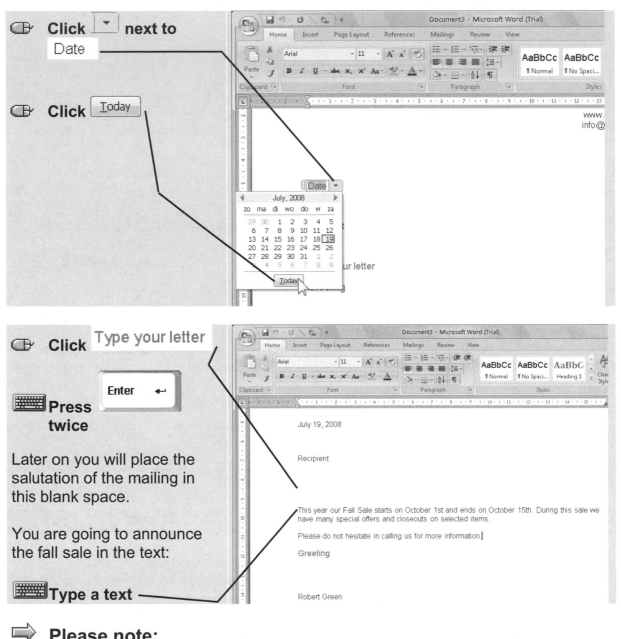

Click ▼ next to Date

Click Today

Click Type your letter

Press Enter **twice**

Later on you will place the salutation of the mailing in this blank space.

You are going to announce the fall sale in the text:

Type a text

⇨ **Please note:**

Do not enter a salutation for your letter; leave the space empty for the moment. The salutation will be added automatically along with the address details of your contacts.

Click ⬛▾ next to *Greeting*

Click **Sincerely,**

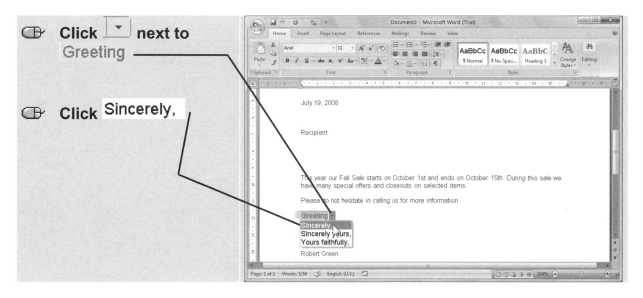

☞ **Save this letter as a *Word* document named *Fall sale* in the *Documents* folder** ✍47

The document is still opened. Now, you are going to send this letter to your contacts using *Business Contact Manager*.

Click the **Mailings** tab

Click **Marketing**

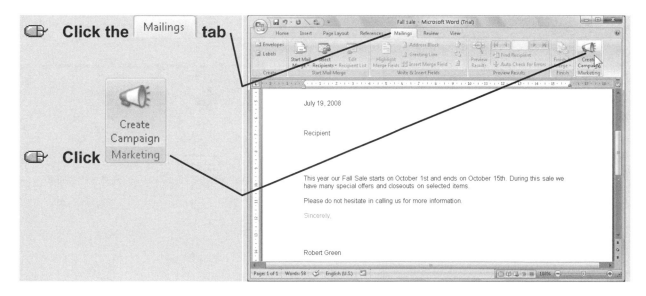

You see the *Business Contact Manager* window:

☞ **Click** [Review and Filter...]

❋ Help! The Business Contact Manager window does not appear.

Click [Fall sale - Marke...] on the taskbar at the bottom of your screen if you do not see the *Business Contact Manager* window.

You see your contacts:

In this example there are two contacts that do not need to receive this mailing:

☞ **Click to remove the check marks for**
Moneypenny, F. **and**
Internal Revenue Service

☞ **Click** [OK]

❋ Help! Other contacts appear.

If you see other contacts in this window, you can remove their check marks too.

💡 Tip

Simple filter

You can use a filter to select the contacts that meet certain conditions. For example, contacts with overdue payments could be excluded from the mailing:

🖰 **Click the** Simple Filter **tab**

🖰 **Click to remove the check mark for** Overdue

To see the result:

🖰 **Click the** Review Results **tab**

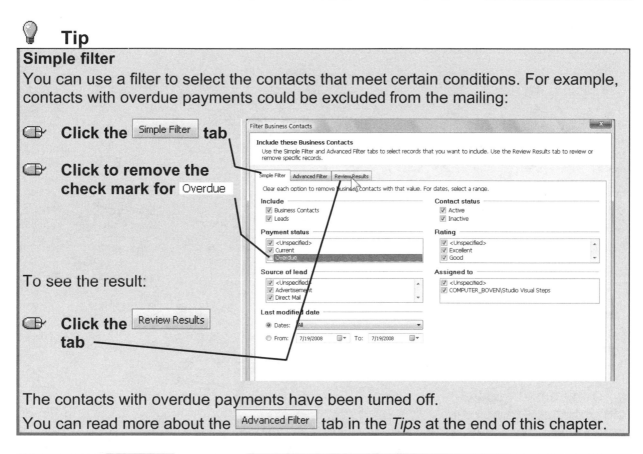

The contacts with overdue payments have been turned off.

You can read more about the Advanced Filter tab in the *Tips* at the end of this chapter.

🖰 **Click** Launch

You see the *Word* window with the letter again. Now you can indicate where the address details should be placed in the letter:

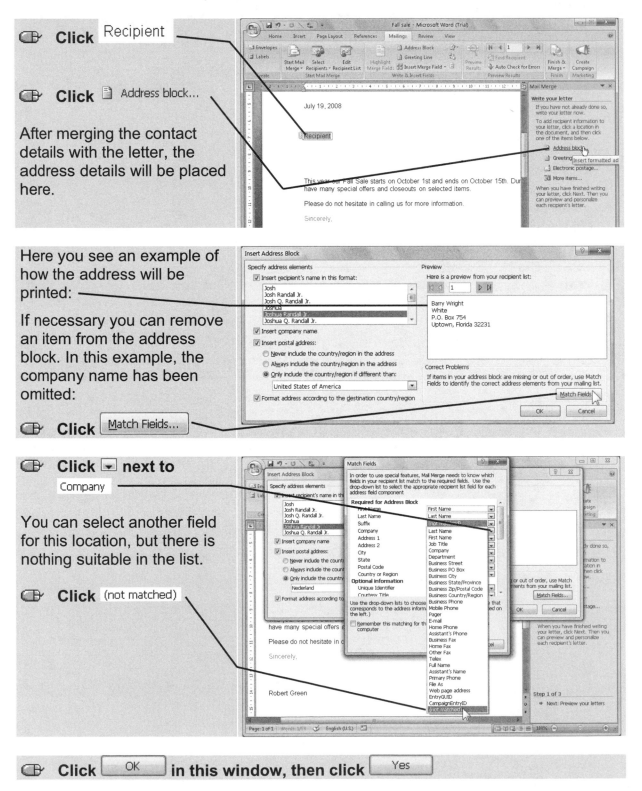

☞ **Click** Recipient

☞ **Click** 📄 Address block...

After merging the contact details with the letter, the address details will be placed here.

Here you see an example of how the address will be printed:

If necessary you can remove an item from the address block. In this example, the company name has been omitted:

☞ **Click** Match Fields...

☞ **Click** ▾ next to

Company

You can select another field for this location, but there is nothing suitable in the list.

☞ **Click** (not matched)

☞ **Click** OK in this window, then click Yes

The address is displayed without the company name:

☞ **Click** `OK`

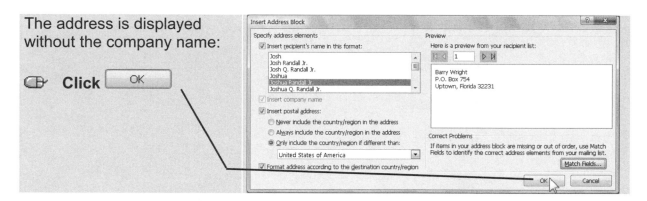

Now you type the salutation:

☞ **Click a blank line above the text**

⌨ **Type:**
Dear Mr. and Mrs.

⌨ **Type a space**

☞ **Click** More items...

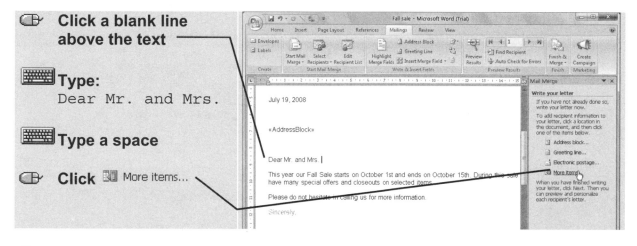

💡 **Tip**

Personal salutation

When you use the mail merge feature only the details that you entered for your contacts can be inserted in the mailing. If you want to use a more personal salutation with the correct title of your contact (like *Mr.*, *Mrs.* or *Ms.*) you have to enter this title when you enter your contact. You can do that in the contact window:

☞ **Click** Full Name...

- Continue reading on the next page -

☞ **Select the correct title**

If the title of your choice is not listed, you can type it yourself.

Here you can select a suffix, for example *Jr., Sr.* or *III*:

🖰 **Click** OK

Check Full Name

Name details

Title: Mr.
First: Barry
Middle:
Last: Wright
Suffix: Jr.

☑ Show this again when name is incomplete or unclear

OK   Cancel

If there is a field missing for a specific detail that you want to show, you can pick one of the fields previously unselected from the group of address fields:

🖰 **Click** ○ Address Fields

🖰 **Click** Last Name

🖰 **Click** Insert

Insert Merge Field

Insert:
● Address Fields   ○ Database Fields

Fields:
Unique Identifier
Courtesy Title
First Name
Middle Name
Last Name
Suffix
Nickname
Job Title
Company
Address 1
Address 2
City
State
Postal Code
Country or Region

Match Fields...   Insert   Cancel

🖰 **Click** Close

⌨ **Type a colon next to**
«Last Name»

🖰 **Click**
Next: Preview your letters

«AddressBlock»

Dear Mr. and Mrs. «Last Name»:

This year our Fall Sale starts on October 1st and ends on October 15th. During this sale have many special offers and closeouts on selected items.

Please do not hesitate in calling us for more information.

Sincerely,

Robert Green

your letter, click a location in the document, and then click one of the items below.
🔲 Address block...
🔲 Greeting line...
🔲 Electronic postage...
🔲 More items...

When you have finished writing your letter, click Next. Then you can preview and personalize each recipient's letter.

Step 1 of 3
➔ Next: Preview your letters
Next wizard step

of 1 | Words: 64 | English (U.S.) | 100%

You see the first address:

To display the next address:

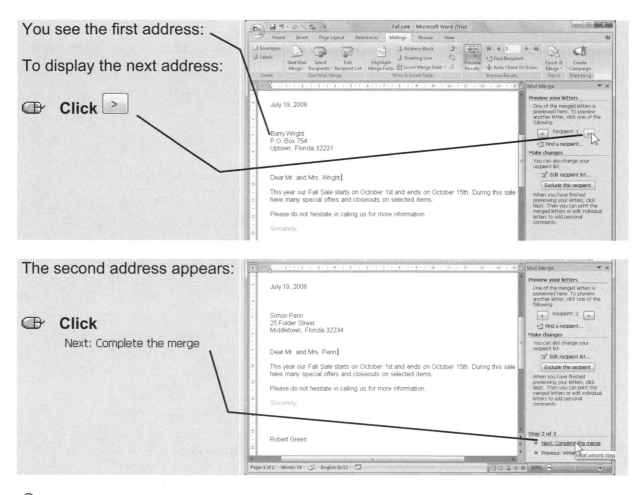

👉 **Click** [>]

The second address appears:

👉 **Click**

Next: Complete the merge

💡 **Tip**

Excluding or re-including contacts from the mailing
If you see contacts that need to be excluded, you may be able to exclude them using the button [Exclude this recipient]. However, this button does not function properly in all versions. Therefore it is better to use the button 📇 Edit recipient list... when you want to exclude contacts or re-include contacts marked as excluded.

When you do a mail merge you can print the letters right now, or you can save them as one big document and print them later. It is a good idea to print at least one letter for a final check:

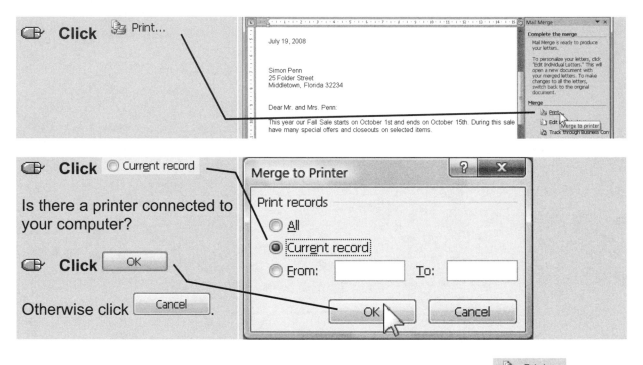

If the print is satisfactory, you can print the complete mailing using 🖨 Print... later.

☞ **Close the document and save it in the *Documents* folder with the name *Fall sale merged*** 🖐47

☞ **Close *Business Contact Manager*** 🖐9

You can track the results of this campaign the same way you practised in *Chapter 2 Customer Relationship Management*.

3.10 Labels

A label is one of the easiest standard documents to create. You can use *Microsoft Word* to create address labels for your contacts in *Microsoft Outlook* or *Business Contact Manager*. The names and the addresses of the contacts are placed on the labels using a mail merge procedure.

Tip

Labels: brand and type

Customized sizes, colors, and shapes of labels are available for almost every need. To ensure good quality when purchasing labels that you will be printing with your printer, make sure that they are designed for the type of printer (laser, inkjet, or dot matrix) you have.

For best results, use one of the label brands and product numbers supported in *Word.* Before you begin to create your labels, check to see if your label's manufacturer and product number are included in the list of vendors. You can find this list by clicking the tab *Mailings,* then *Labels > Options.* Click the drop down list by *Label Vendors* to view the list of product numbers and sizes of the labels for each vendor.

Make sure to have some label sheets on hand for the print exercises.

☞ **Open a new document in *Microsoft Word* 🦶¹⁹**

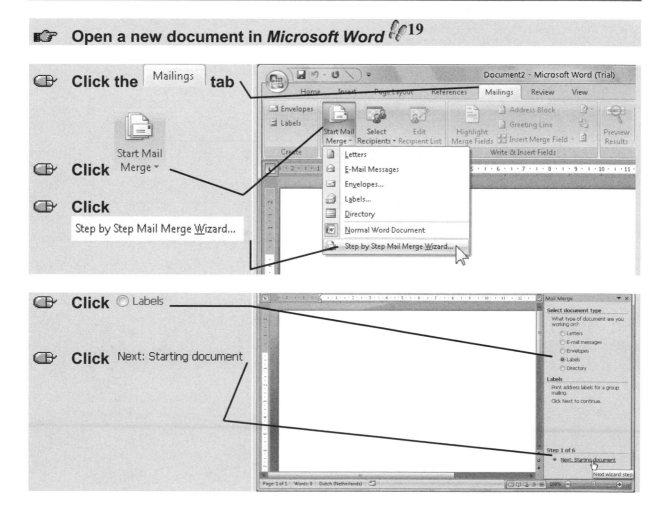

Click the Mailings **tab**

Click Start Mail Merge ▾

Click

Step by Step Mail Merge Wizard...

Click ⦿ Labels

Click Next: Starting document

Click 📄 Label options...

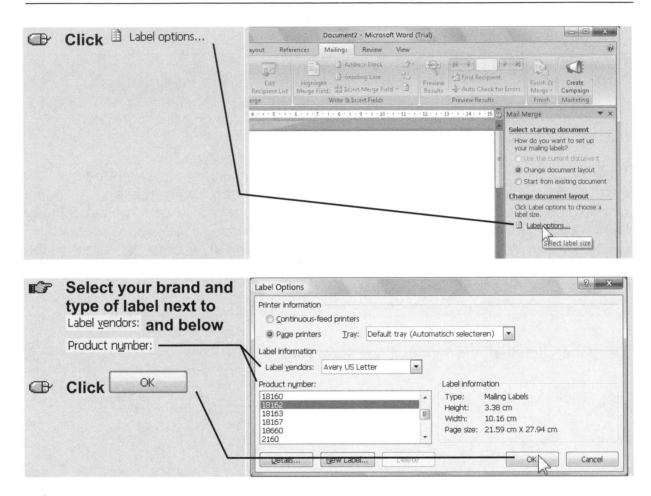

☞ **Select your brand and type of label next to** Label vendors: **and below** Product number:

Click [OK]

➡️ Please note:

All labels have different sizes. If you fail to select the right product number, the labels will not be printed correctly.

You see the label setup on the page:

Click Next: Select recipients

Help! I do not see the label gridlines.

If you do not see the label gridlines, you can display them like this:

- ☞ **Click the** Layout **tab**
- ☞ **Click** 🏢 View Gridlines **in the top left corner**

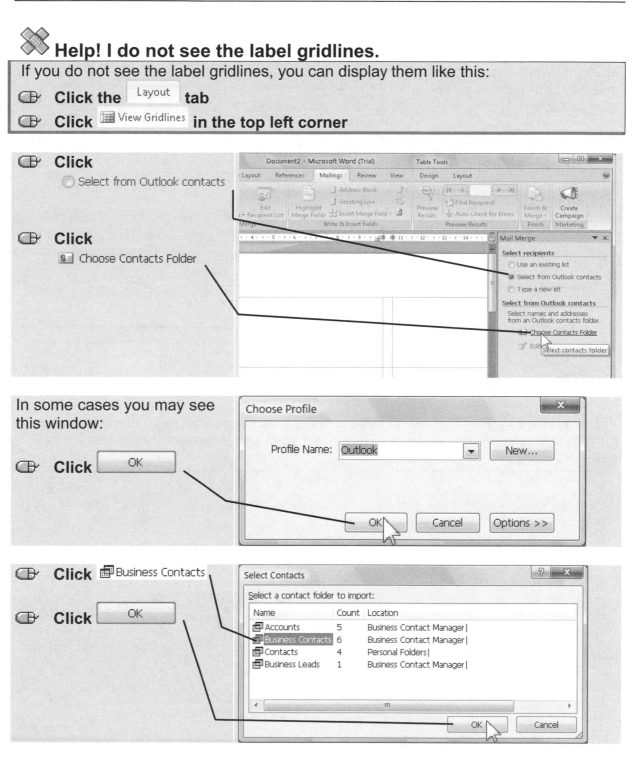

- ☞ **Click**
  - ◉ Select from Outlook contacts

- ☞ **Click**
  - 🔳 Choose Contacts Folder

In some cases you may see this window:

- ☞ **Click** OK

- ☞ **Click** 🏢 Business Contacts

- ☞ **Click** OK

Help! I do not have Business Contact Manager.

If you do not have any business contacts, you can click 🏢 Contacts to use your contacts from *Microsoft Outlook*.

You see your contacts:

In this example, you do not need to print a label for two of the contacts:

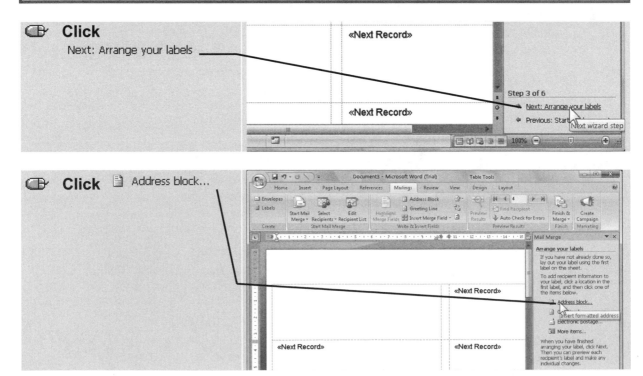

☞ **Click to remove the check marks by**

> Moneypenny   F.

and

> Service   Internal

☞ **Click** `OK`

💡 Tip

Filter

You can use 📇 Filter... to quickly select the contacts that meet certain conditions, for example a zip code or city. You can read more about using filters in the *Tips* at the end of this chapter.

☞ **Click**

> Next: Arrange your labels

☞ **Click** 📄 Address block...

You see an example of the address block that will be printed on the label:

If necessary, you can adjust the way the address block is setup the same way you practiced in the previous section.

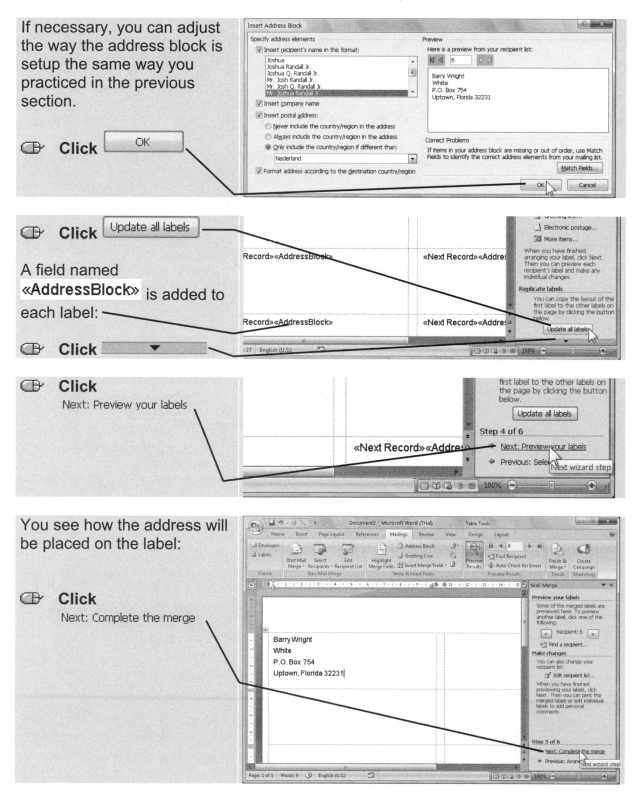

☞ **Click** OK

☞ **Click** Update all labels

A field named «AddressBlock» is added to each label:

☞ **Click** ▼

☞ **Click** Next: Preview your labels

You see how the address will be placed on the label:

☞ **Click** Next: Complete the merge

💡 Tip

Take a step back

If you want to change something in a previous step of the mail merge procedure, you can click ← Previous: in the bottom right corner of the window. This option is available in every step of the mail merge procedure.

👉 **Insert a sufficient number of label sheets into the feed tray of your printer**

To find out which direction the sheets must face, refer to the label packaging for instructions on how to load the label sheets into your printer.

If you want to check the separate labels first, click 🗒 Edit individual labels....

After that you can print the labels the same way you print a normal document.

To print the labels right away:

👉 **Click** 🖨 Print...

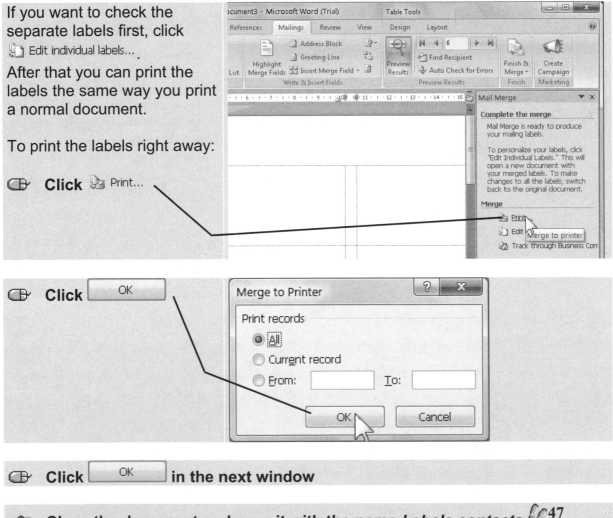

👉 **Click** [OK]

👉 **Click** [OK] **in the next window**

👉 **Close the document and save it with the name *Labels contacts* 📖47**

If you want to print these labels again at a later date, you can use the saved document.

☞ **Open** *Labels contacts* 🐾⁵¹

When you open *Labels contacts* again, you see this window first:

🖱 **Click** Yes

🖱 **Click** OK **in the next window and (if necessary) click** OK **again**

The label page is opened, with the last address in the first label:

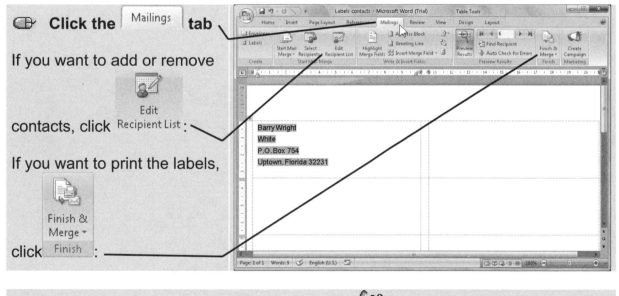

🖱 **Click the** Mailings **tab**

If you want to add or remove

contacts, click Edit Recipient List :

If you want to print the labels,

click Finish & Merge ▾ Finish :

☞ **Close** *Word* **without saving the changes** 🐾⁹

3.11 Customizing Business Cards

Your business card is often the very first thing a prospective client/customer sees about your company. To create a good first impression, it is important to have a professional looking business card. You can use *Microsoft Publisher* to quickly customize your personal business card.

☞ **Open *Publisher*** 🥾¹

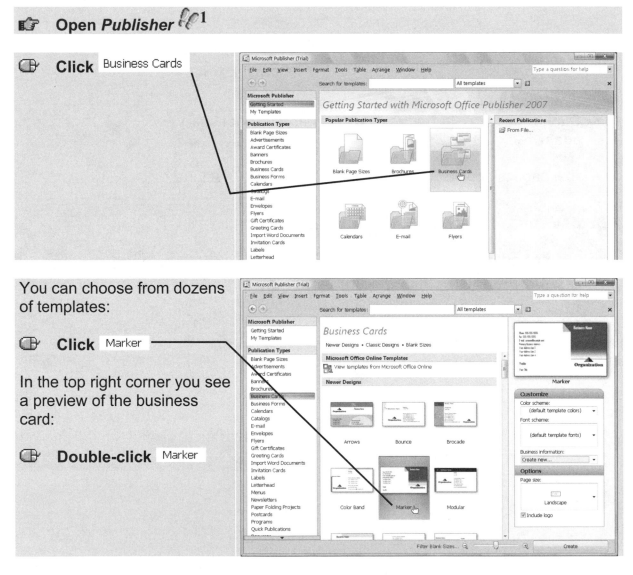

👆 **Click** Business Cards

You can choose from dozens of templates:

👆 **Click** Marker

In the top right corner you see a preview of the business card:

👆 **Double-click** Marker

You can print business cards on special sheets of business card paper. Many suppliers offer special perforated business card paper that allows you to easily separate the cards after printing. Other types of business card paper have to be cut to the right size after printing. Just like when you print labels it is very important to select the correct brand and type of paper to ensure that the text is printed in the right spot.

First select the right size for your business card.

Click Change Page Size...

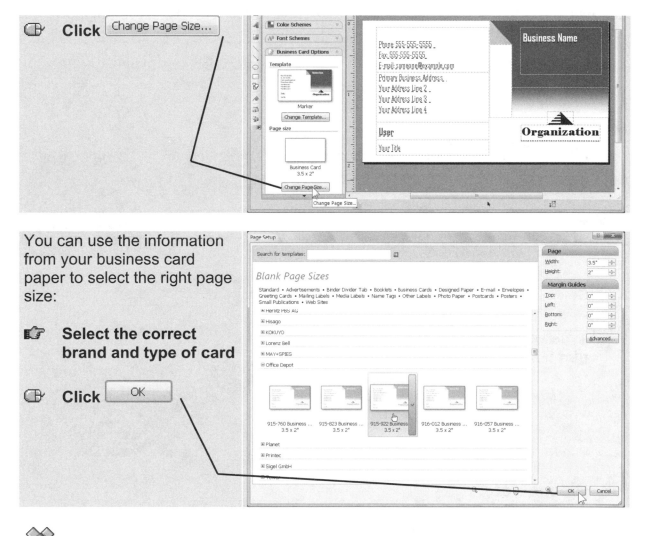

You can use the information from your business card paper to select the right page size:

☞ **Select the correct brand and type of card**

Click OK

✖ Help! The information no longer fits on the card.

If you selected a card that is smaller than the default design of the template, some items may be displayed partly outside the card. You can move these items back to the card yourself:

Click the item

Drag until the item is inside the card again

Repeat this for all items that are outside the card.

➡️ **Please note:**

Layout guides including margin, column, row, and baseline guides will not appear when you print the cards.

Now you can enter your company information:

👆 **Click**

Business Name

three times

⌨️ **Type your company name**

⌨️ **Select** 555-555-5555

⌨️ **Type your phone number**

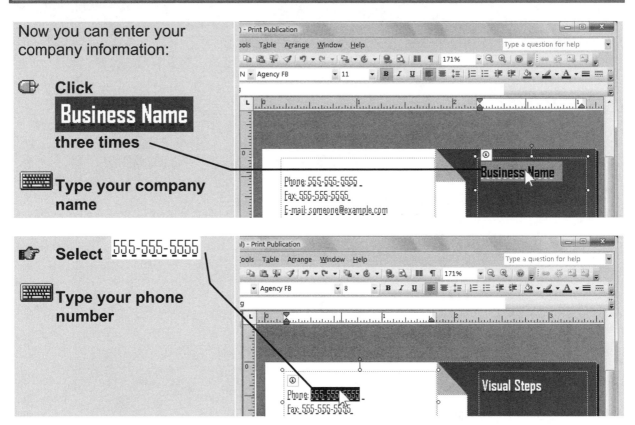

➡️ **Please note:**

Use the same setup and format as you did on your letterhead, not only for your phone number, but also for the way you wrote your company name, address et cetera.

👉 **Enter the rest of your company information as well**

You can remove the fields that you do not use by selecting them and pressing the `Delete` key.

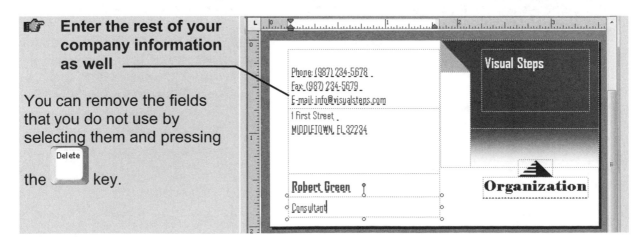

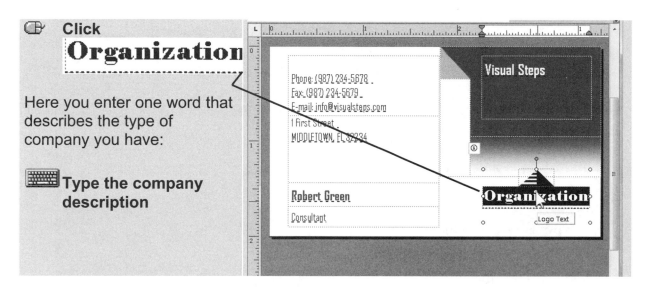

☞ **Click**

Organization

Here you enter one word that describes the type of company you have:

⌨ **Type the company description**

If you have your own company logo, you can add it to the business card:

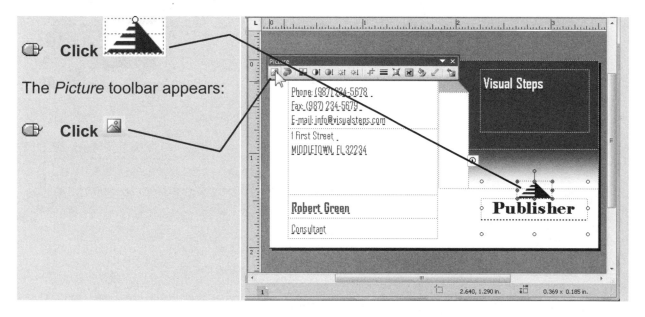

☞ **Click**

The *Picture* toolbar appears:

☞ **Click** 🖼

☞ **Open the folder containing your logo or the folder**

    Practice files Office 2007

    🐾2

You can also use the logo from the *Practice files Office 2007* folder:

☞ **Double-click** Logo

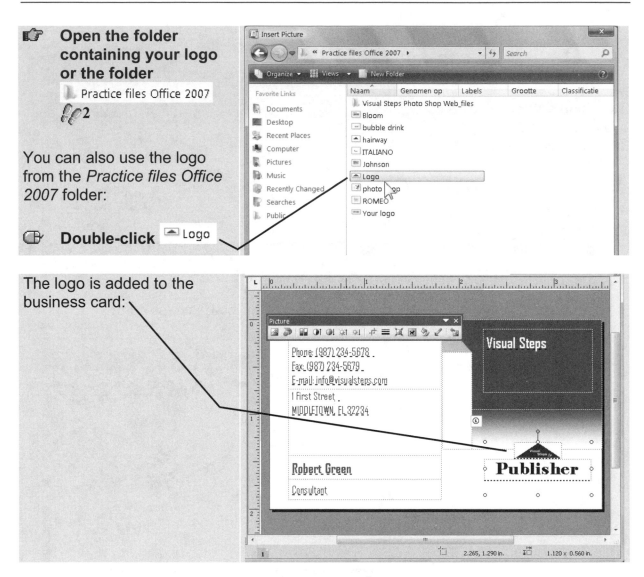

The logo is added to the business card:

There are different ways to customize a business card template:

☞ **Click** Color Schemes

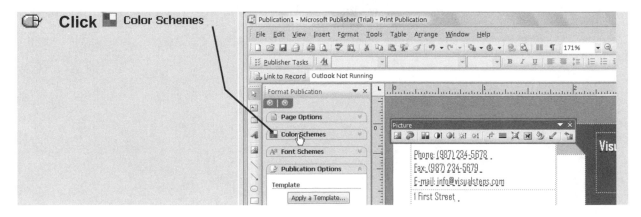

You see different color schemes:

☞ **Click** Verve **for example**

The colors change according to the new color scheme:

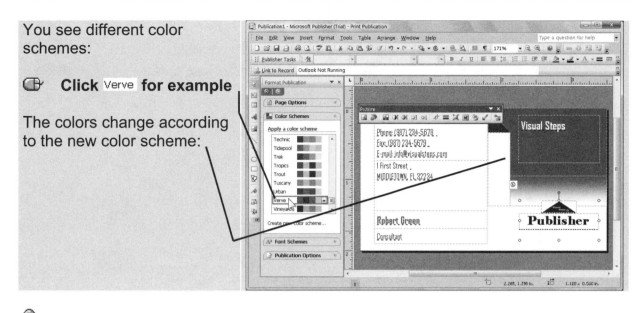

💡 **Tip**

Different font

You can change the font of the entire card at once by clicking Aᵃ **Font Schemes** .
You can also change the font type or text size of one item individually. Select the

text you want to change and use 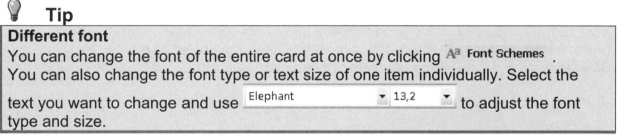 to adjust the font type and size.

As soon as you are satisfied with your design you can save the template:

☞ **Click** File

☞ **Click** Save

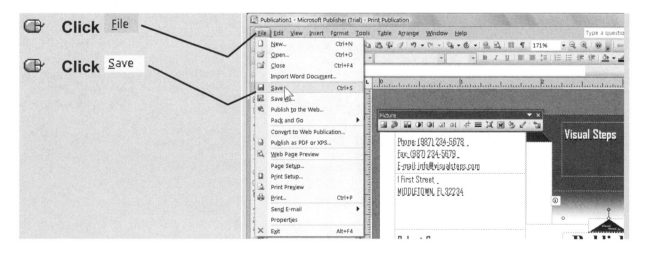

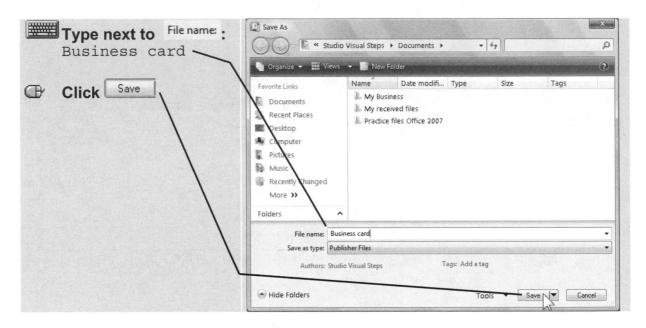

You can print business cards just like any other document. Make sure to insert the paper in the feed tray in the proper orientation. You may need to refer to the directions on the packaging of your business card paper.

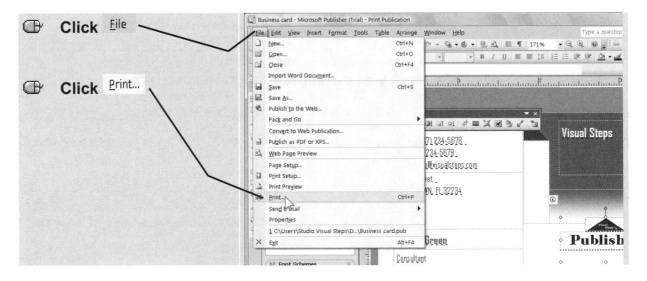

You see a Print Preview:

☞ **Click** [Print]

One page of business cards is printed. Depending on the type of paper you have used, you can either separate the cards from the sheet or cut them to the right size.

In case you are not happy with the print colors, you can adjust your design in *Publisher* before you print a large number of cards. Keep in mind that the screen color and print color may vary somewhat. Always make a test print first.

💡 **Tip**

Experiment with different designs
Now that you have entered your company details in a business card it is very easy to experiment with different business card layouts. When you select another template, your details are automatically displayed on the card. This way you can quickly decide which design you like best. Your company details will also be displayed on other *Publisher* templates right away, for example on envelopes and brochures.

☞ **Close *Publisher*** 𝄞⁹

💡 **Tip**

Online commercial printing services
If you are not happy with the print results of your printer you can consider having your business cards printed professionally. There are many online commercial printing services where you can upload your digital file. Their websites will list the exact specifications for the files you can submit.
Tip: have them print a small batch first to see if the print quality matches your expectations. Pay special attention to the colors, these may vary greatly from what you see on your screen.

3.12 Customizing Invoices

For most companies, the invoice is one of the most important documents. An invoice should look professional, be well-organized and should have a standard layout. Deciding on a suitable layout for your invoice will depend on the line of business you are in, the type of work you do and the type of customers you have. In the practice files, you will find a sample invoice that you can customize for your own company.

➡ **Please note:**

To be able to work through this section you should be able to perform a number of basic tasks in *Excel*. For more information about required prior knowledge you can refer to page 15 of this book. You can also take a look at these basic tasks in *Appendix A* at the end of this book.
If you have not ever worked with *Excel*, then you can start by reading the guide **Basic Knowledge Excel 2007** (PDF file on the website of this book).

☞ **Open** *Excel* 🖐¹

☞ **Open** 📄Sales invoice USA **or** 📄Sales invoice UK **from the folder**
📁 Practice files Office 2007 🖐¹²

In the following examples, the USA version of the invoice will be used. UK readers can perform the same tasks with the UK version of the invoice.

You see only a part of the invoice:

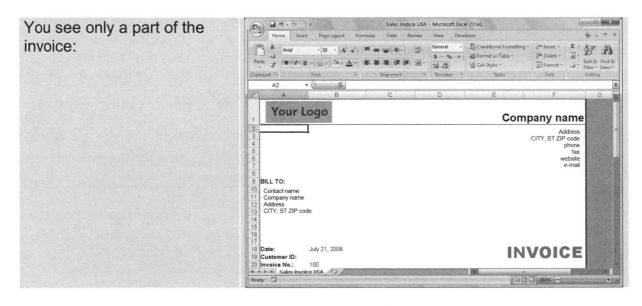

Page layout is very important in an invoice. You can open the Print Preview to take a look at the complete invoice:

☞ **Open the Print Preview** 🐾20

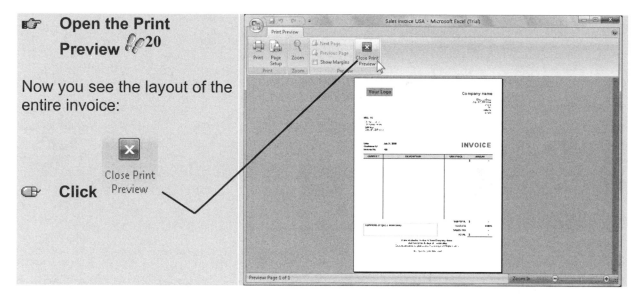

Now you see the layout of the entire invoice:

🖰 **Click** Close Print Preview

In the following steps enter your own company information in the following fields:

🖰 **Click** **Company name**

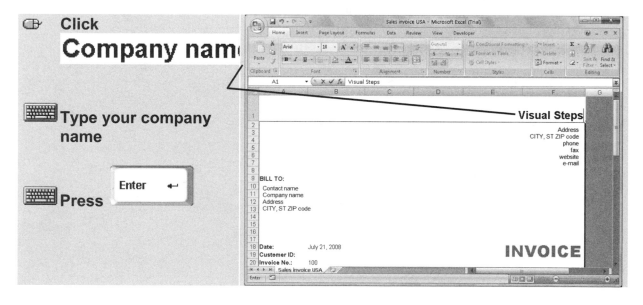

⌨ **Type your company name**

⌨ **Press** Enter ↵

If you have your own company logo you can add it to the invoice. If you do not have a logo, you can remove the sample logo from the invoice:

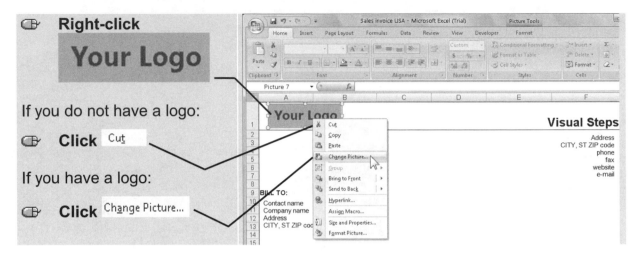

👆 **Right-click**

Your Logo

If you do not have a logo:

👆 **Click** Cut

If you have a logo:

👆 **Click** Change Picture...

After clicking Change Picture... a window appears where you can search the folders on your computer to find your logo:

☞ **Find your logo and double-click it**

Your logo is added to your invoice.

👆 **Click** Address

The full address block is now selected:

👆 **Double-click** Address

Now you can enter your company information:

 Type your company information

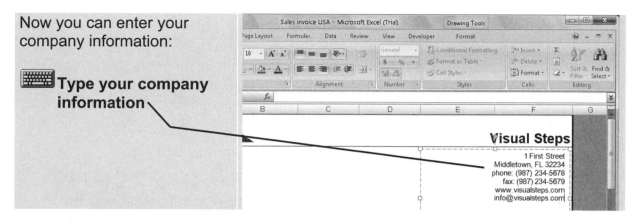

⇨ **Please note:**

Use the same layout and format as you did on your letterhead. Not just for your phone number, but also for the way you write your company name, address et cetera. Many companies will also decide upon a particular font to be used in all their standard documents.

💡 **Tip**

Moving the address block
The address block is placed in a text box. You can move a text box like this:

🖰 **Point to the border of the text box**

The cursor changes into ⬍:

🖰 **Drag the text box to the desired location**

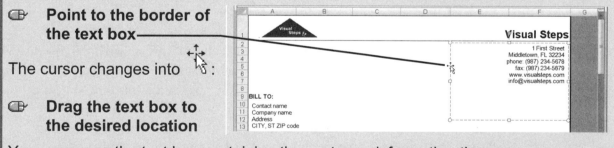

You can move the text box containing the customer information the same way.

🖰 **Drag the scroll bar down**

You see the column headers:

If you want to change a column header:

🖰 **Click a column header**

 Type your own text

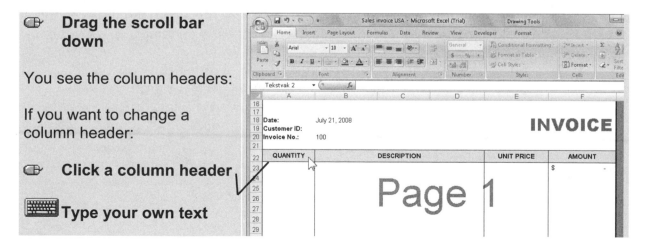

⇨　**Please note:**

In this sample invoice the quantities are displayed without decimal places. If you do calculate in decimals, for example when you bill for hours or measurements, you can format the cell to display one or more decimal places **21**.

The terms you use on your invoice should fit your company and be recognizable for your customers. If you bill per hour or per yard, put that term in the first column header instead of QUANTITY.
UNIT PRICE should then be changed to HOURLY RATE or PRICE PER YARD.

Sales tax and Value Added Tax (VAT)
There is a big difference in taxation in the United States and the United Kingdom.
In the US you usually add *sales tax* to an invoice, in the UK and the rest of Europe a *Value Added Tax* (VAT).

A sales tax is a tax on consumption and is normally a certain percentage that is added onto the price of goods or services that are purchased.
- Sales taxes in the United States are assessed by every state except Alaska, Delaware, Montana, New Hampshire and Oregon. Hawaii has a similar tax although it is charged to businesses instead of consumers.
- In some cases, sales taxes are also assessed at the county or municipal level. There is no national sales tax in the USA.
- Sales tax is usually the responsibility of the merchant to collect and remand to the state, and stated separately (or implicitly added at the time of sale) to consumers.
- Usually only consumers are charged the tax; resellers are exempt if they do not make use of the goods. In some jurisdictions, a reseller's certificate is required to make use of this privilege.
- If a consumer purchases goods from an out-of-state vendor, the consumer's state may not have jurisdiction over the out-of-state vendor and no sales tax would be due. However, the customer's state may make up for the lost sales tax revenue by charging the consumer a use tax in an amount equal to the sales taxes avoided.

- Continue reading on the next page -

Sales taxes change, are added or eliminated frequently. Therefore no list of sales taxes per state has been added to this book. Make sure to check with your state tax authority for the applicable amount of sales tax to charge to your customers. There you can also find information on how to file your sales tax return.

Value Added Tax (VAT) is a tax charged on most business-to-business and business-to-consumer transactions in the UK and Europe.

- If you are a VAT registered business, VAT is a tax on the net value added to your products or services, the difference between the value of your sales and the value of your purchases.
- If you are a non VAT registered businesses or organization, or a consumer, VAT is a tax on your consumption.
- You must register for VAT if your turnover for the previous 12 months is over a specific limit (£67,000 in 2008) or if you think your turnover may soon go over this limit. You may register voluntarily at any time.
- Businesses registered for VAT are in turn reimbursed VAT on their purchases.
- In the UK the standard VAT rate for goods and services is 17.5%. The reduced rate is 5%, and is applicable to for example domestic fuel and power, installation of energy-saving materials, residential conversions, women's sanitary products and children's car seats. Zero rated items (0%) include food (but not meals in restaurants or hot take aways), books and newspapers, children's clothing and shoes and public transport.
- Items that are exempt from VAT include insurance, providing credit, education and training (if certain conditions are met), fund-raising events by charities (if certain conditions are met), and subscriptions to membership organizations.
- You usually account for VAT on a quarterly basis by filling in a VAT return and submitting it to HMRC. You then pay HMRC the excess of your output tax over the VAT you can reclaim as input tax. If the input tax you can reclaim is more than your output tax, you can reclaim the difference from HMRC.
- You can check the website www.hmrc.gov.uk/vat for more information about VAT.

Source: Wikipedia, HM Revenue and Customs

☞ **Drag the scroll bar down**

A sales tax rate of 6% has been added to the sample invoice. To enter the correct sales tax percentage for your state:

☞ **Click** 6.00%

⌨ **Type the correct sales tax percentage**

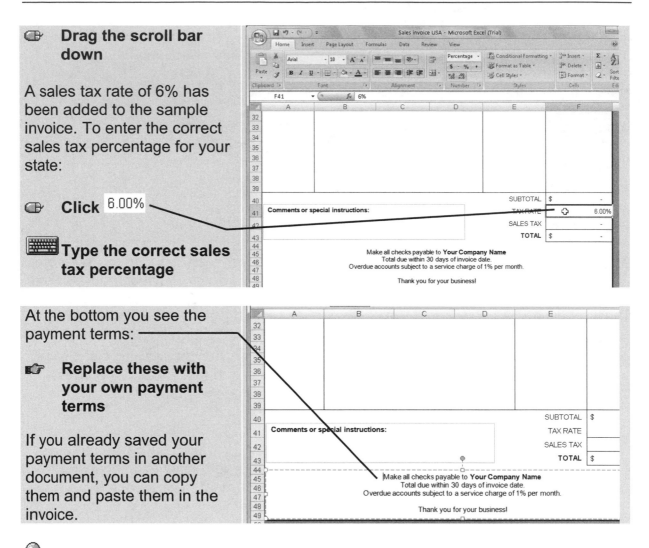

At the bottom you see the payment terms:

☞ **Replace these with your own payment terms**

If you already saved your payment terms in another document, you can copy them and paste them in the invoice.

💡 **Tip**

Payment terms
You will often see invoices that say: 'Payable Upon Receipt', but it is better to avoid that phrase. You do not know when your customer sees the invoice, even if you have sent it by e-mail. When you state the specific payment terms on your invoice, you give your customer a clear idea of how to remit their payment and when payment is due.

Even though you would probably like to get paid quickly, it is not realistic to use an eight day payment term if you work for large companies or government institutions. Especially in large companies the full process of checking and paying invoices may take two to three weeks. It is better to use a thirty day term and immediately send customers who are overdue a reminder. That way you show that you are on top of your bill collection.

When you have finished the design, you can save it. It is a good idea to save the invoice as a template. That way you have a blank invoice every time you open it:

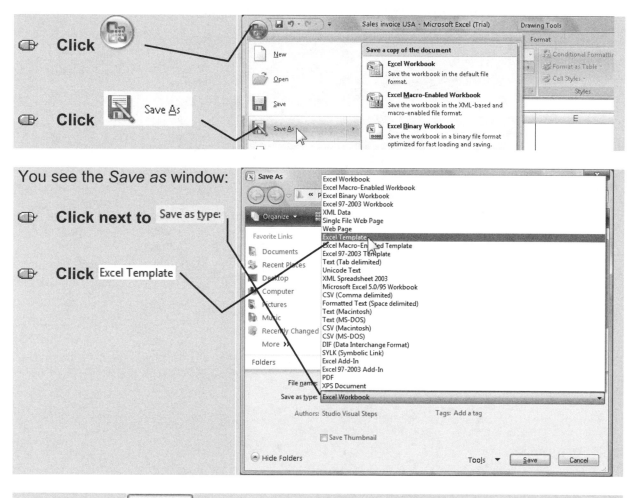

☞ **Click the** Save **button in the window**

☞ **Close the document** ^{9}

⇨ **Please note:**

You have saved your invoice as a template instead of a regular *Excel* document. A template is a document type that creates a copy of itself when you open it. Templates are base documents that you can fill out over and over again, while the original template containing all the standard block elements stays the same. Opening a template is done differently than opening a regular document. You can try that in the next section.

3.13 Making Invoices

You can bill your customers by filling out the invoice template like this:

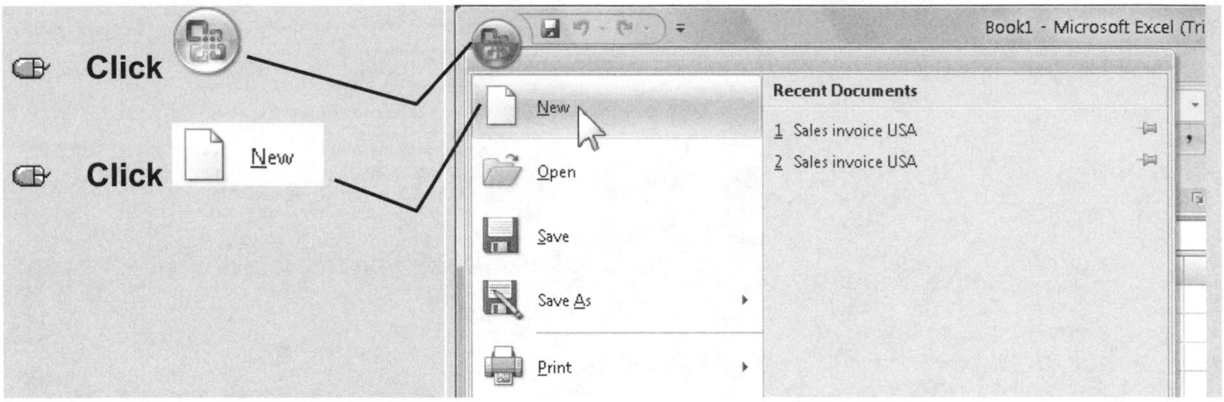

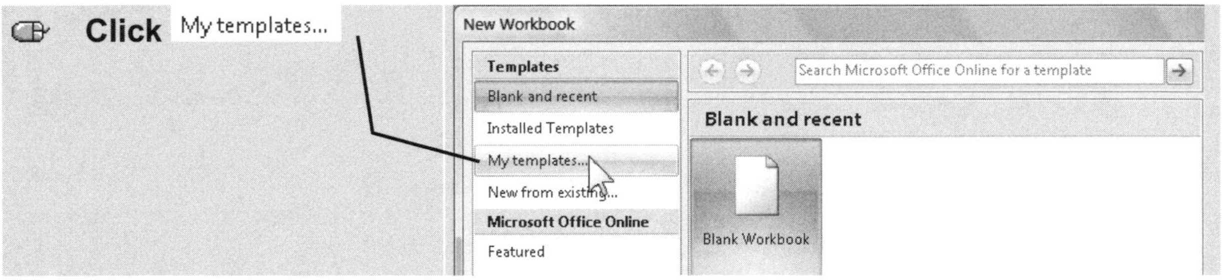

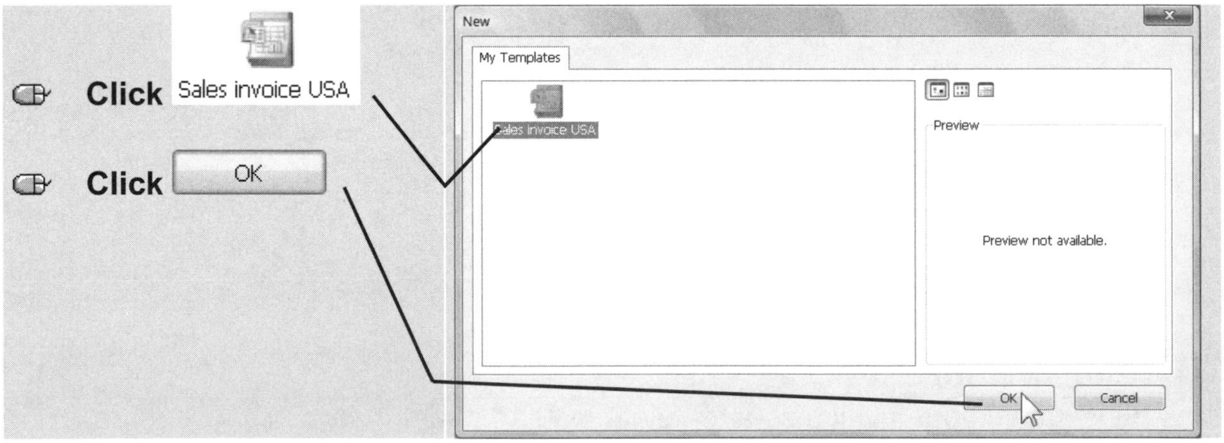

☞ **Click**

☞ **Click** New

☞ **Click** My templates...

☞ **Click** Sales invoice USA

☞ **Click** OK

You see your invoice:

Today's date is entered automatically:

🖰 **Click** Contact name

⌨ **Type the name and address of the customer**

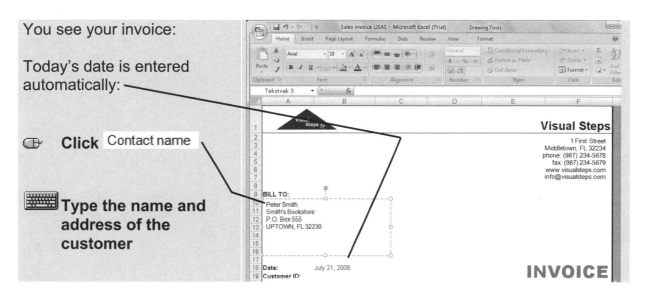

Many companies use unique customer IDs and give each invoice a unique serial number.

🖰 **Click next to** Customer ID:

⌨ **Type the customer ID**

🖰 **Click next to** Invoice No.:

⌨ **Type your invoice number**

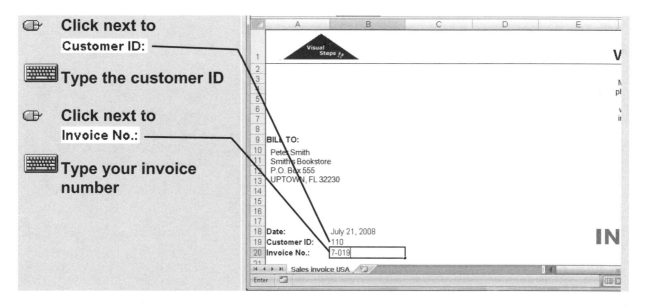

⇨ **Please note:**

Invoices made in the European Community are required to be sequentially numbered by law. The 'invoice number' can be numerical, or it can be a combination of numbers and letters, as long as it forms part of a unique and sequential series. If you are VAT registered, the VAT number, company registration and the registered address of the business is also required on the invoice.

☞ **Drag the scroll bar down**

☞ **Click below** QUANTITY

⌨ **Type the quantity**

⌨ **Press** [Tab]

☞ **Also enter a *Description* and a *Unit Price***

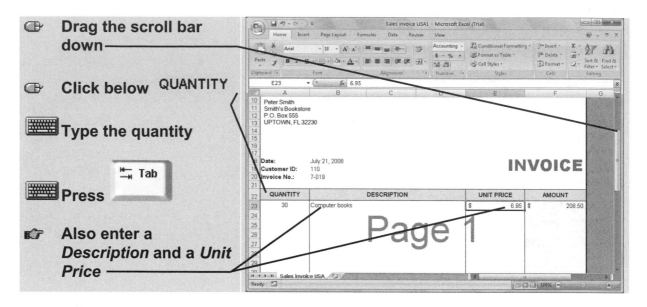

The amount due on this line is calculated automatically. You see that in the column below AMOUNT :

☞ **Use the same method to add a second line to the invoice**

☞ **Drag the scroll bar down**

You see the sales tax or VAT and the total amount due:

☞ **Click below** Comments or special instruct

⌨ **Type a message**

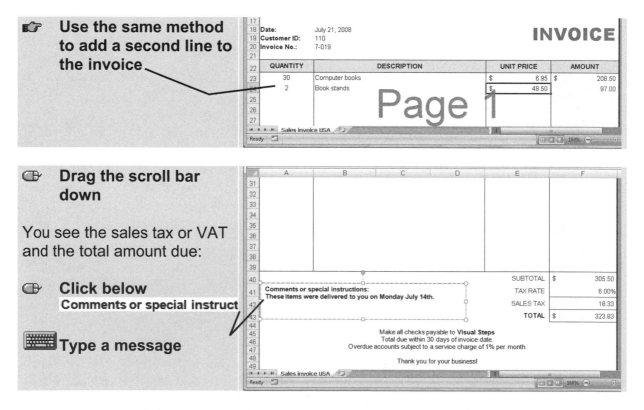

Now you can print the invoice and save it if necessary. If you do not want to save the invoice, do not close the document until you have checked the printed invoice. You may see a typing error on paper that you did not see on your screen.

Usually you print invoices twice: one for your customer and one for your administration.

If you want to save the invoice, use the invoice number as the file name. Create a separate folder named *Invoices* on your computer so that you can store all of your invoices together.

You do not need to save this practice invoice.

☞ **Close *Excel* and do not save the changes** *ℓℓ*[9]

In this chapter you have learned how to create a number of standard documents using *Microsoft Office 2007.* These template documents will save you a lot of time because you can use them over and over again.
By using well-designed standard documents you save time and give your business correspondence a nice professional look.

3.14 Background Information

Glossary

Building blocks	Building blocks are reusable pieces of content or other document parts that are stored in galleries. You can access them and add them to your document at any time.
Filter	Displaying data that answers to certain criteria. For example, you can filter your contacts by a ZIP code in order to display only the contacts that live in that particular ZIP code area. Filtering does not change the data, it only changes the way the data is presented.
Logo	Graphical design to represent a company, brand or product.
Mailing	Standard document that is sent to a selected group. Often personalized with the name, address and other details of the recipient.
Template	A document that is pre-designed with a specific layout and style definition. When a template is opened, a copy of the original template is created automatically.

Source: Windows Help and Microsoft Office 2007 Help

Mailings

Since the introduction of the computer it has become very easy to create mailings. Using your address files and other information, it only takes minutes to create a personalized mailing. But the large quantity of mailings and e-mails may become annoying, resulting in the mailings no longer being read.

To prevent your mailing from meeting with the same fate, it is important to make sure its content is interesting to the recipient. Each mailing should offer something new, instead of repeating the same thing over and over. Try including for example, a special offer that is good for only a limited amount of time, or a contest or a charity drive. These types of things may induce your readers to respond more readily. Always make sure that the contact details of the recipient are correct. When a female recipient reads Mr. in the salutation, your mailing will probably be thrown away unread. Do not use more personal details than absolutely necessary. Referring to someone's upcoming birthday may give the recipient the unwelcome feeling you know everything about him or her.

Estimate

Before a customer accepts your services, you often send an approximate calculation of the anticipated costs first. These types of documents usually have almost the same layout as an invoice. It is easy to create your own versions of these documents by using your invoice template. The differences may be the following:

- An estimate does not have to be numbered and may be titled, *Estimate, Estimate Proposal, Quote, Sales Quote, Quotation* or *Offer* instead of *Invoice.*
- An estimate often contains more explanation or description about the proposed service and type of work that needs to be done. An estimate is not an order yet, so you can make the text a bit more commercial.
- Whether or not to include sales tax or VAT in the estimate will depend on several things. In the US, many states impose a tax on individual sales transactions. Your company may need to register for a sales tax license (also called a seller's permit). This usually applies to businesses involved in selling or leasing tangible property, but, in some states, sales tax applies to services as well. Your customers may also have tax exempt status.
- Depending on the type of service, job or project, certain conditions may be added regarding acceptance of the project or the price.
- Estimates are usually valid up to a certain date or for a specific period (for example thirty days).

As soon as your customer accepts the estimate, you are legally bound to it. Pay close attention to what you write in an estimate.

Terms and conditions

General terms and conditions or terms of service apply to every sale, project, order or delivery you make. Carefully worded documents can protect your company from liability, and should address the key terms and conditions for the provision of information, goods, or services.

The terms you agree with your client ahead of starting work are critical in terms of protecting your business. A good time to present the terms and conditions is when you submit an estimate.

If you print your terms and conditions on the back of the estimate, they can be considered known to the customer upon acceptance of the offer. As a reminder you can also list them on the back of your invoice, but just printing them on your invoice is not enough.

Content controls in Microsoft Word

You have already learned how to add content controls like the drop-down list when you create templates. In addition to the drop-down list there are several other content controls:

Content control	Definition	Example	Restrictions
Rich text	Formatting can be saved by loading, saving, or closing the document.	Use for a short paragraph such as an abstract, a summary, or a legal disclaimer.	No restrictions.
Text	Limited to content that cannot contain any formatting, only plain text.	Use for a simple paragraph.	Limits the formatting to the formatting that is applied around the content control. You can change the formatting by making changes to the surrounding formatting.
Picture	Fills the content control with a single picture.	Use for a drawing, a shape, a chart, a table, a clip art object, or SmartArt.	Limits formatting changes to picture brightness and contrast. Also prohibits users from inserting any other Word objects or any text.
Combo Box	Contains a list that you can edit directly. Formatting can be saved by saving or closing the document.		Like plain text, limits text to a single paragraph that cannot contain any formatting.
Drop-Down List	Contains a list of options defined by the template author when the user activates the drop-down box.	Use this to provide a set of choices, such as a list of names or a set of formatted design elements (such as cover pages or header or footers).	Like plain text, limits text to a single paragraph that cannot contain any formatting.
Date Picker	Contains a calendar control. Limits text to a single paragraph.	Use this to help users enter a date.	Like plain text, limits text to a single paragraph that cannot contain any formatting.
Building Block Gallery	Shows a gallery of formatted design choices that you can add to the content control.	Use this to specify a set of cover pages, headers and footers, page designs, or other building blocks that you add to the Quick Parts gallery.	No restrictions.

Source: Microsoft Office 2007 Help

3.15 Tips

💡 Tip

Filtering

When you create a mailing for your contacts, it's possible that not all of them need to receive it. Earlier in this chapter you learned how to exclude contacts on an individual basis. If there are many contacts that need to be excluded because they do not meet certain requirements, you can select them all at once. You can do so by applying a filter, for example when you launch a marketing campaign in *Business Contact Manager*:

👆 **Click** `Review and Filter...`

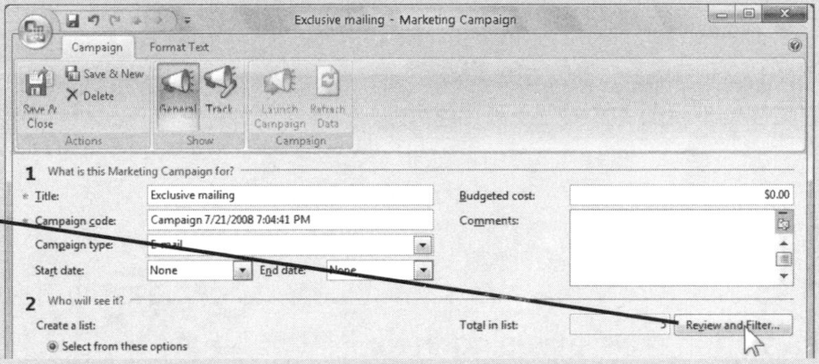

👆 **Click** `Advanced Filter`

👉 **Select** `Business City` **below** `Field name`

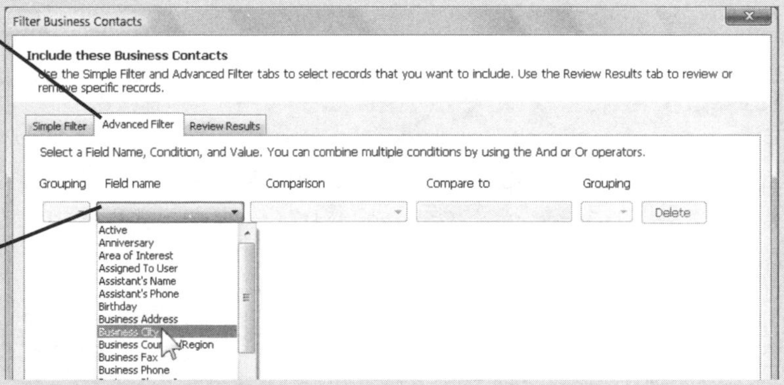

👉 **Select** `Equals` **below** `Comparison`

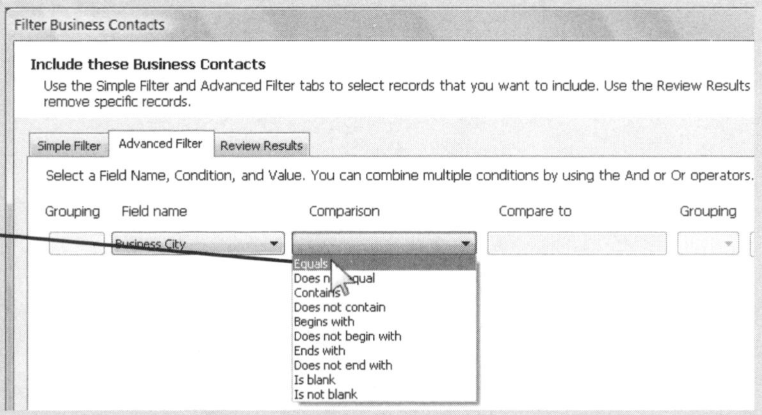

- Continue reading on the next page -

⌨ **Type the city name Uptown below**

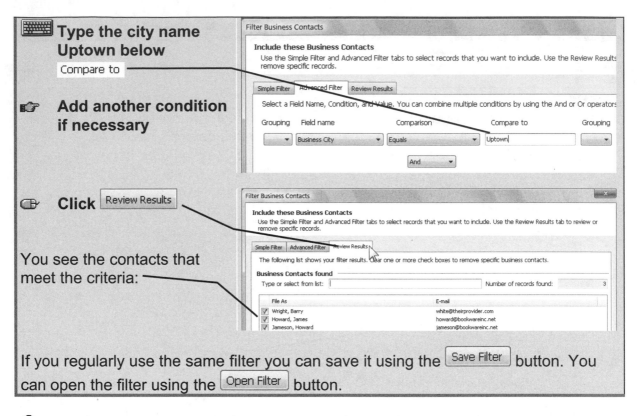

☞ **Add another condition if necessary**

👆 **Click** Review Results

You see the contacts that meet the criteria:

If you regularly use the same filter you can save it using the Save Filter button. You can open the filter using the Open Filter button.

💡 **Tip**

Keeping track of unpaid invoices

If you want to keep track of customer payments without using special accounting software, you can use the tasks in *Outlook*. You enter the invoice with the due date as a task and add a reminder if necessary. As soon as the invoice is paid, you can mark the task as completed.

This method is of course only suitable for companies that do not have a lot of invoices. If you have a lot of invoice it is better to track them in *Excel* or in an accounting program.

Tip

Templates on the Internet
A few templates are pre-installed with *Microsoft Office 2007*. Many more templates are available on the Internet, for example on the *Microsoft* website. On the web page http://office.microsoft.com/en-us/templates you can find a large number of templates divided over many different categories. The UK equivalent of this web page can be found at http://office.microsoft.com/en-gb/templates.

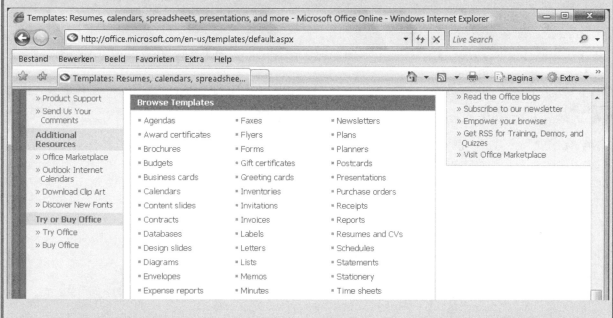

If you cannot find the templates because of changes to the *Microsoft* website, you can try searching the site by typing the term 'templates' in the Search box.

 Tip

Label printer
It can be quite difficult to print a separate label for just one address.

If you need to print separate labels often, a dedicated label printer may be a good investment. You can use it to print labels directly from *Word* and many other programs.

⚓ Tip

Spelling

Use the spelling checker in *Office 2007* wherever you can. You can find the spelling

checker **Spelling & Grammar** on the Review tab.

The spelling checker is usually turned on by default. When a spelling error is made, a wavy red line appears.
Do not blindly trust the spell checker however; a misspelled word will not always be detected.
This sentence for example contains three spelling errors:

Overdue accounts subjects to a servise charged of 1% per month.

The spell checker only recognizes one spelling error: *servise*
The words 'subjects' and 'charged' are not spelled correctly in this sentence, but the spell checker does not pick up on that. These two words do exist in this spelling and can be found in the spell checker's dictionary.

The correct sentence is:
Overdue accounts subject to a service charge of 1% per month.

Spelling and Grammar: English (U.S.)

Not in Dictionary:

Overdue accounts subjects to a servise charged of 1% per month.

Ignore Once | Ignore All | Add to Dictionary

Suggestions:

service
servile
series
serves

Change | Change All | AutoCorrect

Dictionary language: English (U.S.)

☑ Check grammar

Options... | Undo | Cancel

Always thoroughly check your documents for spelling errors - even if you use the spelling checker – or ask someone else to do it for you.

4. Business Administration ⏰ 60 min.

Microsoft Excel is a powerful calculation program that will be a great aid to you as you run your business. It is not an accounting program, but an excellent tool for storing, organizing and manipulating numerical data.

In this chapter you will become acquainted with several sample spreadsheets that can be used to keep track of your petty cash, projects, car expenses, planning et cetera. After reading this chapter first, you can select the sample spreadsheets that are applicable to your business. Most of the spreadsheets already contain sample data that you can add to yourself. This way you can see how the spreadsheet works and what kind of information it provides. When you actually start to use the spreadsheet for your own business, you can delete the sample data.

The fact that you are probably not an accountant or bookkeeper was taken into account when these sample spreadsheets were created. Some spreadsheets may need to be customized before you can use them. In that case you can use the sample spreadsheet as a starting point and add to it yourself.

In this chapter you will learn the following:

- creating and using a tabulated cashbook;
- keeping track of your automobile expenses;
- registering your business miles in a mileage log;
- keeping track of project costs;
- using an hour log;
- creating a time planning for projects or orders;
- comparing the estimated and actual costs of finished projects;
- calculating an annuity;
- compare costs and expenses over several years;
- calculating a sales tax or VAT return.

⇨ **Please note:**

In order to work through this chapter you have to be able to perform basic tasks in *Excel*. Please refer to page 15 for more information. If you don't have any experience with *Excel 2007*, you can work through the PDF file **Basic Excel Knowledge**. You can find this document on the website of this book.
You will also use some of the sample documents that can be found on the website of this book. Check this book's website for possible changes or additional sample files.

➡ **Please note:**

The sample spreadsheets you use in this chapter are – with the exception of the cashbook – not protected. This means you can change the formulas or overwrite them, causing the spreadsheet not to function properly anymore. If necessary copy the spreadsheet again from the website of this book. Then you will be able to start over fresh with the original sample spreadsheet.

4.1 Creating a Tabulated Cashbook

Creating and maintaining a cashbook is very easy in *Excel*. There are different types of cashbooks. A cashbook that uses a series of columns for revenues and expenses provides an easy way to keep up with the incoming and outgoing of cash in your business. In this section you are going to work with this type of cashbook.

➡ **Please note:**

In order to work through this chapter you need to be able to perform basic tasks in *Excel*. Please refer to page 15 for more information. If you don't have any experience with *Excel 2007*, you can work through the PDF file **Basic Excel Knowledge**. You can find this document on the website of this book.

☞ **Open** *Excel* ¹

☞ **Open** Cashbook US with sales tax **or** Cashbook UK with VAT **from the folder**
    Practice files Office 2007 ₡₡12

➡ **Please note:**

The folder Practice files Office 2007 from the website of this book is needed for this chapter. Make sure you have copied the folder to your computer. You can read how to do that in *Chapter 1 Preparation.*

In the following examples the US version of the cashbook will be used. UK readers can perform the same tasks in the UK version of the cashbook.

The worksheet containing the cashbook is opened:

You see the layout of the cashbook:	

Before you start using the cashbook, you can customize the columns for your business. If you do not use personal deposits for example, you can remove that column. To be able to do so you need to turn off the worksheet protection first:

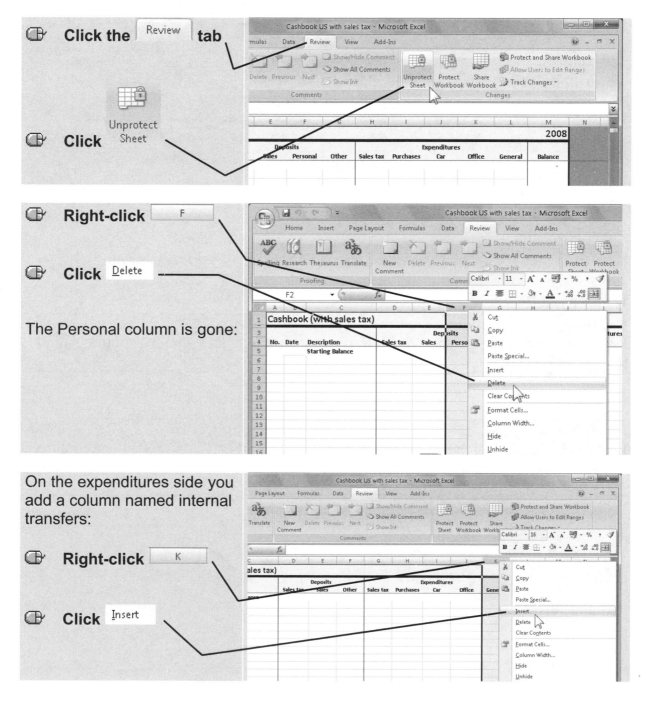

Click the Review tab

Click Unprotect Sheet

Right-click F

Click Delete

The Personal column is gone:

On the expenditures side you add a column named internal transfers:

Right-click K

Click Insert

A bank deposit is an example of an *internal transfer.* It is not expenditure since the money is taken from petty cash. At a later time the same amount is added to your bank account.

There is a new empty column:

☞ **Click cell K4**

⌨ **Type:**
Int. transf.

⌨ **Press** | Enter ← |

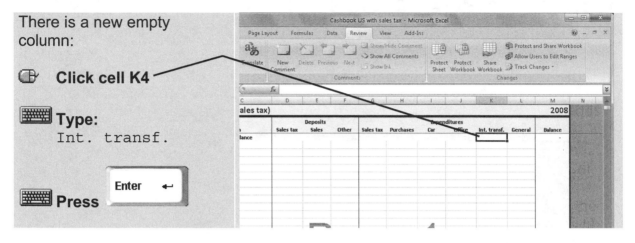

☞   **If necessary, adjust the other columns for use in your business**

💡 **Tip**

Changing column names
If there is a column that you do not use, you can change its name to a name you do use. That way you do not have to add or remove columns.

💡 **Tip**

No VAT
In the UK cashbook there are two columns for received and paid VAT. If you are not registered for VAT, you can remove the VAT columns or rename them. In that case you enter all amounts including VAT.

The big advantage of this type of cashbook is that you can quickly display the totals of each category of deposits and expenditures. You use the summary on the *Totals* worksheet for that:

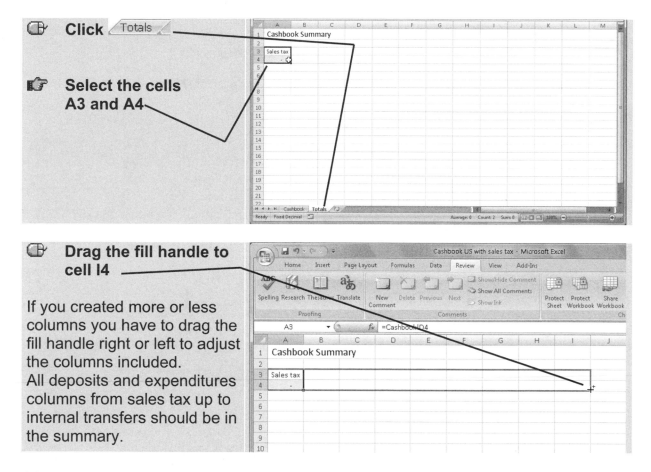

Click Totals

☞ **Select the cells A3 and A4**

Drag the fill handle to cell I4

If you created more or less columns you have to drag the fill handle right or left to adjust the columns included.
All deposits and expenditures columns from sales tax up to internal transfers should be in the summary.

You have created a customized cashbook that is ready for use in your business. You can save this cashbook as a template that you can use over and over again. First you turn on the worksheet protection:

☞ **Open the** Cashbook **worksheet** 𝄞23

Click Protect Sheet

If necessary you can type a
password to protect the
worksheet layout or formulas
from unwanted changes:

That is not necessary if you
are the only one who uses
the cashbook.

Click OK

Click

Point to Save As

Click

Excel Workbook
Save the workbook in the defa
format.

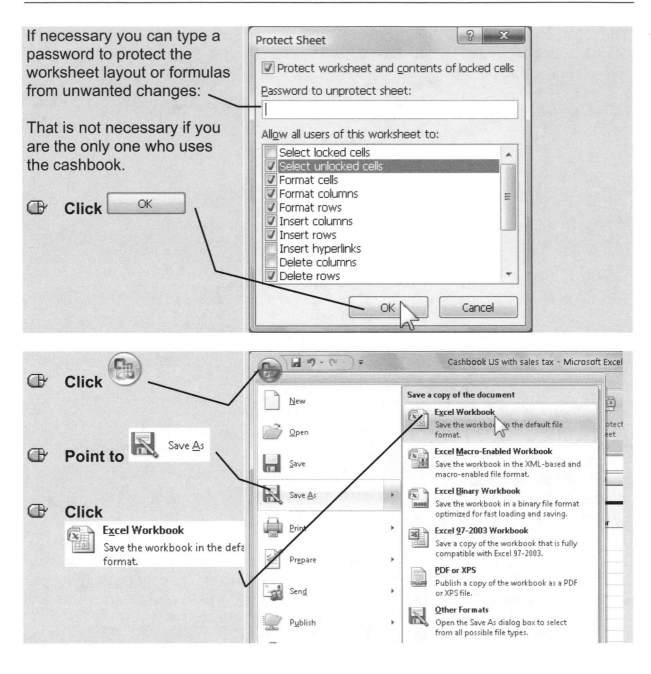

Click next to Save as type:

Click Excel Template

Click Save

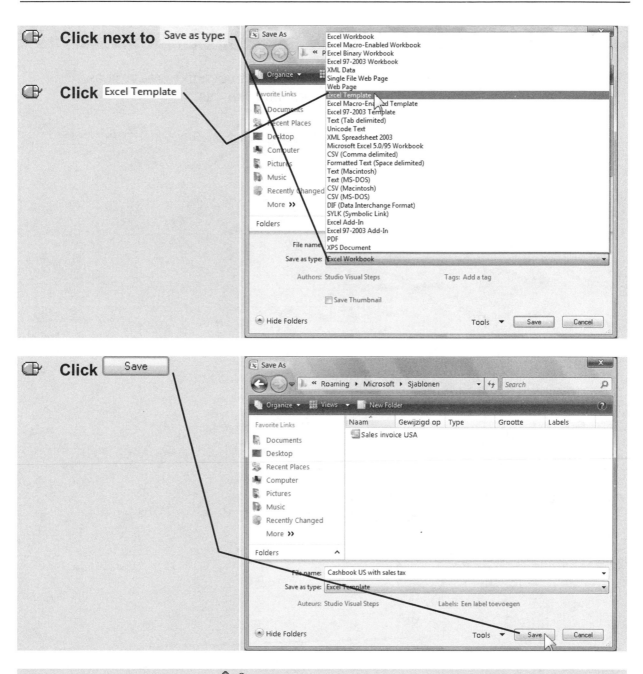

☞ **Close the document** 🐾⁹

⇨ **Please note:**

You have saved your cashbook as a template instead of a regular *Excel* document. A template is a document type that creates a copy of itself when you open it. You can use it over and over again, while the original template stays the same. There is a difference between opening a template and opening a regular *Excel* document. You can try that in the next section.

4.2 Recording Cash Transactions

You can use the cashbook you created in the previous section to record cash transactions. You can open your cashbook template like this:

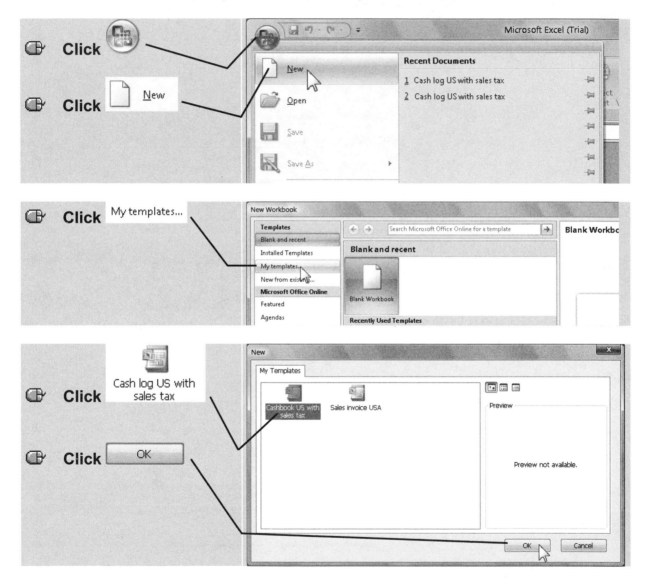

You see your cashbook:

As an exercise you can enter a couple of transactions:

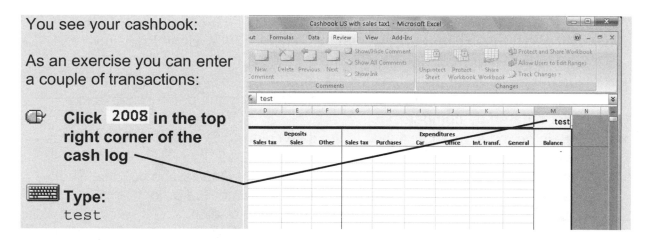

☞ **Click** 2008 **in the top right corner of the cash log**

⌨ **Type:**
test

The cashbook is protected so you can only access the cells that you have made editable:

⌨ **Press** ⭾ Tab

Cell B5 in the Date column is selected:

⌨ **Type:** 01/01

⌨ **Press** ⭾ Tab

Cell M5 in the Balance column is selected:

⌨ **Type:** 100

This is the amount of cash you started with today.

On the next rows you can enter your cash deposits and expenditures by date in the order with which they occurred. When you do, pay attention to the following:

- Enter only one transaction per row.
- Number the deposit or expenditure receipts in ascending order. Write that number in the No. column and on the receipt. Keep the paper receipts in a folder ordered by number.
- You do not have to enter a year in the date column. *Excel* automatically adds the current year to the date.
- Type an exact description of the transaction in the Description column. The description 'car expenses' is useless, since you enter the amount in the Car column anyway. A better description is insurance or gas.
- In the US: for items you sold you enter the amount excluding sales tax in the Sales column, and the sales tax in the Sales tax column. If you paid sales tax on an item you bought, enter the amount excluding sales tax in the correct expenditure column. Enter the amount of sales tax in the Sales tax column.
- In the UK: if you are VAT registered you have to keep track of the amount of VAT you paid and received. For items you sold you enter the amount excluding VAT in the Sales column. For items you bought you enter the amount excluding VAT in the correct expenditure column. Enter the amount of VAT in the VAT column for either sales or expenditures.
- Many goods and services are sold inclusive of VAT, with the VAT element shown separately on the invoice or receipt. Sometimes however products or services are sold including VAT where the amount of VAT is not shown separately at the time of sale. When this is the case, buyers must still accurately calculate the VAT they can reclaim from HM Revenue & Customs (HMRC) and suppliers must still accurately calculate the VAT they must pay to HMRC.
- The balance is automatically calculated in the Balance column. Make sure to regularly check if the amount listed in the Balance column corresponds to the amount of money in the cash box.

As an exercise, try entering a couple of transactions. For example these:

No.	Date	Description	Deposits			Expenditures					
			Sales tax	Sales	Other	Sales tax	Purchases	Car	Office	Int. transf.	General
	01/01	**Starting Balance**									
E1	01/01	Gas				3.00		50.00			
E2	01/02	Lunch				1.08					18.00
D1	01/03	Sale to P. Smith	30.00	500.00							
E3	01/03	Bank deposit								400.00	
D2	01/04	Sale to R. Jones	6.00	100.00							
E4	01/05	Battery				4.80		80.00			

After that the cashbook looks like this:

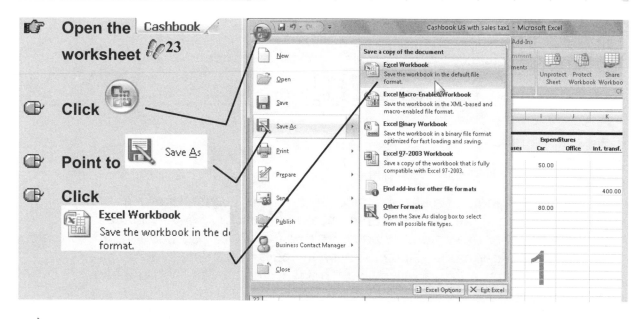

☞ **Open the** Totals **worksheet** 👣23

You see the totals for each column:

This way you can always check your total cash deposits and expenditures.

☞ **Open the** Cashbook **worksheet** 👣23

🖱 **Click**

🖱 **Point to** Save As

🖱 **Click**

Excel Workbook
Save the workbook in the d‹
format.

➡ **Please note:**

This cashbook extends to row 1,000. In case you need more rows, you can turn off the worksheet protection and copy the cells A1:E1 further down. You can also create separate cashbooks per period, for example one per quarter or one every six months.

Click Documents

Type:
Cashbook test

Click [Save]

Save As

← → ⊽ 🔲 ▸ Studio Visual Steps ▸ Documents ▸   ⊽ ✦ʄ Search   𝒫

🔲 Organize ▾ 🔳 Views ▾ 🔲 New Folder   ⓘ

Favorite Links | Naam | Gewijzigd op | Type | Grootte | Labels |
|---|---|---|---|---|
| 🔲 Documents | 🔲 Practice files Office 2007 | | | |
| 🔲 Desktop | | | | |
| 🔲 Recent Places | | | | |
| 🔲 Computer | | | | |
| 🔲 Pictures | | | | |
| 🔲 Music | | | | |
| 🔲 Recently Changed | | | | |
| More ▸▸ | | | | |

Folders   ∧

File name: Cashbook test   ⊽
Save as type: Excel Workbook   ⊽

Auteurs: Studio Visual Steps   Labels: Een label toevoegen

☐ Save Thumbnail

▴ Hide Folders   Tools   [Save] [Cancel]

☞ **Close the cashbook** ℓ⌀⁹

💡 **Tip**

Bank log
You can also use this cashbook sample spreadsheet to keep track of your bank account(s). You must record your bank transactions in a separate log. You should not combine bank and cash transactions in one log.

Cashbook
You keep a cashbook for a specific period, for example a year or a quarter, type the year or the period in the top right corner instead of 'test' and save your cashbook with that name. For example *Cashbook 2008* or *Cashbook first quarter 2008*. Create a separate subfolder named *Administration* in your *Documents* folder to store your cashbook and other administrative files. That way you can easily find these files again.
Since your cashbook is an important part of your administration, you are legally bound to save it for a specific period of time. This time depends on what the records are used for. Check the IRS website at www.irs.gov or the HMRC website at www.hmrc.gov.uk for the applicable period in your specific situation.
Usually the period you have to save your records is longer than the expected lifespan of your computer. Therefore it is advisable to print the cashbooks and store them in a folder. In that case, make sure to define which part of the cashbook you want to print, otherwise all 1,000 lines will be printed.

4.3 Automobile Expenses

Do you know how much your car costs each mile that you drive? Often it is more than you think, so it is a good idea to keep track of your automobile expenses. You can do that using the *Excel* file *Automobile expenses* from the *Practice files Office 2007* folder.

☞ **Open** 📊Automobile expenses (Miles) **or** 📊Automobile expenses (KM) **from the folder** 📁 Practice files Office 2007 👣**12**

You see the *Per mile* worksheet:

⌨**Type your initial mileage in cell B4**

This can be the mileage when you bought the car or the mileage at the moment you start keeping track of the costs.

⌨**Type the current mileage in cell B5**

Enter the other data on the other worksheets.

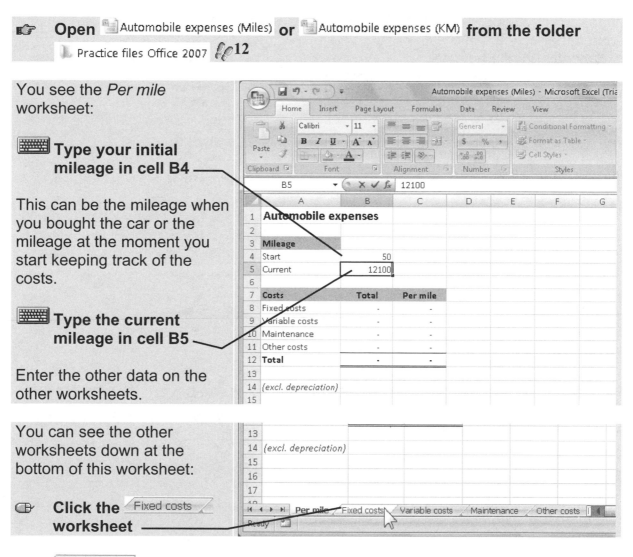

You can see the other worksheets down at the bottom of this worksheet:

👆 **Click the** Fixed costs **worksheet**

The Fixed costs worksheet is opened.

⇨ **Please note:**

If you are registered for VAT and can reclaim VAT, enter the amounts excluding VAT in the following worksheets. If you are not registered for VAT you enter the amounts including VAT. If you use your personal car you enter the costs including VAT.

First enter the fixed costs, for example your insurance, motor vehicle tax (US), road tax (UK) and (if applicable) lease payments.

☞ **Enter the fixed costs**

For a leased car you enter your lease costs here as well. If you financed your car with a loan, enter only the interest payments, not the payback.

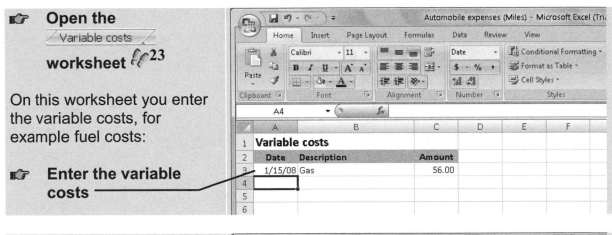

☞ **Open the**
Variable costs
worksheet 👣²³

On this worksheet you enter the variable costs, for example fuel costs:

☞ **Enter the variable costs**

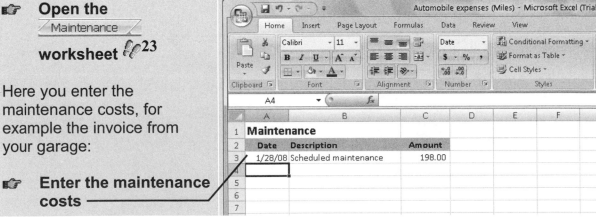

☞ **Open the**
Maintenance
worksheet 👣²³

Here you enter the maintenance costs, for example the invoice from your garage:

☞ **Enter the maintenance costs**

☞ **Open the** [Other costs]
worksheet *𝓁𝓁23*

Other costs may be tolls, speeding tickets or parking fees.

☞ **Enter the other costs**

	A	B	C	D	E	F
1	**Other costs**					
2	**Date**	**Description**	**Amount**			
3	1/17/08	Speeding ticket	80.00			
4						
5						
6						

💡 **Tip**

Depreciation
Depreciation is a large part of the cost of a car. The exact depreciation can only be determined when the car is sold, but you can enter the estimated cost of depreciation into the *Other costs* worksheet each month. In that case ask your bookkeeper what the estimated monthly depreciation cost is.

☞ **Open the** [Per mile]
worksheet *𝓁𝓁23*

You see the total costs and the costs per mile:

B5 · *fx* 12100

	A	B	C	D	E	F
1	**Automobile expenses**					
2						
3	**Mileage**					
4	Start	50				
5	Current	12100				
6						
7	**Costs**	**Total**	**Per mile**			
8	Fixed costs	96.00	0.008			
9	Variable costs	56.00	0.005			
10	Maintenance	198.00	0.016			
11	Other costs	80.00	0.007			
12	**Total**	**430.00**	**0.036**			
13						
14	*(excl. depreciation)*					

These averages are not very reliable when you just start entering the costs, but they will become more precise as time passes.
If you entered real figures you can save the *Automobile expenses* workbook:

☞ **Close the *Automobile expenses* workbook and save the changes** *𝓁𝓁9*

If you just used the workbook to practice, you do not have to save the changes.

4.4 Mileage Log

Generally it is advisable to keep a mileage log of your business or personal miles.
If you use a company car you need this log to be able to bill your customers.
If you use your personal car for work, you need the number of business miles to be able to deduct your automobile expenses for the business use of your car.
In the *Practice files 2007* folder you find a sample mileage log that you can use to keep track of the distances you drive.

☞   **Open** 🗐 Mileage log **from the folder** 📁 Practice files Office 2007 👣¹²

A mileage log can look like this in *Excel*:

You see the *Distances* worksheet:

☞   **Open the** Distances **worksheet**

Here you see the distances you drove. The total distance is calculated automatically.

☞   **Open the** Destinations **worksheet** 👣²³

✖ HELP! I see little green triangles.

The little green triangle you may see in the top left corner of a cell ⌐‾‾ is an error indicator. It means that there may be a problem with a formula in a cell. In the model you are using, the main problem is that the cell contains a formula, but no data yet. They will disappear when you enter the data.

For now, you can hide these error indicators like this:

👉   **Click** 🅱, 🔲 Excel Options

👉   **Click** Formulas

👉   **Click to remove the check mark for** 🔲 Enable background error checking **below Error Checking**

The background error checking feature can be very useful when you build worksheets with formulas yourself. In that case you can repeat the above steps to turn it on again.

Here you see the locations you visit on a regular basis and their roundtrip distance:

⌨ **Type a location in cell A4**

⌨ **Type the distance in cell B4**

☞ **Open the** Distances **worksheet** 👣23

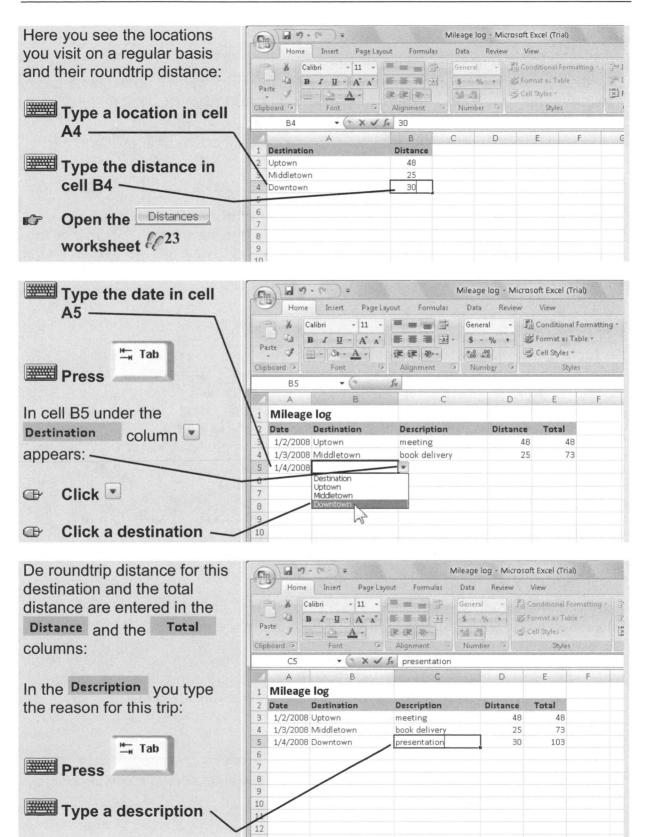

⌨ **Type the date in cell A5**

⌨ **Press** ⇥ Tab

In cell B5 under the Destination column ▼ appears:

🖱 **Click** ▼

🖱 **Click a destination**

De roundtrip distance for this destination and the total distance are entered in the Distance and the Total columns:

In the Description you type the reason for this trip:

⌨ **Press** ⇥ Tab

⌨ **Type a description**

💡 **Tip**

> **Adding to the Destinations worksheet**
> On the *Destinations* worksheet you enter the destinations you visit on a regular basis and their roundtrip distance. This information is automatically displayed in the drop-down list in the `Destination` column on the *Distances* worksheet.
> You do not have to enter locations you visit only once, or special routes. Otherwise the drop-down list will become very long. In that case you can just type the destination and the distance in the cell. The total is then calculated automatically.

Using this mileage log you can quickly and easily keep track of your business miles. Either for billing your customers or for registering the business miles you drove with your personal car. This worksheet contains formulas up to row 100. In case you need more rows you can copy the cells A1:E1 further down.

> **Deducting automobile expenses**
> In the US, automobile expenses are deductible at actual cost or the standard mileage allowance. Actual costs would include lease payments or depreciation deductions, plus gas, insurance, washes, tires and repairs, and maintenance. If the car is financed, you can deduct the business portion of the interest. The business portion is calculated by the miles used for business compared to total miles the car is used in the year. This means you have to keep track of the business miles you drive, no matter how you deduct your automobile expenses.
>
> If you work from home, business use of the car starts when you leave your home to visit clients, go to the bank or the office supply store, plus all your trips in between. If you do not want to keep track of your actual expenses, you can claim the standard allowance (in 2008, this was 58.5 cents per business mile).
>
> For more information about the business use of a car, visit the IRS website http://www.irs.gov/taxtopics/tc510.html. To find the current standard mileage rate on the www.irs.gov website, search for 'standard mileage rate'.
>
> In the UK: Information about business expenses and dispensations can be found at the Business link website www.businesslink.gov.uk. Use the search terms 'Treatment of vehicle expenses for the purposes of self assessment' to find information about the business use of your car.
> *Source: www.irs.gov; www.hmrc.gov.uk; www.businesslink.gov.uk*

If you entered actual mileage information you can save the *Mileage log* workbook, otherwise you do not need to save the changes:

☞ **Close the workbook and save the changes** 𝓁𝓁⁹

4.5 Projects

To determine if a project is profitable, you will need to keep track of the costs. Especially for projects that run for a longer period of time. In the *Practice files Office 2007* folder you can find the *Projects* workbook that you can use to keep track of the costs of a project.

☞ **Open** 📊Projects **from the folder** 📁 Practice files Office 2007 ✍**12**

You see the *Project* workbook. The worksheet *Project costs* is opened:

The **Costs** column contains the materials or other purchases you use for this project:

The **Time** column contains the time you (or a machine) spend on this project:

Below **Hourly rate** you enter your hourly rate or that of the machine:

Below **Total** the total amount is calculated from the three previous columns:

	A	B	C	D	E	F	G
1	**Project:**						
2	**Date**	**Description**	**Costs**	**Time**	**Hourly rate**	**Total**	
3	2/01/08	Material	500.00			500.00	
4	2/01/08	Preparation		1:30	40.00	60.00	
5	3/01/08	Installation	100.00	2:00	50.00	200.00	
6						-	
7						-	
8						-	
9						-	
10						-	
11						-	
12						-	
13						-	
14						-	
15						-	

In each row you can enter the costs, the hours or both.

💡 **Tip**

Project name or number

Enter the project name or the project number in cell B1 next to **Project:**. If you have multiple projects you can save each project in a separate workbook.

This workbook contains an additional worksheet:

☞ **Open the** `Summary` **worksheet** ℓℓ²³

Here you see the total actual costs of the *Project costs* worksheet.

If you enter the estimated costs, the variance is calculated in money/time and as a percentage.

	A	B	C	D	E	F
1	**Summary**					
2		**Estimated**	**Actual**	**Difference**		
3	**Costs**	700.00	600.00	-100.00	-14.3%	
4	**Time**	3:00	3:30	0:30	16.7%	
5	**Total**	850.00	760.00	-90.00	-10.6%	
6						
7						

☞ **Open the** `Project costs` **worksheet** ℓℓ²³

You can enter data up to row 20. In case you need more rows, you can copy A20:F20 further down.

	A	B	C	D	E	F
1	**Project:**					
2	**Date**	**Description**	**Costs**	**Time**	**Hourly rate**	**Total**
3	2/01/08	Material	500.00			500.00
4	2/01/08	Preparation		1:30	40.00	60.00
5	3/01/08	Installation	100.00	2:00	50.00	200.00
6						-
7						-
8						-

⇨ **Please note:**

In *Excel* you enter time values using a colon (:) between the hours and minutes. To enter the number of hours and the number of minutes, look at these examples:
- 45 minutes is entered as 0:45;
- 1 hour and 50 minutes is entered as 1:50;
- If you would enter 0:75, *Excel* reads that as 1 hour (60 minutes) and 15 minutes, so 1:15.

This means you do not have to recalculate the times in hourly segments. Because of the colon *Excel* recognizes that you are entering an amount of time.

When you keep track of projects it is important to discover where the actual costs differ from the estimated costs. This will help you make a better calculation on your next project.

☞ **Close the workbook** ℓℓ⁹

4.6 Hour Log

You can use an hour log to track the total number of hours you have worked for your company. Using the hour log you can for example check if you billed all billable hours. You can find the *Hour log* workbook in the *Practice files Office 2007* folder:

☞ **Open** Hour log **from the folder** Practice files Office 2007 🐾**12**

You see the *Hours* worksheet from the *Hour log* workbook:

Type the date in cell A6

Press ⇥ Tab

In cell B5 ▾ appears:

👆 **Click** ▾

👆 **Click a description**

You can also type a description yourself.

Type an explanation in cell C6

Type the time in cell D6

Press ⇥ Tab

The total time is calculated:

☞ **Copy cells A100:E100 further down if you need more rows**

💡 Tip

Invoice number
Enter the invoice number in the Invoice column as soon as you have sent the invoice. That way you can quickly see which hours still need to be invoiced.

☞ **Open the** Descriptions **worksheet** ℓℓ²³

You can enter standard descriptions that you use often in column A:

These descriptions automatically appear in the drop-down list in cell B6 on the *Hours* worksheet.

💡 Tip

Changing the order of the descriptions
The drop-down list in cell B6 displays the descriptions in the same order. If you move the descriptions you used most to the top of the list, you can select these quicker when you log your hours.

You can keep an hour log for separate periods. You can create a separate log for the hours you worked each year.

You can close this workbook. You only need to save the changes if you made changes that are useful for your business.

☞ **Close the workbook without saving the changes** ℓℓ⁹

4.7 Time Planning

Planning your time is necessary to finish a current project on time or to be able to decide if you can accept a new order. In the following model you see an example of a planning:

☞ **Open** 📄 Planning **from the folder** 📁 Practice files Office 2007 ℓℓ¹²

You see the *Project* worksheet of the *Planning* workbook:

On this sheet you enter information about one project, in which each different task has to be performed after the one before.

When you enter the first start and end date yourself, the next start date is entered automatically.

In the next rows you enter the end date. The number of work days is calculated automatically when you enter the end date.

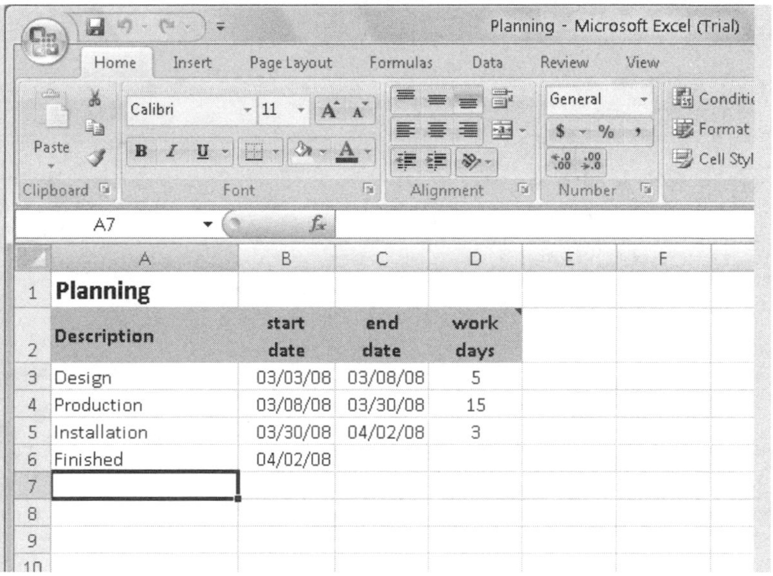

	A	B	C	D	E	F
1	**Planning**					
2	**Description**	**start date**	**end date**	**work days**		
3	Design	03/03/08	03/08/08	5		
4	Production	03/08/08	03/30/08	15		
5	Installation	03/30/08	04/02/08	3		
6	Finished	04/02/08				
7						

☞ **Copy cells A22:D22 further down in case you need more rows**

💡 **Tip**

Calculating the end date
You can also use the *Goal seek* feature to have the end date calculated:

👆 **Click the** Data **tab**

👆 **Click the cell you want to have calculated below** work days

👆 **Click** What-If Analysis ▾

👆 **Click** Goal Seek...

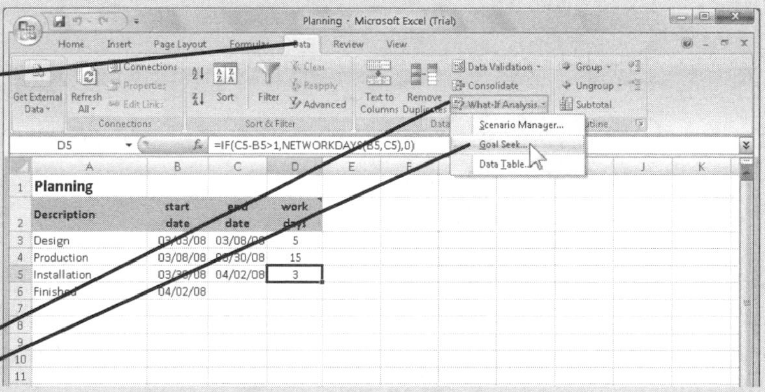

- Continue reading on the next page -

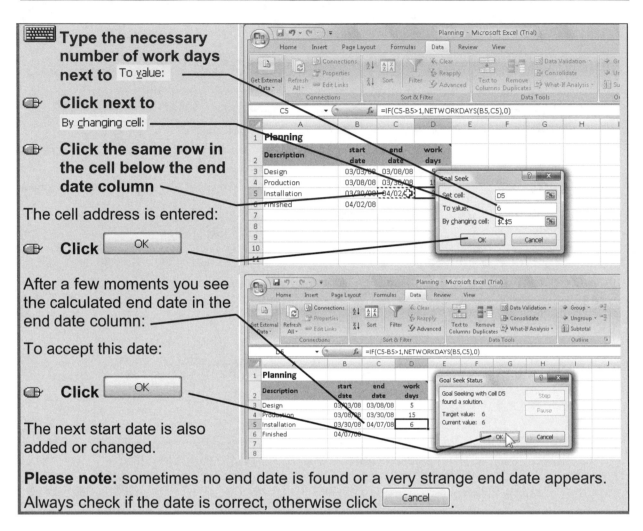

⌨ **Type the necessary number of work days next to** To value:

☞ **Click next to** By changing cell:

☞ **Click the same row in the cell below the end date column**

The cell address is entered:

☞ **Click** OK

After a few moments you see the calculated end date in the end date column:

To accept this date:

☞ **Click** OK

The next start date is also added or changed.

Please note: sometimes no end date is found or a very strange end date appears. Always check if the date is correct, otherwise click Cancel .

On the *Planning* worksheet you enter your subsequent jobs or projects. Here you can see if there is space in your planning for new projects, or when you can start accepting new projects.

☞ **Open the** Planning **worksheet** ℓℓ²³

This sheet works the same as the *Project* worksheet. The work days are calculated automatically when you enter the end date.

	A	B	C	D	E	F
1	**Planning**					
2	Description	start date	end date	work days		
3	Order 1	03/03/08	03/08/08	5		
4	Order 2	03/08/08	04/05/08	20		
5	Order 3	04/05/08	04/23/08	13		
6			04/23/08			
7						
8						

☞ **Close the workbook** ℓℓ⁹

You do not need to save the changes in this practice file if you did not enter any real data.

4.8 Actual Cost

By comparing the estimated and actual costs of finished projects, you can improve your estimates for new projects. You can make the comparison in the *Actual cost* workbook, using the information from the *Projects* worksheet you used before. On the *Projects* worksheet you recorded the details for each project. On the *Actual cost* worksheet you create an overview of all your projects:

☞ **Open** Actual cost **from the folder** Practice files Office 2007 *ℓ*ℓ**12**

You see the *Actual cost* workbook:

In the Description column you enter the name of the project.

Below **Actual** you enter the real cost and below **Estimated** you enter the estimated costs or the contract value.

The values in the other columns are calculated automatically:

☞ **Copy cells A22:E22 further down if you need more rows**

☞ **Close the workbook** *ℓ*ℓ**9**

You do not need to save the changes in this practice file if you did not enter any real data.

4.9 Financing

When you buy business equipment like a machine or a car you will often need to finance the investment through a small business loan. A characteristic of this type of loan is that it is long-term and the payment is usually the same amount. In the beginning you pay a lot of interest and pay back little on the principal, at the end of the term it is the other way round.

It is not easy to calculate the monthly or quarterly payments, but *Excel* has a built-in formula for that. If you enter the loan information in the following model, you can see right away how much you pay for every installment and how much interest you pay in total:

☞ **Open** Financing **from the** Practice files Office 2007 **folder** *12*

You see the details you have to enter for the loan:

⌨ **Type the principal in cell B4**

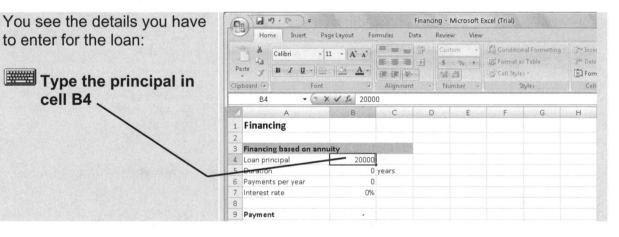

⌨ **Type the duration of the loan in cell B5**

⌨ **Type the number of annual payments in cell B6**

For monthly installments you type 12, for quarterly installments you type 4. If you pay once a year, you type 1.

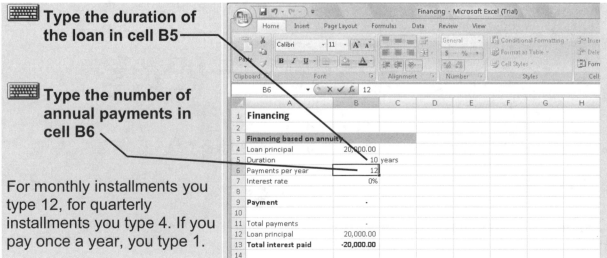

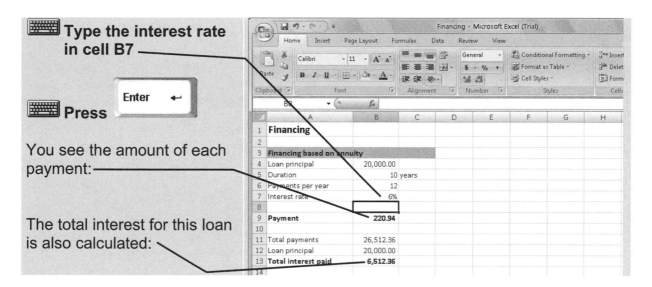

Type the interest rate in cell B7

Press [Enter ←]

You see the amount of each payment:——

The total interest for this loan is also calculated:◄

The payment calculated here may be slightly different at your bank. This can be caused by an amount being rounded off differently, or if the payment is done at the beginning or at the end of the period.

☞ **Close the workbook** $\ell\ell^9$

If you entered useful data, you can save the changes.

4.10 Comparative Figures

If you use accounting software to do your bookkeeping, you may be able to create reports with comparative figures. Your accountant may provide these reports for you periodically.

You can also create reports with charts in *Excel*. With an *Excel* report, you have the added advantage that you can change the numbers without affecting your bookkeeping. You immediately see the effects on your costs and profits when you change an item. You can also use the report to create an estimate for next year. Take a look at this model:

☞ **Open** Comparative figures **from the** Practice files Office 2007 **folder** $\ell\ell^{12}$

You see the *Amounts* worksheet from the *Comparative figures* workbook:

You see an example of the revenues and expenses for three years for a fake company:

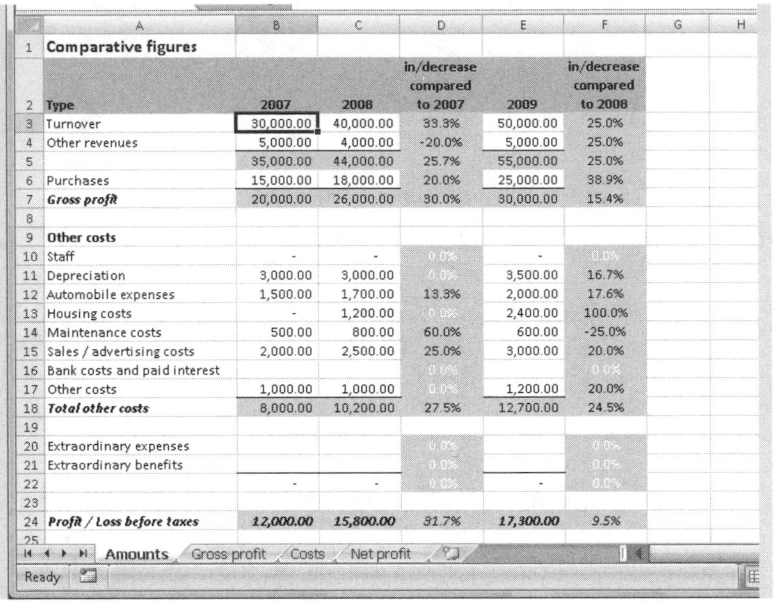

	A	B	C	D	E	F	G	H
1	Comparative figures							
2	Type	2007	2008	in/decrease compared to 2007	2009	in/decrease compared to 2008		
3	Turnover	30,000.00	40,000.00	33.3%	50,000.00	25.0%		
4	Other revenues	5,000.00	4,000.00	-20.0%	5,000.00	25.0%		
5		35,000.00	44,000.00	25.7%	55,000.00	25.0%		
6	Purchases	15,000.00	18,000.00	20.0%	25,000.00	38.9%		
7	*Gross profit*	20,000.00	26,000.00	30.0%	30,000.00	15.4%		
8								
9	**Other costs**							
10	Staff	-	-	0.0%	-	0.0%		
11	Depreciation	3,000.00	3,000.00	0.0%	3,500.00	16.7%		
12	Automobile expenses	1,500.00	1,700.00	13.3%	2,000.00	17.6%		
13	Housing costs	-	1,200.00	0.0%	2,400.00	100.0%		
14	Maintenance costs	500.00	800.00	60.0%	600.00	-25.0%		
15	Sales / advertising costs	2,000.00	2,500.00	25.0%	3,000.00	20.0%		
16	Bank costs and paid interest			0.0%		0.0%		
17	Other costs	1,000.00	1,000.00	0.0%	1,200.00	20.0%		
18	*Total other costs*	8,000.00	10,200.00	27.5%	12,700.00	24.5%		
19								
20	Extraordinary expenses			0.0%		0.0%		
21	Extraordinary benefits			0.0%		0.0%		
22		-	-	0.0%	-	0.0%		
23								
24	*Profit / Loss before taxes*	12,000.00	15,800.00	31.7%	17,300.00	9.5%		
25								

Amounts / Gross profit / Costs / Net profit

Ready

⇨ **Please note:**

The cells with blue backgrounds contain formulas. Do not enter data in these cells. If you do, you will overwrite the formulas and the calculations will no longer be correct.

You can customize this report for your company in three steps:

Step 1 Adjust the descriptions of revenues and costs in column A Type.

Step 2 Change the years above the columns to the years you want to compare.

Step 3 Enter the data from your accounting software or from the report you received from your accountant.

💡 **Tip**

Budget

You can also use the last column to enter the estimated amounts for the coming year, for example if you want to create a report for a bank.

This workbook also contains multiple worksheets:

☞ **Open the** Gross profit
worksheet 🦶23

You see the turnover, other
revenue and purchases
displayed in a chart:

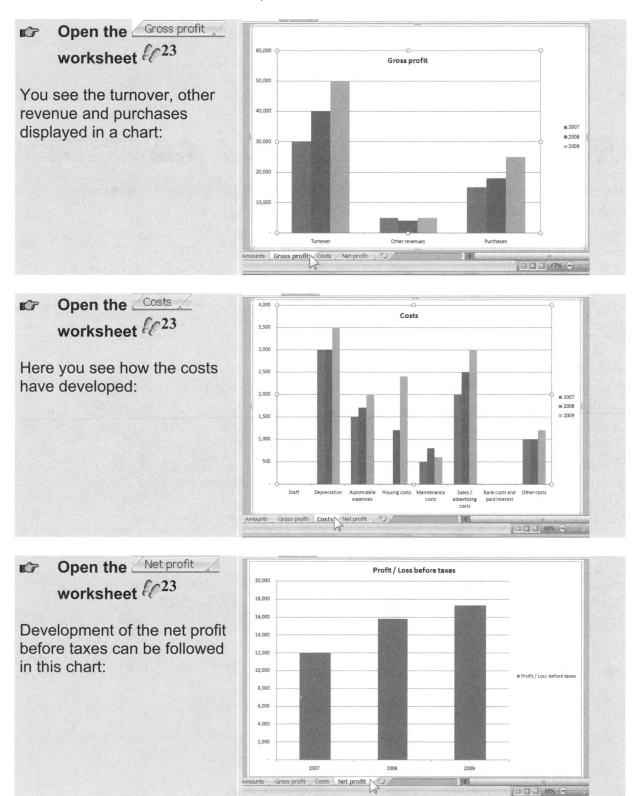

☞ **Open the** Costs
worksheet 🦶23

Here you see how the costs
have developed:

☞ **Open the** Net profit
worksheet 🦶23

Development of the net profit
before taxes can be followed
in this chart:

When you adjust the amounts on the *Amounts* worksheets, the charts change accordingly.

If you entered your own figures:

☞ **Close the workbook and save the changes** 🦶⁹

4.11 Filing a Sales and Use Tax Return

If you file your own Sales and use tax return, you can use the following model to calculate the amount payable beforehand.

⇨ **Please note:**

If you are in the UK and you file a VAT return instead, you can skip this section and continue reading *section 4.12 Filing a VAT Return*.
If you are not VAT registered you can skip both sections and continue reading the background information at the end of this chapter.

⇨ **Please note:**

Each US state has different requirements for filing sale and use tax returns. Some states may still accept a return on paper or by phone; others require an online sales and use tax return.

The forms used by each state are also different, as well as the sales and use tax percentages and possible municipal or county discretionary surtaxes.
Therefore the model used in this section may not reflect the actual requirements for your location. Check with your local tax authority for more information.

⇨ **Please note:**

Filing a sales and use tax return is not difficult, but does require some tax and accounting knowledge. If you do not have that knowledge you can ask your bookkeeper for help.

☞ **Open** Sales and use tax return **from the** Practice files Office 2007 **folder** 🦶¹²

You see the layout of the Sales and use tax return model:

⌨ **Type the return period in cell E1**

⌨ **Type the applicable sales tax rate in cell E2**

☞ **Enter the applicable amounts**

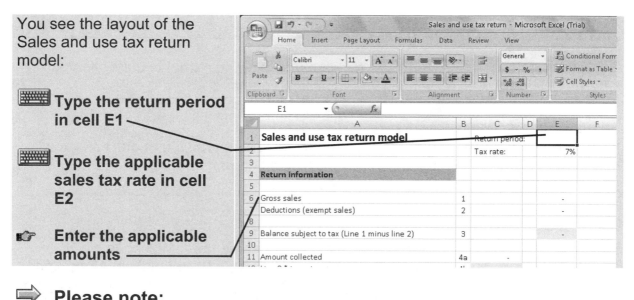

⇨ **Please note:**

The cells with blue backgrounds contain formulas. Do not enter data in these cells. If you do, you will overwrite the formulas and the calculations will no longer be correct.

🖰 **Drag the scroll bar down**

Here you see bottom part of the worksheet. The total tax due is calculated automatically:

	A	B	C	D	E	F
3						
4	**Return information**					
5						
6	Gross sales	1			-	
7	Deductions (exempt sales)	2			-	
8						
9	Balance subject to tax (Line 1 minus line 2)	3			-	
10						
11	Amount collected	4a	-			
12	Line 3 * tax rate	4b	-			
13						
14	Sales tax due (enter the greater of Line 4a or Line 4b)	4			-	
15						
16	Taxable purchases (include Use tax on Internet and out-of-state untaxed purchases)	5	-			
17						
18	Use tax due	6				
19						
20	Total tax due	7				
21						

☞ **Close the workbook** 🦶⁹

If you entered useful data, you can save the changes.

4.12 Filing a VAT Return

If you file your own VAT return, you can use the following model to calculate your VAT payable and VAT reclaimable/deductible beforehand.

⇨ **Please note:**

If you are in the US, or you are in the UK and you are not registered for VAT, you can skip this section and continue reading the background information at the end of this chapter.

⇨ **Please note:**

Filing a VAT return is not difficult, but does require some tax and accounting knowledge. If you do not have that knowledge, you can also appoint someone (for example your accountant or bookkeeper) as your VAT agent. Your authorized agent can act on your behalf to register for VAT, file your VAT returns and deal with HMRC on other VAT matters. However, even if you use an agent, you are still legally responsible for registering for VAT, filing your VAT returns and paying VAT on time.

Of course you can also ask your bookkeeper for help and file your own VAT return. On the HMRC website you can also register to file your VAT return online. Check http://www.hmrc.gov.uk/demo/organisation/VAT-online/ for a demo.

☞ **Open** VAT return **from the** Practice files Office 2007 **folder** $\ell\ell$12

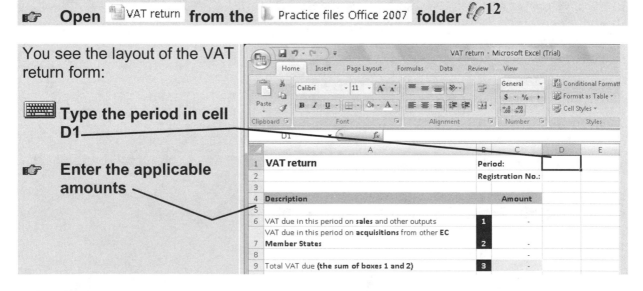

You see the layout of the VAT return form:

⌨ **Type the period in cell D1**

☞ **Enter the applicable amounts**

⇨ **Please note:**

The cells with blue backgrounds contain formulas. Do not enter data in these cells. If you do, you will overwrite the formulas and the calculations will no longer be correct.

⌨ **Drag the scroll bar down**

Here you see the bottom part of the worksheet. The total VAT due and the net VAT to be paid or reclaimed are calculated automatically:

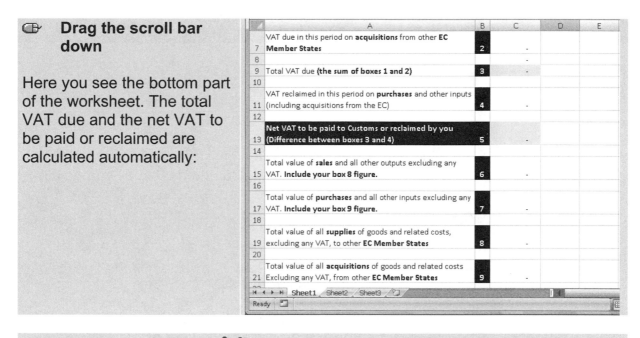

☞ **Close the workbook** ₰⁹

If you entered useful data, you can save the changes.

☞ **Close** *Excel* ₰⁹

In this chapter you have learned to work with a number of practical workbooks that you can use to do part of your administrative tasks.

These workbooks contain many useful formulas that will save you time doing research and performing calculations.

The website with this book contains the original files. If you somehow delete the formulas by mistake, you can start over with the original workbook files from the website.

4.13 Background Information

Glossary	
Depreciation	Spreading the investment cost of an asset over the lifespan of that asset. If a machine costs $ 8,000 and has an estimated life span of 5 years, then each year gets a 1/5 share = $ 1,500 of the costs.
Internal transfer	Money that is on its way from a petty cash fund to a bank account or the other way around. Or money that is on its way between two company bank accounts.
Template	A pre-developed worksheet layout containing fonts, visual styles and formulas. When a template is opened, a copy of the original template is created automatically.
VAT	Value Added Tax, a tax charged on most business-to-business and business-to-consumer transactions in the UK and Europe. VAT is levied on a VAT registered business as a fraction of the price of each taxable sale they make. Businesses registered for VAT are in turn reimbursed VAT on their purchases. Businesses not registered for VAT do not charge VAT on their sales, pay VAT on their purchases and cannot reclaim this VAT.

Calculating or working?

You can use *Excel* to make countless calculations, but you have to interpret the outcome yourself or with help from your bookkeeper.

Circumstances may arise that will force you to accept an order, even though you know you will not make a profit. For example to be able to get that new customer, or to retrieve some of the costs of machines that would stand still otherwise. In a slow period, you may have to lower your hourly rate.

Checking your cash balance
The balance at the end of the last row of your cash ledger is the amount that should physically be present in your cash box. It is advisable to count the money in your cash box from time to time, to make sure there still is a match.

Small differences are normal and may have arisen from payments being rounded off. Large differences may be caused by:
- failing to record deposits if there is a surplus in your cash box;
- failing to record expenditures when there is a deficit, or maybe you lost some receipts;
- theft from the cash box if there is a deficit.

It is not possible to have a negative balance. You can overdraw your checking account with the bank, but that is not possible in a petty cash fund. You cannot spend more money than you have. In a tax audit, the IRS will always check if you have a negative cash balance somewhere. If that is the case, it may be an indication for revenues that are not reported.

4.14 Tips

 Tip

Business wallet
Even if you handle most of your financial affairs by bank, there will always be times that you pay or receive something in cash. For example for parking or for lunch on the road. It is a good idea to use a separate wallet for your business expenses and receipts. The expenditure receipts can then be recorded in your cashbook.

Using your personal wallet for business expenses is asking for trouble, because the completeness cannot be checked. You are required to maintain a cashbook for tax purposes, and you cannot do that if you mix your personal and business cash.

Tip

Website for small businesses
Microsoft has a special website for small businesses:
www.microsoft.com/smallbusiness. Here you will find additional information about
using *Microsoft* programs in your company, along with many business templates
such as a business plan, cash flow statements, brochures, newsletters and
datasheets.
On this website you can also subscribe to a free e-mail newsletter at the bottom of
the page *Insight: Microsoft Small Business Newsletter* is a monthly newsletter
containing business insights and exclusive software tips, articles from experts in
small business, free software downloads and special offers.

Tip

DIY saves money (1)
Some of the figures you calculated in this chapter can also be obtained from your
bookkeeper. In that case you will find the added cost on his invoice. By doing some
calculations yourself, you can save on administrative expenses. Furthermore, you
know your own company best, so it is easier for you to collect certain data than it is
for an outsider like your bookkeeper. And you learn from it as well.

It is also a disadvantage that you receive the information from your bookkeeper at a
later time. In many cases your administration is processed quarterly, which may be
too late to take action.

Tip

DIY saves money (2)
A huge part of your administrative tasks and their costs is entering data into an
accounting program. In many cases you can do that yourself.

Most new accounting software has special versions for clients of accountants and
bookkeepers. Online bookkeeping or eBookkeeping is a new trend. You enter your
data online. You do not have to be a trained bookkeeper to be able to do that, but it
is advisable to ask your bookkeeper to help you get started.
After you enter the data, your accounts are then prepared by your bookkeeper. Ask
your bookkeeper or accountant for more information.

5. Advertising and Business Presentations

🕐 60 min.

Informing (potential) customers about your company is an important part of running a business. Whether it is a simple advertisement or a complete business presentation, you want to let your customers know what you can do for them.

Using *Publisher* you can easily create an advertisement, flyer or brochure. Templates that you adapt to your company style can help you get started. In this chapter you can learn how to do that by creating a brochure.

You can use *Word* to create a simple newsletter. *Word* contains many templates for newsletters, brochures and other standard documents that you can customize for your own needs. In this chapter you will create a newsletter based on a sample newsletter. You can also read how to send a newsletter using *Business Contact Manager*.

PowerPoint is a program you can use to create professional business presentations. You also use templates for that, enabling you to create a slideshow in a short period of time. You can play this presentation on your computer screen, or show it to a larger audience on a projection screen.

In this chapter you will learn to:

- create a brochure;
- save the brochure for (commercial) printing;
- create a newsletter;
- send a newsletter by e-mail;
- create a business presentation;
- play a business presentation;
- print a hand-out for a presentation.

5.1 Brochure, Advertisement and Flyer

You are going to create a brochure with the program *Publisher 2007*. A brochure is a folded leaflet that you can fill with information about your company and your products or services.

When you use a template or a sample brochure that you customize, you can quickly and easily create a brochure. The same thing goes for creating an advertisement or flyer. Customizing an existing template or sample is always quicker than creating a new one from scratch.

Tip

A template also contains the formatting information of the document. By consistently using the same templates, you establish a recognizable house style and identity for your business. This is also known as *branding*.

☞ Open *Publisher* ⓵¹

In the start window you can choose among a wide range of built-in templates available in *Publisher*.

On the left side of the window you see the publication types:

☞ Click Brochures

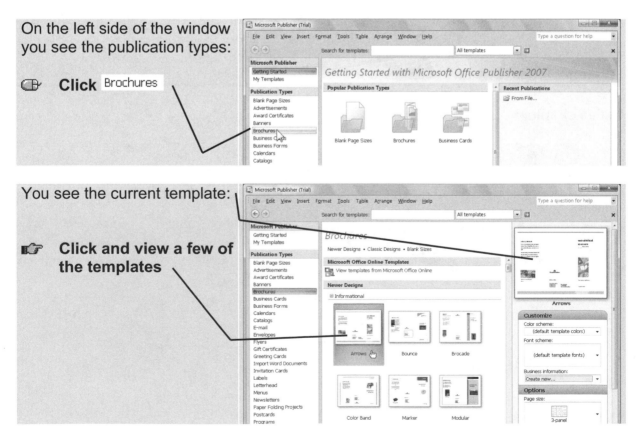

You see the current template:

☞ **Click and view a few of the templates**

Publisher comes with an assortment of templates for brochures and other publication types. You can work with these templates or modify them to meet your needs.

In this exercise you do not need to use one of these templates. You can open a sample brochure template from the *Practice files Office 2007* folder instead:

➡️ **Please note:**

The folder *Practice files Office 2007* can be found on the website with this book. In *Chapter 1 Preparation* you can read how to copy this folder to your PC.

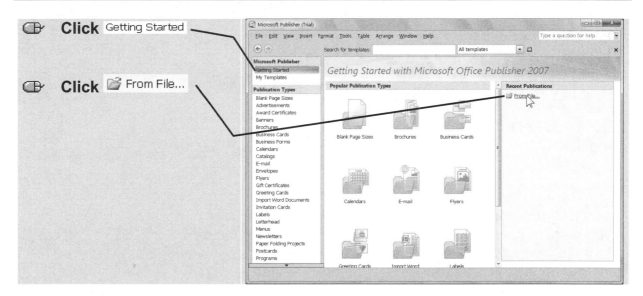

You see the *Open Publication* window:

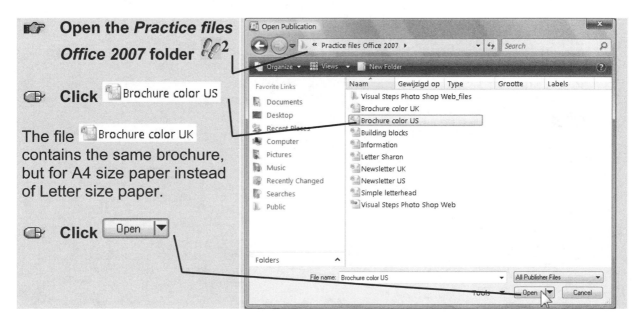

Brochure color consists of one horizontal page with three columns. You can enter information on the front and back side of the paper. Here you see the first page of *Brochure color*:

On the left you see the Task pane:

To see the back of the brochure:
☞ **Click** [2]

To see the front of the brochure again:
☞ **Click** [1]

The page size of this US brochure is Letter (landscape):

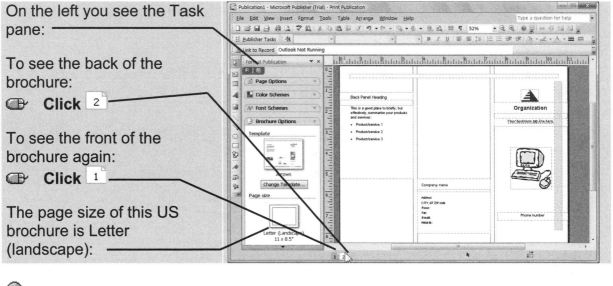

💡 Tip

Changing the page size
If you want to change the page size, it is best to do that at the beginning so you can adapt the layout to the new page size right away. For an advertisement you should know the range of size requirements before you start.

In the bottom left corner of the window:

☞ **Click** Change Page Size...

To select a standard size:

☞ **Click the desired size**

To create a custom size:

☞ **Click** Create custom page size...

This brochure is folded in three parts after printing, so it is important to pay attention to the correct layout. The texts in the sample brochure help you with that.

A brochure contains a number of objects and guides such as text boxes, images and colored rectangles. You can see that when you take a closer look at the brochure:

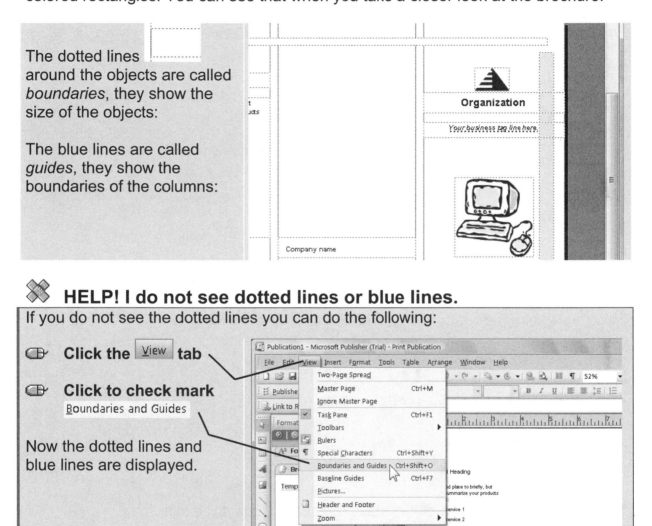

The dotted lines around the objects are called *boundaries*, they show the size of the objects:

The blue lines are called *guides*, they show the boundaries of the columns:

HELP! I do not see dotted lines or blue lines.

If you do not see the dotted lines you can do the following:

☞ **Click the** View **tab**

☞ **Click to check mark** Boundaries and Guides

Now the dotted lines and blue lines are displayed.

You can customize these objects and guides. You can change the contents of text boxes and images, as well as their size and location in the brochure.

💡 Tip

Would you like to create a brochure for your own business right away? Then use your own logo and add applicable texts in the next exercises. Pay attention to the font as well; use the font you selected for your letterhead for example.

You start by changing the text in a text box:

🖱️ **Double-click**
   `Organization` ─────

The word is selected.

⌨️ **Type:**
   Photo Specialist

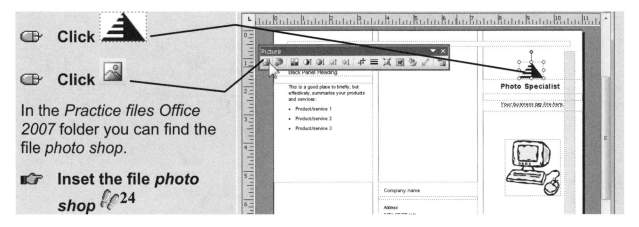

Now you can replace the logo:

🖱️ **Click** 📐 ────

🖱️ **Click** 🖼️ ────

In the *Practice files Office 2007* folder you can find the file *photo shop*.

☞ **Inset the file *photo shop* 👣²⁴**

The logo that is inserted is quite small. You can enlarge it like this:

🖱️ **Point to a circle on one of the corners of the logo** ─────

The mouse pointer changes into ↖:

🖱️ **Drag** ↖ **until the logo has the right size**

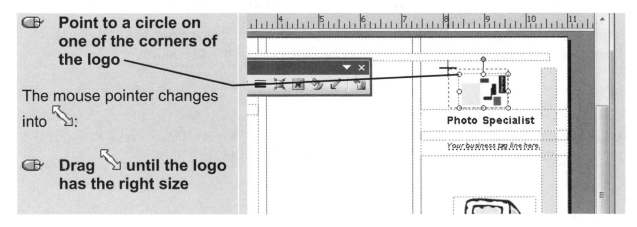

When the logo has the right size you can move it to the right location:

☞ **Point to the logo**

The mouse pointer changes into ✥:

☞ **Drag the logo to the right location**

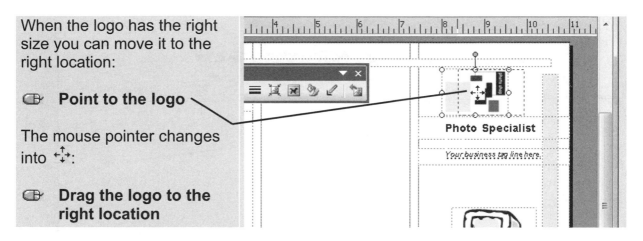

To enhance your brochure you can add an extra image. You can select one of the photos or images that are on your computer:

☞ **Right-click**

☞ **Click** Change Picture

☞ **Click** From File...

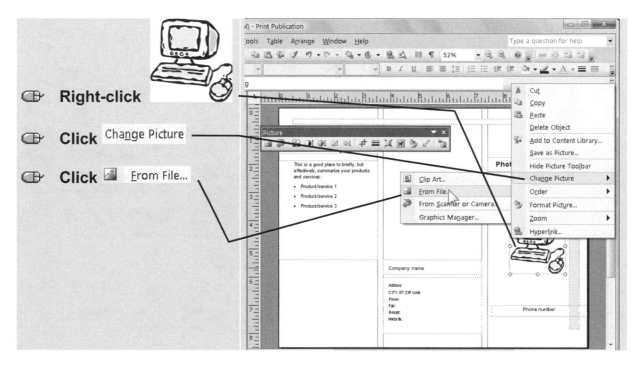

In the *Practice files Office 2007* folder you will see the file *Camera*.

☞ **Insert the file *Camera***
  ⏚12

If necessary you can enlarge or move the image the same way you did with the logo.

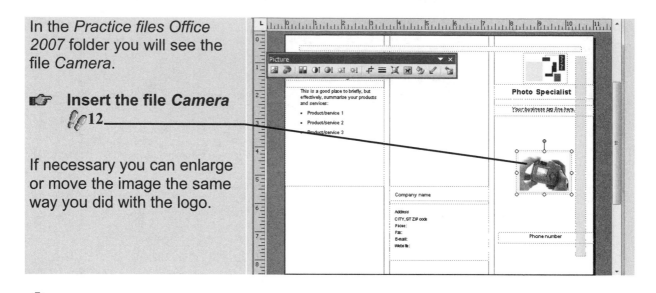

💡 **Tip**

Adding new images
In the example you have replaced an image, but you can also add new images. Like this:

👆 **Click somewhere in the brochure**

👆 **Click the** Insert **tab**

👆 **Click** Picture

👆 **Click** 🖼 From File...

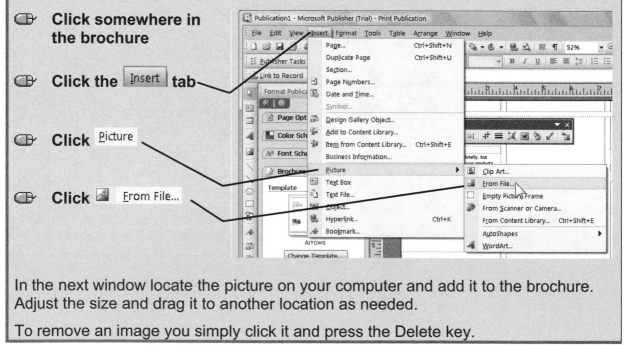

In the next window locate the picture on your computer and add it to the brochure. Adjust the size and drag it to another location as needed.

To remove an image you simply click it and press the Delete key.

You have changed a text and two images in the brochure. Now you can try adding a new text box:

Click Insert

Click Text Box

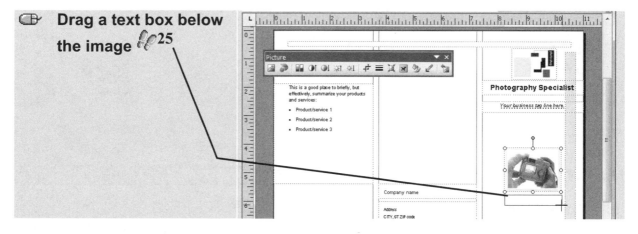

To drag a text box on the brochure, you need to hold the mouse button down. Position the text box so that it is below the image you just added:

Drag a text box below the image 25

Select the font and the font size for the text:

Click next to
Times New Roman

Click Arial

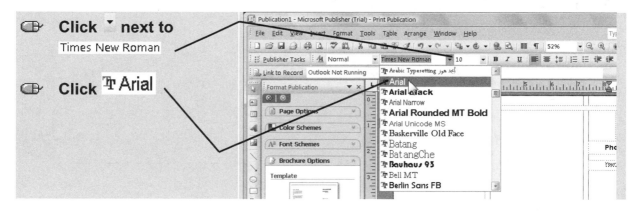

Click ˇ next to 10

Click 12

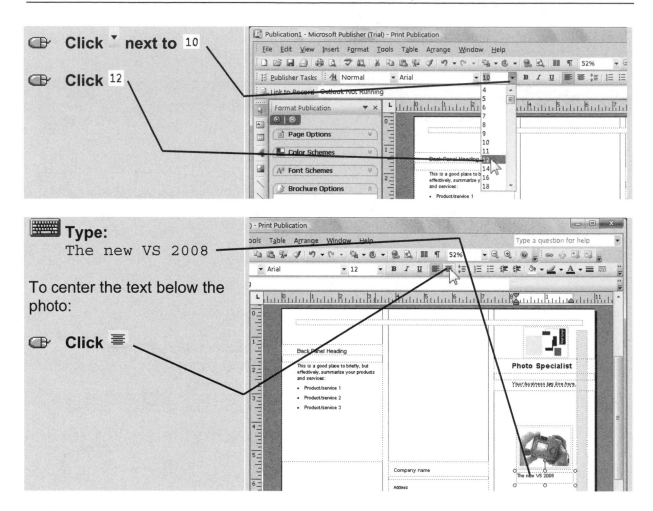

⌨ **Type:**
The new VS 2008

To center the text below the photo:

Click ≡

You can also easily customize existing texts:

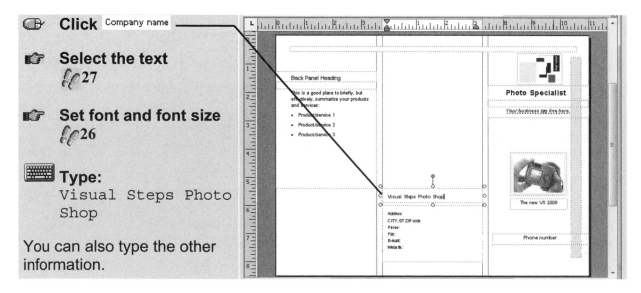

Click Company name

☞ **Select the text**
🦶27

☞ **Set font and font size**
🦶26

⌨ **Type:**
Visual Steps Photo
Shop

You can also type the other information.

💡 Tip

Larger letters
Often the text is hard to read while you type. You can zoom in by pressing F9. If you press F9 again the text goes back to the original size.

Texts are typed in text boxes. If the text box is too big or too small you can adjust the size:

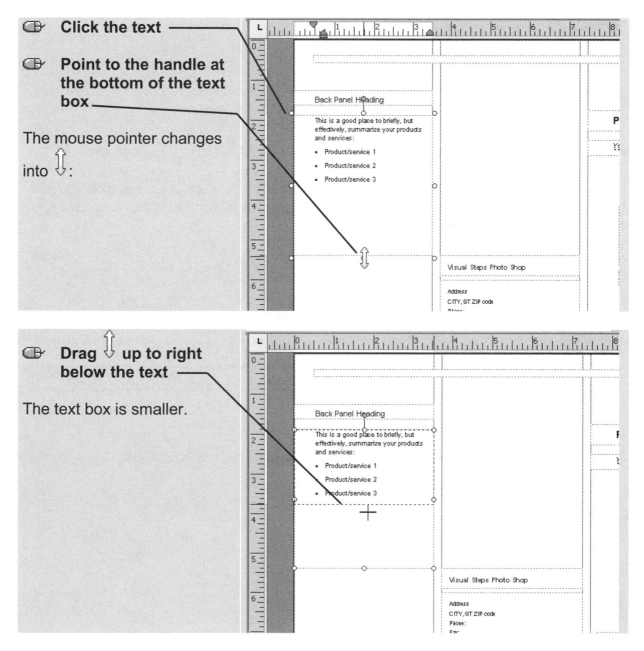

👆 **Click the text** ————

👆 **Point to the handle at the bottom of the text box**

The mouse pointer changes into ⇕:

👆 **Drag ⇕ up to right below the text** ————

The text box is smaller.

If you want to add a short text, you can just type it in the text box. If you have saved (longer) texts about your company in *Word*, you can insert those like this:

☞ **Select all text in the text box**

🖰 **Click** `Insert`

🖰 **Click** `Text File...`

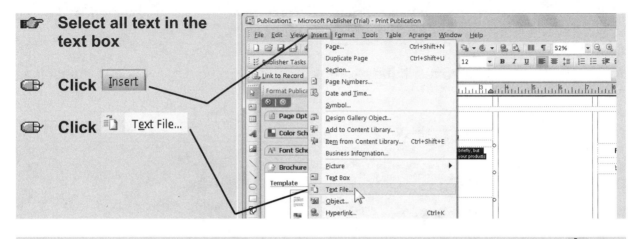

☞ **Insert the file *Information* from the *Practice files Office 2007* folder** 📖12

The text does not fit in the text box. *Publisher* asks if you want to use *autoflow*. This means the text automatically flows to the next text box when the first one is full. You do not want to use that feature:

🖰 **Click** `No`

The inserted text doesn't fit in this box. Do you want to use autoflow?

To have Publisher automatically flow text throughout your publication, asking for confirmation before it flows into existing boxes, click Yes. To connect boxes yourself, click No. For information on connecting text boxes, press F1.

The text is inserted. 🄰⋯ indicates that the text does not fit in the text box:

🖰 **Place the mouse pointer on the handle at the bottom of the text box**

Now the mouse pointer looks like this ⇕:

🖰 **Drag the mouse pointer down**

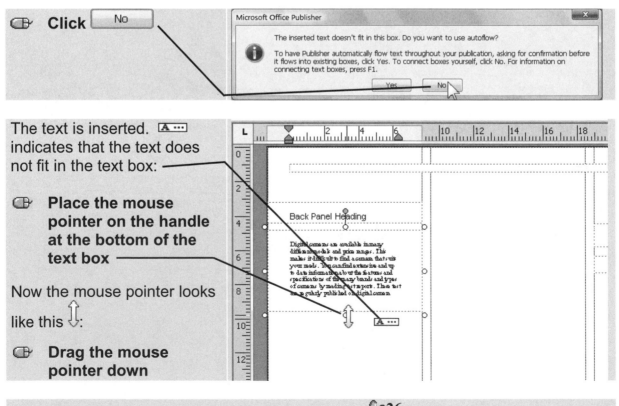

☞ **Adjust the font and font size if necessary** 📖26

💡 Tip

Pasting text
You can also paste (portions of) texts from other files into the brochure. You can read more about this in the *Tips* at the end of this chapter.

You now know how to modify text and images. You can do this the same way for the other texts and images in this brochure. If you are already working on a real brochure for your company you can do that now.

☞ Modify the other texts and images on the front and the back of the brochure

After that you can continue to format the brochure. You can select another color scheme for this brochure. The color scheme decides the color of the guides, such as the rectangles in the layout grid.

🖰 **Click**

    ■ **Color Schemes** ⌃

🖰 **Click a color scheme**

The color of the rectangles in the brochure has changed.

To close the list of color schemes:

🖰 **Click** ⌃

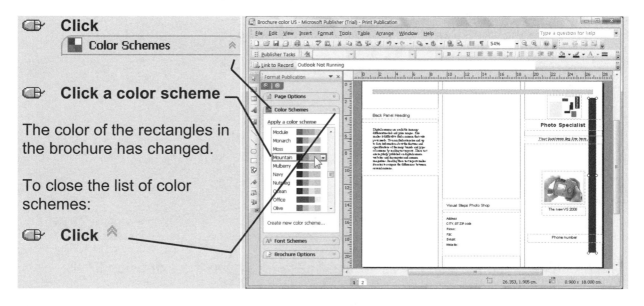

⊗ HELP! I do not see the Task pane.

If you do not see the Task pane on the left side of the *Publisher* window you can do the following:

🖰 **Click** `View`

🖰 **Click to check mark**
    `Task Pane`

Now the Task pane is displayed again.

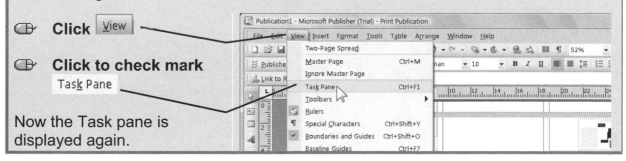

You have learned how to quickly customize a sample brochure. Now you can save the brochure:

☞ **Click** File

☞ **Click** Save As...

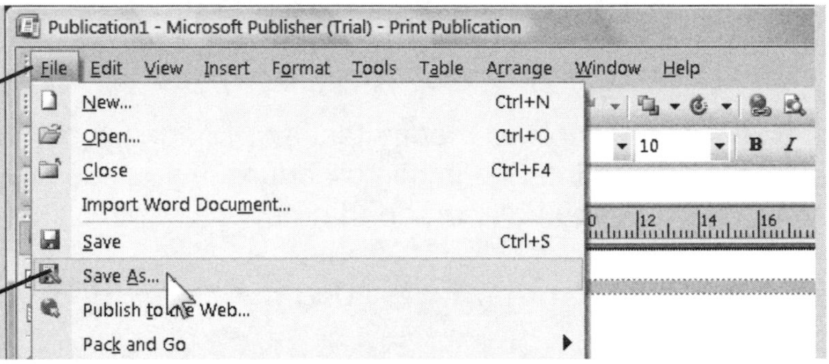

☞ **Click** 📄 Documents

You can also select another folder to save the brochure.

☞ **Click** Save

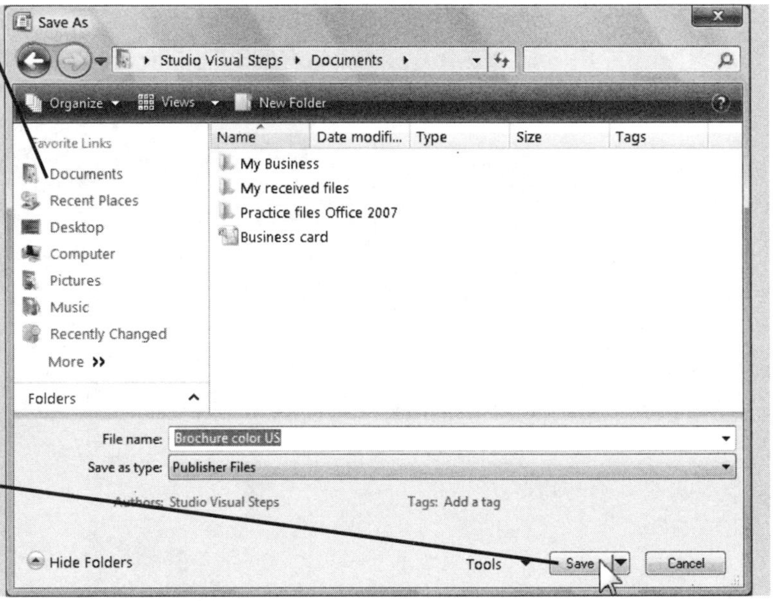

The brochure is stored as a *Publisher* file. These files have the extension .PUB.
A .PUB file can only be opened in *Publisher.*
You can easily print a *Publisher* file yourself.
If you want to have your brochure printed by a commercial printer, it is best to save the file as a PDF (Portable Document Format) file. PDF files cannot be changed by others, so you can be sure that your brochure is printed exactly as you created it.

➡️ **Please note:**

To be able to save a file as a PDF file, you will need to install an add-on first. You can read how to do that in *Chapter 1 Preparation*.

You are going to save this brochure as a PDF file:

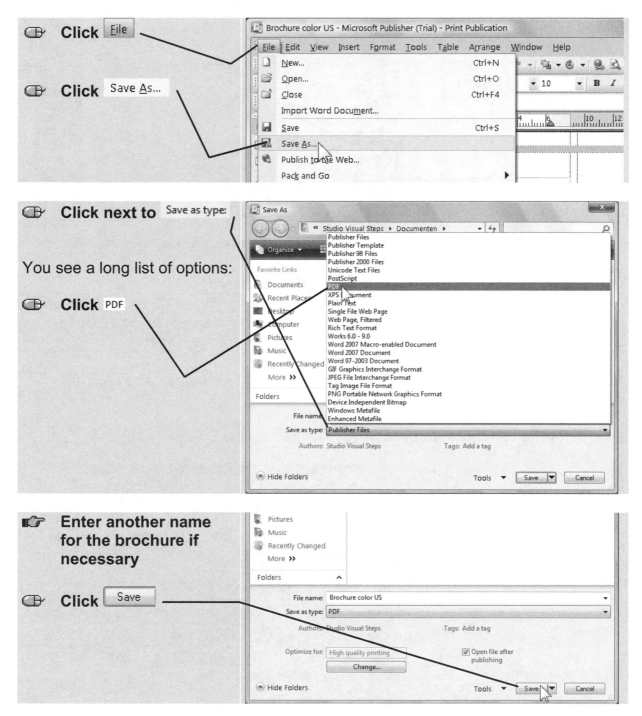

The file is saved as a PDF file with the extension .PDF.

The PDF file is automatically opened in the program *Adobe Reader*.

The free program *Adobe Reader* needs to be pre-installed on your computer before you try to open the document.

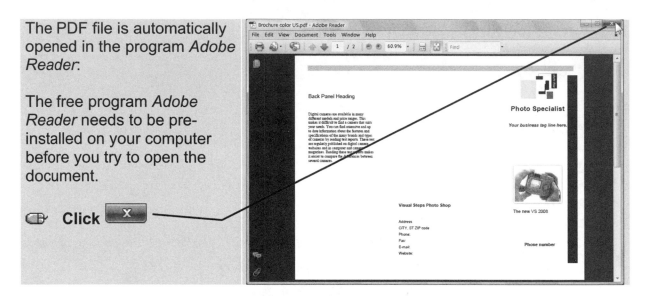

☞ Click ⬛ X ⬛

❖ HELP! I do not have Adobe Reader on my PC.

If you do not yet have the free program *Adobe Reader* on your PC, you can install it from the website of *Adobe*. A step by step description of the installation procedure can be found on the webpage **www.visualsteps.com/adobereader**

The brochure is ready to be sent to a commercial printer. You can also print the brochure yourself, if you want.

☞ Print the brochure if necessary

After printing and folding, the front of the brochure looks like this:

☞ Close *Publisher* ⁹

5.2 Creating a Newsletter

A newsletter is an easy way to send information to your business relations. In just a few steps you can create a newsletter that can be sent by mail or e-mail.

☞ **Open** *Word* 🦶¹

☞ **Open the document** 📄Newsletter US **or** 📄Newsletter UK **from the folder** *Practice files Office 2007* 🦶¹²

The content of these documents is the same, only the page size is different.

  Please note:

The *Practice files Office 2007* folder can be found on the website of this book. In *Chapter 1 Preparation* you can read how to copy this folder to your computer.

☞ **Save the document in the** *Documents* **folder with the name** *Example newsletter* 🦶⁴⁷

You see a simple newsletter with two pages:

👆 **Click the** View **tab**

👆 **Click** 📄 Two Pages

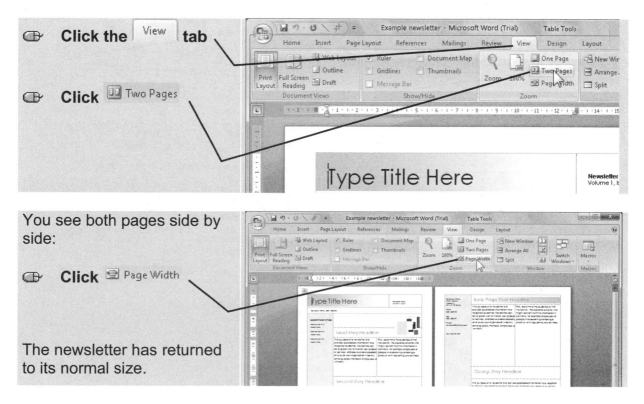

You see both pages side by side:

👆 **Click** 📄 Page Width

The newsletter has returned to its normal size.

You can use this newsletter as a basis for your own newsletter. If you want, you can use your own texts instead of the sample texts used in this section.
You start with the title of your newsletter:

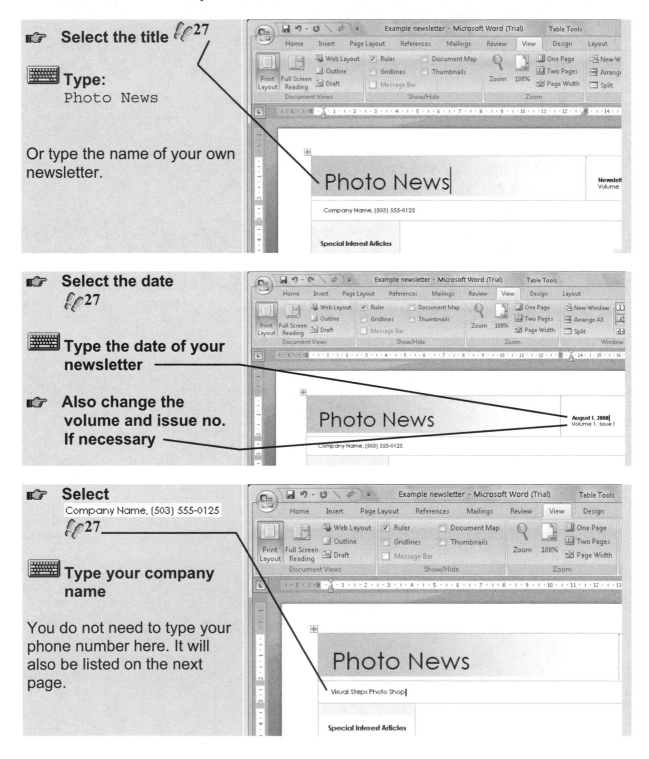

☞ **Select the title** 🦶27

⌨ **Type:**
Photo News

Or type the name of your own newsletter.

☞ **Select the date** 🦶27

⌨ **Type the date of your newsletter**

☞ **Also change the volume and issue no. If necessary**

☞ **Select**
Company Name, (503) 555-0125
🦶27

⌨ **Type your company name**

You do not need to type your phone number here. It will also be listed on the next page.

You can change the formatting of the text the way you are used to do in *Word*. You can make the company name stand out a bit more like this:

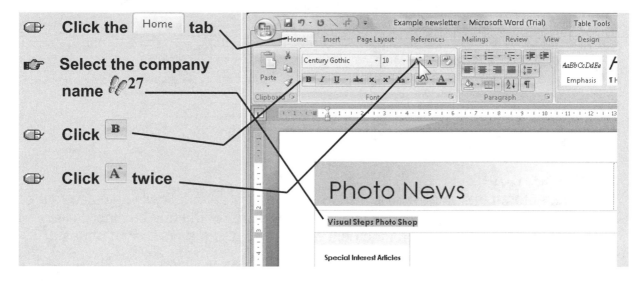

☞	**Click the** Home **tab**
☞	**Select the company name** 🦶27
☞	**Click** B
☞	**Click** A˄ **twice**

Now you can adjust the contents of the newsletter:

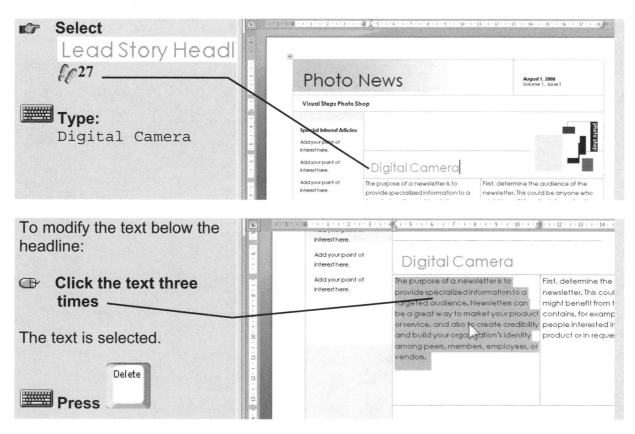

Select Lead Story Headl 🦶27

Type: Digital Camera

To modify the text below the headline:

☞ **Click the text three times**

The text is selected.

Press Delete

The box is empty now.

⌨ **Type your own text**

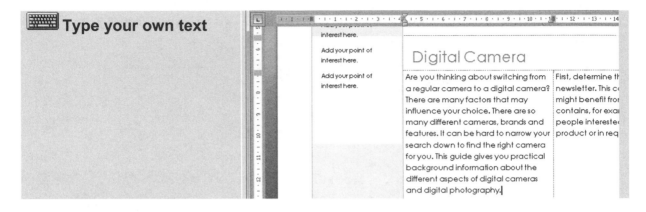

➡ **Please note:**

The text is entered into a table. The size of every box is automatically adjusted to the amount of text. If you enter a large piece of text, the size of the text box increases. This may have consequences for the next news items and the number of pages. If necessary, divide a longer text over two columns.

You can also add images to the newsletter:

🖱 **Click the box next to the text you entered three times**

The text is selected.

⌨ **Press** Delete

🖱 **Click the** Insert **tab**

🖱 **Click** Picture

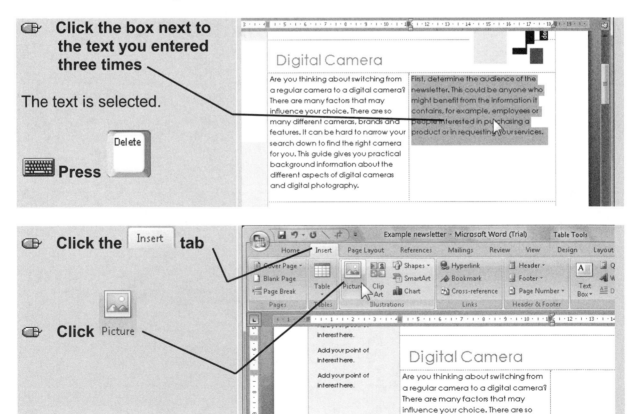

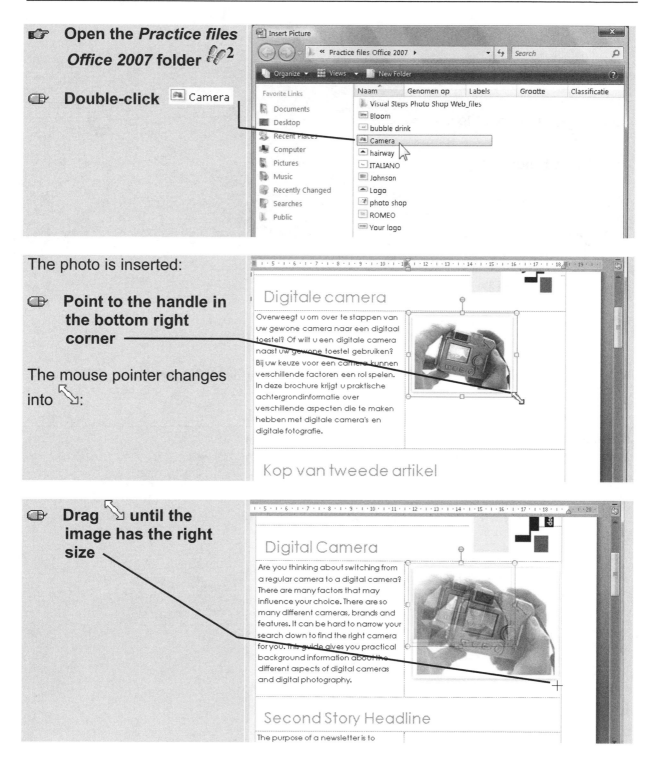

☞ **Open the *Practice files Office 2007* folder** 👣²

🖱 **Double-click** 📷 Camera

The photo is inserted:

🖱 **Point to the handle in the bottom right corner**

The mouse pointer changes into ↖:

🖱 **Drag ↖ until the image has the right size**

If you have texts saved in other *Word* documents, you can insert those as well:

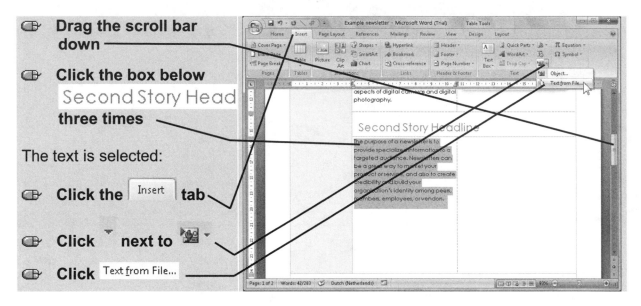

☞ **Drag the scroll bar down**

☞ **Click the box below** Second Story Head **three times**

The text is selected:

☞ **Click the** Insert **tab**

☞ **Click** ⏷ **next to** 📄⏷

☞ **Click** Text from File...

👣 **Insert the file *Information* from the *Practice files Office 2007* folder** 👣**12**

💡 **Tip**

Inserting parts of text files
You can use copy and paste to insert part of a text from another file. The method to do this is described for *Publisher* in the *Tips* at the end of this chapter.

The font and the font size are not the same as the other text. You can correct that like this:

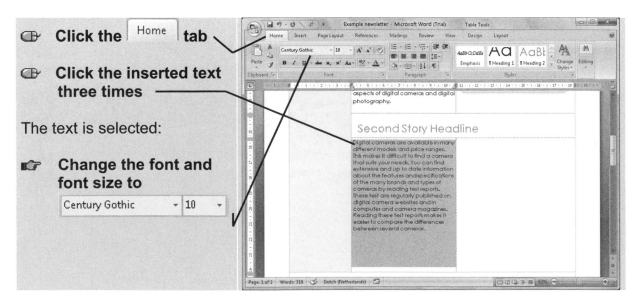

☞ **Click the** Home **tab**

☞ **Click the inserted text three times**

The text is selected:

👉 **Change the font and font size to**

Century Gothic   ⏷ | 10   ⏷

💡 Tip

Font and font size
If you want to know the font or font size of another text, insert the pointer somewhere inside it and click. You will see the settings for that part of the text right away.

👆 **Click the text** ——————

You see the font and the font size for that text:

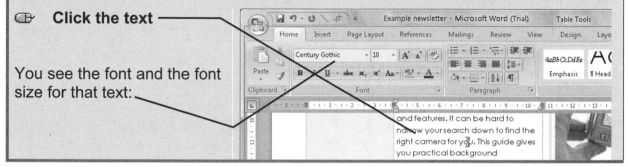

✖ HELP! The line spacing is also different.

When you add a text from another document, the line spacing can also be different. You can adjust the line spacing of a text like this:

👆 **Click the** ┌ Home ┐ **tab**

👆 **Click the text** ——————

A menu appears where you can select different types of line spacing:

☞ **Select the same line spacing for each text box**

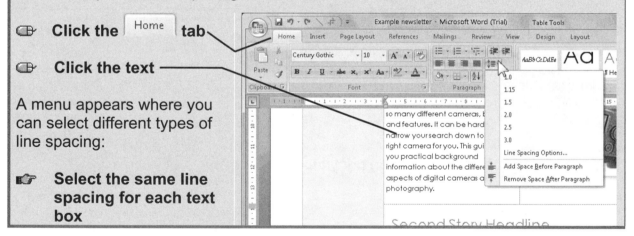

☞ **Adjust the other text boxes and add new images if necessary**

Now you can finish the other information in the newsletter:

List the topics of the newsletter in the top left corner:

👆 **Drag the scroll bar up**

☞ **Click the box and replace the text**

On page 2, enter your company information. In the top left corner of the page:

☞ **Click the box and replace the text**

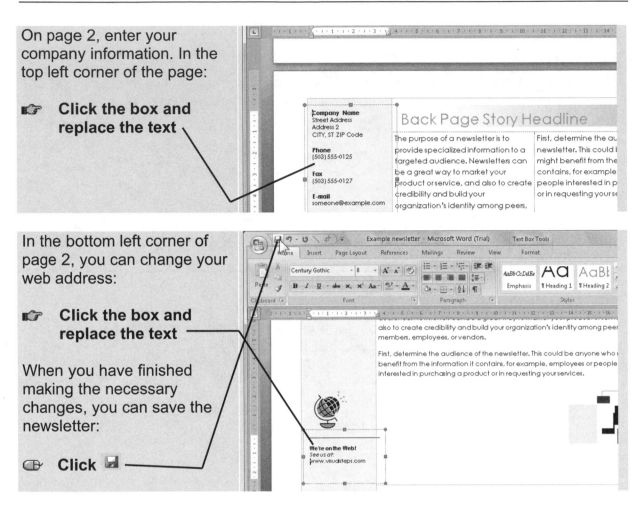

In the bottom left corner of page 2, you can change your web address:

☞ **Click the box and replace the text**

When you have finished making the necessary changes, you can save the newsletter:

 Click 💾

The newsletter is finished. You can print it to send it to your customers.

☞ **Print the newsletter** 👣⁴⁸

You can also send this newsletter as an e-mail newsletter to your contacts in *Business Contact Manager*.

⇨ **Please note:**

To be able to do the next set of exercises, *Business Contact Manager* must be installed on your computer. In *Chapter 1 Preparation* you can read how to install it. It is also advisable to work through the basic tasks of *Business Contact Manager* that are covered in *Chapter 2 Customer Relationship Management*.
If you do not have this program on your computer you can skip the next set of exercises and continue reading in the section that follows.

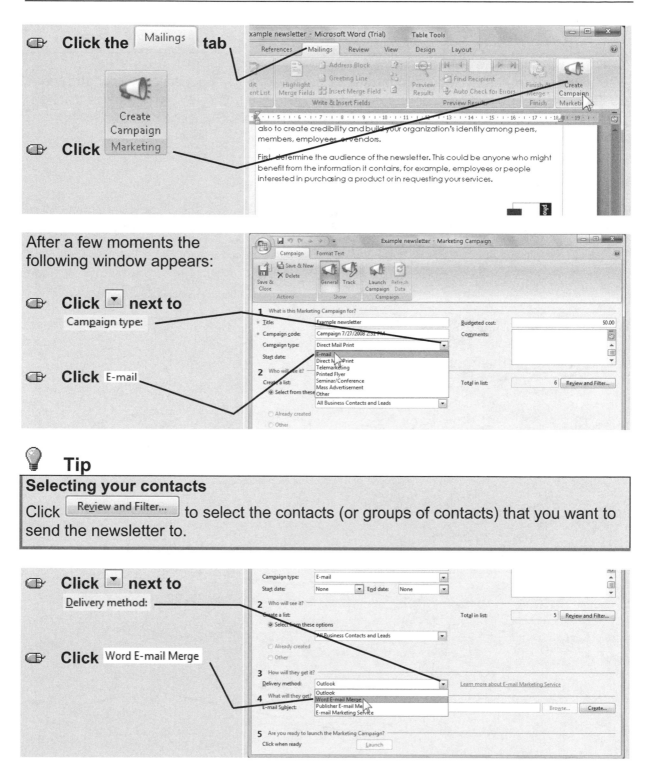

🔘 **Click the** ⌈Mailings⌉ **tab**

🔘 **Click** ⌈Create Campaign Marketing⌉

After a few moments the following window appears:

🔘 **Click** ▼ **next to** Campaign type:

🔘 **Click** ⌈E-mail⌉

💡 **Tip**

Selecting your contacts

Click ⌈Review and Filter...⌉ to select the contacts (or groups of contacts) that you want to send the newsletter to.

🔘 **Click** ▼ **next to** Delivery method:

🔘 **Click** ⌈Word E-mail Merge⌉

💡 Tip

Tracking the results
The newsletter is launched as a marketing campaign. If necessary you can add the costs in this window. The responses that you get from this newsletter can be tracked and registered the same way you practiced in *Chapter 2 Customer Relationship Management*.

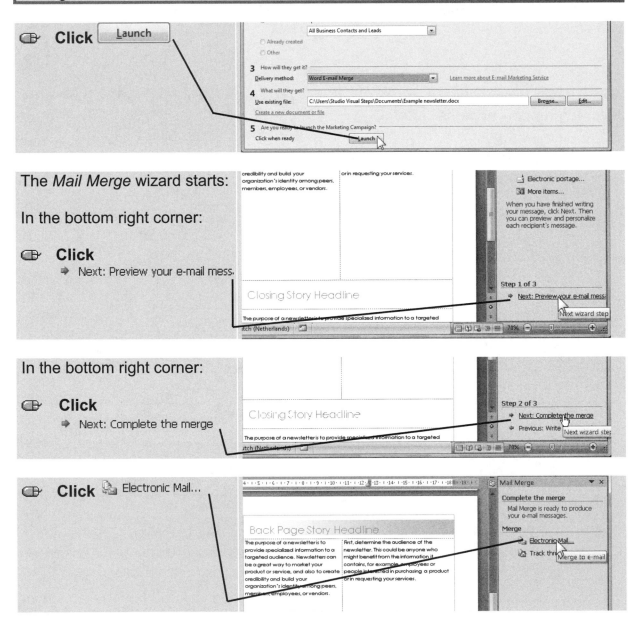

🖱 **Click** [Launch]

The *Mail Merge* wizard starts:

In the bottom right corner:

🖱 **Click**
➡ Next: Preview your e-mail mess.

In the bottom right corner:

🖱 **Click**
➡ Next: Complete the merge

🖱 **Click** 🖳 Electronic Mail...

☞ **Select the text next to**

Subject line: ✍²⁷

⌨ **Type the subject**

🖯 **Click** [OK]

Merge to E-mail	? ✕
Message options	
To:	Email ▾
Subject line:	Newsletter
Mail format:	HTML ▾
Send records	
◉ All	
○ Current record	
○ From: [ ] To: [ ]	
	[OK] [Cancel]

An e-mail message containing the newsletter is created for each contact. The messages are sent by *Outlook*.

If you do not have a permanent Internet connection the newsletters are placed in your *Outbox*. If there is a connection, the messages are sent immediately and you can find them in the *Sent Items* folder.

💡 **Tip**

Wrong addresses
Pay attention to the *Mail System Error – Returned Mail* messages you receive. Use these returned messages to update the information about your contacts.

💡 **Tip**

Check the newsletter you sent
No matter how well you checked everything; there may still be something wrong that only becomes visible after sending the newsletter. Always make sure to send a copy to your own e-mail address as well. That way you know what the recipients have received. If you added yourself as a contact, this is done automatically.

⇨ **Please note:**

The newsletter is sent in the HTML format. Some people have restricted the reception of HTML documents, and will only receive the text of the message. It is also possible that the recipient uses another type of computer or operating system that does not show all elements of HTML documents. That is why you should always include some form of contact information within the actual text of the newsletter, such as your website, fax or phone number.

☞ **Close *Word* and save the changes** ✍⁹

☞ **Close *Business Contact Manager*** ✍⁹

5.3 Business Presentations

You can use *PowerPoint* to create digital presentations. You can play a presentation through your laptop and view it on an external screen by means of a beamer. A company presentation is one of the important ways that your company values and brand can be communicated. You can run your company or product presentation as a continuing slide show at trade show exhibits. Or copy your presentations onto CD ROMs for use as extra sales and marketing tools for (potential) customers. You can customize the contents of a presentation to suit your individual needs.

☞ **Open** *PowerPoint* 🖐¹

You see the first slide of your presentation:

On the left side you see miniatures of the slides in your presentation: ⎯⎯

At the bottom there is some space for notes or explanations. These could be used as reminders when you run the presentation: ⎯⎯

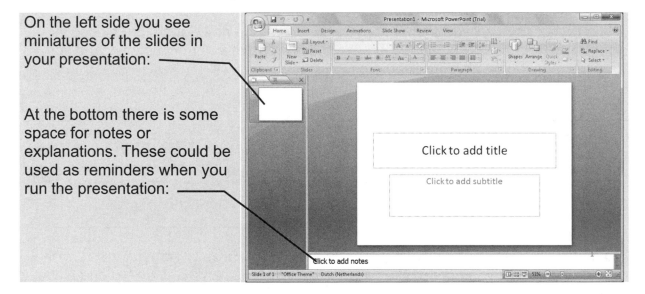

You are going to create a presentation about fictitious products. If you prefer, you can enter information about your own business, products or services.

💡 **Tip**

Standard presentations
On the Internet you can find a large number of templates for standard presentations. In the *Tips* at the end of this chapter you can read how to use these. Most likely these presentations will need some customization for your own company or product, so it is a good idea to work through this section anyway.

Instead of a white background, you can select one of the themes:

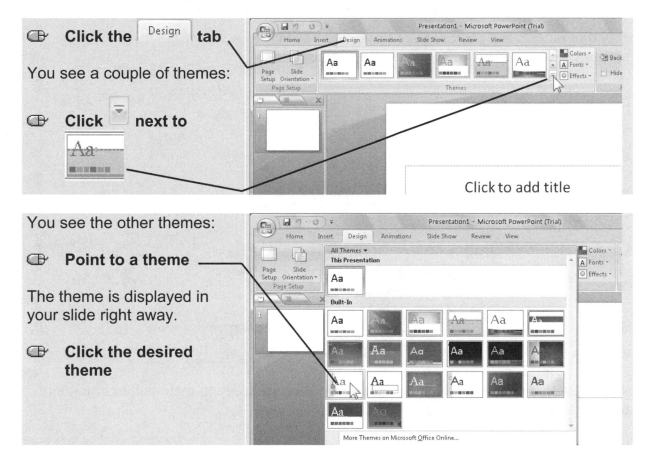

- Click the Design tab

You see a couple of themes:

- Click ⌄ next to Aa

You see the other themes:

- Point to a theme

The theme is displayed in your slide right away.

- Click the desired theme

Themes are combinations of layout, colors and fonts. In each theme you can adjust the colors and the font:

⇨ **Please note:**

If you selected another theme the effects may be different on your screen.

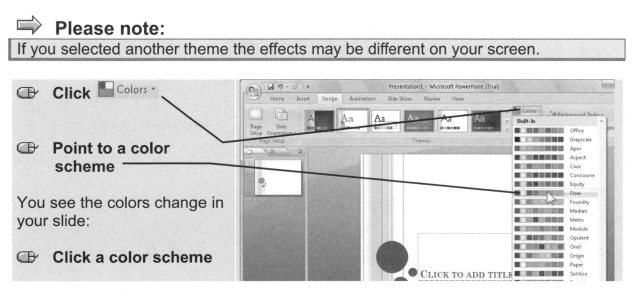

- Click Colors

- Point to a color scheme

You see the colors change in your slide:

- Click a color scheme

💡 Tip

The right colors
Pay attention to the colors of your logo and possible images you use in your presentation when you select a color scheme.

☞ **Click** 🅰 Fonts ▾

☞ **Point to a font**

You see the font change in the slide:

☞ **Click the desired font**

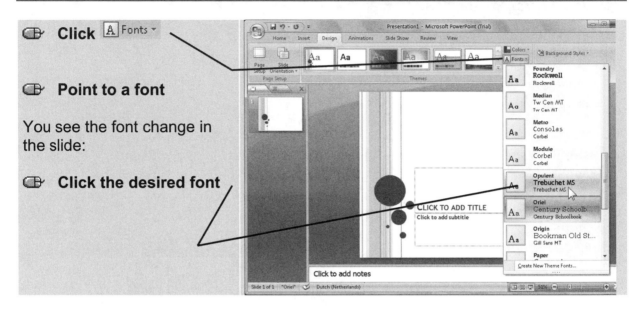

When you are done customizing the theme, you are ready to modify the contents of the slide:

☞ **Click the title box**

⌨ **Type:**
Visual Steps Photo
Shop

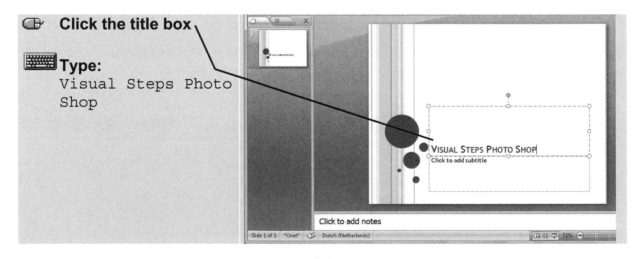

✖ Help! I see uppercase letters.

The theme you selected may contain the setting which displays all titles as capitals. If you do not want to use capitals, you can select another theme.

Click the subtitle box

Type:
Your Photo
Specialist Since
50 Years

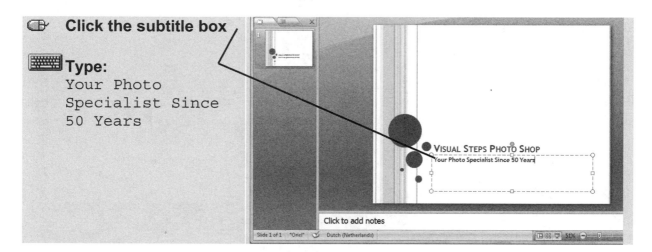

You can also add elements to a slide yourself, like a logo:

Click the Insert tab

Click Picture

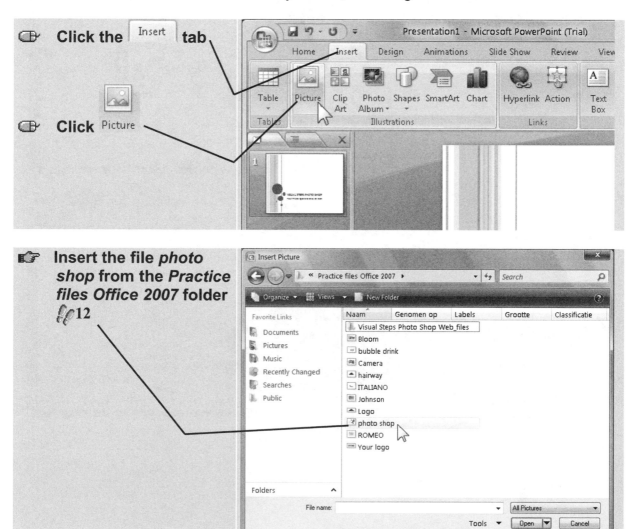

Insert the file *photo shop* from the *Practice files Office 2007* folder
&&12

The logo is added to the slide:

Now you can make the logo a bit smaller.

☞ **Point to the handle in the lower right corner**

The mouse pointer changes into ⬉:

☞ **Drag ⬉ until the logo has the desired size**

Now you can move the logo to the right location:

☞ **Point to the logo**

The mouse pointer changes into ✛:

☞ **Drag the logo to the right location**

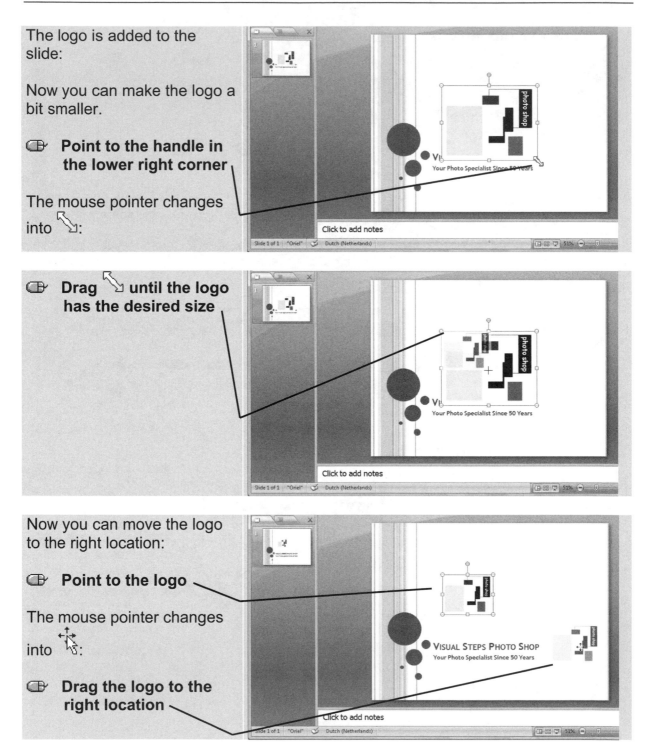

The first slide is finished. You can save this presentation:

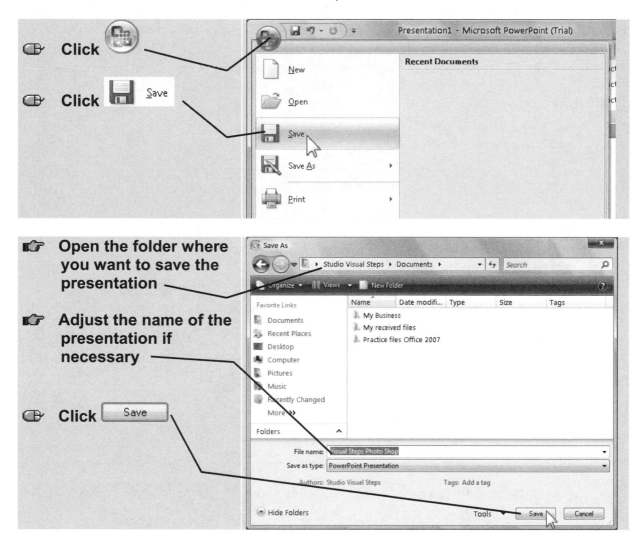

☞ **Click**

☞ **Click** 💾 **Save**

☞ **Open the folder where you want to save the presentation**

☞ **Adjust the name of the presentation if necessary**

☞ **Click** Save

Now you can add a second slide:

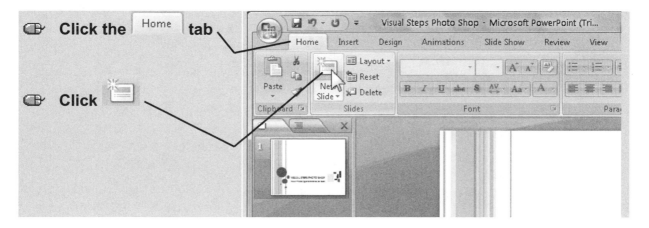

☞ **Click the** Home **tab**

☞ **Click**

Each new slide has a default layout containing a title box and below that a second box:

👆 **Click the title box**

⌨️ **Type:**
Digital
Photography

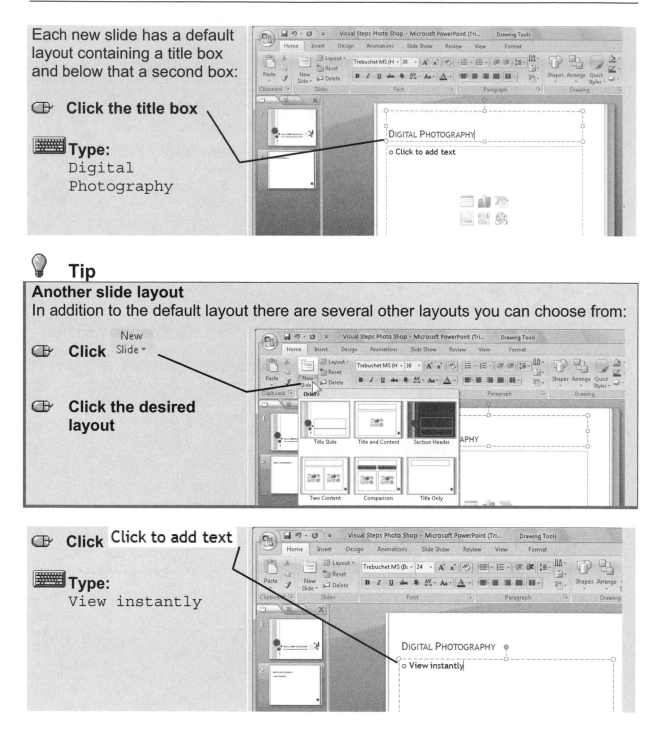

💡 **Tip**

Another slide layout
In addition to the default layout there are several other layouts you can choose from:

👆 **Click** New Slide ▾

👆 **Click the desired layout**

👆 **Click** Click to add text

⌨️ **Type:**
View instantly

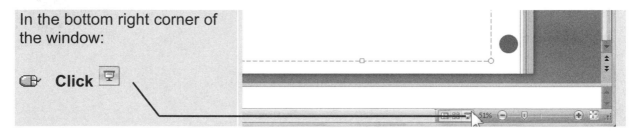

Press `Enter ↵`

A second bullet appears automatically:

Type:
`Transfer to computer`

On the left side of the *PowerPoint* window you see a miniature of this slide. You can also view this slide full screen:

In the bottom right corner of the window:

☞ **Click** 🖳

💡 **Tip**

View slide
You can view the actual size of a slide by double-clicking the slide in the left part of the window.

The slide is displayed full screen:

To go back to the normal display of the *PowerPoint* window:

Press `Esc`

DIGITAL PHOTOGRAPHY

o View instantly
o Transfer to computer

The slide does not look very attractive yet. You can improve the slide by adding color to the title box and the text box:

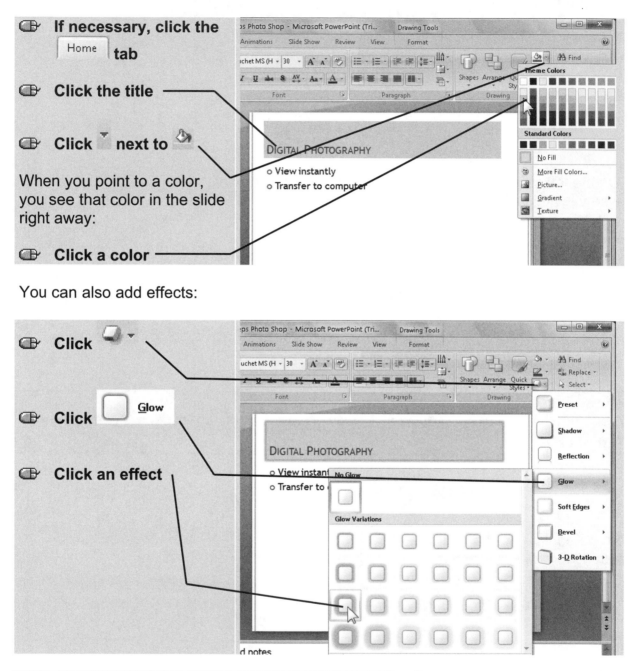

☞ **If necessary, click the** `Home` **tab**

☞ **Click the title**

☞ **Click ▼ next to** 🪣

When you point to a color, you see that color in the slide right away:

☞ **Click a color**

You can also add effects:

☞ **Click**

☞ **Click** `Glow`

☞ **Click an effect**

👉 **View the slide full screen, then close that view** 🦶32

You can also add color to the text box this way. Be careful not to make the colors to distracting, it is the text that is the most important part of your slide.

💡 Tip

Adjusting the size of text boxes

If you add color to a box, the entire box is colored. If the box becomes a lot bigger than the text it contains, you can adjust the size of the box. You can do that the same way you adjust the size of an image:

🖱️ **Click inside the box** ──────

🖱️ **Point to a handle** ╲

The mouse pointer changes into ↖↘:

🖱️ **Drag** ↖↘ **until the box has the desired size**

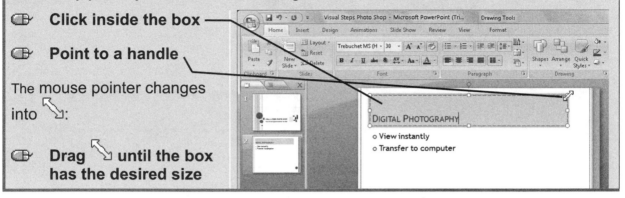

The second slide is finished for now. It is a good habit to save your presentation after every slide you finish.

☞ **Save the presentation** 𝕃𝕃⁴⁹

☞ **Create a new slide** 𝕃𝕃²⁹

🖱️ **Click the title box** ──────

⌨️ **Type:**
The New VS2008

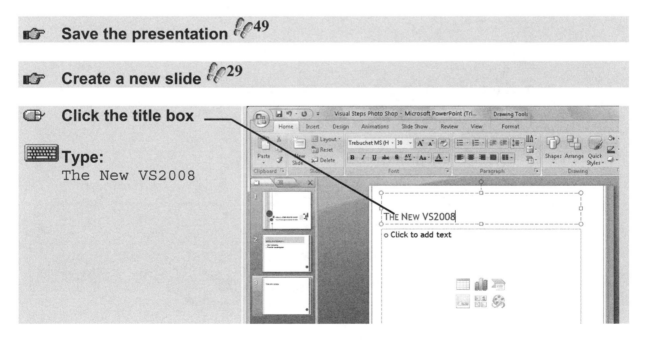

You add an image to this slide:

☞ **Click** 🖼️

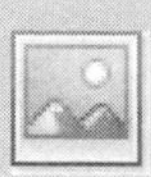

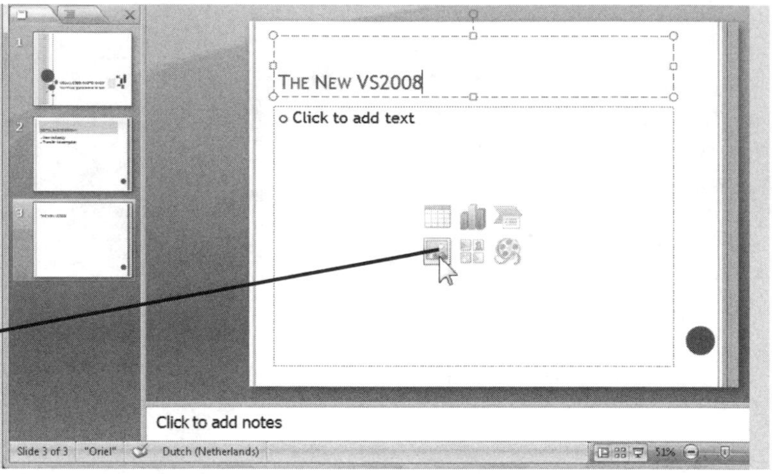

Adding elements to a slide
You can add the following elements to a slide:

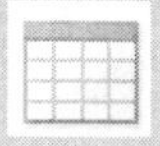

🔲 table;

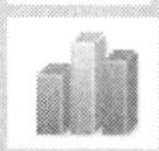

📊 chart;

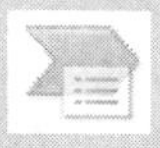

🔖 *SmartArt* graphic (these are simple symbols);

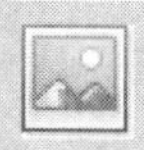

🖼️ picture;

🖼️ *Microsoft Office* clip art;

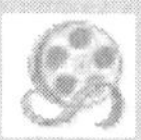

🎞️ a media clip, for example a video clip.

☞ **Insert the file *Camera* from the folder *Practice files Office 2007*** 📎¹²

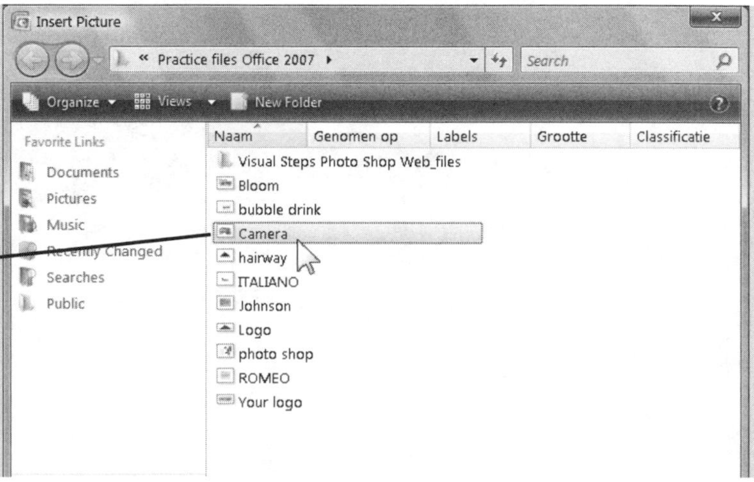

Naam	Genomen op	Labels	Grootte	Classificatie
Visual Steps Photo Shop Web_files				
Bloom				
bubble drink				
Camera				
hairway				
ITALIANO				
Johnson				
Logo				
photo shop				
ROMEO				
Your logo				

Favorite Links: Documents, Pictures, Music, Recently Changed, Searches, Public

☞ **Enlarge the image**
  ℓℓ30

☞ **Center the image on the slide** *ℓℓ31*

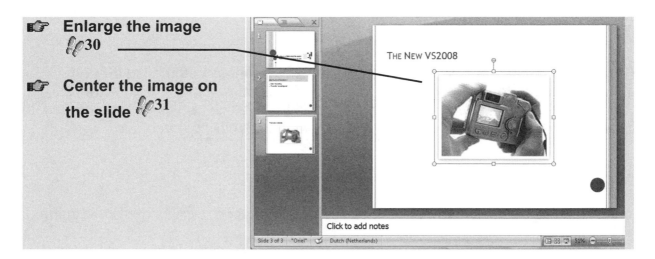

To be able to create a caption below the image you need to add a text box first:

🖱 **Click the** Insert **tab**

🖱 **Click** Text Box

The mouse pointer changes into ↓:

🖱 **Drag the size of the text box below the image**

⌨ **Type:**
  Back

🖱 **Click** ≣

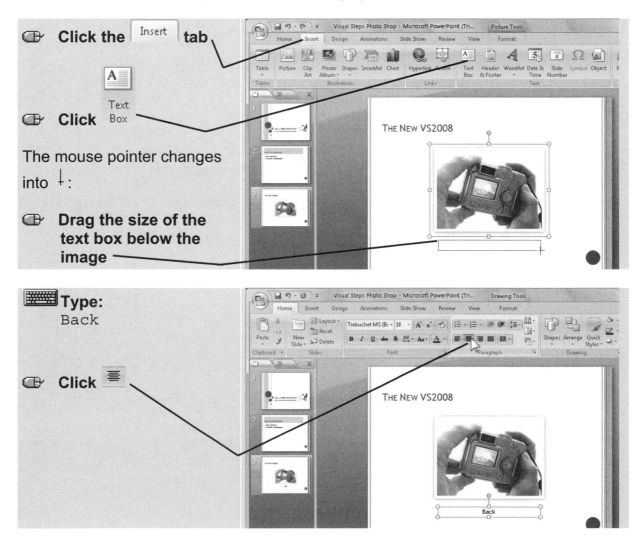

💡 Tip

Legibility

You can format the text in the same way you have been accustomed to in *Word*. Just click on the formatting buttons or tabs in the top portion of the window (this is called the *Ribbon* in *Office 2007*). Keep in mind that legibility is very important for a presentation. Small letters or stylish fonts may not be legible to everyone.

👉 **Save the presentation** 🖑⁴⁹

If you want to go back to another slide in your presentation, click its miniature in the left pane:

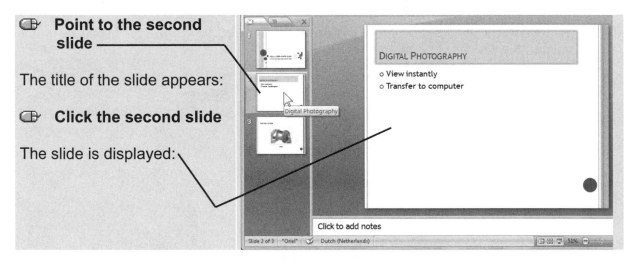

☞ **Point to the second slide** ————

The title of the slide appears:

☞ **Click the second slide**

The slide is displayed:

When you have a large presentation, use the slide sorter to jump directly to a particular slide:

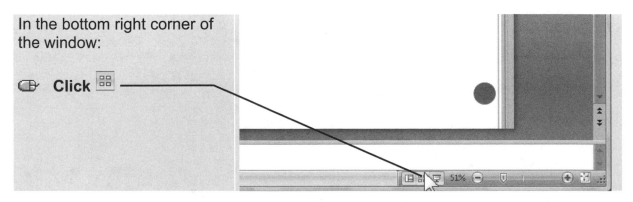

In the bottom right corner of the window:

☞ **Click** ⊞ ————

You see the slides:

Double-click the first slide

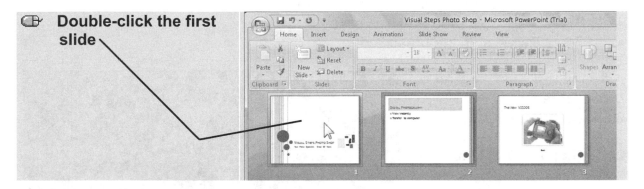

You see the first slide again. You can also play the presentation as a slide show:

In the bottom right corner of the window:

Click 🖳

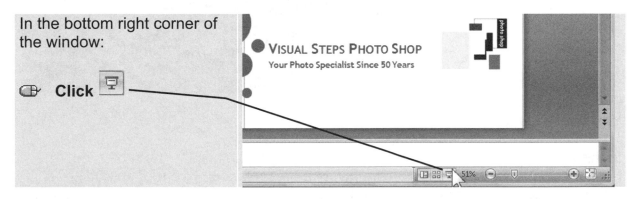

➡ **Please note:**
The slide show commences at the slide you were viewing. If that is not the first slide, you do not see the first part of the presentation.

The first slide is displayed:

To go to the next slide:

Click a random spot on the slide

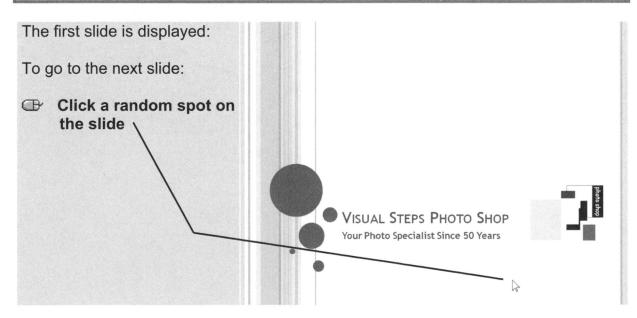

You can also use the keyboard:
- Press Enter or PageDown for the next slide.
- Press PageUp for the previous slide.
- Press Esc to stop the presentation.

After the last slide you see a black screen with `End of slide show, click to exit.`.

☞ **Click the black screen**

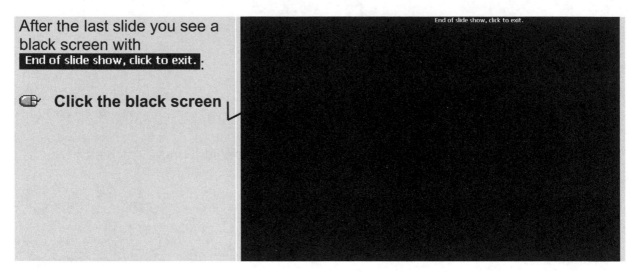

You see the first slide again.

In this example you had to click a slide or press a key to display the next slide. That is the best way to do it when you are giving a presentation in front of an audience. Another option is to set the next slide to appear automatically. You can also set the amount of time the slide is displayed. This allows you to give more viewing time to a slide containing a lot of information.

☞ **Click the** Slide Show **tab**

☞ **Click** 🕮 Rehearse Timings

In the top left corner the display time is tracked in seconds:

When you think the slide has displayed for a long enough period:

👆 **Click** ➡

Repeat the previous steps for the next few slides.

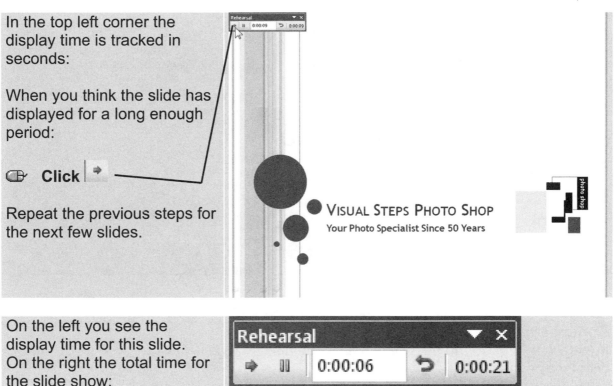

On the left you see the display time for this slide. On the right the total time for the slide show:

After the last slide you see this window:

👆 **Click** Yes

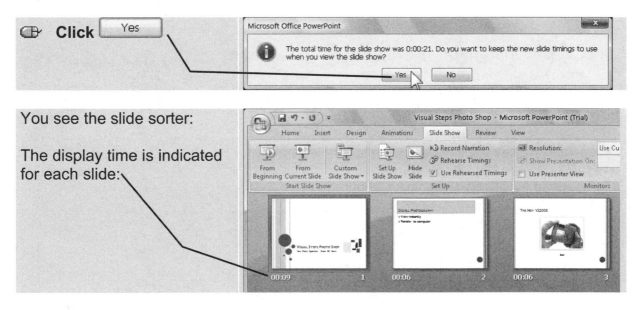

You see the slide sorter:

The display time is indicated for each slide:

Now you no longer have to click to go to the next slide. When the set display time has elapsed, the next slide will appear. You can give that a try:

☞ **Play the slide show** 🦶³²

💡 Tip

Adjusting the time setting of a slide
To adjust the time setting of a particular slide, do the following:

☞ **Click the slide**

☞ **Click the** Animations **tab**

To adjust the time:

☞ **Click ‡ next to**
Automatically After:

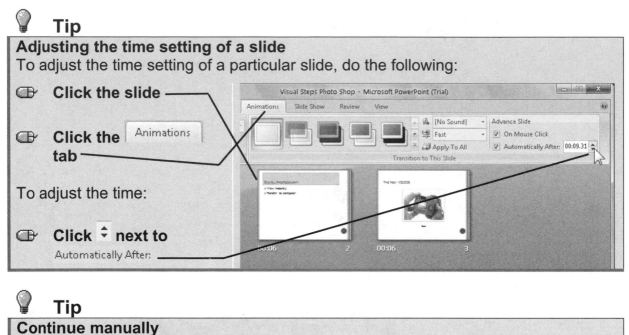

💡 Tip

Continue manually
If you want to go to the next slide before the display time is finished, you can click with the mouse.
If you temporarily do not want to use the time setting, you can turn it off:

☞ **Click the** Slide Show **tab**

☞ **Click ☑ in front of**
Use Rehearsed Timings

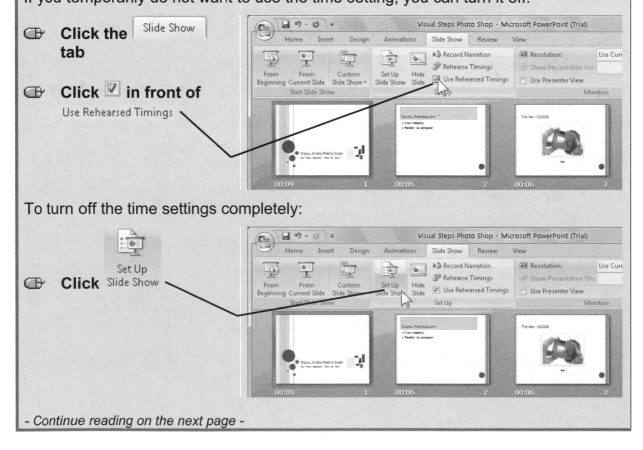

To turn off the time settings completely:

☞ **Click** Set Up Slide Show

- Continue reading on the next page -

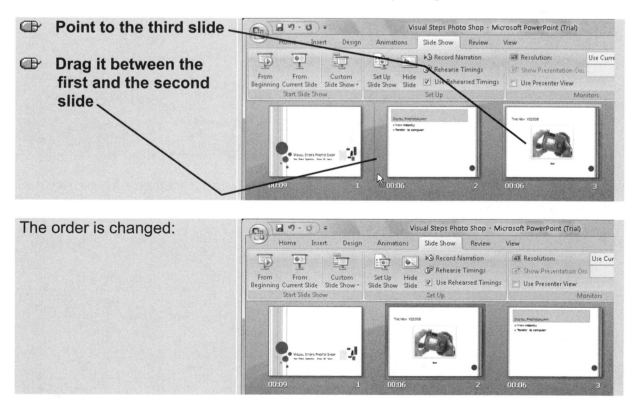

Even after you created a presentation, you can still change it. For example, you can change the order in which the slides are presented by using the slide sorter:

Point to the third slide

Drag it between the first and the second slide

The order is changed:

💡 Tip

Inserting or deleting slides

You can insert a new slide next to an existing slide like this:

🖰 **Right-click next to a slide**

🖰 **Click** New Slide

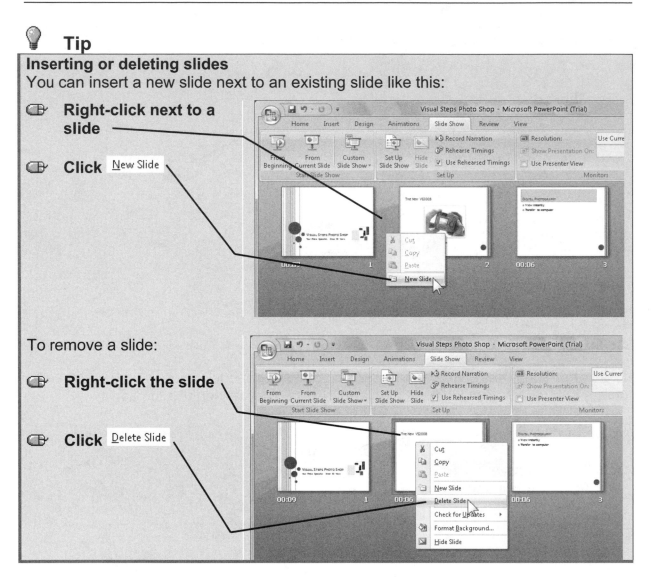

To remove a slide:

🖰 **Right-click the slide**

🖰 **Click** Delete Slide

Instead of displaying the next slide right away, you can add transition effects between the slides. Like this:

🖰 **Click the** Animations **tab**

🖰 **Click** ⯆ **next to** 🖼

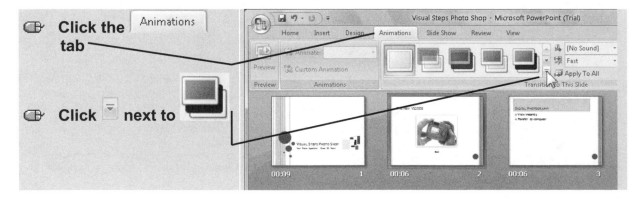

⌔ **Click a transition**

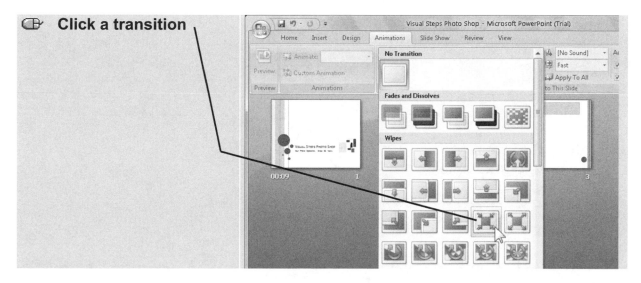

The transition is set for this slide. To apply this transition for the entire presentation:

⌔ **Click** 🔲 Apply To All

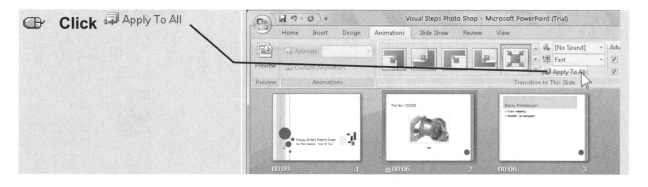

☞ **Play the slideshow starting at the first slide** 👣³²

☞ **Save the slide show** 👣⁴⁹

The presentation is ready to be played on your computer or projected by a beamer. It is often a good idea to make a hand-out for the audience with a copy of the slides, if necessary with space for their own notes:

⌔ **Click**

⌔ **Click** 🖨 Print

⌔ **Click** **Print Preview**

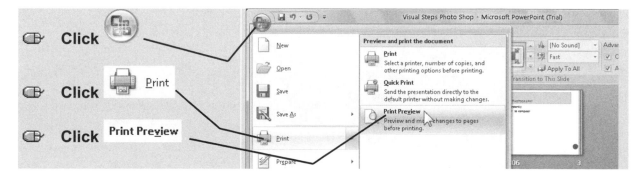

You see the first slide:

☞ **Click** Slides ▼
below Print What:

☞ **Click the desired layout, for example**
Handouts (3 Slides Per Page)

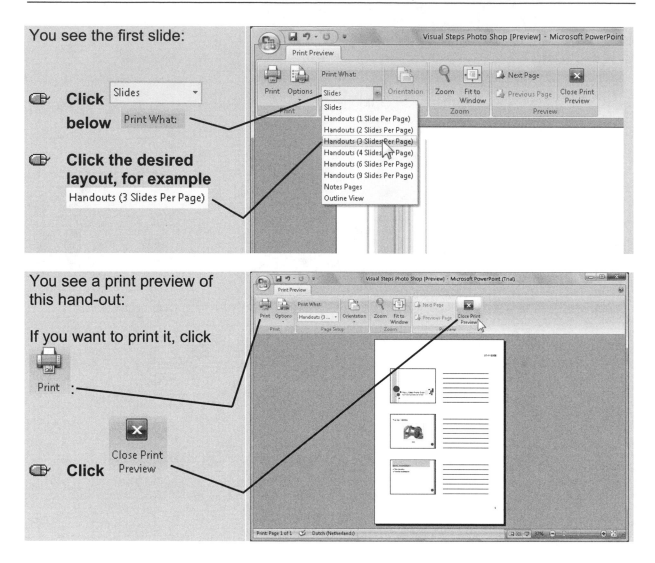

You see a print preview of this hand-out:

If you want to print it, click

Print :

☞ **Click** Close Print Preview

💡 Tip

Footer

The hand-outs are printed on blank sheets. You can also add headers and footers to the hand-outs, for example with the title of the presentation:

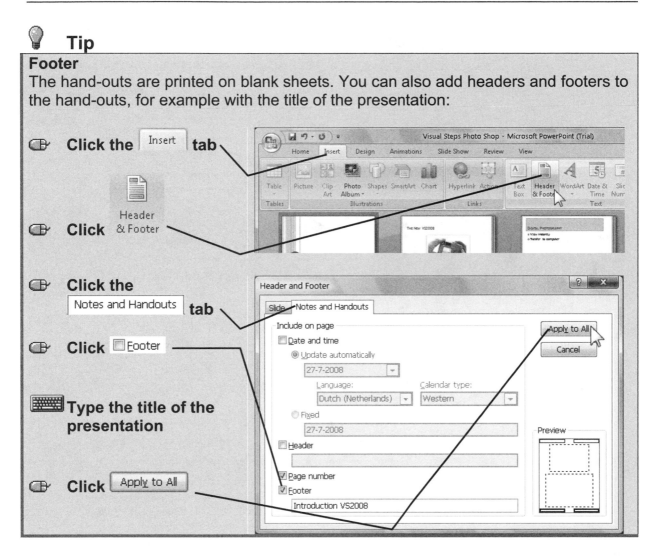

Click the `Insert` tab

Click `Header & Footer`

Click the `Notes and Handouts` tab

Click `☐ Footer`

⌨ **Type the title of the presentation**

Click `Apply to All`

You can also copy the presentation to a CD ROM to play it on another computer or to send it to customers as a means of advertising for your product or service.

➡ **Please note:**

If you do not want to burn a CD ROM, you can just read through the following steps.

Click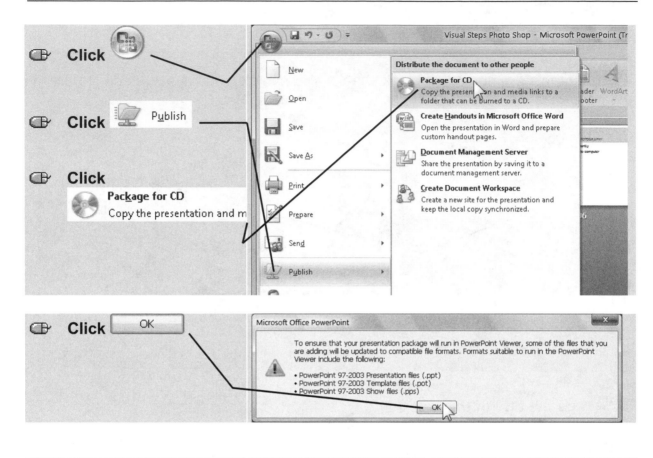

Click Publish

Click

Package for CD
Copy the presentation and m

Click OK

Type the name of the presentation

Click Copy to CD

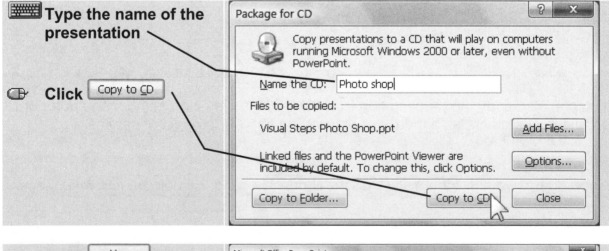

Click Yes

☞ **Insert a blank CD ROM in your burner**

The presentation is burned to CD ROM:

> Copying Files to CD
>
> Preparing to burn the CD...
>
> [progress bar]
>
> Cancel

Click [Yes] if you want to burn another CD ROM.

Otherwise:

☞ **Click** [No]

> **Microsoft Office PowerPoint** ✕
>
> ❓ The files were successfully copied to the CD.
> Do you want to copy the same files to another CD?
>
> Yes | No

☞ **Remove the CD ROM from your burner and close the drawer**

☞ **Click** [Close]

> **Package for CD** ? ✕
>
> 💿 Copy presentations to a CD that will play on computers running Microsoft Windows 2000 or later, even without PowerPoint.
>
> Name the CD: [Photo shop]
>
> Files to be copied:
>
> Visual Steps Photo Shop.ppt   Add Files...
>
> Linked files and the PowerPoint Viewer are included by default. To change this, click Options.   Options...
>
> Copy to Folder...   Copy to CD   Close

The CD ROM is ready and can be played on other computers. It is not necessary to have *PowerPoint* installed on these computers to view the presentation. The CD ROM version of the presentation is read-only, it cannot be further modified.

➡️ **Please note:**

When you insert the CD ROM in a CD or DVD drive it is started like this:

👉 **Insert the CD ROM**

After a few moments this window appears:

👉 **Click**

After a few moments this window appears:

👉 **Click** [Accept]

The presentation starts after that.

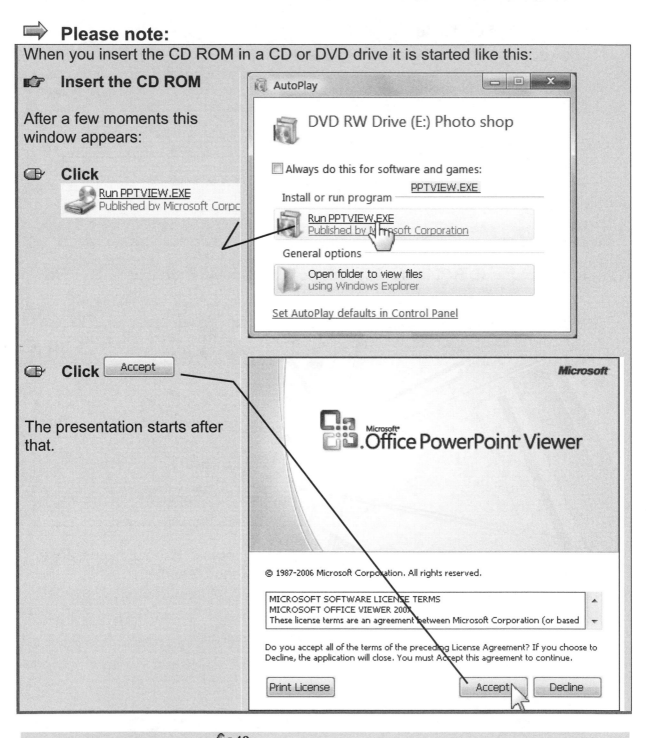

👉 **Save the slideshow** 🦶⁴⁹

👉 **Close *PowerPoint*** 🦶⁹

5.4 Background Information

Glossary

Brochure	Folded flyer with information about your company, products or services.
HTML format	Programming language used to create documents for the web. HTML defines the structure and layout of a web document by using a variety of tags and attributes.
PowerPoint Viewer	Program you can use to view a *PowerPoint* presentation on a computer that does not have *PowerPoint* installed. The presentation can only be viewed with this program, not changed.
Template	A file that contains information about the theme, the layout and other elements of a document or presentation. A template can be used as a model for new documents or presentations.
Theme	A set of design elements including colors, fonts and effects. The 'look and feel' of the presentation. A theme can be applied to the entire presentation or to selected slides.

Source: Windows Help and Microsoft Office 2007 Help

PDF format

PDF (*Portable Document Format*) is a fixed-layout electronic file format that preserves document formatting and enables file sharing. The PDF format ensures that when the file is viewed online or printed, it retains exactly the format that you intended, and that data in the file cannot easily be changed. The PDF format is also useful for documents that will be reproduced by using commercial printing methods.

To view a PDF file, you must have a PDF reader installed on your computer. One reader is the *Adobe Reader*, available from *Adobe Systems*. A step by step description of the installation procedure can be found on the webpage **www.visualsteps.com/adobereader**

After you save a file as PDF, you cannot use your *Office 2007* release program to make changes directly to the PDF file. You must make changes to the original file in the program in which you created it and save the file as PDF again.

Source: Windows Help and Microsoft Office 2007 Help

Which program for which document?
Word, *Publisher* and *PowerPoint* offer specific solutions for documents and content. Use the program that suits your document best:

Type of document you want to create	Use this program	Reason
Graphically rich print and e-mail newsletters	*Publisher*	Precise control over positioning text with images and other design elements.
Printed and digital newsletters with large amounts of text	*Word*	Simple text entry with many formatting options.
Graphically rich catalogs	*Publisher*	Pre-designed catalog publications and the *Mail and Catalog Merge Wizard*.
Greeting cards	*Publisher*	Greeting card types and designs you can customize for all your business and personal needs.
3 or 4 panel brochures or flyers	*Publisher*	Many designs to choose from with optional space for customer addresses, and order, response, or sign-up forms.
Posters or banners	*Publisher*	Poster and banner designs with easy width and height choices to match your needs.
Presentations	*PowerPoint*	Slide presentations with little text, images, charts et cetera that are viewed on a computer screen or projection screen.
Business cards	*Publisher*	Design types to match all of your business communications and marketing materials.
Design publications to be commercially printed	*Publisher*	Support for large jobs that require the services of a commercial printer, including composite CMYK PostScript output and advanced print settings for better color separations.
Documents with a table of contents and index	*Word*	Indexing and table of contents features allow you to create a professional published document.
Long documents	*Word*	Features specific to research papers, business plans, or other longer documents including page numbering, footnotes, endnotes, and annotations.
Short, simple documents (memos or letters)	*Word*	Templates and Wizards that allow you to choose style and function, as well as content for the documents you write every day.

Source: Microsoft Office Help

5.5 Tips

💡 **Tip**

Inserting fragments from other text files

If you want to use fragments of text from other documents in your newsletter or brochure, you can use the *Windows* functions copy and paste:

In the source document:

☞ **Select the text** 🖐️²⁷

👆 **Right-click the text**

👆 **Click** `Copy`

☞ **Open the source document**

👆 **Right-click the desired insertion point**

👆 **Click** `Paste`

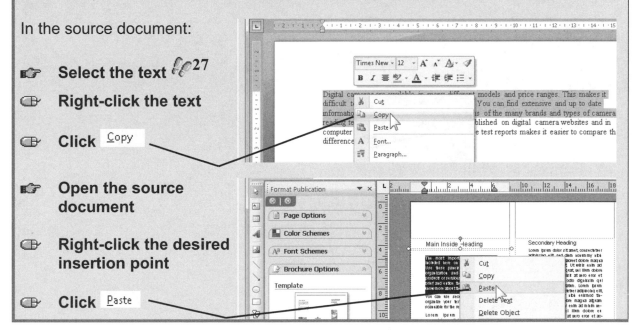

💡 Tip

Templates for PowerPoint presentations
PowerPoint contains a large number of standard presentations. The presentations are grouped by subject. Try selecting one of these templates as a starting point for your own presentation. You will need an Internet connection to access the templates:

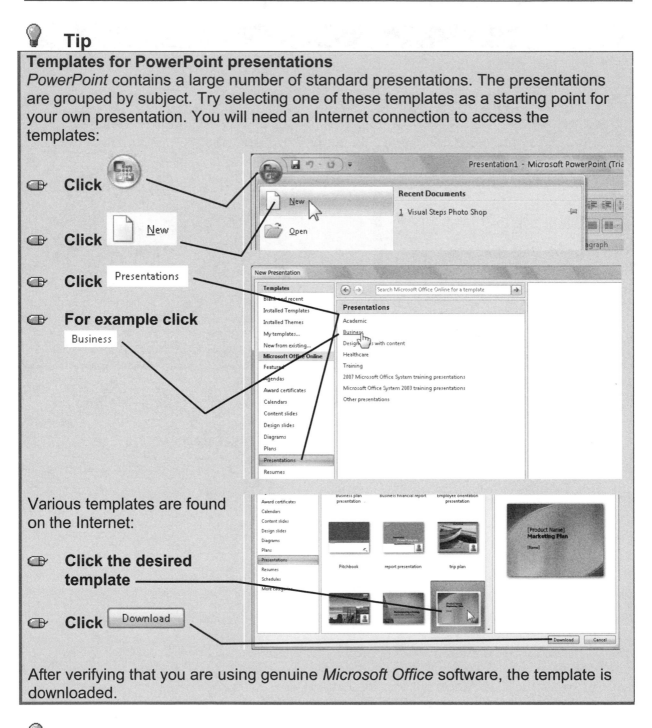

☞ **Click**

☞ **Click** New

☞ **Click** Presentations

☞ **For example click** Business

Various templates are found on the Internet:

☞ **Click the desired template**

☞ **Click** Download

After verifying that you are using genuine *Microsoft Office* software, the template is downloaded.

💡 Tip

Presentation on the Internet
You can also place a presentation you created in *PowerPoint* on the Internet. You can learn how to do that in the next chapter.

6. Your Website

 60 min.

When it comes to presenting your company, the Internet is a very important medium. You can use your own website to show your products and services to your customers. Your website may be the first introduction to your business activities for potential customers. In some lines of work the international aspect is also very interesting. Your website can be viewed anywhere in the world. If you want to, you can even offer your products and services globally.

If you want to have an extensive website where people can fill out order forms and make online payments, you can hire a specialized company to create one for you. If you just want a simple website to present your company, you can make it yourself using *Publisher* or *PowerPoint*.

Before you start creating a website, it is important to think about what you want to accomplish with your website. In the *Background Information* at the end of this chapter you can find some pointers for creating your own website.

In this chapter you learn the following:

- how to create a website in *Publisher*;
- how to publish your website on the Internet;
- how to make changes to your website;
- how to save a *PowerPoint* presentation as a website;
- how to publish a presentation on the Internet.

⇨ Please note:

In this chapter the emphasis is on publishing and maintaining a website. The tasks involved in creating the webpages and/or the presentation are only briefly covered in this chapter. If you want to learn more about those tasks, you can read through *Chapter 5 Advertising and Business Presentations* again.

6.1 Creating a Simple Website

You can create a simple website using the program *Microsoft Publisher*. That is easy to do when you use a template and the *Easy Website Builder* wizard.

☞ **Open *Publisher*** 👣¹

You use a template to create your website:

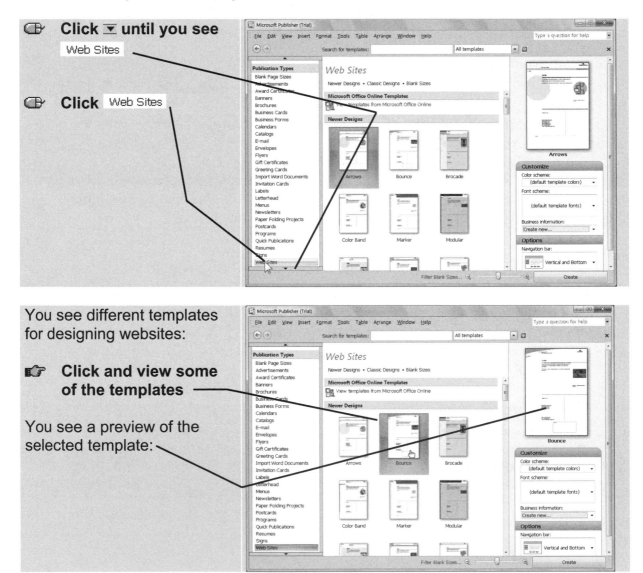

🖰 **Click ▼ until you see**
   Web Sites

🖰 **Click** Web Sites

You see different templates for designing websites:

☞ **Click and view some of the templates**

You see a preview of the selected template:

Click the desired template, for example *Capsules*

A template contains certain colors and fonts that you can change. If you want to use different colors for your website:

Click ⏷ below

Color scheme:

Click the desired color scheme

If you want to use another font:

Click ⏷ below

Font scheme:

Click the desired font

Click ⏷ below

Business information:

Click Create new...

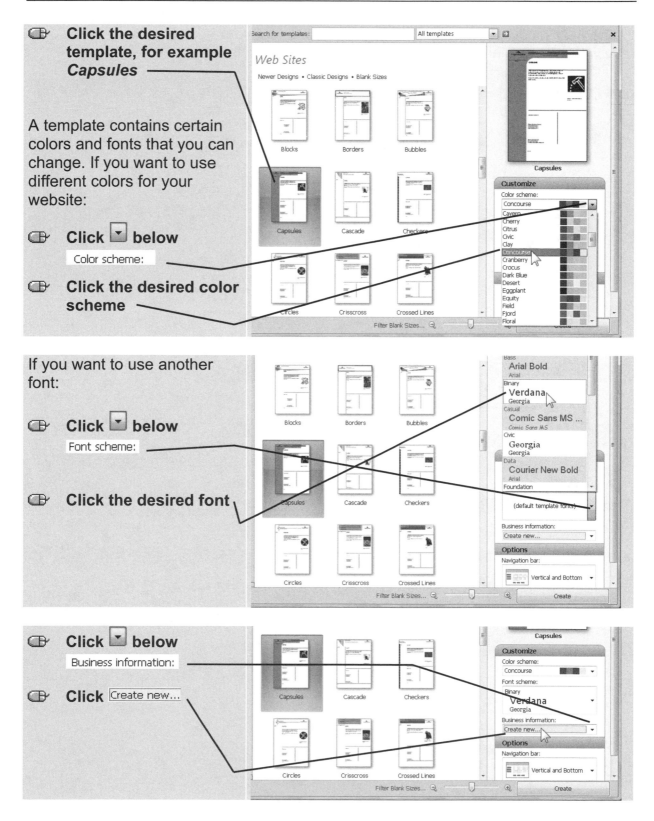

In the next window you enter some information about your business. You can also use your own business information instead of the sample text.

⌨ **Type next to**
Business Information set name: **:**
Photo Shop

⟶ **Click below**
Organization name: **three times**

The text is selected.

⌨ **Type:**
Visual Steps Photo Shop

☞ **Adjust the other information as well**

Now you can add a logo:

🖰 **Click** Add Logo...

☞ **Insert the file *photo shop* from the folder *Practice files Office 2007*** 👣12

You see the logo:

🖰 **Click** Save

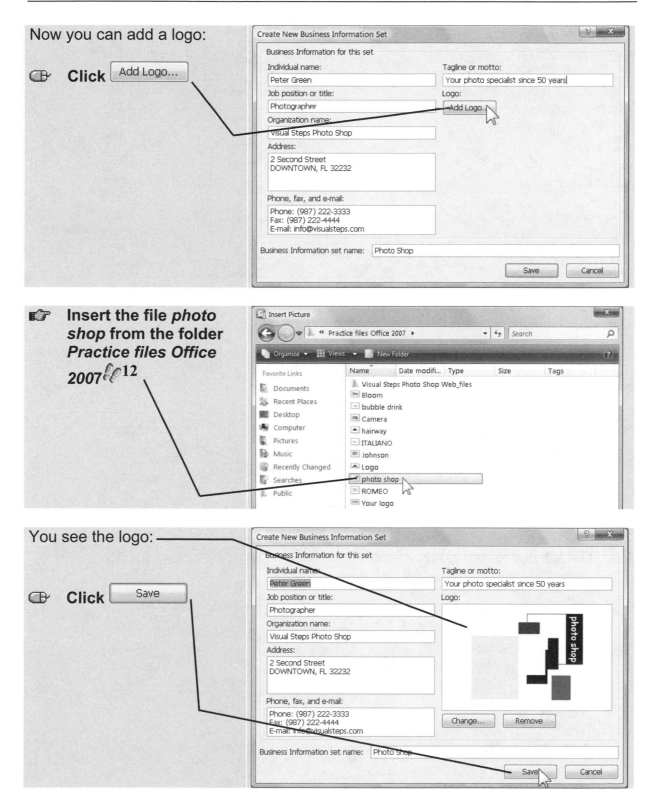

You see your logo in the preview:

You have inserted the basic information for the website. Now you can create the website:

☞ **Click**

[Create]

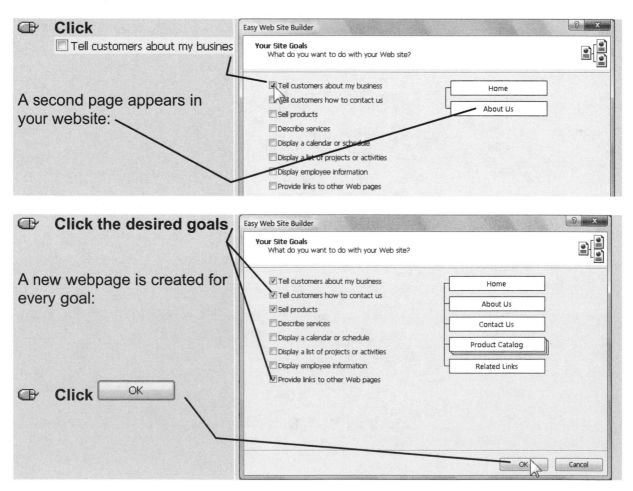

The *Easy Web Site Builder* wizard helps you to customize your website. First select the goals of your website:

☞ **Click**

☐ Tell customers about my busines

A second page appears in your website:

☞ **Click the desired goals**

A new webpage is created for every goal:

☞ **Click** [OK]

The website is created. You see the first webpage.
You can adjust the text and images on a webpage like this:

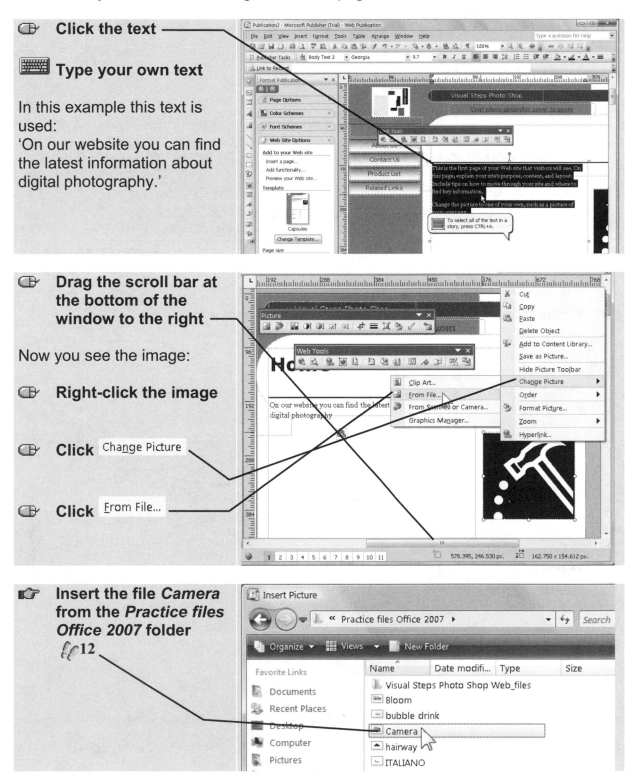

Click the text

Type your own text

In this example this text is used:
'On our website you can find the latest information about digital photography.'

Drag the scroll bar at the bottom of the window to the right

Now you see the image:

Right-click the image

Click Change Picture

Click From File...

Insert the file *Camera* from the *Practice files Office 2007* folder
12

The photo is added: ——

☞ **Adjust the size if necessary** 🐾30

☞ **Move the photo to another location if necessary** 🐾31

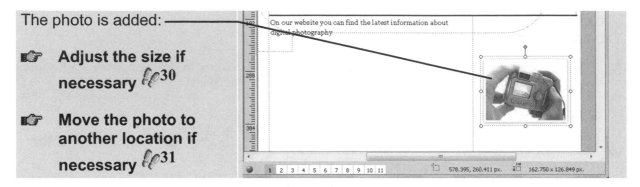

If you finished working on the first webpage you can start working on page 2.

At the bottom of the window:

🖱 **Click** 2

You see the second page:

☞ **Adjust the text and the image**

🖱 **Click** 4

You see the fourth page. Here you can enter product information:

☞ **Adjust the text and the image for the first product**

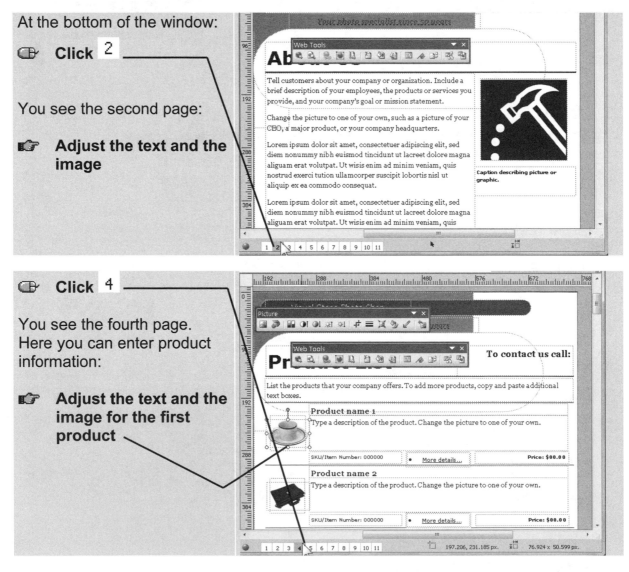

On this page you only describe the main features of the product. The visitor of the website can click the image or More details... to access more information.

💡 **Tip**

Recognizable texts
Replace the default headers and texts by text that fits your company. Replace 'Product list' by 'Cameras' for example.

💡 **Tip**

Which page?
When you point to a page number, a mini window appears to indicate the type of page.

👉 **Point to the page number**

You see Product List :

💡 **Tip**

More products
In case you want to add more products to your website you can add extra pages:

👉 **Click** Insert a page...

👉 **Click** Products

👉 **Click** Product List with Links

👉 **Click** OK

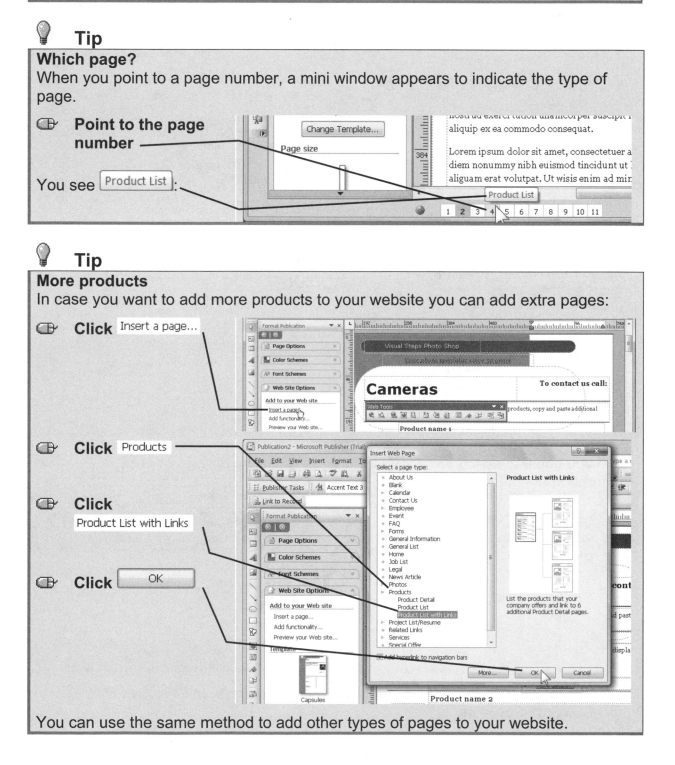

You can use the same method to add other types of pages to your website.

You can remove the boxes you do not use:

- ☞ **Point to the border of a text box** ⎯⎯⎯

The mouse pointer changes

into 🖙:

- ☞ **Right-click that border**

- ☞ **Click** Delete Object

- ☞ **Remove all unwanted objects**

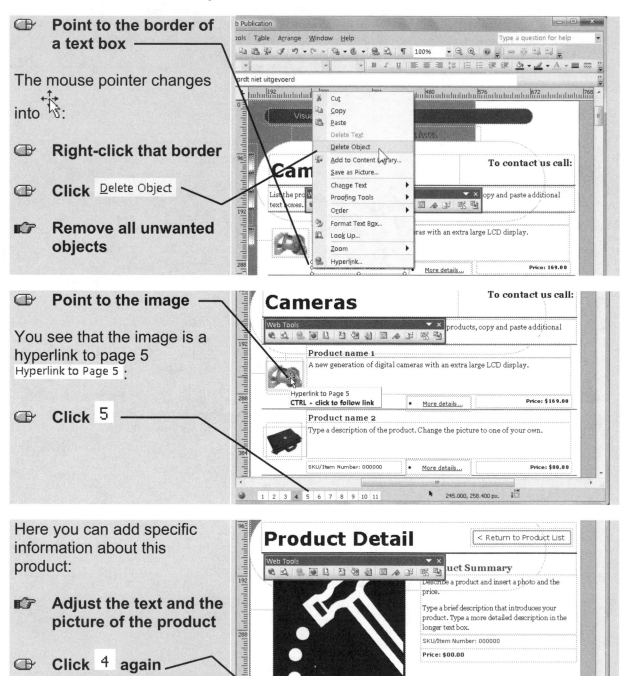

- ☞ **Point to the image** ⎯⎯

You see that the image is a hyperlink to page 5 Hyperlink to Page 5 :

- ☞ **Click** 5 ⎯⎯

Here you can add specific information about this product:

- ☞ **Adjust the text and the picture of the product**

- ☞ **Click** 4 **again** ⎯⎯

- ☞ **Adjust the product information, adjust the images and remove the unwanted objects**

Most websites contain a page with links to other companies, for example the manufacturer of your products. You can place these links on the Related Links page. In this example a link is created to the website of publisher Visual Steps. You can use your own text and link instead.

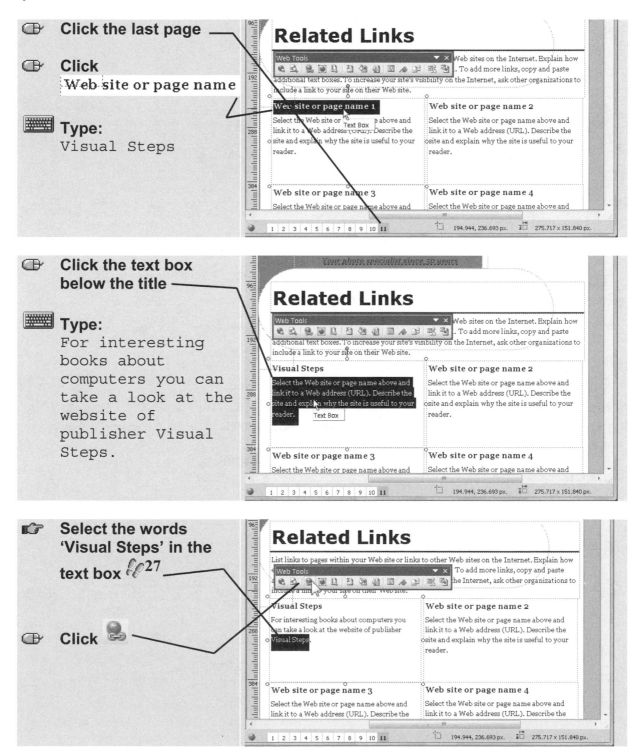

☞ **Click the last page**

☞ **Click**
Web site or page name

⌨ **Type:**
Visual Steps

☞ **Click the text box below the title**

⌨ **Type:**
For interesting books about computers you can take a look at the website of publisher Visual Steps.

☞ **Select the words 'Visual Steps' in the text box** ℓℓ27

☞ **Click** 🌐

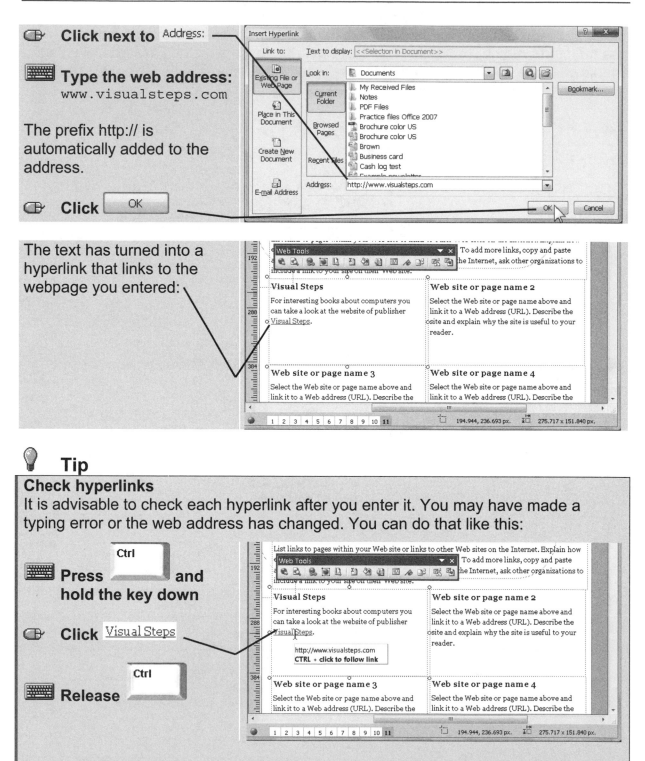

Click next to Address:

Type the web address:
www.visualsteps.com

The prefix http:// is automatically added to the address.

Click OK

The text has turned into a hyperlink that links to the webpage you entered:

💡 Tip

Check hyperlinks
It is advisable to check each hyperlink after you enter it. You may have made a typing error or the web address has changed. You can do that like this:

Press **Ctrl** and hold the key down

Click Visual Steps

Release **Ctrl**

Internet Explorer opens and you see the page the hyperlink links to.

You can save the website:

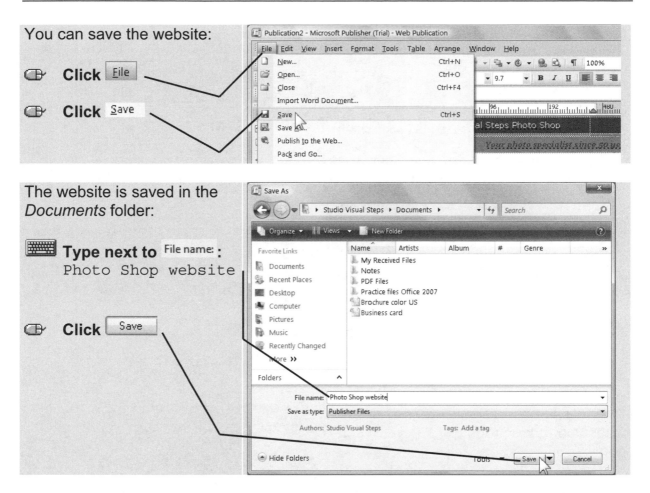

The website is saved in the *Documents* folder:

6.2 Previewing the Website

To see what the website will look like on the Internet, you can open a preview. Like this:

Internet Explorer opens and you see this page of your website:

☞ **Click** Home

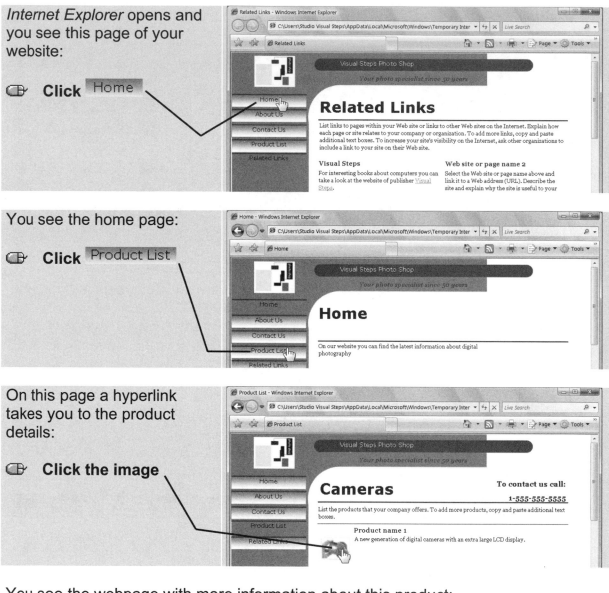

You see the home page:

☞ **Click** Product List

On this page a hyperlink takes you to the product details:

☞ **Click the image**

You see the webpage with more information about this product:

☞ **Check all pages and hyperlinks of your website**

☞ **Write down all errors**

When you have finished checking your website:

☞ **Click** X

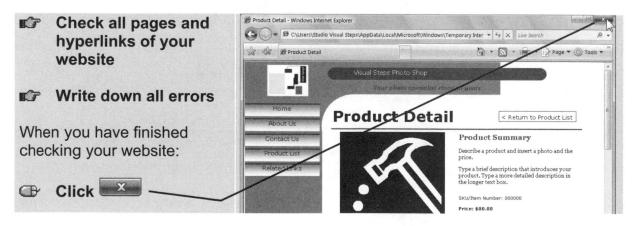

You see your design in *Publisher* again.
Now you have the opportunity to make changes before you publish your website.
You can use the error checklist you just made for that.

☞ **Correct all errors**

☞ **Save the website** $\ell\ell^{50}$

In the next section you can read how to publish the website to the Internet.

6.3 Publishing the Website to the Internet

If you are content with your website you can publish it to the Internet. Look up the information about your web space beforehand. You need the location details (your host name, usually an FTP address) where you can upload the website, and the account information such as a user name (or user id) and password. You should have received these details from your *hosting provider*. A hosting provider is an Internet Service Provider (ISP) that mainly provides web space for websites.

⇨ **Please note:**

In order to work through the exercises in this section you need a working Internet connection. You also need web space from a hosting provider to be able to publish the website to the Internet. They provide the Internet access, storage space on a web server and a web address (formally called Universal Resource Locator and abbreviated as *URL*). The URL is what your visitor's need to enter in a browser program such as *Internet Explorer* in order to be able to surf to your website. Your hosting provider also gives you information about where the website should be uploaded, a user name and a password.

Many ISPs offer a limited amount of free web space to their subscribers. In most cases you do not have your own domain name for this kind of web space. In the *Background Information* at the end of this chapter you can read more about domain names and web space.
If you do not have a hosting provider yet you can just read through this section.

You can use *Publisher* to publish your website by doing the following steps:

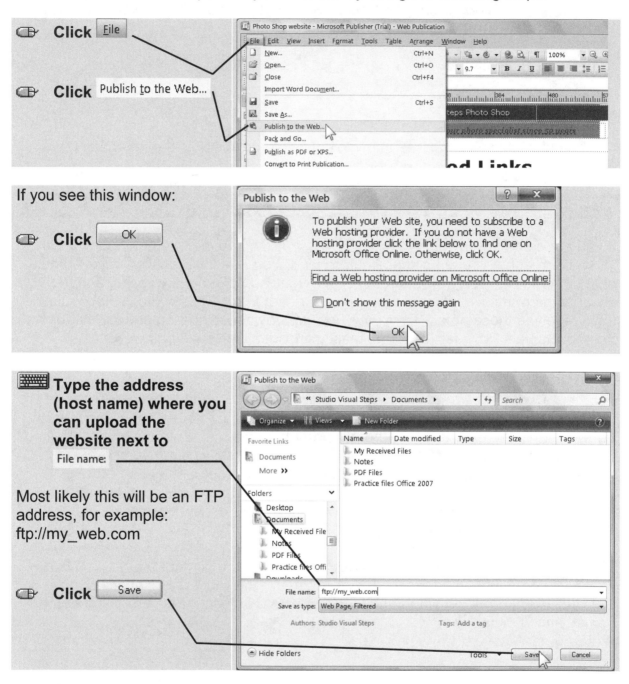

HELP! What is the right address.

In the information you received from your hosting provider you will find the address needed to upload your website to the web server. This address usually begins with ftp://. Ask your hosting provider for assistance if you cannot find the address.

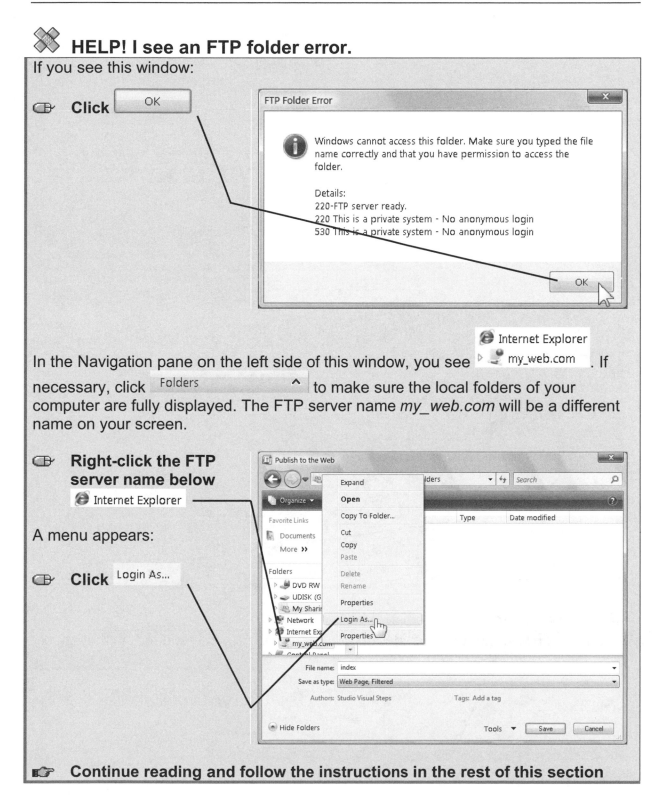

HELP! I see an FTP folder error.

If you see this window:

⊕ **Click** OK

FTP Folder Error

Windows cannot access this folder. Make sure you typed the file name correctly and that you have permission to access the folder.

Details:
220-FTP server ready.
220 This is a private system - No anonymous login
530 This is a private system - No anonymous login

OK

In the Navigation pane on the left side of this window, you see 🌐 Internet Explorer ▷ 🖥️ my_web.com . If necessary, click Folders ^ to make sure the local folders of your computer are fully displayed. The FTP server name *my_web.com* will be a different name on your screen.

⊕ **Right-click the FTP server name below**
🌐 Internet Explorer

A menu appears:

⊕ **Click** Login As...

Publish to the Web

Organize ▼

Favorite Links
📄 Documents
More ≫

Folders
▷ 💿 DVD RW
▷ 💾 UDISK (G
🖥️ My Sharin
▷ 🖧 Network
▷ 🌐 Internet Ex
▷ 🖥️ my_web.com

Expand
Open
Copy To Folder...
Cut
Copy
Paste
Delete
Rename
Properties
Login As...
Properties

Type   Date modified

File name: index
Save as type: Web Page, Filtered
Authors: Studio Visual Steps   Tags: Add a tag

🔺 Hide Folders   Tools ▼   Save   Cancel

☞ **Continue reading and follow the instructions in the rest of this section**

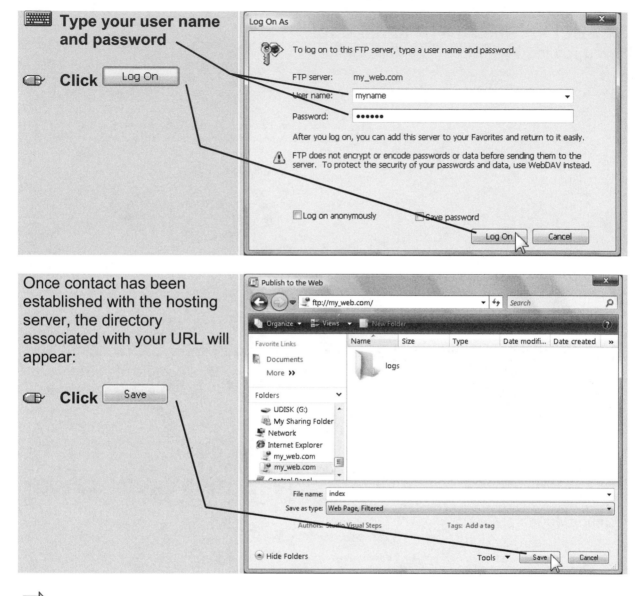

Type your user name and password

Click `Log On`

Once contact has been established with the hosting server, the directory associated with your URL will appear:

Click `Save`

➡️ **Please note:**

Depending on your hosting provider other information may be required. In that case follow the instructions on your screen.

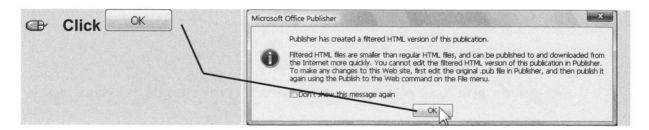

Click `OK`

⌨ **Type your user name and password (again)**

🖰 **Click** `OK`

The files are now uploaded to the server. This may take some time.

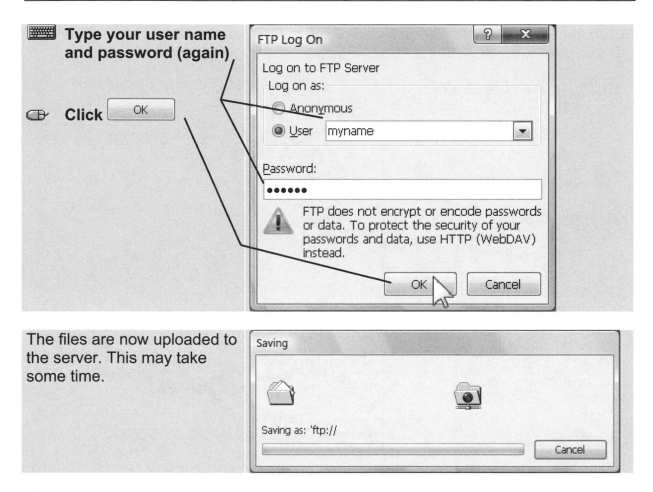

🩹 HELP! I see a Windows Security Alert.

If this is the first time you are trying to publish something to the Internet using *Publisher*, the program may be blocked by *Windows Firewall*. You can give *Publisher* permission to accept incoming network connections:

🖰 **Click** `🛡 Unblock`

Your screen goes dark and you need to give *Windows* permission to continue:

🖰 **Click the** `Continue` **button**

As soon as your files have been saved (uploaded) to the web server you can check if your website is online. You need the web address (the URL) of your website for that.

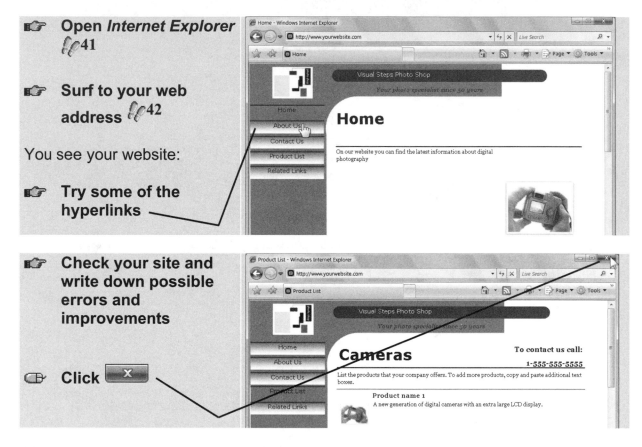

☞ **Open** *Internet Explorer* 𝓵𝓵41

☞ **Surf to your web address** 𝓵𝓵42

You see your website:

☞ **Try some of the hyperlinks**

☞ **Check your site and write down possible errors and improvements**

☞ **Click** [X]

You see the *Publisher* window again.

When you have a website for your own business you will probably want to make regular changes from time to time. You can do that using these steps:

Step 1 Start *Publisher*. Open the website files that are stored locally on your PC.
Step 2 Make changes to the webpages.
Step 3 Save the website in the local folders of your PC.
Step 4 Republish the website using the same steps outlined earlier.

⇨ **Please note:**

Do not delete the website files from your computer. If you do, you can no longer make changes to your website.

☞ **Close** *Publisher* 𝓵𝓵9

In the next section you can practice making changes to your website.

6.4 Making Changes to the Website

A website that is created in *Publisher* can easily be maintained and changed. You must make sure you have the original website files on your computer. Be sure not to delete these files!

☞ **Open *Publisher* $\ell\ell^1$**

☞ **Open your website $\ell\ell^{33}$**

💡 **Tip**

Recently used files
You can quickly open a recently used file from the *Recent Publications* window:

☞ **Click the file**

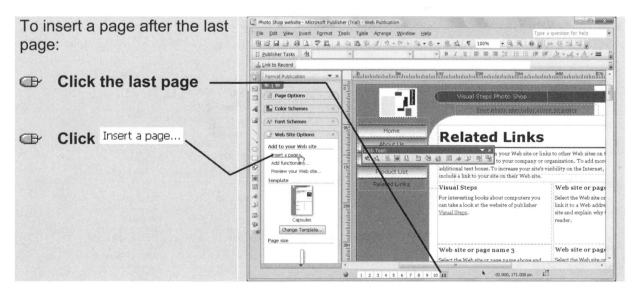

You can change the information on your website for example by adding new products and special offers or updating prices.
You can also add new pages, for example, you may want to publish a news article or a press release. A new page is always added after the page that is visible in the window.

To insert a page after the last page:

☞ **Click the last page**

☞ **Click** Insert a page...

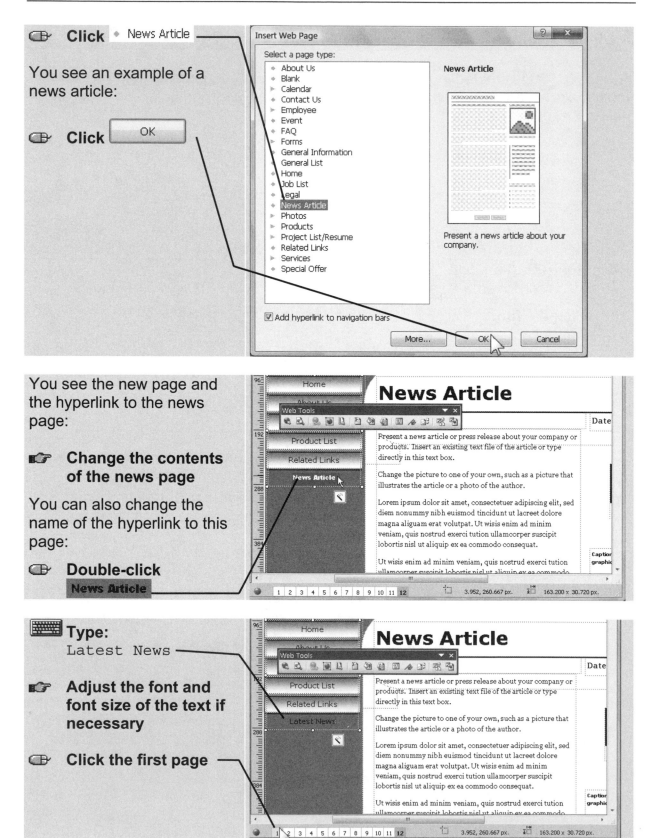

☞ **Click** ◆ News Article

You see an example of a news article:

☞ **Click** [OK]

You see the new page and the hyperlink to the news page:

☞ **Change the contents of the news page**

You can also change the name of the hyperlink to this page:

☞ **Double-click**
News Article

⌨ **Type:**
Latest News

☞ **Adjust the font and font size of the text if necessary**

☞ **Click the first page**

The hyperlink is adjusted on all pages:

As you can see, the font and font size of this hyperlink are different:

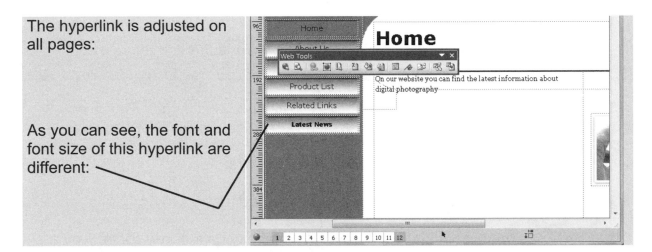

☞ **If necessary, adjust the font and font size of the new hyperlink to your liking**

Before you publish the changes you can check the website preview.

☞ **Preview your website** 𝒸ℓ³⁴

If you are happy with the results you can save the changes to the website:

☞ **Save the changed website** 𝒸ℓ⁵⁰

💡 **Tip**

Removing a webpage
You can remove a webpage like this:

☞ **Open the webpage you want to remove**

🖝 **Click** Edit

🖝 **Click** Delete Page

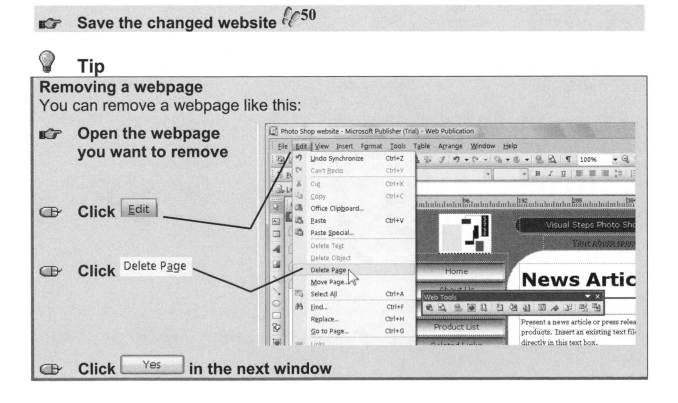

🖝 **Click** Yes **in the next window**

⇨ **Please note:**

If you do not have a hosting provider yet you can just read through the rest of this section.

After previewing and checking your website you can publish it again. *Publisher* publishes the website incrementally, that means that only the recent changes are uploaded and it takes you less time to do the publishing. This is especially helpful when you have a large website with many files or folders.

☞ **Publish the website the same way you learned in the previous section**

Since there is already data present in your web directory on the web server, you are asked at some point during the process if you want to replace it:

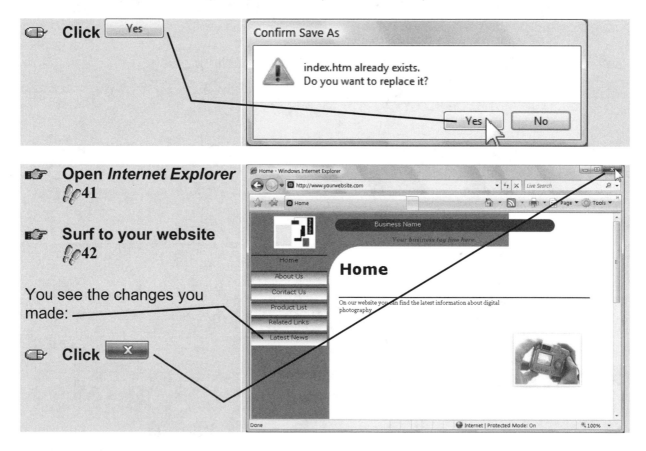

☞ **Click** `Yes`

Confirm Save As

⚠ index.htm already exists.
Do you want to replace it?

`Yes`   `No`

☞ **Open** *Internet Explorer*
🦶41

☞ **Surf to your website**
🦶42

You see the changes you made: ──

☞ **Click** `X`

HELP! I still see the old website.

There are different reasons why you may still see the old website after publishing your new website.
Some hosting providers need some time to process the new information, so it takes a while for the new website to appear.
It is also possible *Internet Explorer* does not retrieve the website from the Internet, but from the memory of your PC instead. In that case you can use the refresh command to get the latest version:

In the top right corner of the *Internet Explorer* window:

Click

Experience has shown that many new websites once published are no longer updated. This is the reason why there is a great deal of inaccurate information and sometimes altogether useless websites on the Internet.
You have seen that it is very easy to update a website in *Publisher*. Use the skills you have acquired to regularly update your website, to keep it interesting for your business relations and other visitors.

Close *Publisher* $\ell\ell^9$

6.5 Publishing a PowerPoint Presentation to the Internet

In the previous section you published a website created in *Publisher* to the Internet. It is also possible to publish a presentation created in *PowerPoint* to the Internet. You can try that with the *PowerPoint* presentation you created in *Chapter 5 Advertising and Business Presentations*. Or you can use a presentation from the *Practice files Office 2007* folder.

Please note:

In order to work through the exercises in this section you need a working Internet connection. You also need web space from a hosting provider to be able to publish the website to the Internet. They provide the Internet access, storage space on a web server and a web address (Universal Resource Locator, abbreviated as URL) so visitors can visit your website. Your hosting provider also gives you information about the location where the website should be uploaded, a user name and a password.
If you do not have a hosting provider yet you can just read through the next section.

⇨ **Please note:**

If you already published a website to your web directory on the web server of your hosting provider, you cannot perform the tasks in this chapter right away. You can only publish one website to your web directory. Before you can publish a completely new website, you must first remove the files from the previous website.
Please refer to the *Tip Managing your website files on the web server of the hosting provider* on page 315 at the end of this chapter.

☞ **Open *PowerPoint*** 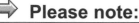^{1}

☞ **Open your own presentation or *Visual Steps Photo Shop Web* from the *Practice files Office 2007* folder** ^{12}

⇨ **Please note:**

Certain *PowerPoint* functions for presentations do not work very well or do not work at all when you publish the presentation to the Internet. Various kinds of animations, effects and action settings are known to be problematic. Make sure to test your presentation on the Internet after publishing it.

First you will need to save the presentation as a webpage:

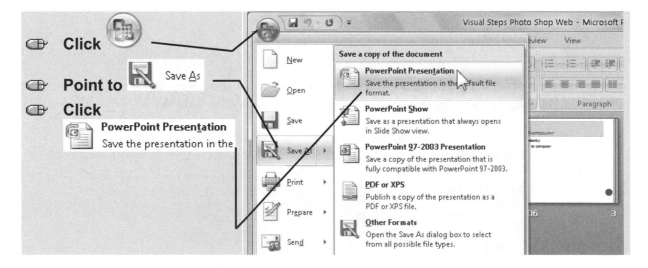

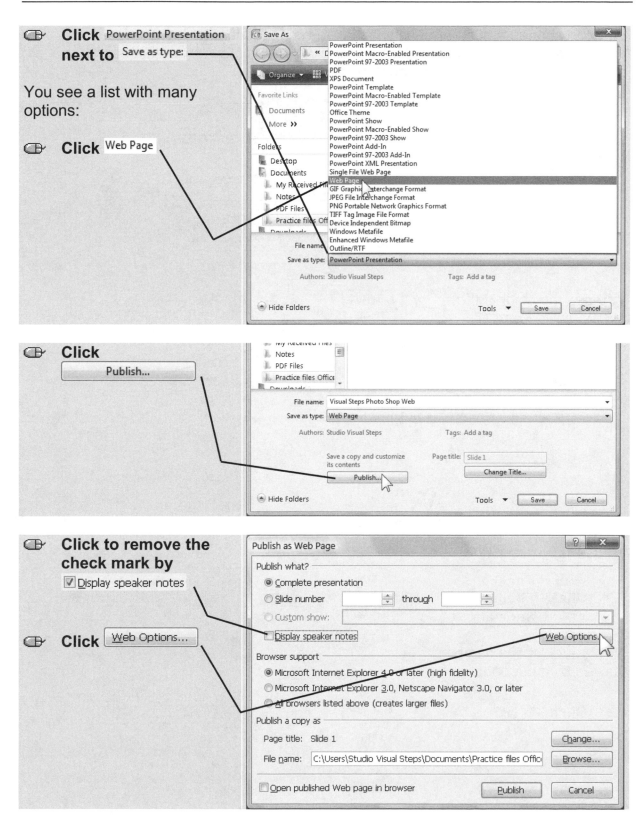

You can change a number of settings in the web options. The layout of the presentation, for example, will look better if you display the navigation bar in the colors of the presentation instead of black and white:

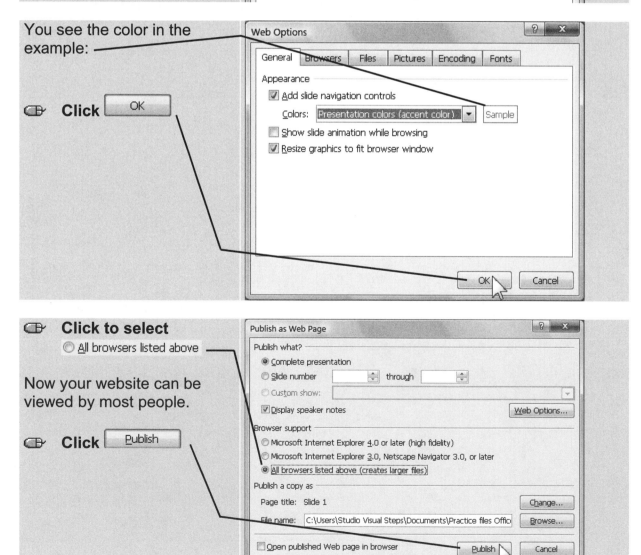

☞ **Click** ▾ **next to** Colors:

☞ **Click**
Presentation colors (accent color)

You see the color in the example: ──

☞ **Click** OK

☞ **Click to select**
○ All browsers listed above ──

Now your website can be viewed by most people.

☞ **Click** Publish

The presentation has been saved as an HTML file. This means it can now be published to the Internet. This HTML file can be found in the same folder as the original *PowerPoint* presentation. You can publish the website using an FTP utility or the FTP function of *Internet Explorer*. This last method works like this:

⇨ **Please note:**

To be able to perform the tasks in this section you need some experience in working with folder windows in *Windows Vista*. If you do not have enough experience with that you can just read through this section. The website with this book also contains a file where you can read more about working with a folder window.
Often your hosting provider will recommend a special FTP utility you can use to upload your website to the Internet. These FTP utilities are usually easier to use.

☞ **Open *Internet Explorer* 𝒞41**

☞ **Surf to the FTP server of your hosting provider 𝒞35**

✖ **HELP! What is the address of the FTP server.**

The FTP address (also called host name) where you can upload your website can be found in the information you received from your hosting provider. Usually this address begins with ftp://
If you cannot find that address you can contact your hosting provider.

You may see a log on screen right away:

⌨ **Type your user name and password**

☞ **Click** Log On

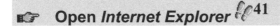

Log On As

To log on to this FTP server, type a user name and password.

FTP server: my_web.com

User name: myname

Password: ••••••

After you log on, you can add this server to your Favorites and return to it easily.

⚠ FTP does not encrypt or encode passwords or data before sending them to the server. To protect the security of your passwords and data, use WebDAV instead.

☐ Log on anonymously   ☐ Save password

Log On   Cancel

You see the root page:

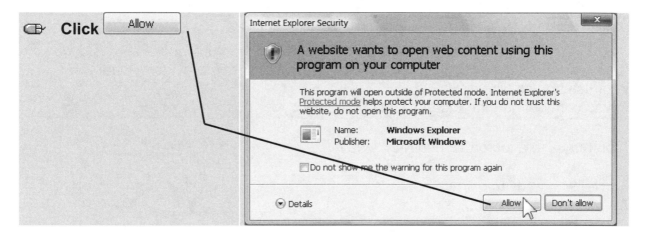

☞ **Click** 📝 Page ▼

☞ **Click**

   Open FTP Site in Windows Explore

⇨ **Please note:**

The option Open FTP Site in Windows Explorer works only with an address that starts with ftp://.

You may see an *Internet Explorer* security message about opening web content:

☞ **Click** [Allow]

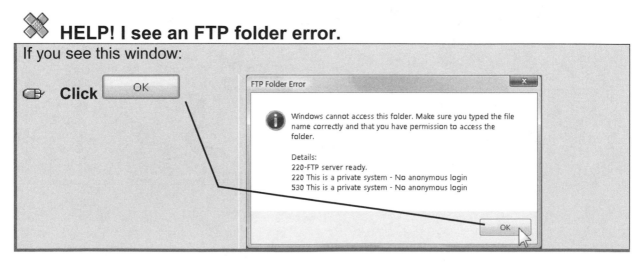

Internet Explorer Security

A website wants to open web content using this program on your computer

This program will open outside of Protected mode. Internet Explorer's Protected mode helps protect your computer. If you do not trust this website, do not open this program.

   Name: **Windows Explorer**
   Publisher: **Microsoft Windows**

☐ Do not show me the warning for this program again

⊙ Details   [Allow] [Don't allow]

🩹 HELP! I see an FTP folder error.

If you see this window:

☞ **Click** [OK]

FTP Folder Error

Windows cannot access this folder. Make sure you typed the file name correctly and that you have permission to access the folder.

Details:
220-FTP server ready.
220 This is a private system - No anonymous login
530 This is a private system - No anonymous login

[OK]

In the Navigation pane on the left side of the window you see ![Internet Explorer my_web.com]. If necessary, click ![Folders ^] to make sure the local folders of your computer are fully displayed. The FTP server name *my_web.com* will have a different name on your screen.

☞ **Right-click the FTP server name below**

![Internet Explorer]

A menu appears:

☞ **Click** ![Login As...]

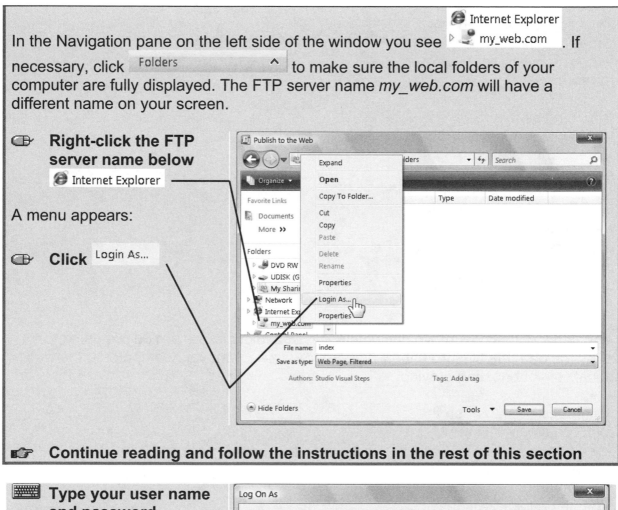

☞ **Continue reading and follow the instructions in the rest of this section**

⌨ **Type your user name and password**

☞ **Click** ![Log On]

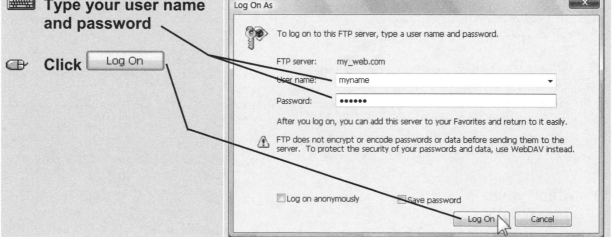

Once contact has been established with the hosting server, the directory associated with your URL will appear:

You can use this folder window to remove files and folders from your web directory in the same way you have become accustomed to in *Windows*. You can do that for example when you want to completely remove a previously published website. That is not necessary in this example.

You can locate, copy, move and delete files in a folder window. You are going to copy (upload) the files from the *PowerPoint* website from your computer to the web server of your hosting provider.

The first step is to open the folder that contains the HTML version of your *PowerPoint* presentation. Use the Navigation pane on the left side of the folder window to do this:

☞ **Open the folder that contains the presentation**

You see the contents of the folder:

☞ **Click your presentation**

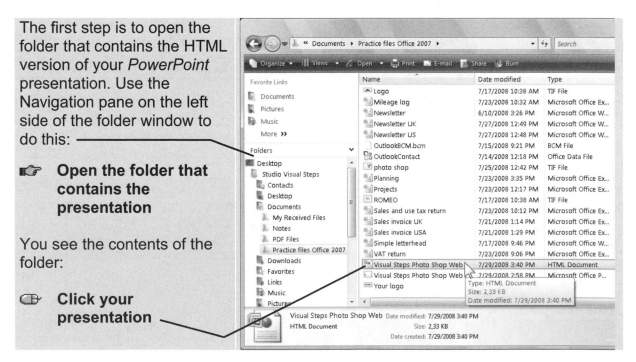

The HTML file you just selected only contains the pages of the presentation, without the images and special effects. These images and special effects are stored in a separate subfolder with the same name as your presentation. You need to publish this subfolder as well.

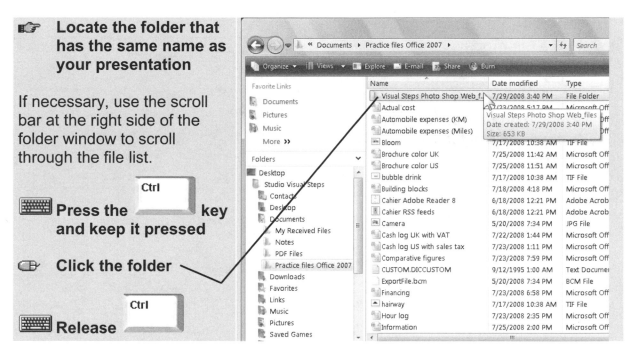

☞ **Locate the folder that has the same name as your presentation**

If necessary, use the scroll bar at the right side of the folder window to scroll through the file list.

⌨ **Press the** Ctrl **key and keep it pressed**

🖱 **Click the folder**

⌨ **Release** Ctrl

You have selected both the file and the subfolder. They will stay selected as long as you do not click anything else.
Now you can return to the FTP location in the Navigation pane of the left side of your folder window. You can find it below 🌐 Internet Explorer. Most likely, you will need to use the scroll bar of the Navigation pane to be able to see the right folder:
Make sure not to click a folder in the Navigation pane!
If you do, you will have to go back and reselect the file of your *PowerPoint* website and the accompanying subfolder once more.

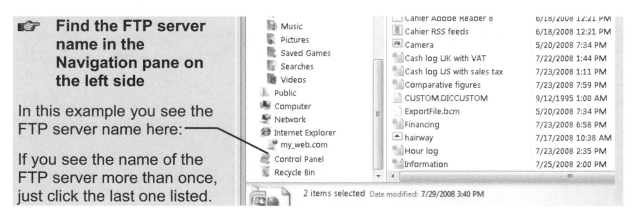

☞ **Find the FTP server name in the Navigation pane on the left side**

In this example you see the FTP server name here:

If you see the name of the FTP server more than once, just click the last one listed.

Now you are going to copy the selected file and the subfolder of your *PowerPoint* website to the web server. You do that by dragging and dropping the files from your local folder to the directory of files shown in the pane on the right side of the window (this is your website directory – it contains the files and folders of your web space on the web server). Follow the next instructions carefully:

☞ **Place the mouse pointer on the selected file or folder**

👆 **Press the left mouse button and hold it down**

👆 **Drag your presentation to the directory on the web server**

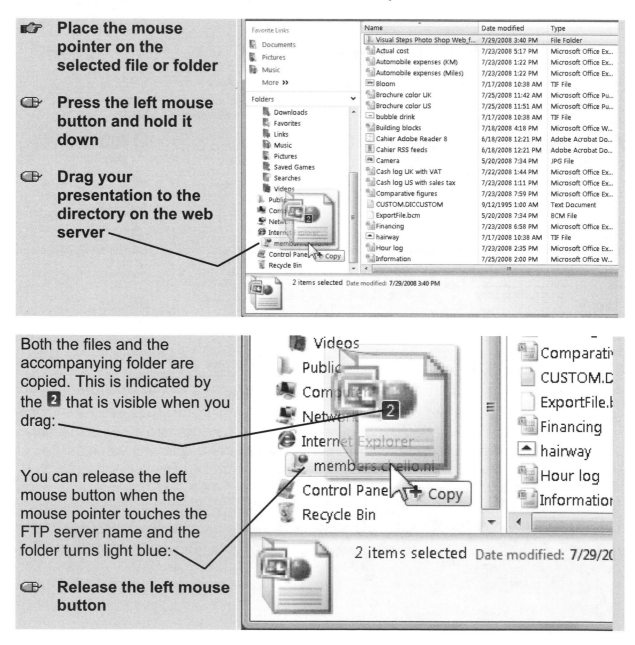

Both the files and the accompanying folder are copied. This is indicated by the **2** that is visible when you drag:

You can release the left mouse button when the mouse pointer touches the FTP server name and the folder turns light blue:

👆 **Release the left mouse button**

The file and subfolder will now be copied to the web server.

You can follow the progress in this window:

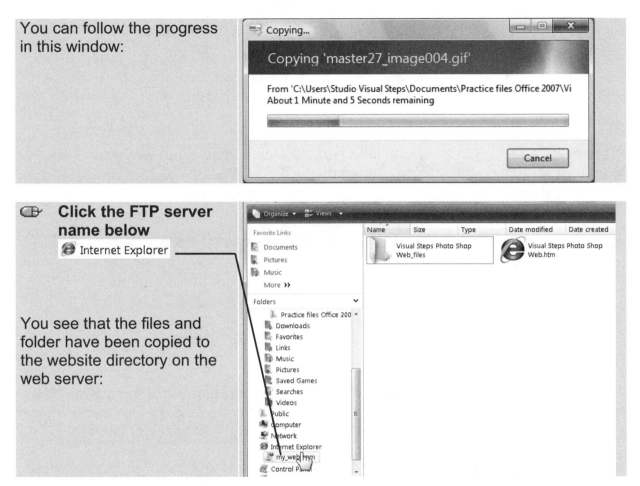

☞ **Click the FTP server name below**

🔵 Internet Explorer

You see that the files and folder have been copied to the website directory on the web server:

The home page of a website must be named *index*. The file named *index* is the first file that web browsers such as *Internet Explorer* will read. This is why you must change the name *Visual Steps Photo Shop Web* to *index*:

☞ **Right-click**

🔵 Visual Steps Photo Shop Web.htm

☞ **Click** Rename

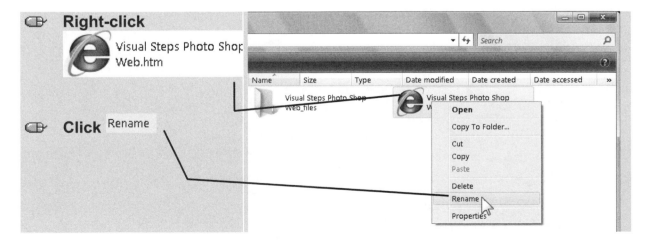

Type: index

Press Enter ↵

➡ **Please note:**

If another file named *index.htm* is found in your web directory you will need to remove it or rename it first. You can remove a file like this:

👆 **Right-click the file**

👆 **Click** Delete

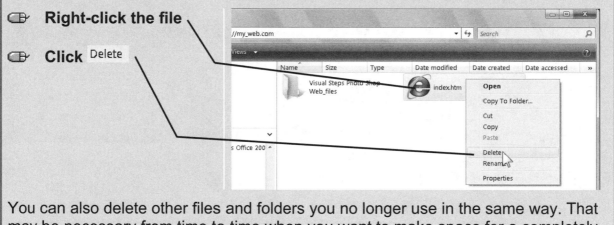

You can also delete other files and folders you no longer use in the same way. That may be necessary from time to time when you want to make space for a completely new website in your web directory.

You can close the folder window now:

👆 **Click** X

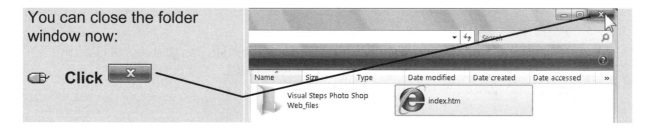

You see the *Internet Explorer* window again. You can view your website on the Internet to see the result of your efforts:

☞ **Surf to your own web address** 42

You see your *PowerPoint* website:

You can go to a specific slide by clicking the hyperlink:

To see the entire slideshow you can click 🖳 Slide Show in the bottom right corner:

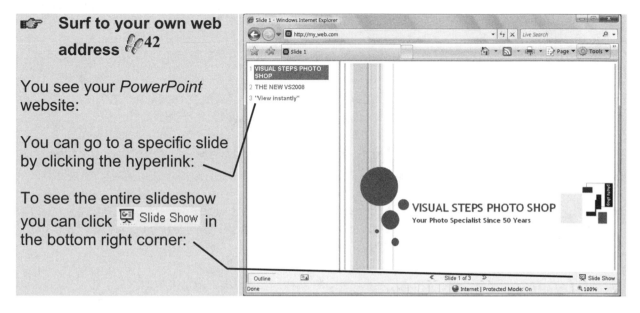

If you are done viewing your website:

☞ **Close *Internet Explorer*** 9

☞ **Close *PowerPoint*** 9

⇨ **Please note:**

Each time you change your presentation you must upload it again to your directory on the web server. It may be necessary to remove the files of your existing presentation before you can do that. The *Windows* operating system does not accept files with the same name and shows an error message if necessary.

⇨ **Please note:**

There are many graphic illustrations and photos to be found on the Internet. You may want use some of these on your own website or in other publications. Keep in mind that many of these images may require (written) permission from the owner before you can use them.

In this chapter you have learned how to create a website in *Publisher*. You have also learned how to open a *PowerPoint* presentation, add some modification and save it as a website. Both of these programs are suitable for creating simple websites.

6.6 Background Information

Glossary

Browser	A software program used to display webpages and to navigate the Internet. *Internet Explorer* is a web browser.
FTP	File Transfer Protocol (FTP) is a protocol used to transfer files over the Internet.
Hosting provider	An Internet Service Provider that provides Internet access, storage space on a web server, and a Uniform Resource Locator (URL) to a website owner.
HTML format	A text markup language used to create documents for the web. HTML defines the structure and layout of a web document by using a variety of tags and attributes.
Hyperlink	Link to another location on a website or to another website.
Internet Service Provider (ISP)	A company that provides access to the Internet, usually for a fee. The most common ways to connect to an ISP are by using a phone line (dial-up) or broadband connection (cable or DSL). An ISP provides a telephone number, a user name, a password, and other connection information so that users can access the Internet through the ISP's computers. An ISP typically charges a monthly or hourly connection fee. Many ISPs provide additional services such as e-mail accounts, web browsers, and a limited amount of web space for you to host a website.
Publish/Upload	Publishing or uploading is the process of transferring files and folders from your computer to another computer.

Source: Windows Help and Microsoft Office 2007 Help

Plan your website
Before you create your website, ask yourself these questions:

- **Who do I want to visit my website?**
  The answer to this question depends on who your audience is: potential business clients, potential fund-raisers or volunteers for your organization, members of a professional society, or another group of people. You need to know who your audience is and focus on them. Your business and your targeted audience will decide the contents and the 'look and feel' of your website. A website targeted for children or young adults will have a different look and feel than a site targeted for an older audience.

- **What do I want my website to accomplish?**
  Ask yourself what essential information your audience needs to know. For a business, this can be information about your products and services, or examples of previous projects or jobs done.

- **Which program?**
  Deciding which program to use to create your website depends on your specific needs. *Publisher* is an excellent program if you want to quickly create, publish, and manage a simple website. If your website needs interactivity or database-driven content, so that visitors can respond to a web log (blog) or purchase items with a credit card, *Publisher* may not be the best tool.

- **Do I have the time, knowledge and drive to create a website myself?**
  Planning and creating a good website takes time. You not only need to learn how to work with the program, you need to collect material for your website, write text and create the website. After that you will need to update the website regularly.

Contents of your website
Anyone who visits your website wants to find interesting and up-to-date information. You can use your website to:
- offer information to (potential) customers about products or services;
- introduce new products and services and announce special offers;
- create name awareness, brand awareness and good public relations;
- publish additional information about products and services;
- give technical support to customers or workgroups, for example by publishing user manuals and product spec sheets.

Design your website in such a way that visitors are able to quickly find all the information they need. Do not forget to make your contact information, such as address, telephone number and travel directions if necessary easy to find.

- Continue reading on the next page -

Layout, look and feel

What kind of layout and look and feel are suitable for your company and which tone do you want to use to convey your message to your audience?

You need to know your visitors, write from their point of view, and use the same language that they do. Also consider your branding. If your business branding represents authority and years of experience, irreverent humor will not be consistent with your branding. Keep the following in mind:

- use 'you' and 'your' frequently so your visitors know that their needs come first.
- get your main points across in the headings and subheadings;
- keep sentences and paragraphs short to reinforce scanning and readability;
- refine your text so that it captures your visitors' attention, holds their interest, answers their questions, overcomes their objections, and compels them to action;
- you also want to make sure that all potential customers can see, read and enjoy your website the way that you designed it. Some people turn off graphics so they can see only text. Others have dial-up connections to the Internet, so graphics on a webpage increase the page download time.

Maintenance of your website

It is also important that your website remains interesting to your visitors. Usually this takes up most of the time. For example:
- update the pages of your website frequently to keep them interesting;
- send newsletters that complement the material on your website, and include links to your website;
- provide web-based incentives such as web-only promotions or downloadable screen savers, or offer games or other downloads.

Source: Windows Help and Microsoft Office 2007 Help

Web space, web hosting and domain name

There are two kinds of Internet Service Providers (ISPs). The first group gives you access to the Internet so you can surf and e-mail. The other group offers web space on their server where you can place your website. They are called web hosting providers.

If you have a regular Internet subscription with an ISP, a limited amount of free web space is available as an extra service. This is enough for most people who only want to create a simple website. In that case your web address will partly consist of the name of the provider, for example: www.yourprovider.com/yourusername

If you want to create a website for your business, this may not be enough. You may want more web space, your own domain name for your website (for example www.yourcompanyname.com) or special features such as the possibility of using a guestbook, forum or an order form. Then you will need a hosting provider.

Hosting providers offer different kinds of packages, from basic (with little extras) to extensive business packages. For a simple website the most inexpensive package is usually enough.
Another service offered by a hosting provider is domain name registration. This will allow you to direct people to a website with a more easily recognizable address, usually for just a small monthly fee.

If you want to check if the domain name you have in mind for your business is still available you can check the following website:
www.directnic.com/search

6.7 Tips

💡 **Tip**

Small images
Sending large or high quality images over the Internet may take some time.
High quality is usually not necessary for images that are used on the Internet.
It is best to use images with the **.JPG** file extension for your website. These are
compact and have good quality. If you want to use an image that has the **.BMP** file
format you can use *Paint* or another drawing program to convert it to a file format
more suitable for the Internet.

💡 **Tip**

Register with a search engine
In order for people to quickly find the product or service you offer, you can register
your website with search engines. Most search pages contain a link for doing this:

☞ **Surf to**
   www.google.com

👆 **Click** Business Solutions

You see the various business
solutions offered by *Google*.
Some of these options are
free, others are paid
services.

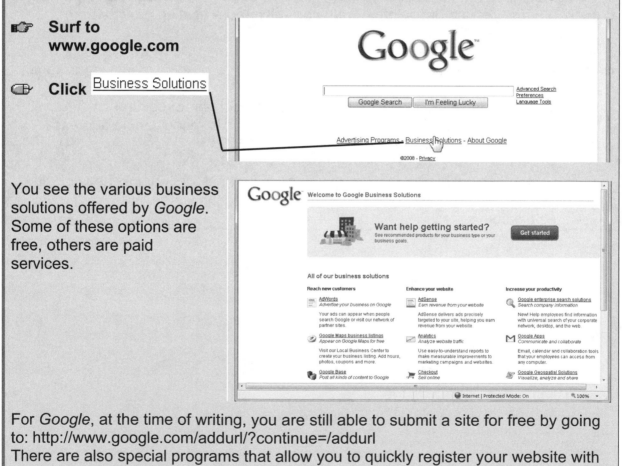

For *Google*, at the time of writing, you are still able to submit a site for free by going
to: http://www.google.com/addurl/?continue=/addurl
There are also special programs that allow you to quickly register your website with
a large number of search engines.

💡 Tip

Inserting HTML-code

You can find many graphic images and animations on the Internet which may be added to your own website. Examples of these animations are banners, counters, weather maps et cetera. In order to add one of these images to your website you will need to copy its HTML code to your website. You can only do this if the person who offers the image grants you permission to do so, for example in the form of a special button. You will find the instructions for copying the code there.

You can add the copied code to your *Publisher* website like this:

👉 **Open the desired page**

👆 **Click** `Insert`

👆 **Click** `HTML Code Fragment...`

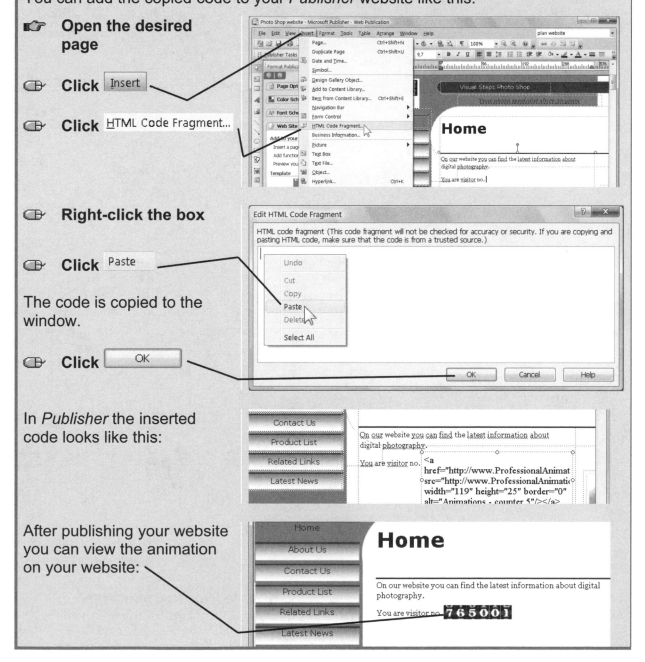

👆 **Right-click the box**

👆 **Click** `Paste`

The code is copied to the window.

👆 **Click** `OK`

In *Publisher* the inserted code looks like this:

After publishing your website you can view the animation on your website:

💡 Tip

Making changes to the business information on your website
When your business information changes, for example a new telephone number, you will want to update your website. If you created your website in *Publisher* you can do that like this:

👆 **Click** Edit

👆 **Click** Busi̲ness Information...

👆 **Click** Edit...

👉 **Make the necessary changes**

👆 **Click** Save

In the *Business Information* window:

👆 **Click** Update Publication

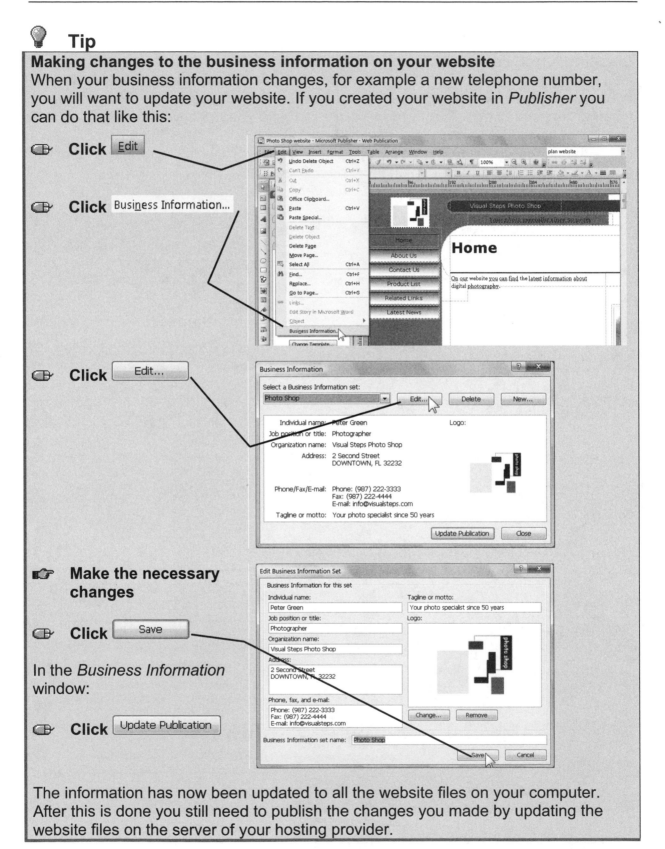

The information has now been updated to all the website files on your computer. After this is done you still need to publish the changes you made by updating the website files on the server of your hosting provider.

💡 Tip

Managing your website files on the web server of the hosting provider
A website you published is physically located on the web server of your hosting provider. When you make changes to your website, you might want to manually remove any unnecessary files from the server. For example after removing all of the hyperlinks to a particular webpage, because that page is no longer up-to-date. You can remove the page itself, with all accompanying files (such as images), from the server in order to save space. You can do that using an FTP utility or the convenient FTP feature inside *Internet Explorer*.

If you use *Publisher*, you see the files and folders on the web server when you publish a website (please refer to *Section 6.3 Publishing the Website to the Internet*).

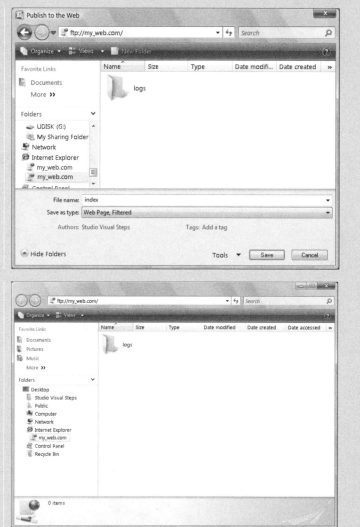

If you use *PowerPoint*, you see the files and folders on the web server when you go to your FTP site name (please refer to *Section 6.5 Publishing a PowerPoint Presentation on the Internet*).

You can open the folders and remove the unnecessary files the same way you remove files in *Windows*. The folders you see and the name of the folder(s) that contain your files may be different for each hosting provider. Please refer to the information you received from your hosting provider. If you are having difficulties you can contact your provider's helpdesk.

Notes

Write your notes down here.

7. Windows Vista Maintenance, Security and Backups ⏱ 100 min.

It is essential to secure the data on all of the computers used in your business. You should also take precautions for restoring data in case of problems or theft. Companies have been known to go bankrupt as a result of computer problems or data loss. Make sure to take the necessary precautions to prevent this from happening in your company.

This chapter focuses on how to safely store the data on your computer and how to work with your computer in a safe manner. Being safe means that you regularly create backups and protect user accounts with passwords. You will also learn how to protect your computer from viruses and other dangers that may be encountered by Internet use.

The hard disk of your computer is the central location where everything is stored. You need to check the reliability of the disk regularly and do a little spring cleaning every now and then. You can do that using the tools *Disk Cleanup*, *Disk Defragmenter* and *Error Checking*.

At the end of this chapter you will read about what to do when you are having problems with your computer.

In this chapter you will learn how to:

- create, use and set passwords for user accounts;
- check your security settings;
- set up a firewall and use *Windows Update*;
- protect your computer against viruses and spyware;
- create a complete, full or incremental back-up;
- create and restore system restore points;
- clean up your hard disk and check it for errors;
- solve common problems.

 Please note:

The 100 minutes mentioned above is the approximate amount of time it will take to read this chapter. If you are going to perform the tasks described in this chapter you will need extra time. This will depend on the particular task you want to carry out.

⇨ **Please note:**

This chapter has been written for *Windows Vista*. On a *Windows XP* PC some of the options work a little differently.

If you use *Windows XP*, you can refer to the PDF documents on the website with this book:

- **PDF Guide User Accounts**
- **PDF Guide System Restore and Backup**
- **PDF Guide System Maintenance**

Also on the website of this book you will find supplemental PDF documents that contain 3 additional chapters:

- **PDF Guide Writing Data CDs**
- **PDF Guide Folders, Documents and Files**
- **PDF Guide Computer Security**

You can only open these PDF files using a special code. Please refer to *section 1.5 Copying the Practice Files to Your Computer* and *section 1.6 Opening the PDF files from the Website* to see how you can open the files.

In order to print these documents, you need to have *Adobe Reader* on your computer. If you do not have this free program on your computer, you can read on the webpage **www.visualsteps.com/adobereader** how to install this program.

7.1 Types of User Accounts

User accounts make it possible to share a computer with several people and still maintain your own files and settings. Each person accesses their user account with a user name and possibly a password.

A user account is a collection of information that tells *Windows Vista* what files and folders you are allowed to access, what changes you can make to the computer, and your personal preferences, such as your desktop background or color theme.

Tip

Separate user accounts for business and personal use
If you are the only user of your computer, you can create separate user accounts to separate the business data on your computer from your personal data. Depending on the user name you use to log on, you will see either your business or your personal data.
If your computer is used by more people, this is a good way to protect your business data. Keep in mind that this is not completely fool proof: another user may be able to find a way to access the data.

There are three different types of user accounts:

- **Standard user account:** allows you to use most of the capabilities of the computer, but permission from an administrator is required if you want to make changes that affect other users or the security of the computer. For example, you cannot install software and hardware or delete files that are required for the computer to work.

- **Administrator account:** allows you to make changes that will affect other users. Administrators can change security settings, install software and hardware, and access all files on the computer. Administrators can also make changes to the other user accounts.

- **Guest account:** an account for users who do not have a permanent account on your computer. It allows people to use your computer without having access to your personal files. People using the guest account cannot install software or hardware, change settings, or create a password.

You can switch accounts while you work, but only if you have access to the other account. If you do not know the password, you cannot enter the other account.

⇨ **Please note:**

Many actions in this chapter require that you are logged in as an administrator. If you are not, there are certain tasks you cannot perform or you are asked to enter the administrator password. If your PC is part of a network, you may not be able to perform all tasks. Ask the system administrator for the available options if necessary.

7.2 Changing a User Name

When you start *Windows Vista* for the very first time, for example on a new computer, you enter the information for your user account in a wizard.

A user account shows the name you entered for the user. This name can easily be changed in the window *Manage Accounts*. You reach this window through the *Control Panel*:

☞ **Open the *Control Panel* ℓℓ³⁶**

🖒 **Click**
  🛡 Add or remove user accounts

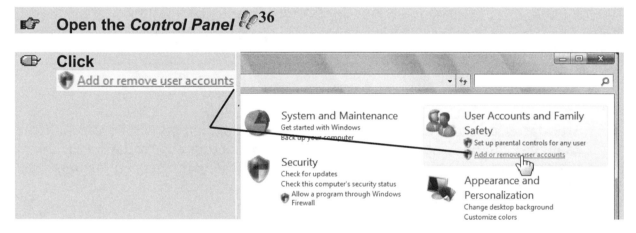

Your screen goes dark and you see the *User Account Control* window where you need to give your permission to continue.

🖒 **Click**   Continue

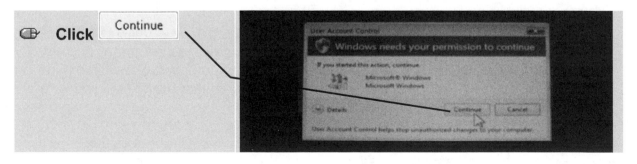

HELP! I see another window.

If you see this window, it means you are using a standard user account. With a standard user account you cannot access the window *Manage Accounts*.
Users with a standard account need to enter the password that has been set for the administrator account in order to be able to continue with this task:

☞ **Type the administrator password**

⏺ **Click** `OK`

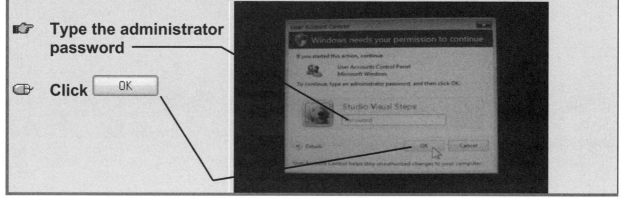

In the window *Manage Accounts* you see every user account that is used on this computer. If you did not add any extra user accounts, only your account or the account named *User* is active. The account *User* was created when *Windows Vista* was installed.

⏺ **Click your user account**

    Studio
    Administrator

You see the account type:

In this example the account name is *Studio*. You will see a different name on your computer.

You can change the name of your user account like this:

⏺ **Click**
`Change the account name`

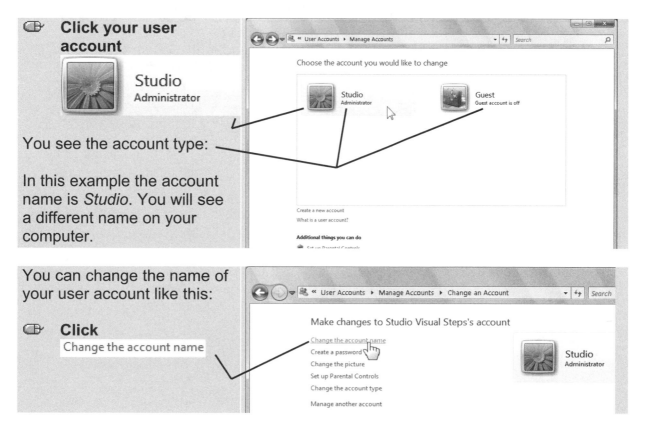

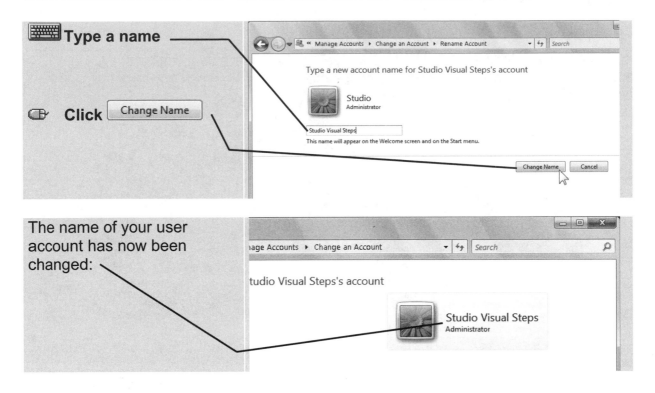

7.3 Choosing Another Picture

Windows Vista displays a small image for every user account. You can change this image like this:

In this window you see the images available for user accounts in *Windows Vista*. You can try changing the current picture to the picture of the dog:

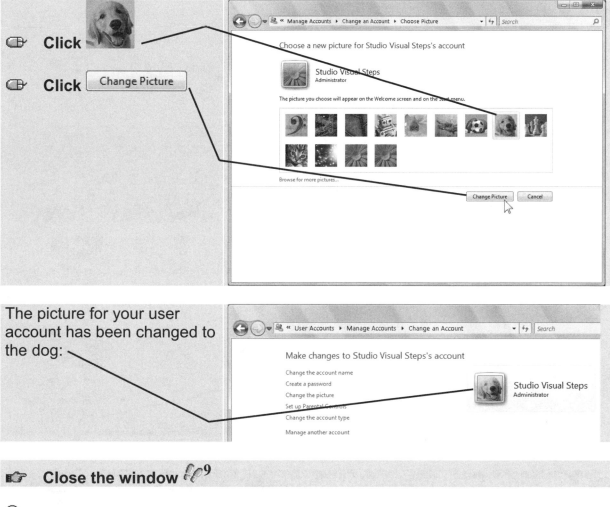

☞ **Click**

☞ **Click** Change Picture

The picture for your user account has been changed to the dog:

☞ **Close the window** 𝒶𝒷⁹

💡 **Tip**

Use your own image or logo
Instead of using the standard images provided by *Windows Vista*, you can also set your own photo or image as the picture for your user account. You can use your company logo for your business account for example. Like this:

- Continue reading on the next page -

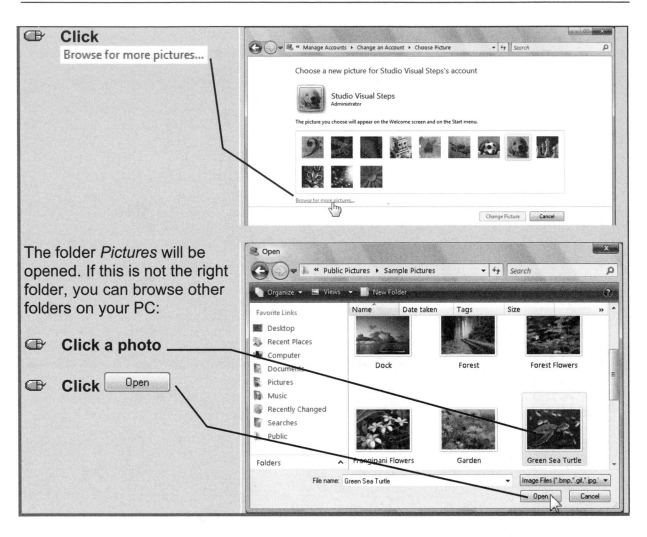

Click
Browse for more pictures...

The folder *Pictures* will be opened. If this is not the right folder, you can browse other folders on your PC:

Click a photo

Click [Open]

7.4 Creating a New User Account

In just a few steps, you can create a new user account in the window *Manage Accounts*.

☞ **Open the *Control Panel*** $\ell\ell^{36}$

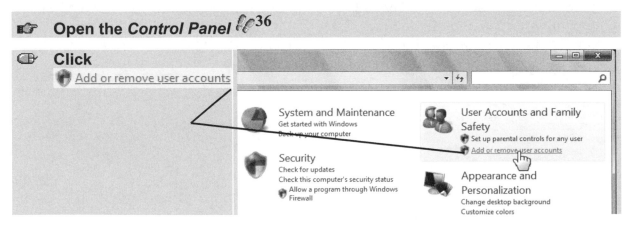

Click
🛡 Add or remove user accounts

If your screen goes dark and you are asked for permission to continue:

☞ **Click** Continue

Click Create a new account

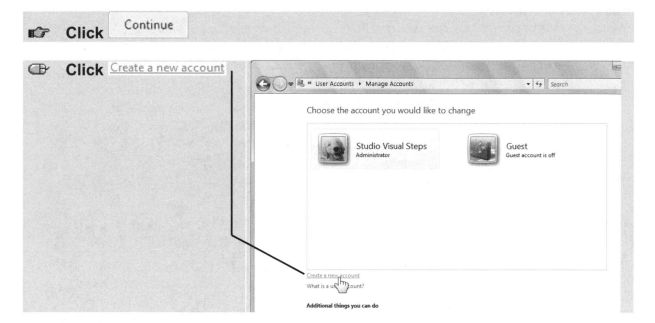

In the next window you can enter the user name and account type for the new user account. For this exercise, choose the standard user account:

⌨ **Type a name in this box, for example:**
Mary

Click the option
⦿ Standard user

Click Create Account

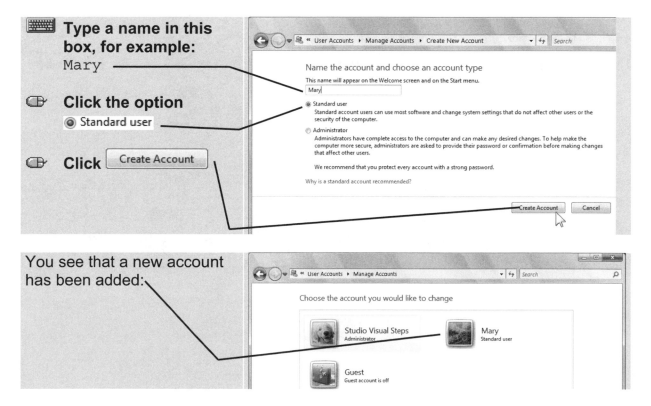

You see that a new account has been added:

💡 Tip

Fast user switching

Windows Vista offers the option to quickly switch between users. This is very useful if you are working on the computer and another user wants to check his e-mail, or if you want to take a quick look at your company or personal information. You do not have to close all your programs and log off. In *Windows Vista* you can switch to another user account and then return to your account.

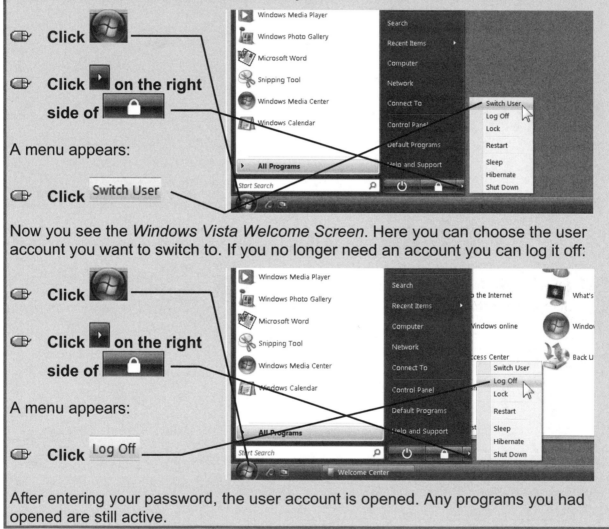

☞ **Click**

☞ **Click** ▶ **on the right side of** 🔒

A menu appears:

☞ **Click** Switch User

Now you see the *Windows Vista Welcome Screen*. Here you can choose the user account you want to switch to. If you no longer need an account you can log it off:

☞ **Click**

☞ **Click** ▶ **on the right side of** 🔒

A menu appears:

☞ **Click** Log Off

After entering your password, the user account is opened. Any programs you had opened are still active.

7.5 Deleting a User Account

If one of the users no longer uses the computer, you can remove his or her account. To be able to delete a user account, you must have an administrator account or the administrator password.

 Please note:

When you remove a user account, the mail settings associated with this account are lost, as well as any saved e-mails, or files in the folders *Documents, Favorites*, *Pictures*, *Videos* and *Music* and the files on the desktop.
Before you permanently delete the account, *Windows Vista* will ask if you want to save this information.

You can remove the new user account you just created like this:

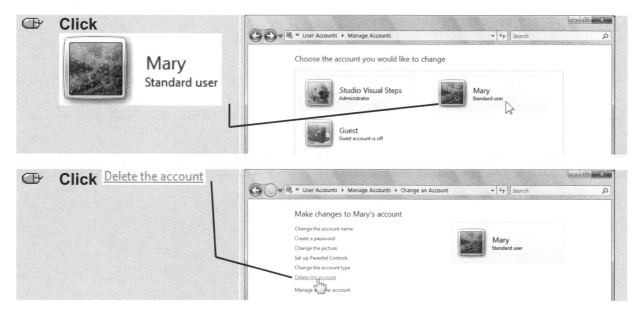

Windows Vista now asks what should be done with the files from this user. You can choose to save or delete the files in the folders *Documents, Favorites*, *Pictures*, *Videos* and *Music* and the files on the desktop. If you choose to save the files, they will be placed on your desktop in a folder with the name of the deleted user account.

Finally, you are asked if you are sure you want to delete the account:

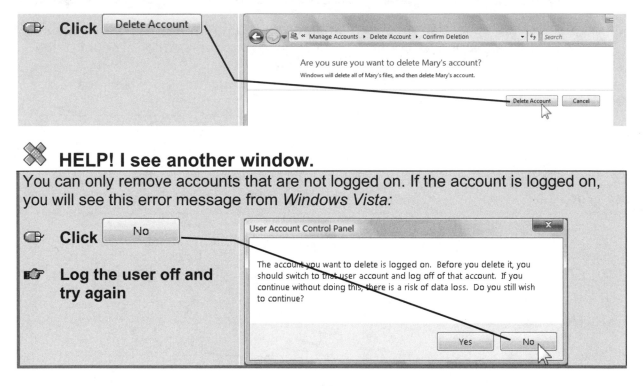

HELP! I see another window.

You can only remove accounts that are not logged on. If the account is logged on, you will see this error message from *Windows Vista:*

☞ **Log the user off and try again**

7.6 Creating a Password for a User Account

Every user account can be protected with a password. If you want to make sure nobody can change your settings, you should create a password for your user account. You can do that like this:

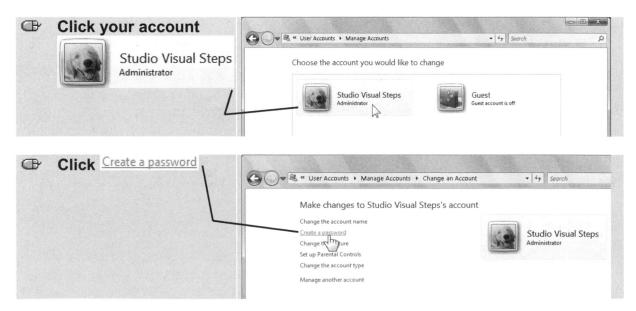

⇨ **Please note:**

A password is only useful when others cannot easily guess it. Use at least seven characters, combining letters and digits. Keep in mind that every user on your computer can see your password hint on the *Welcome Screen*. Keep your hint vague enough so that others cannot guess your password.

⌨ **Type your password here**

⌨ **Type your password again here**

⌨ **Type your password hint here**

☞ **Before you continue, write down your password**

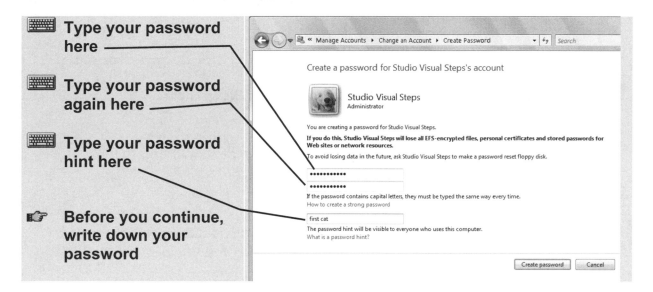

When you have entered your password and password hint, and you have written down your password, you can let *Windows Vista* activate the password:

🖱 **Click** Create password

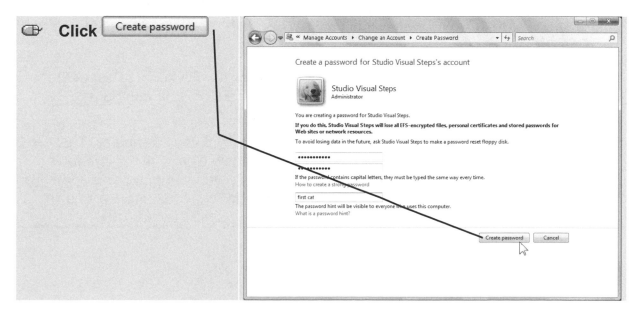

HELP! I see another window.

If you entered two different passwords, you will see:

> **User Account Control Panel**   [x]
>
> The passwords you typed do not match. Please retype the new password in both boxes.
>
>   [OK]

Type your password in both boxes again

⇨ Please note:

Your password only protects your account; other users cannot log on to the computer using your name.

When another user tries to open your *Personal folder*, he sees this window:

> **Studio Steps**   [x]
>
> ⚠   You don't currently have permission to access this folder.
>
>   Click Continue to get access to this folder.
>
>   [🛡 Continue] [Cancel]

When a user with a standard user account clicks [🛡 Continue], he is prompted to enter the administrator password.

When an administrator clicks [🛡 Continue], he can access the *Personal folder* of the other user! You see why it is better to give the other users on your computer a standard user account instead of an administrator account.

Suppose you created a folder C:\Letters on the hard disk of your computer. This folder can be opened by all other users. Using the window *Computer* or *Windows Explorer* they can view what is stored on the hard disk of the computer and open this folder. So always keep your personal files and folders in (a subfolder of) your own *Personal folder*!

💡 Tip

Shared documents
It is still possible to share documents even when all users have a standard user account that is protected by a password. You can use the folder *Public Documents* for this. Every user can open this folder. This is how you save a document to the *Public Documents* folder in the window *Save*:

☞ **Click** ▼ Browse Folders

☞ **Click** 📁 Public

☞ **Double-click** 📁 Public Documents

☞ **Click** Save

7.7 Changing a Password

When you protect your user account with a password, it is a good idea to change this password regularly. Like this:

☞ **Click** Change the password

In the next window you must enter your current password first. This is to make sure that you really are the user that is allowed to change the password. Then you can enter your new password and password hint:

⌨ **Type your current password**

⌨ **Type your new password**

⌨ **Type your new password again**

⌨ **Type a password hint for your new password**

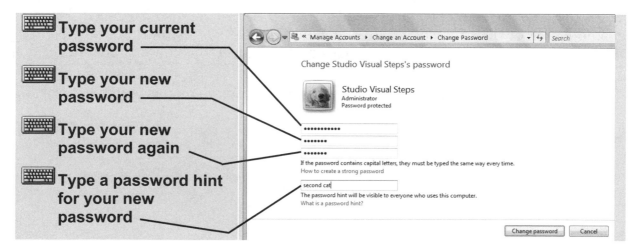

☞ **Write down your new
password**

☞ **Click** `Change password`

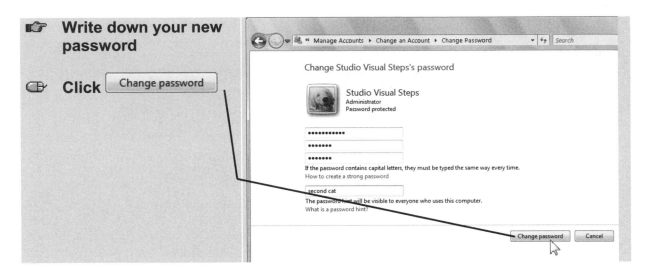

The password has been changed. Next time you log on to the computer, you will
need to enter the new password.

☞ **Close the *User Accounts* window** ℓℓ⁹

7.8 Creating a Password Reset Disk

There is always a possibility that you could forget your password. Even if the
password hint does not help you to remember the password, it is good to have
something else to fall back on. You can create a *password reset disk* that you can
use to log on to *Windows Vista.* Then you can create a new password. You only have
to create this disk once, no matter how often you change your password later.

⇨ **Please note:**

Although the term 'disk' is used in the windows, you will probably want to use some
other kind of portable media, such as a USB stick. A USB stick is also called USB
memory stick or USB flash drive. Most new Vista PCs will probably not even have a
floppy disk drive as diskettes are gradually being replaced by other storage media.

To go to the window where you can find the option to create a password reset disk:

☞ **Open the *Control Panel* ℓℓ³⁶**

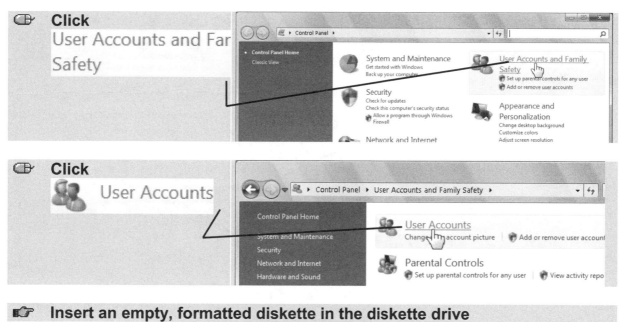

Click
User Accounts and Far
Safety

Click
User Accounts

☞ **Insert an empty, formatted diskette in the diskette drive**
Or:
☞ **Insert a USB stick in the USB port of the computer**

If you select this option, you will need to wait a moment for the USB stick to be recognized by *Windows Vista*.

You will see a message in the lower right corner of your screen:

☞ **If necessary, close the *AutoPlay* window** 🐾⁹

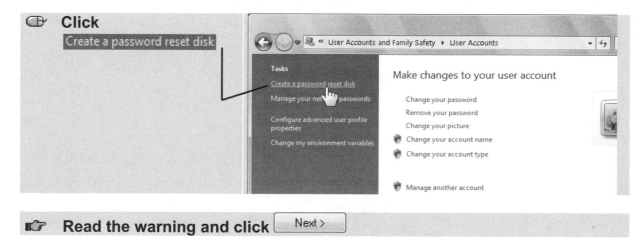

Click
Create a password reset disk

☞ **Read the warning and click** [Next >]

Now you can choose the drive where the password reset disk is to be created:

In this example a USB stick
connected to port E: is used:

☞ **Click** ▾

☞ **Click** Removable Disk (E:)

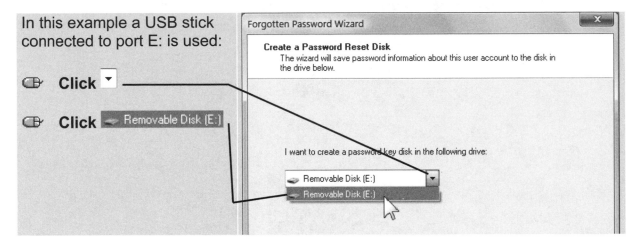

☞ **Click** Next >

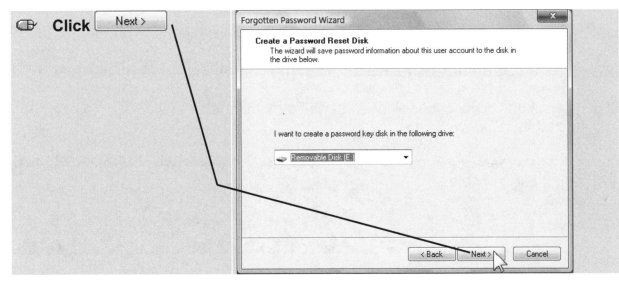

⌨ **Type your current
password here**

☞ **Click** Next >

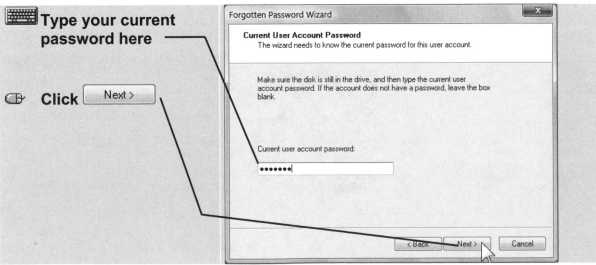

Now the *Forgotten Password Wizard* writes the reset information to the diskette or the USB stick:

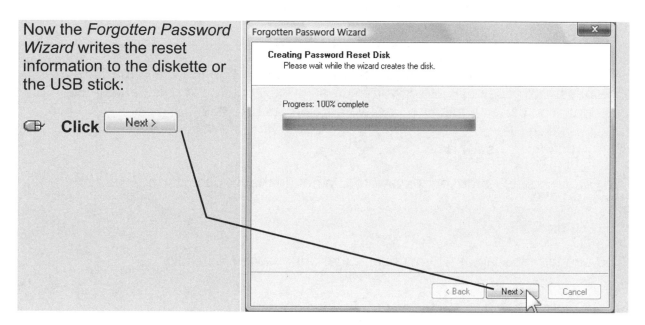

☞ **Click** Next >

When the diskette or USB stick is ready:

☞ **Click** Finish

☞ **Close the** *User Accounts* **window** $\ell\ell^9$

⇨ **Please note:**

Make sure other users do not have access to your password reset disk. Anyone could use this USB stick to log on to your account.

✖ HELP! I did not create a password reset disk.

If you have lost your password and you have not created a password reset disk, you will no longer be able to log on to your computer.
The (other) administrator can set a new password for you. In this procedure you will permanently lose part of your settings: your personal certificates, access to e-mail messages and saved passwords for websites.

Are you the only computer administrator? Then you will need to reinstall *Windows Vista* on your computer.

💡 Tip

Using the password reset disk

When you lose your password, you can no longer log on in the *Welcome Screen*. The password reset disk allows you to create a new password outside your own account. You can use this new password to log on. Like this:

👆 **Click your user name**

You are asked to enter your password. Do not do that yet. Instead:

👆 **Click** ➡️

You see the message that your user name or password is invalid.

👆 **Click** `OK` **to leave this window**

👆 **Click *Reset password***

Now you see the first window of the *Password Reset Wizard*:

👉 Insert the password reset disk or connect the USB stick to your computer

👆 **Click** `Next >`

In the window that appears, you can select the drive where you placed the password reset disk in:

👆 **Click** ▾ **and then the drive you want to use, for example** `Removable Disk (E:)`

👆 **Click** `Next >`

Now you can enter your new password and password hint.

- Continue reading on the next page -

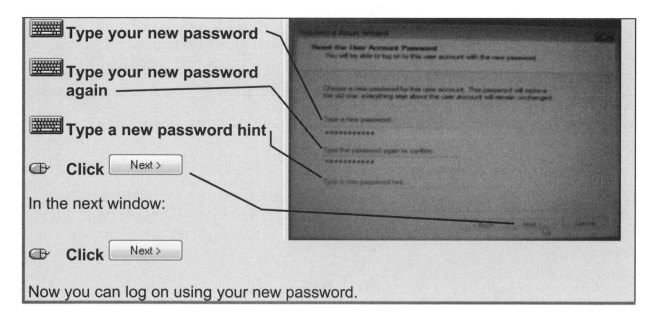

⌨ **Type your new password**

⌨ **Type your new password again**

⌨ **Type a new password hint**

🖰 **Click** [Next >]

In the next window:

🖰 **Click** [Next >]

Now you can log on using your new password.

7.9 User Account Control

You have already been introduced to *User Account Control* in *Windows Vista*. This feature causes your screen to darken and you must give your permission to continue. This will prevent changes being made to your computer by users who do not have permission to do so. When you see a message from *User Account Control*, read through it carefully. Make sure that the name that is displayed corresponds to the task you want to perform or the program you want to open.

In a darkened screen you can see several different messages from *User Account Control*:

Windows needs your permission to continue
You see this message when you start a *Windows* function or program that can affect other users of this computer.

A program needs your permission to continue
This message is displayed when you open a program that is not part of *Windows*, but does have a valid digital signature (electronic security). This means you can assume this program is legitimate.

An unidentified program wants access to your computer
This message is displayed when you open an unknown program that does not have a valid digital signature from its publisher. This means that you are unable to check if the program is legitimate. It does not necessarily indicate danger, as

many older, legitimate programs do not have signatures. However, you should use extra caution and only allow this program to run if you obtained it from a trusted source, such as the original CD or a publisher's website.

⊗ This program has been blocked

When your computer is connected to a network, the network administrator can block programs from running on your computer. To run this program, you can contact your administrator and ask to have the program unblocked.

If you want to use the full potential of *User Account Control*, you should create a standard user account for each user of the computer (including yourself). With this type of account you have sufficient rights to send e-mails, edit photos or surf the Internet.

You keep one administrator account that you protect with a password. It is advisable to (have the other users) do the same for the standard user accounts.

When a user who has a standard user account tries to install software for example, the screen will go dark. *Windows* will ask for the password of the administrator account. This way software cannot be installed without your knowledge and permission.

The user with the standard user account must enter the administrator password to be able to continue with this task:

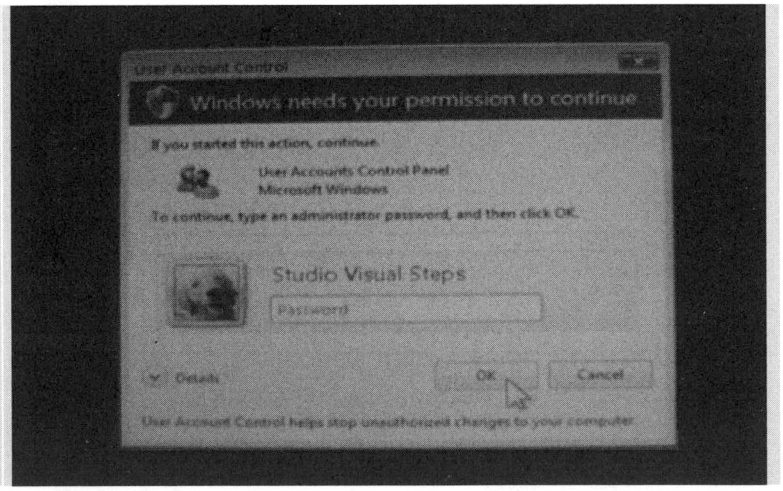

The administrator password must be entered each time before tasks can be performed that might:
- affect the settings of the computer;
- change the settings of other users.

💡 **Tip**

User accounts as a security measure
Even if you are the only person that works with your computer, it is still advisable to set up user accounts. This way you can prevent easy access to your data in case of theft of your computer.

7.10 Removing a Password

If you decide you do not need to protect your user account with a password, you can remove the password.

☞ **Open the *Manage Accounts* window** 🦶³⁷

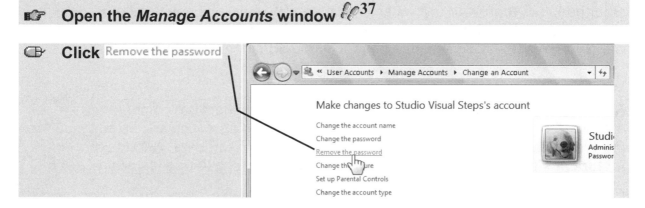

Windows Vista checks if you are really the user that is allowed to remove the password. That is why you must type the password first:

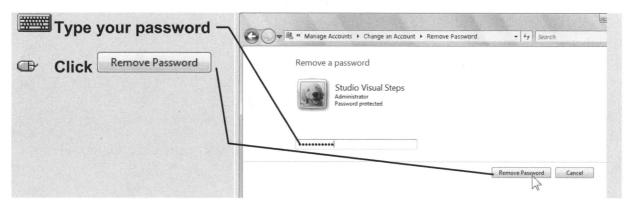

Now your password has been removed.

☞ **Close all windows** 🦶⁹

⇨ **Please note:**

If you decide later on to set a password for your account, do not forget to create a new password reset disk!

7.11 Windows Security Center

It is very important to effectively protect your computer, especially when you regularly use the Internet. A good security system reduces the risk of viruses and other malicious software from entering your computer.

A computer that is infected with a virus is very annoying: not only for you, but also for other people. When your computer is infected with malicious software, other computers can also become infected. That can happen when you send an e-mail or when you exchange files using a CD, DVD or USB stick.

⇨ **Please note:**

As a computer user you are responsible for protecting your own computer. Your computer should be protected by a firewall and should also regularly be scanned for the presence of viruses and other malicious software. **Windows Vista does not include a virus scanner!** This means you have to purchase and install an antivirus program yourself.

The *Security Center* is your central location for computer security. The *Security Center* checks the security settings of your computer and keeps track of updates to *Vista*. You can open the *Security Center* like this:

☞ **Open the *Control Panel* ℓℓ^{36}**

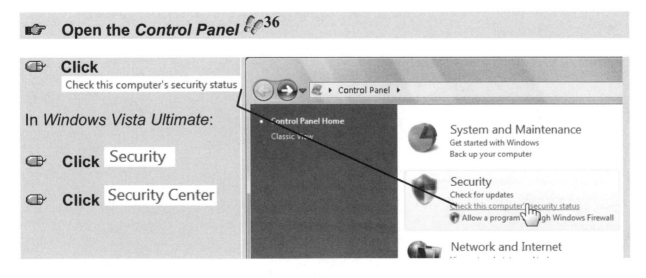

☐ **Click**
Check this computer's security status

In *Windows Vista Ultimate*:

☐ **Click** Security

☐ **Click** Security Center

In this window you see the status of the four most important components of your computer's security:

- *Firewall*
- *Automatic updating*
- *Malware protection*
- *Other security settings*

For each component you see the current status:

- On ⊙ or OK ⊙ These items do not need your attention. In this example all components have this (green) status.
- Check settings ⊙ The *Security Center* is unable to detect a program. You see the red warning. Possibly an antivirus program has not been installed, or the installed program is not recognized by *Windows Vista*.
- Off ⊙ You see this status if you switched off an item manually.

The settings of your computer may be different than what you see in this example.

7.12 Windows Firewall

A firewall is software or hardware that manages the incoming and outgoing data traffic between your computer and the Internet and/or other networks. Depending on your firewall settings, data traffic is either blocked or allowed to pass through to your computer.

⇨ **Please note:**

The word *firewall* sounds safer than it actually is: a firewall **does not** protect your computer against viruses. If your e-mail program is allowed access to the Internet through your firewall, you can still receive an e-mail with an attachment that contains a virus. The firewall does not check the content of the data traffic, it only checks if the traffic runs according to the rules you have set.

 Click Windows Firewall

In this example *Windows Firewall* is used.
Some antivirus programs have their own firewall. In that case you will see different windows on your screen than in this book.

☞ **Click** Change settings

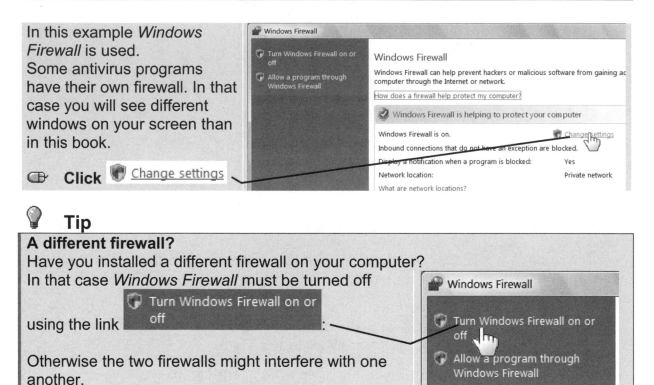

💡 **Tip**

A different firewall?
Have you installed a different firewall on your computer?
In that case *Windows Firewall* must be turned off

using the link Turn Windows Firewall on or off :

Otherwise the two firewalls might interfere with one another.

Your screen goes dark and you see the window *User Account Control* where you need to give your permission to continue.

☞ **Click** Continue **in the *User Account Control* window**

You see that *Windows Firewall* is turned on:

You can check the option ☐ **Block all incoming connections** when you connect to a less secure network such as a public network at an airport:

When this option is not checked, programs on the Exceptions tab are allowed access to your computer.

☞ **Click the** Exceptions **tab**

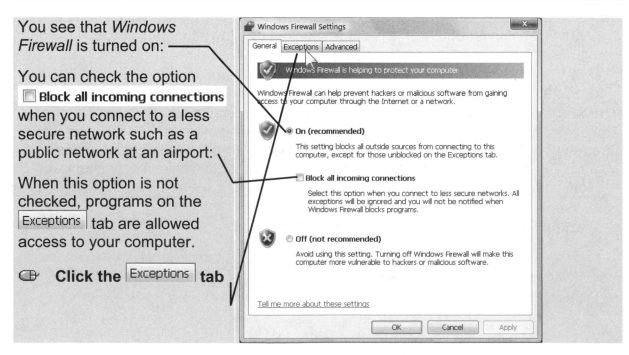

If you are using a program that has to receive data from the Internet or a network, the firewall will ask if you want to allow the connection. For each allowed connection, an exception is added to this list:

You can use the button Add program... to add exceptions directly:

You do not have to change these settings now:

👈 **Click** Cancel

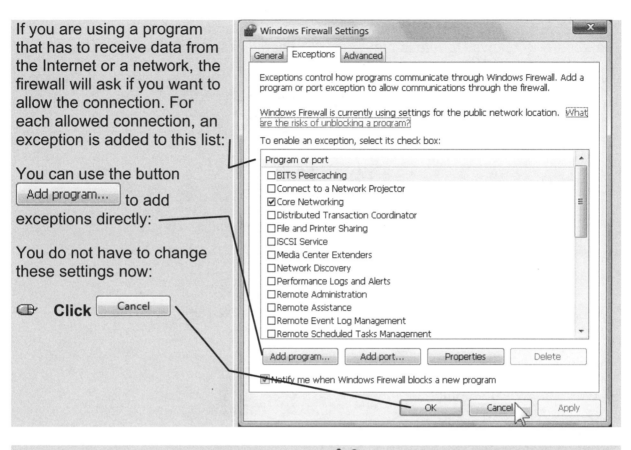

📧 **Close the** *Windows Firewall* **window** $\ell\ell^9$

7.13 Windows Update

A very important part of the *Security Center* is *Windows Update*. This is a system that checks if you are using the most recent version of *Windows Vista*. *Windows Vista* is constantly being modified, expanded and made more secure. The additions and improvements are dispersed by *Microsoft* in the form of *software updates*. You can download these updates for free if you are using a legitimate version of *Windows Vista*.

➡️ **Please note:**

Microsoft **never** sends software updates by e-mail. Anyone who receives an e-mail claiming to contain *Microsoft* software or a *Windows* update is strongly advised not to open the attachment and immediately delete the e-mail. Do not forget to delete it from the folder *Deleted items* as well. Mails like that are sent by criminals who try to install malicious software on your computer.

If you want to make sure your version of *Windows Vista* stays up-to-date, you should make sure *Windows Update* is turned on. You can turn this option on like this:

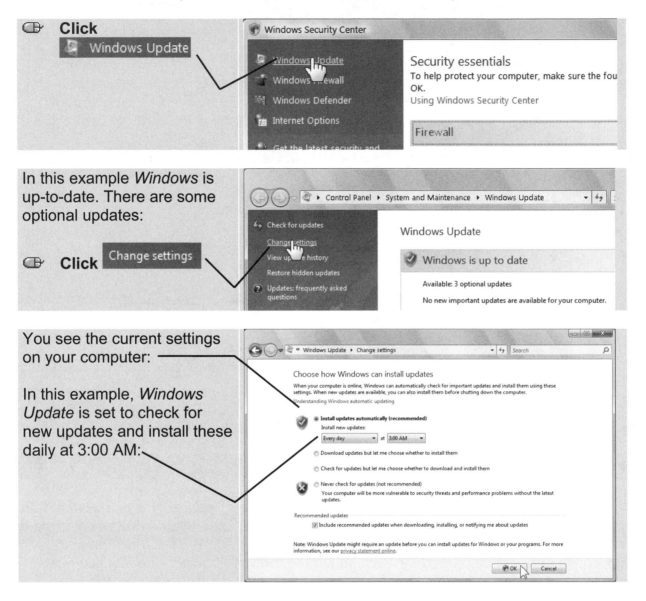

Click Windows Update

In this example *Windows* is up-to-date. There are some optional updates:

Click Change settings

You see the current settings on your computer:

In this example, *Windows Update* is set to check for new updates and install these daily at 3:00 AM:

It is a good idea to select the ◉ **Install updates automatically (recommended)** setting.
In that case you always use the latest version of *Windows Vista*. You can change the time for downloading and installing updates to a moment that is most convenient for you.

If the computer was turned off at that time, the check will take place the next time the computer is turned on. The updates are then automatically downloaded and installed. *Windows* places a notification about this at the bottom of the screen, but in most cases you can just keep on working. For critical updates it may be necessary to restart your computer after downloading and installing the updates.

Did you change a setting?

☞ **Click** [🛡 OK]

Your screen goes dark; *Windows* needs your permission to continue. You can use the button [Continue] to give permission.

If you have not changed anything:

☞ **Click** [Cancel]

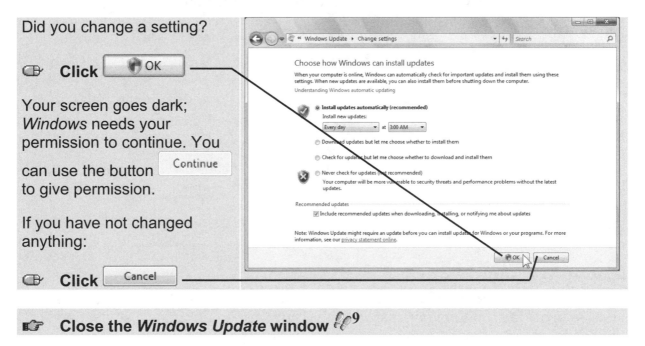

☞ **Close the *Windows Update* window** ‿‿⁹

7.14 Malware Protection

Malware is short for 'malicious software', software that is designed to deliberately harm your computer. Viruses, worms, spyware and Trojan horses are forms of malware. These types of software are an increasing threat to every computer connected to the Internet. The source of infection may be an attachment to an e-mail message or a file downloaded from the Internet. Your computer can also become infected by exchanging USB sticks, CDs or other storage media.

If you did not install an antivirus program, a message like this will appear at the bottom of your screen from time to time:

Check your antivirus software status ✕
avast! antivirus 4.7.942 [VPS 000723-2] is turned off.
Click this notification to fix the problem.

The *Malware protection* component of *Windows Security Center* indicates whether or not an up-to-date antivirus program is installed on your computer.

Click

Malware protection

In this example the antivirus program ⬤ avast! antivirus is used:

The antispyware program ▦ Windows Defender is also active:

➡ **Please note:**

If you work without a good antivirus program, your PC and the PCs of the people you are in contact with are seriously at risk. Using online banking is also not safe, leading to financial risks as well.

Automatic updates are essential for an antivirus program. You can usually obtain a subscription for a year or longer to do this. When that period has elapsed you will need to pay again to continue the subscription. If you do not do that, your program will quickly become outdated and is no longer safe.

💡 Tip

No antivirus program yet?

If you did not install an antivirus program on your computer, or your subscription has expired, you can go to the website of some well-known manufacturers like this:

🖱️ **Click** Find a program

The website *Windows Vista Security Software Providers* is now open. Here you can download free trial versions of antivirus programs that are compatible with *Windows Vista. Compatible* means that the program will definitely work in *Windows Vista.* The length of the free trial period depends on the supplier and usually varies between thirty and ninety days.

👉 **Click a program name**

👉 **Follow the instructions for downloading and installing the program**

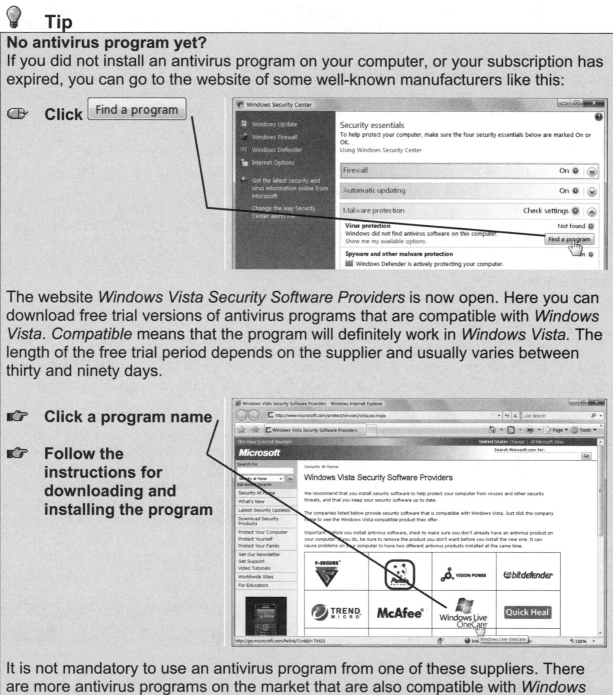

It is not mandatory to use an antivirus program from one of these suppliers. There are more antivirus programs on the market that are also compatible with *Windows Vista*. Other manufacturers will also offer a free trial period. Other well-known manufacturers that are not mentioned on the *Windows Vista Security Providers* website are:

- Norman: www.norman.com
- Avast: www.avast.com

Be sure to check the service pages of your Internet Service Provider. Some ISPs offer free downloads of well-known antivirus programs as part of your subscription.

7.15 Windows Defender

Most Internet users will occasionally take advantage of one or more of the many free programs offered on the Internet. However, many people do not realize that some of these applications can contain components that gather information about users and send the information to the software's creators, for example about the websites you visit.
It is even more annoying when settings on your computer are changed, like a different home page in your Internet browser or the insertion of an extra toolbar. Programs that do these kinds of things are called *spyware*.

Windows Defender is a program from *Microsoft* that is packaged with *Windows Vista*. You can use it to find and remove known spyware from your PC. Its continuous protection prevents the unnoticed installation of spyware on your computer while you surf the Internet.

➡ **Please note:**

Windows Defender does **not** protect your computer against viruses!
There is no antivirus program packaged with *Windows Vista*. This means you have to purchase and install one yourself. In the previous sections you can read more about antivirus programs.

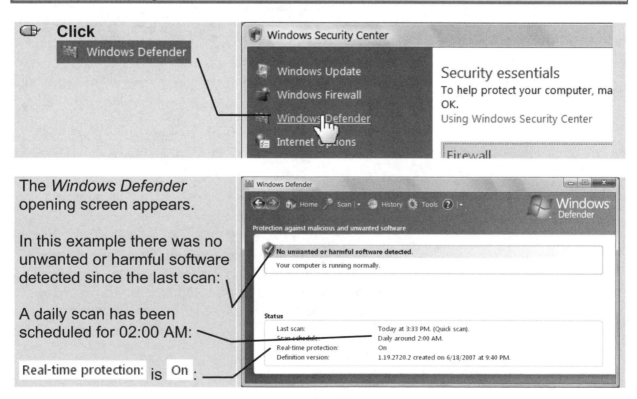

☞ **Click** Windows Defender

The *Windows Defender* opening screen appears.

In this example there was no unwanted or harmful software detected since the last scan:

A daily scan has been scheduled for 02:00 AM:

Real-time protection: is On :

The real-time protection will alert you as soon as spyware attempts to install itself on your computer. *Windows Defender* works closely together with *Windows Update*: as soon as there are new spyware definitions available they are downloaded and installed. Because the program is constantly updated, it works with the latest known information. By default an extra check is made before a scan (automatic or manual) is performed.

You can take a look at the *Windows Defender* settings to verify this:

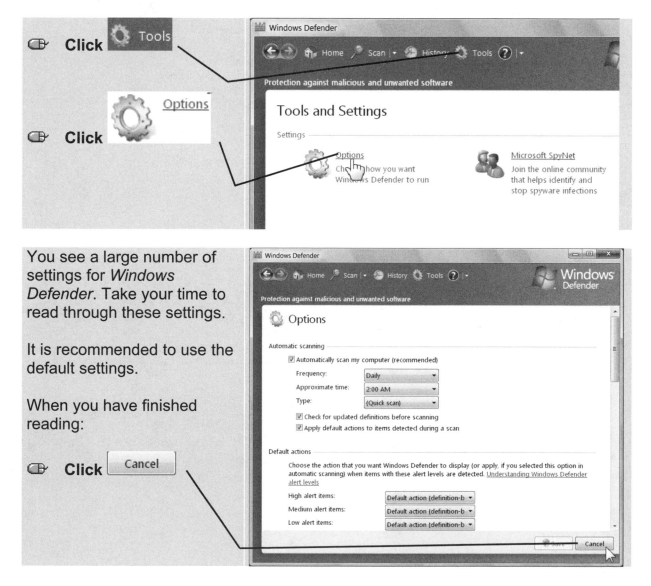

Click Tools

Click Options

You see a large number of settings for *Windows Defender*. Take your time to read through these settings.

It is recommended to use the default settings.

When you have finished reading:

Click Cancel

💡 Tip

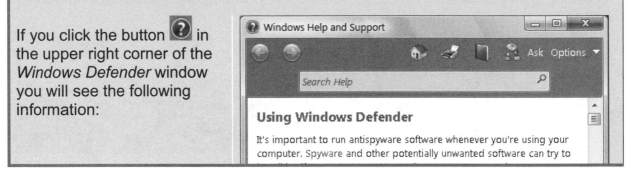

Help and Support
In *Windows Help and Support* you will find more information about spyware and using *Windows Defender*.

If you click the button 🔘 in the upper right corner of the *Windows Defender* window you will see the following information:

In *Windows Defender* you can choose between three scan types:

- Quick Scan : only scans locations where spyware is most likely to be found.
- Full Scan : scans all files and folders on your computer.
- Custom Scan... : only scans the folders you specify.

You can start a quick scan like this:

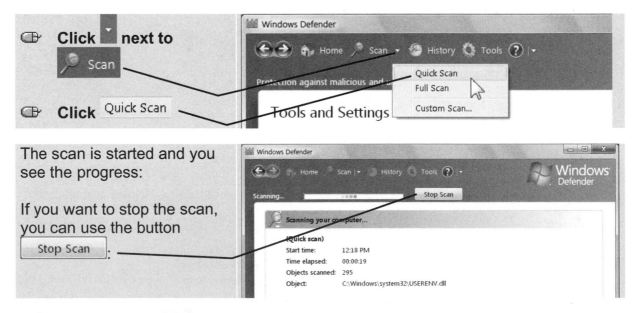

☞ **Click** 🔽 **next to** 🔍 Scan

☞ **Click** Quick Scan

The scan is started and you see the progress:

If you want to stop the scan, you can use the button Stop Scan :

A full scan can take fifteen to thirty minutes, depending on the speed of your computer and the number of files. The quick scan takes a lot less time.
If nothing is found, you see this message:

🛡️ **No unwanted or harmful software detected.**

Your computer is running normally.

If something is found, you will see a message like the one in this example:

An item was found with alert level `Severe` :

Windows Defender advises to remove the item:

In this part of the window you can read detailed information about the item that was found:

In addition to `Remove` you have three other options:

- `Ignore` : select this option if you are certain you want to keep the item.
- `Quarantine` : select this option if you are not sure about an item. The item will be placed in a folder where it can do no harm. If it turns out to be something you need, you can put it back where it belongs.
- `Always allow` : select this option if you are familiar with the item and you are sure you want to keep it. The item will no longer be shown in future scans.

If more than one item was found on your computer, you can select a different action for each separate item. With the button `Apply Actions` you can carry out the selected actions at once. If you would rather just remove all items in one go, you can use the button `Remove All`.

When you have removed the item for example, you see this:

Name	Alert level	Action	Status
🛡 Tool:Win32/EICAR_Test_...	Severe	Remove	Succeeded

☞ **Close the *Windows Defender* window** 𝒶𝓁⁹

☞ **Close the *Windows Security Center* window** 𝒶𝓁⁹

7.16 The Backup and Restore Center

Making regular backups (copies) of your files is essential for your business. Try to think of what you may lose if your PC would crash or become infected by a virus. This might be all of your important business and financial records, correspondence, et cetera.

Windows Vista has a central location where you can create backups: the *Backup and Restore Center*. Here you can setup what kind of backup you want to create, and the interval for when it should be done.
You open the *Backup and Restore Center* like this:

☞ **Open the *Control Panel* ℓℓ³⁶**

⇨ **Please note:**

To be able to do the exercises in this chapter you need one or more recordable CDs or DVDs. You can also use an external hard disk. This can be connected to the USB port of your computer.

☞ **Click**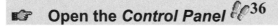

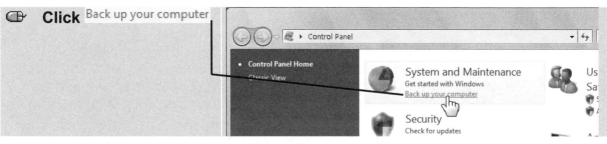

In this example you see the window *Backup and Restore Center* of *Windows Vista Home Premium*:

In *Windows Vista Home Basic* you see a similar window.

If you have you created a backup previously, the date of the last backup will be displayed here:

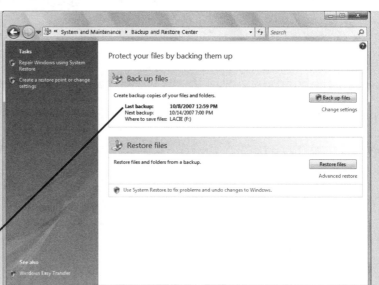

If you have *Windows Vista Ultimate*, you see this window which shows extra features for creating and restoring a *Complete PC Backup*:

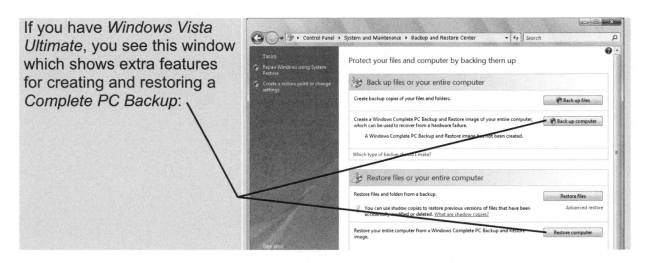

7.17 Windows Complete PC Backup

Windows Vista Ultimate contains the program *Windows Complete PC Backup*. You can use this program to create a complete backup of your computer.

⇨ Please note:

Do you have *Vista Home Basic* or *Vista Home Premium*? Then you can just read through this section.

Windows Complete PC Backup creates a backup image, which contains copies of your programs, system settings, and files. You can use this backup image to restore the contents of your computer if your hard disk crashes or your computer suddenly stops working. A complete backup is also known as a *recovery CD*.

To be able to create a *Windows Complete PC Backup* image, your hard disk must be formatted to use the NTFS File System. In *Windows Help and Support* you can find more information on this subject.

☞ Click
🛡 Back up computer

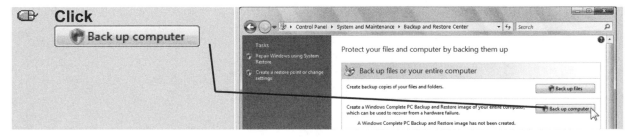

Your screen goes dark. You see the window *User Account Control* where you need to give your permission to continue.

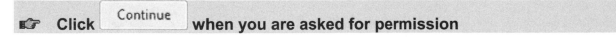

☞ Click Continue **when you are asked for permission**

Then you see the next window:

In this window you can choose where you want to save the backup: on a (external) hard disk or DVD.

Please note: if you save the backup to an external hard disk, that disk must also be formatted to use the NTFS file system. If that is not the case, you will see a warning that the disk is not a valid location for a backup.

In this example the backup is saved to DVD:

When you have made your choice:

☞ **Click** Next

Windows Complete PC Backup

Where do you want to save the backup?

Windows Complete PC Backup creates a backup copy of your entire computer, including programs, system settings, and files. Your entire computer can be restored using the Windows Recovery Environment.

○ On a hard disk

Files (D:)

● On one or more DVDs

DVD RW Drive (E:)

Next   Cancel

You see the disks in your computer that can be included in the backup. In this example there are two. You may see a different list on your PC or another window.

☞ **Click the disk(s) you want to include in the backup**

☞ **Click** Next

Windows Complete PC Backup

Which disks do you want to include in the backup?

The disk that Windows is installed on will always be included in the backup. You cannot include the disk that you are saving the backup to. We recommend including all of the disks that contain Windows files, programs, and personal data.

Your backups are being saved on DVD RW Drive (E:).

Disk	Total size	Used space
☑ Local Disk (C:) (System)	60.0 GB	26.0 GB
☑ Files (D:)	172.9 GB	6.8 GB

Next   Cancel

In the next window you see how many DVDs you need for the complete backup. In the example the backup will take five to nine DVDs:

If you want to start creating the backup, click

Start backup :

If you want to cancel the backup, click Cancel :

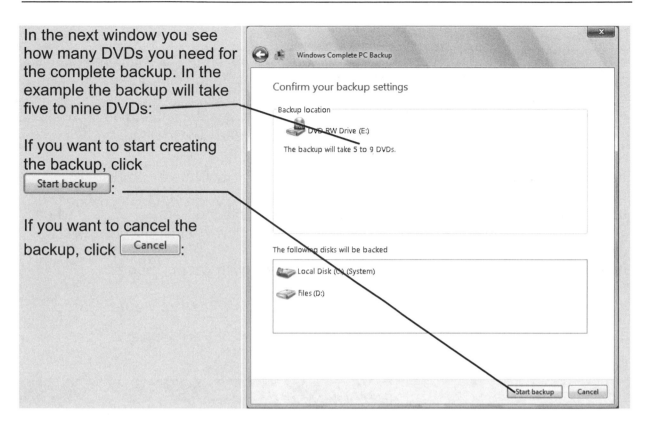

When you start the backup, a number of windows will guide you through this procedure. Follow the instructions in each window. At the end of the procedure you will have a number of DVDs or an external hard disk with a complete backup of your current system. Be sure to store this backup in a secure place.

If you ever need to restore the backup you can start the procedure from the *Backup and Restore Center*.

You can use the button

Restore computer :

You will be guided through the procedure by a number of windows. Follow the instructions in each window.

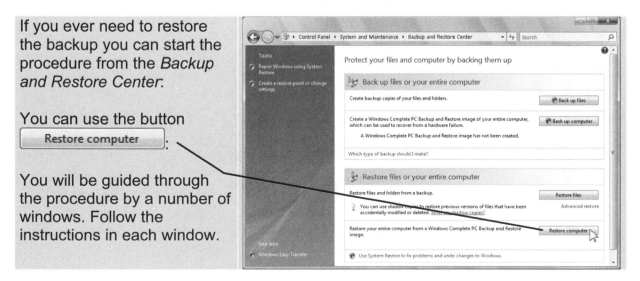

⇨ **Please note:**

When you restore your computer from a *Windows Complete PC Backup* image, it is a complete restoration. You cannot select individual items to restore, and all of your current programs, system settings, and files will be replaced.
It is important to make regular backups to secure your recent work and your business administration, etcetera. In the next sections you can read how to do that.

Windows Vista Home Basic and *Home Premium* do not facilitate a complete PC backup. However in some cases this is done automatically using a separate program that has been added by the computer manufacturer. This program will appear when you start the computer for the first time. In that case follow the instructions in each window and store the backup in a secure place.
If necessary, refer to the documentation you received with your computer.

☞ **Close all windows until you see the *Backup and Restore Center* window again** 𝓵𝓵⁹

7.18 Backing Up Files

In the *Backup and Restore Center* of *Vista* you can create a backup of your own files. Backing up the files that are important to you helps to protect them from being permanently lost or changed in the event of accidental deletion, a short circuit, fire, theft, or a software or hardware failure. If any of those things occur and your files are backed up, you can easily restore those files.
You see the window *Backup and Restore Center*:

You are going to create a file backup:

☞ **Click** [🔲 Back up files]

HELP! I see an error message.

Do you have a laptop or notebook and you see this window?

You cannot create a backup when your laptop is running on battery power. This is to prevent problems and unreliable backups when the battery runs out during the backup process.

☞ **Click** ⬜ OK

☞ **Plug in your laptop**

☞ **Open the window** *Backup and Restore Center* ℰℰ³⁸

☞ **Click** 🛡 Back up files

Your screen goes dark. You see the window *User Account Control* where you need to give your permission to continue.

☞ **Click** Continue

In this window you can choose the location where you want to save the backup:

In this example a DVD drive is selected.

☞ **Click** ▼

☞ **Click the CD or DVD drive you want to use**

☞ **Click** Next

Which location?

Deciding on which location to save your backup depends on the setup of your computer. Take the following into account:

- It is not possible to save the backup to the same drive or disk you are trying to back up. It is also not possible to save the backup to the disk where *Windows Vista* is installed. That makes sense because if problems arise, you would not be able to use your original files or your backup.

- You can save a backup to another disk/drive of your computer.

- If the hard disk is divided into several partitions, it is possible to back up to another partition. It is not advisable to use this as your only backup, because it is still the same hard disk. If problems do arise you will be unable to use this disk. Combine this method with regular backups to another location.

- You cannot back up files to a USB stick. USB sticks are meant for temporary storage and are not suitable for backups.

- Backing up files to diskettes or tape drives is also not possible.

The most suitable storage media for backups are external hard disks, CDs or DVDs.

If you have multiple hard disks in your computer, you see this window:

Here you see the disks in the computer that can be included in the backup. In this example there are two. You may see a different list on your computer.

☞ **Click the disk(s) you want to include in the backup**

☞ **Click** [Next]

Back Up Files

Which disks do you want to include in the backup?

The disk that Windows is installed on will always be included in the backup. You cannot include the disk that you are saving the backup to. We recommend including all of the disks that contain Windows files, programs, and personal data.

Your backups are being saved on DVD RW Drive (E:).

Disk	Total size	Used space
☑ Local Disk (C:) (System)	60.0 GB	26.0 GB
☑ Files (D:)	172.9 GB	6.8 GB

[Next] [Cancel]

In the next window you can select which types of files to be included in the backup, regardless of where they are located on the hard disk.
To get more information about a file type that can be included in the backup, you point at the file type:

Point to Music

You see a description of the files that belong to this file type:

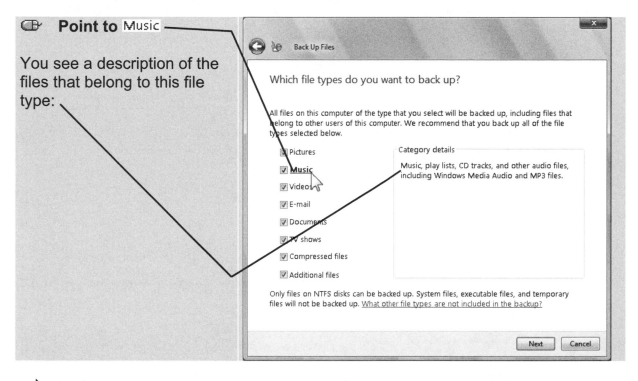

Please note:

In order to create a backup of your business files and administration it is important to select *E-mail*, *Documents* and *Additional files.* Many administrative programs also have their own backup facilities. Use those to create periodic backups of that program. Often these backups have additional possibilities to restore parts of the administration for example.

You may decide not to back up certain categories. Perhaps you are already using another method to back up certain types of files, or maybe the files are no longer important to you.

For example, you decide not to include recorded TV shows in the backup:

☞ **Click** TV shows

The check mark ☑ next to TV shows has disappeared.

☞ **Click** Next

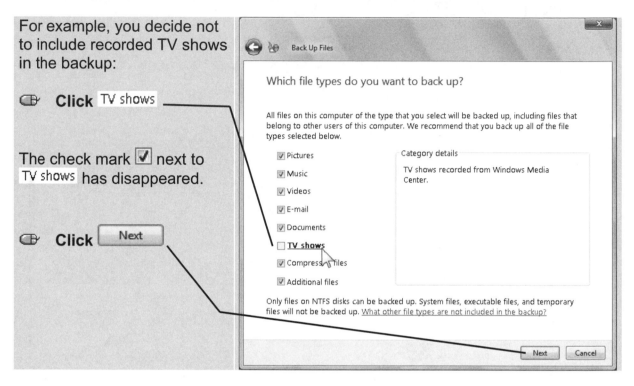

Backups should be created on a regular basis. In the next window you can select how often you want to create a backup. Deciding on how much time should elapse between backups depends on how important the files are and how often they change.

⇨ **Please note:**

Automatic backups are not available in *Windows Vista Home Basic*. The next window will not be shown in this edition. You will have to make the backup yourself using the *Backup and Restore Center*. *Windows Vista* will frequently remind you to create a backup.

You see the current settings:

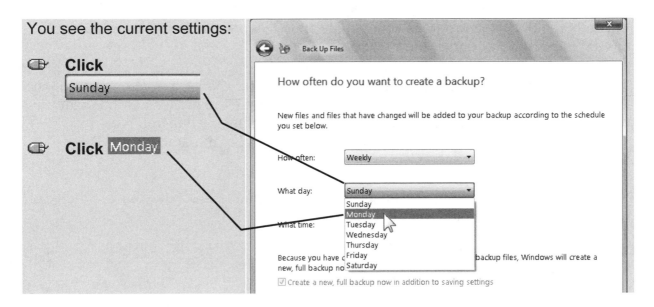

👆 **Click**
Sunday

👆 **Click** Monday

The backup will be created weekly on Mondays, at the time you specify. If the computer is not turned on at that time, the backup procedure will continue as soon as you turn on your computer.

A window will appear where you are asked to insert the CD or DVD that is to be used for the backup. If you have decided to use an external hard disk, the backup will be created automatically when the disk is connected to the computer.

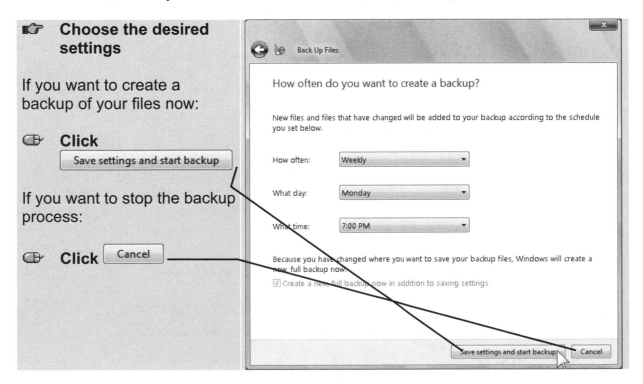

👉 **Choose the desired settings**

If you want to create a backup of your files now:

👆 **Click**
Save settings and start backup

If you want to stop the backup process:

👆 **Click** Cancel

While the backup is in progress you can continue to work on the computer. Do not turn off the computer during the backup procedure.

If it is necessary to interrupt the backup process, click ⟨Stop backup⟩. When you open the *Backup and Restore Center* again, you can continue the process at the point where it was interrupted the last time. This will also happen when you have to interrupt the backup process because you have run out of the amount of CDs or DVDs necessary to save the files.

When you start the backup, you will be guided through the procedure by a number of windows. Follow the instructions in each window.

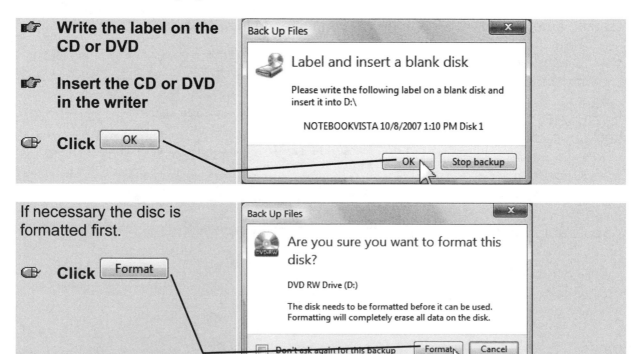

You see that the backup is being prepared:	**Back Up Files** [≈] [×] Preparing to backup

After a short while you are asked to insert a disc in your CD or DVD writer. In this window you see the label you should write on the disc. Always use a special CD marker to avoid damaging the disc.

☞ **Write the label on the CD or DVD**

☞ **Insert the CD or DVD in the writer**

☞ **Click** ⟨OK⟩

Back Up Files
Label and insert a blank disk
Please write the following label on a blank disk and insert it into D:\

NOTEBOOKVISTA 10/8/2007 1:10 PM Disk 1

⟨OK⟩ ⟨Stop backup⟩

If necessary the disc is formatted first.

☞ **Click** ⟨Format⟩

Back Up Files
Are you sure you want to format this disk?

DVD RW Drive (D:)

The disk needs to be formatted before it can be used. Formatting will completely erase all data on the disk.

☐ Don't ask again for this backup   ⟨Format⟩ ⟨Cancel⟩

⇨ **Please note:**

When the disc is formatted, all data on the disc is erased.

During the formatting process you see this window:

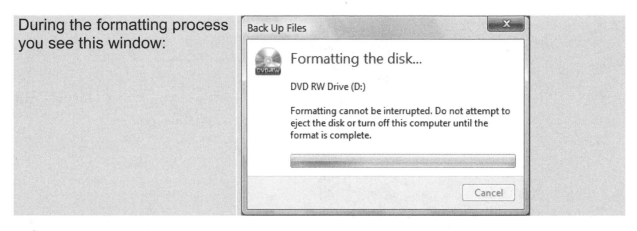

Back Up Files

Formatting the disk...

DVD RW Drive (D:)

Formatting cannot be interrupted. Do not attempt to eject the disk or turn off this computer until the format is complete.

Cancel

⇨ **Please note:**

As stated in the previous window, you cannot interrupt the formatting process!

When the disc is formatted, the backup starts automatically. You can follow the progress in this window:

Back Up Files

Creating a shadow copy

⇨ **Please note:**

If you need more discs for your backup, the backup program will ask you to insert the next disc. Follow the instructions in the window and write the correct label on each disc. This way you will be able to restore the backup in the right order later.

When the backup is finished, you see the status window:

You see when the last backup was made and (possibly) when the next one will be made:

☞ **Click** ☒

Backup Status and Configuration

Back Up Files

Restore Files

Automatic file backup is turned on

Windows will scan your computer for new and updated files and add them to your backup based on the schedule you set.

What file types are not included in the backup?

Backup status

ⓘ The last file backup was successful.

Backup location: DVD RW Drive (D:)

Last successful backup: 10/8/2007 1:23 PM
Next backup: 10/8/2007 7:00 PM

 Back up now
   Scan for new or updated files and add them to your backup.

 Change backup settings
   Adjust your current backup settings or start a new, full backup.

Automatic backup is currently   [Turn off]
on

You see the *Backup and Restore Center* again:

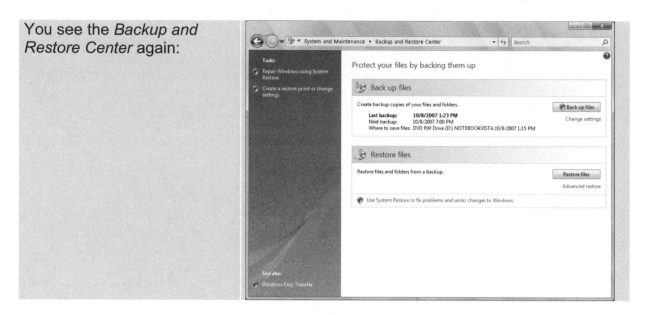

💡 Tip

If you want to change the backup schedule or the settings for file types to be included in the backup, click `Change settings` in this window.

7.19 Incremental Backup

The first time you start the backup procedure a new, full backup is created. The next time you can choose to limit the backup to include only those files that have been modified or added since the last backup. This is called an incremental backup and saves a lot of time and disk space.

⇨ Please note:

A full backup is **not** the same as the *Windows Complete PC Backup* that was described in *section 7.17 Windows Complete PC Backup*. In a full backup, *Windows* and all programs and settings are not backed up.

You can also create an incremental backup yourself, for example when important data has changed on your computer.
The settings for file types that are included in the backup can remain unchanged.
Start by doing the following:

☞ **If necessary, open the *Backup and Restore Center* ℰℰ³⁸**

Click [🗁 Back up files]

The screen goes dark and you need to give your permission to continue.

Click [Continue]

If you have not yet inserted a disc for your backup in the writer, *Windows Vista* will ask you to do that now.

During the backup process you see a small window just above the notification area on the right side of the taskbar:

🗁 File backup is running ✕
Click to view backup progress.

1:33 PM

✶ HELP! I do not have enough discs.

If you do not have enough discs to complete the backup, you can interrupt the backup process and continue later.

During this backup you can also continue working. Because this is not a full backup, it can be done very quickly.

When the backup has completed, you see this message in the notification area:

🗁 File backup has completed successfully ✕
Click to close this balloon.

1:35 PM

⇨ Please note:

When you use incremental backups, you also need to keep the discs with the previous backups. Together these discs are a full backup. Do not throw away or overwrite these discs, otherwise you will no longer have a complete backup.

♀ Tip

After a few incremental backups the number of discs for the backup may have become very large. Restoring the backup will become more difficult, since you have to restore parts of different discs.

In that case it is advisable to create a new full backup periodically and use that to do incremental backups again. Do not use the current discs; you may need them if creating the new backup goes wrong.

Also read *section 7.22 New Full Backup* and in the *Background Information* of this chapter the text called *Grandfather – father – son backups*.

7.20 Restoring a Backup

Whenever you need to restore a backup you use the *Backup and Restore Center*. It is best to just read through this section. Do not follow these actions unless you really want to restore a backup, for example after data loss.

☞ **If necessary, open the *Backup and Restore Center*** 📚^{38}

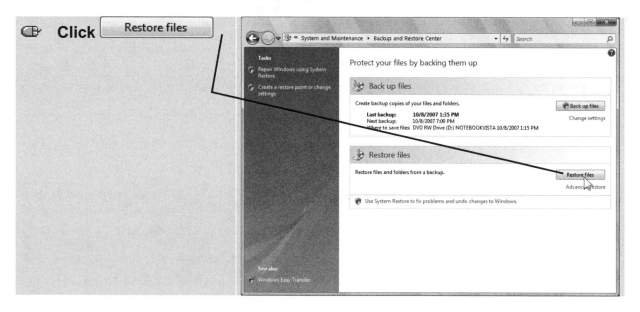

Usually you want to restore the most recent backup. If you want to solve a problem that was present for a longer period, it may be necessary to restore an older backup. This means you will lose the changes that you have made after that backup was made.

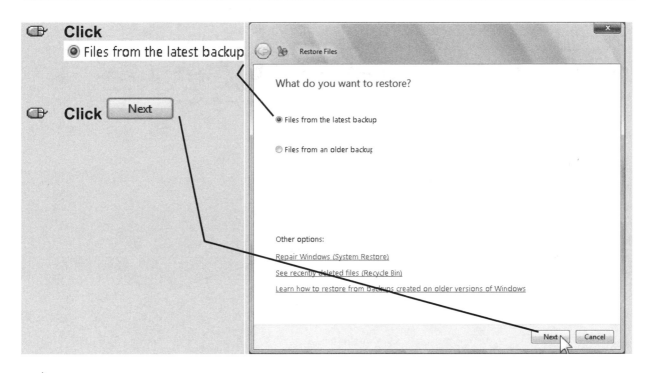

Click ◉ Files from the latest backup

Click Next

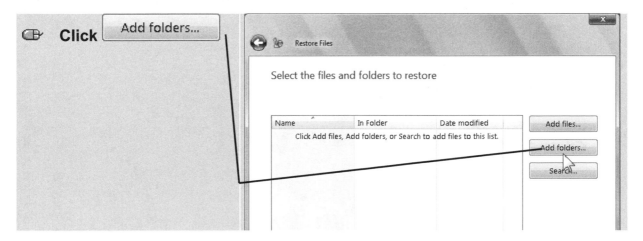

⇨ **Please note:**

The backup program only restores files, not programs. In order to repair or reinstall a program you will need the installation discs for that program.

Now you can choose which files or folders you want to restore. To restore your music files, you do the following:

Click Add folders...

☞ **Click** Music

☞ **Click** Add

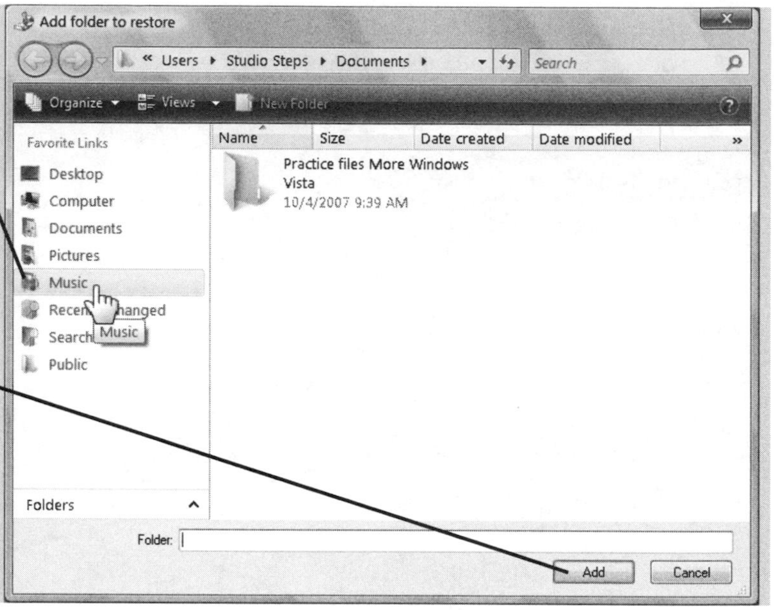

💡 Tip

If you want to restore all the files on a disk, click Computer and then click the disk you want to restore, for example C: .

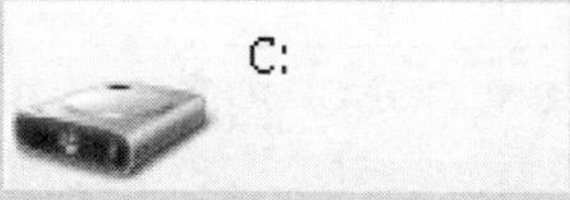

Repeat these actions if you want to restore more disks. Keep in mind that only data files are restored, not program files or parts of *Windows Vista*.

The folder Music has been added and will be restored:

☞ **Repeat these steps for each folder you want to restore**

☞ **Click** Next

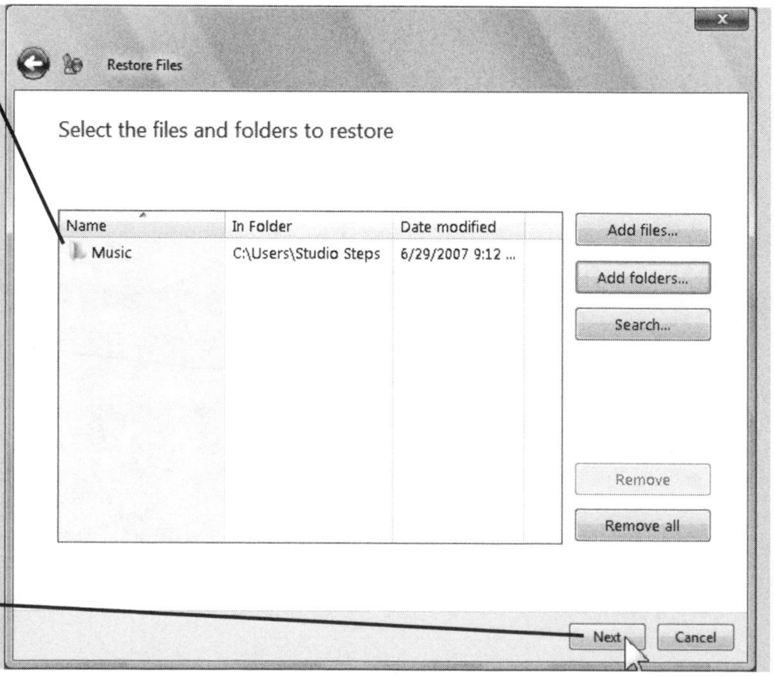

In most cases, the files you restore have to replace the original files on the disk. However, it is possible to restore the files to another location, for example when the original hard disk is damaged.

In this example the files are restored to the original location:

☞ **Click** Start restore

Restore Files

Where do you want to save the restored files?

◉ In the original location

○ In the following location:

[   ] Browse...

☐ Restore the files to their original subfolders
☐ Create a subfolder for the drive letter

Start restore   Cancel

⇨ **Please note:**

If your backup consists of more than one disc, you will be prompted to insert the other discs during the procedure. Make sure to insert the correct disc. You will see the label of the necessary disc in the window.

When the restore process has completed, you see this window:

☞ **Click** Finish

Restore Files

Successfully restored files

Finish

Now you see the *Backup and Restore Center* again.

✖ HELP! Restoring the files went very quickly.

The length of the restoration process depends on the amount of data. If it went very quickly, it does not mean that nothing has happened. There were probably very few music files that had to be restored.

You will see that the restoration process takes longer next time, for example when you restore photo or video files.

7.21 Automatic File Backup

When you have set an automatic file backup for a specific time, *Windows Vista* will create the backup automatically if the computer is on at that time. If the computer is not on at that time, the backup will be created as soon as the computer is turned on.

⇨ Please note:

Just read through this section, so you will know what to do when the automatic file backup starts.

✖ HELP! I have lost a disc.

If you have lost one or more backup discs, the backup is no longer usable. In that case you will need to create a new full backup.

As soon as *Windows Vista* wants to create an automatic file backup, you are notified in the lower right corner of your desktop:

If you want to create the backup:

☞ **Click the notification**

You see this window:

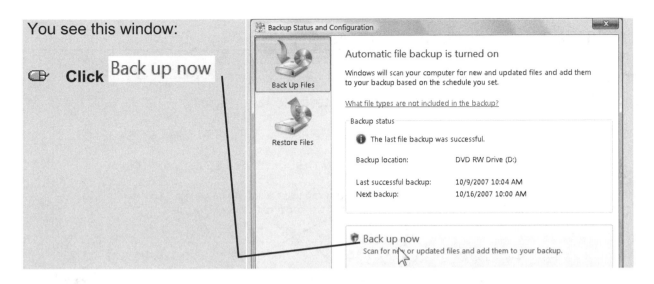

➾ **Click** Back up now

💡 **Tip**

You can still change the settings for your backup, for example the file types to include in the backup. To do so, click Change backup settings .

The screen goes dark and you need to give your permission to continue:

➾ **Click** Continue

Because the necessary backup disc is probably not in the writer yet, you are asked to insert the (first) backup disc:

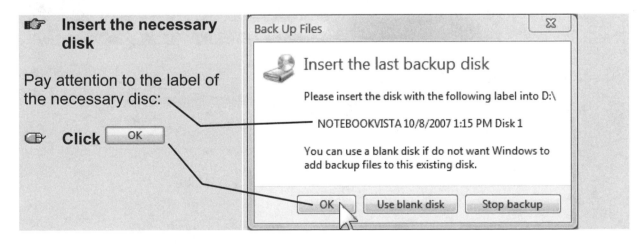

☞ **Insert the necessary disk**

Pay attention to the label of the necessary disc:

➾ **Click** OK

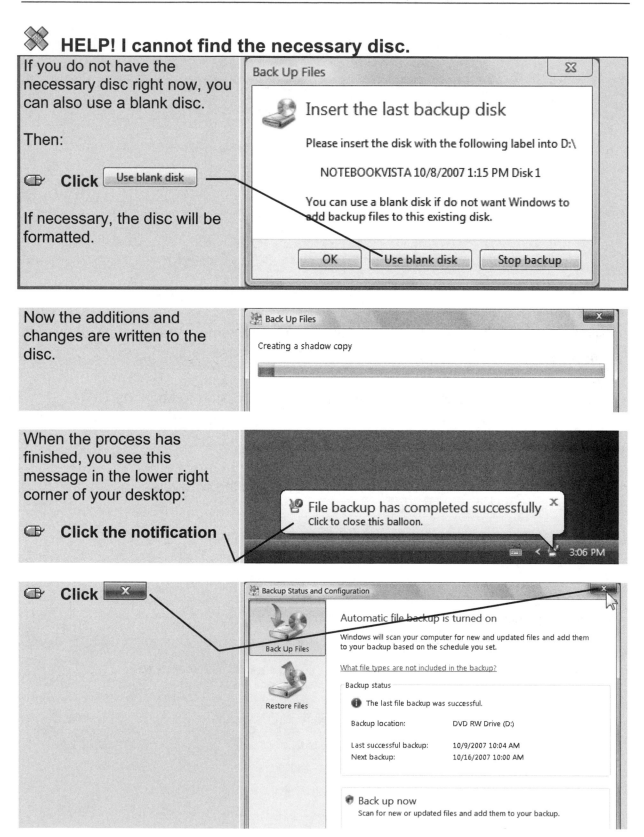

✖ HELP! I cannot find the necessary disc.

If you do not have the necessary disc right now, you can also use a blank disc.

Then:

☞ **Click** `Use blank disk`

If necessary, the disc will be formatted.

Back Up Files ⊠

💿 Insert the last backup disk

Please insert the disk with the following label into D:\

NOTEBOOKVISTA 10/8/2007 1:15 PM Disk 1

You can use a blank disk if do not want Windows to add backup files to this existing disk.

[OK]   [Use blank disk]   [Stop backup]

Now the additions and changes are written to the disc.

Back Up Files   ✕

Creating a shadow copy

When the process has finished, you see this message in the lower right corner of your desktop:

☞ **Click the notification**

📝 File backup has completed successfully ✕
Click to close this balloon.

⌨ < 3:06 PM

☞ **Click** ✕

Backup Status and Configuration   ✕

Automatic file backup is turned on

Windows will scan your computer for new and updated files and add them to your backup based on the schedule you set.

What file types are not included in the backup?

Back Up Files

Backup status

ℹ The last file backup was successful.

Backup location: DVD RW Drive (D:)

Last successful backup: 10/9/2007 10:04 AM
Next backup: 10/16/2007 10:00 AM

Restore Files

🔘 Back up now
Scan for new or updated files and add them to your backup.

7.22 New Full Backup

To avoid the need of having to restore a large number of backup discs (the full backup and the incremental backups) it is advisable to create a full backup on a regular basis, for example monthly. When you create a new, full backup you have a new, more recent version.

⇨ **Please note:**

Do not use your old backup discs yet, use other discs to create the new full backup instead. If something goes wrong when the new backup is made, you may need your previous backup. Do not reuse your old discs until the new backup is completed successfully.
Also read *Grandfather – father –son backups* in the *Background Information* at the end of this chapter.

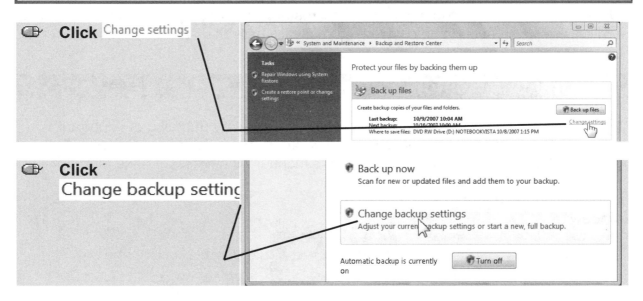

⊨ **Click** Change settings

⊨ **Click**
     Change backup setting

Your screen goes dark and you need to give your permission to continue:

⊨ **Click** Continue

☞ **Close the window** *Backup Status and Configuration* ℓℓ⁹

💡 **Tip**

If you do not want to create automatic full backups anymore, click ⎡ 🕐 Turn off ⎤.

This will start the wizard you were introduced to in *section 7.18 Backing Up Files*. The settings you enter in this wizard replace your previous settings.

7.23 System Restore

Backing up your files helps to protect them from being lost or changed in the event of computer problems or accidental deletion. Sometimes, the installation of a program or a driver can cause an unexpected change to your computer or cause *Windows* to behave unpredictably. In that case your files are still intact, but *Windows* is not reliable anymore.

Restoring a backup of your files does not solve that problem. Restoring a complete PC backup or recovery CD will make your computer work properly again, but you will lose all of your personal files and any programs that were recently installed.

System Restore creates automatic restore points to help you restore your computer's system files to an earlier point in time. These restore points contain information about registry settings and other system information that *Windows* uses. When *Windows Vista* no longer works properly, you can try restoring your computer's system to an earlier date when everything did work correctly. Usually this solves the problems.

7.24 Creating Restore Points

Windows Vista creates automatic restore points every day and also at important moments, for example, when you install new programs or devices. At crucial moments you can also create restore points manually if necessary. Like this:

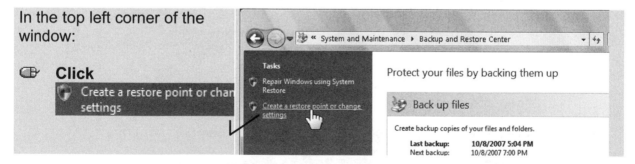

In the top left corner of the window:

☞ **Click** Create a restore point or change settings

Your screen goes dark and you need to give your permission to continue.

☞ **Click** Continue

You see when the last restore point was created:

👆 **Click**
🖳 Local Disk (C:) (System)

Usually this is the disk where *Vista* is installed.

👆 **Click** Create...

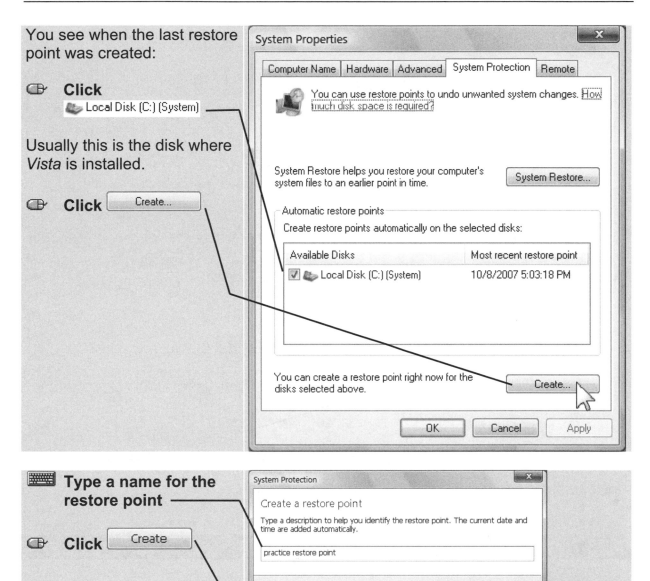

⌨️ **Type a name for the restore point**

👆 **Click** Create

💡 **Tip**

Include a date or another clear description in the name of the restore point. That way you know when a restore point was created if you want to restore it.

While the restore point is created you see this window:

When the restore point is created:

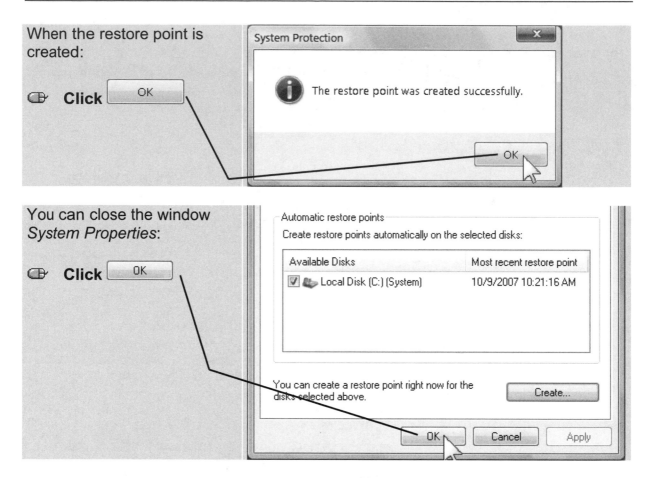

☞ **Click** OK

You can close the window *System Properties*:

☞ **Click** OK

You see the window *Backup and Restore Center* again.

7.25 Restoring Restore Points

In the *Backup and Restore Center* you can repair *Windows* using *System Restore*.

⇨ **Please note:**

When you use *System Restore* your computer will be restarted. Make sure to close all your programs and save your work before you start *System Restore*.

☞ **Click**
Repair Windows using System Restore

Your screen goes dark and you need to give your permission to continue.

Click [Continue]

After a few moments the wizard *System Restore* starts:

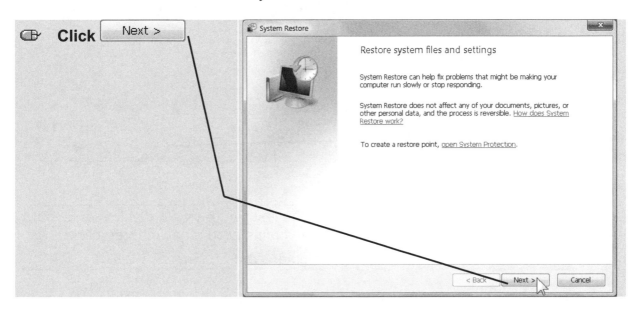

Click [Next >]

HELP! I see another window.

Do you see this window?

Then:

Click
   ● Choose a different restore point

Click [Next >]

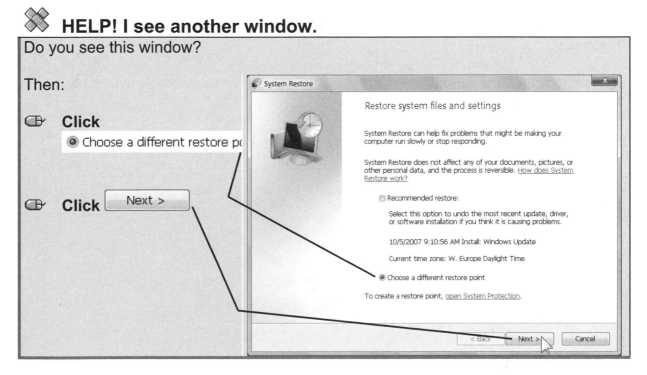

☞ **Click the restore point you want to use** ⎯⎯⎯

☞ **Click** `Next >`

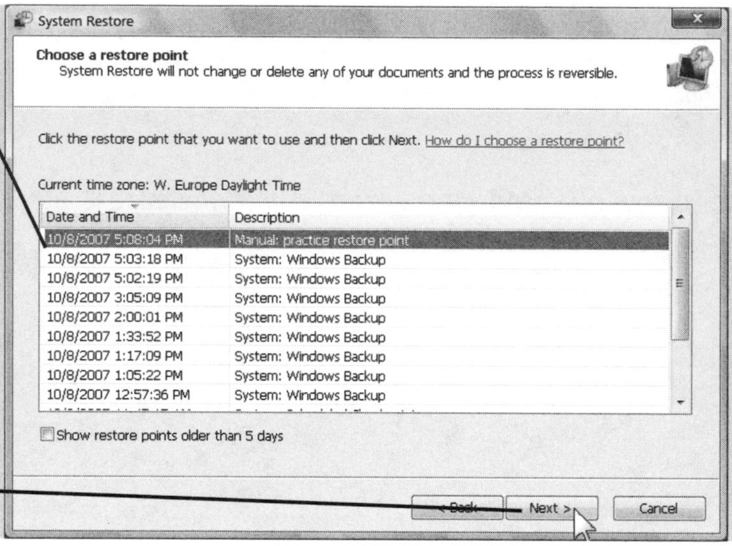

⇨ **Please note:**

> By default, only the restore points created in the last five days are displayed. If your problem started before that, for example after you installed a new printer, click ☐ Show restore points older than 5 days to see the older restore points as well.

If you have several hard disks in your computer, you can select the disks you want to restore in the next window. You always need to restore the disk that contains *Windows Vista*. In most cases that will be the (C:) disk. Restoring any other disk is optional.

In this example there is only one hard disk. In the next window, you will need to confirm your restore point.

☞ **Click** `Finish`

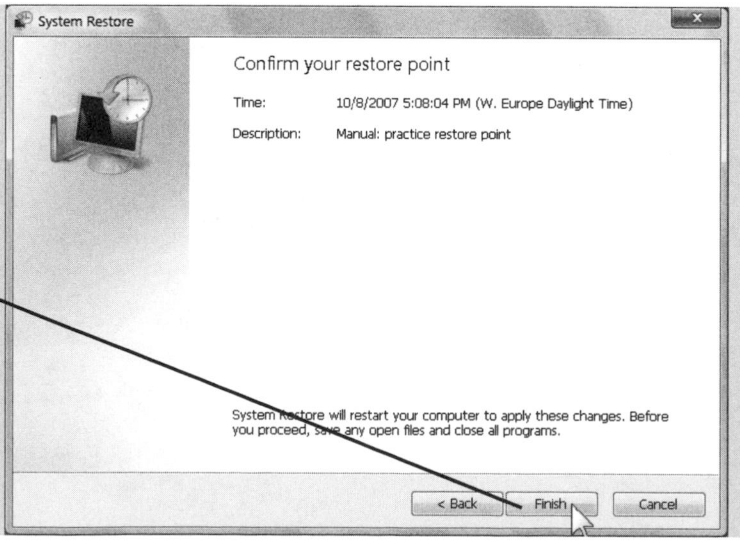

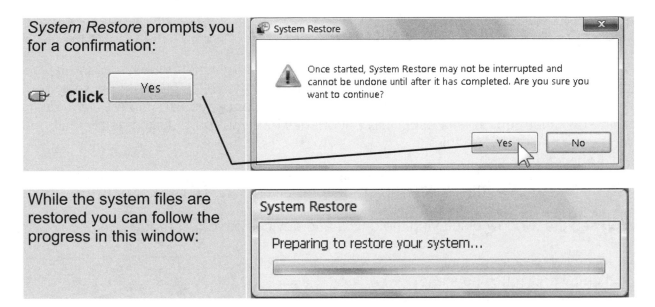

System Restore prompts you for a confirmation:

☞ **Click** Yes

While the system files are restored you can follow the progress in this window:

When *System Restore* has completed, *Windows Vista* is shut down and restarted. When you see the desktop again, you see this message:

☞ **Click** Close

In most cases *Windows* will now function normally again.

7.26 Cleaning Your Hard Disk

When you frequently use your computer, more and more files gradually accumulate on the hard disk. For the most part this happens automatically, for example when you surf the Internet. To improve your computer's performance, you should regularly do some disk cleanup. This is especially important when your hard disk is getting full. You can check that like this:

☞ **Open the *Computer* window** ʕʕ³⁹

You see the window displaying the drives and devices of your computer:

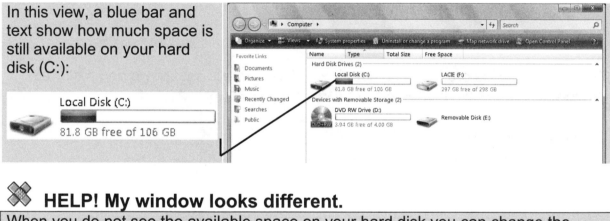

In this view, a blue bar and text show how much space is still available on your hard disk (C:):

Local Disk (C:)
81.8 GB free of 106 GB

✖ HELP! My window looks different.

When you do not see the available space on your hard disk you can change the view of the window:

☞ **Click** ▼ **next to** ▦ Views

☞ **Click** ▦ Tiles

💡 Tip

10% free
A common rule of thumb is that you should keep at least 10% of the disk capacity free, but preferably more. Experience shows that the computer becomes slower when the hard disk is fuller than that. Also, some programs may start causing problems. Many programs use the hard disk for temporary data storage. When there is not enough free space, temporary data cannot be stored and the programs will not function properly.

You can also display the available space on your hard disk like this:

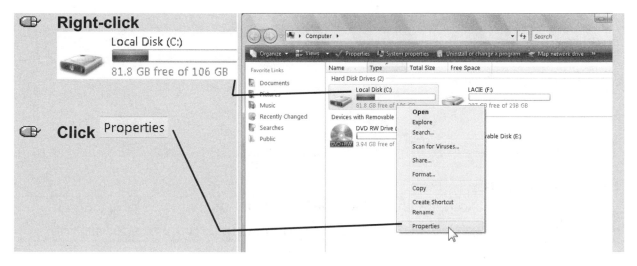

Right-click

Local Disk (C:)

Click Properties

The *Local Disk (C:) Properties* window is opened.

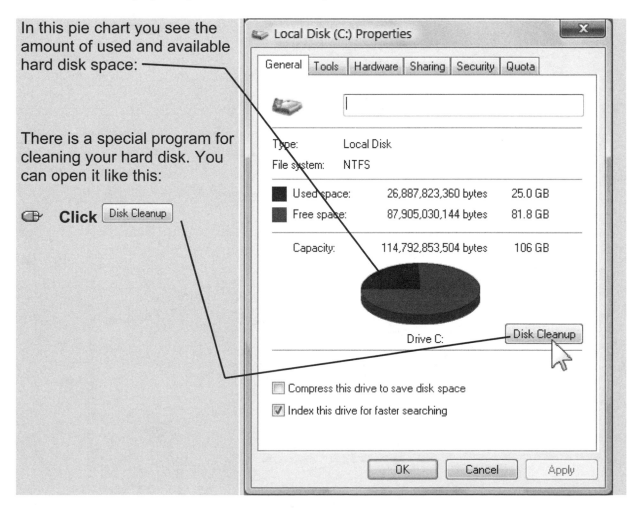

In this pie chart you see the amount of used and available hard disk space:

There is a special program for cleaning your hard disk. You can open it like this:

Click Disk Cleanup

Now *Vista* asks which files you want to clean up.

You choose to clean up your own files only:

☞ **Click**

→ My files only

Disk Cleanup Options   x

🗜 Choose which files to clean up

→ My files only

● Files from all users on this computer

Cancel

⇨ **Please note:**

Disk cleanup may take quite some time if you have not done it for a long time or if the disk is very full. Click Cancel if you want to run disk cleanup at another time.

Now a calculation is made to determine how much space can be freed:

Disk Cleanup   x

🗜 Disk Cleanup is calculating how much space you will be able to free on (C:). This may take a few minutes to complete.

Calculating...

Cancel

Scanning: System error memory dump files

In this window you can choose which file types you want to delete:

If you want to do a full cleanup, check if every line that has a file size displayed is also check marked ☑:

Use the scroll bar to see the other lines as well:

☞ **Click OK**

🗜 Disk Cleanup for (C:)   x

Disk Cleanup

🗜 You can use Disk Cleanup to free up to 1.29 GB of disk space on (C:).

Files to delete:

☐ 🗎 Hibernation File Cleaner	765 MB	▲
☐ 🗎 Debug Dump Files	98.3 MB	▤
☑ 🗎 Recycle Bin	24.6 MB	
☐ 🗎 Setup Log Files	14.2 KB	
☐ 🗎 System error memory dump files	98.3 MB	▼

Total amount of disk space you gain: 24.6 MB

Description

Downloaded Program Files are ActiveX controls and Java applets downloaded automatically from the Internet when you view certain pages. They are temporarily stored in the Downloaded Program Files folder on your hard disk.

View Files

How does Disk Cleanup work?

OK   Cancel

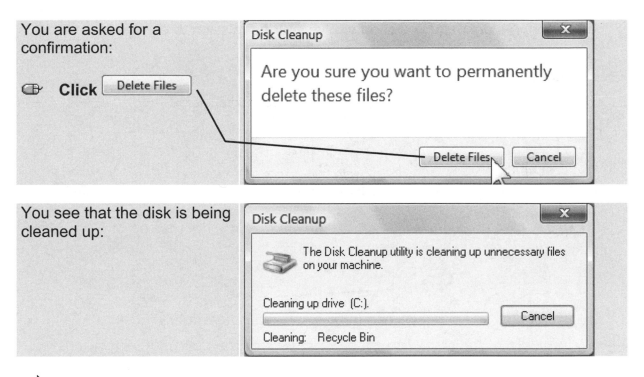

You are asked for a confirmation:

☞ **Click** `Delete Files`

Disk Cleanup

Are you sure you want to permanently delete these files?

`Delete Files`　`Cancel`

You see that the disk is being cleaned up:

Disk Cleanup

The Disk Cleanup utility is cleaning up unnecessary files on your machine.

Cleaning up drive (C:).

`Cancel`

Cleaning:　Recycle Bin

⇨ **Please note:**

If your computer contains more hard disks or if your hard disk is divided into multiple partitions, you need to perform these tasks for each disk or partition separately.

7.27 Error Checking

The hard disk is one of the few mechanical parts of the computer. Most other parts are electronic. Normal use causes wear and tear on the hard disk or makes it less reliable. You can use *Error Checking* to check the quality of the hard disk, mark unreliable parts and restore previously stored data there if possible.

☞ **Click the** `Tools` **tab**

☞ **Click** `Check Now...`

Local Disk (C:) Properties

Security | Previous Versions | Quota
General | Tools | Hardware | Sharing

Error-checking

This option will check the volume for errors.

`Check Now...`

Defragmentation

This option will defragment files on the volume.

Your screen goes dark and you need to give your permission to continue:

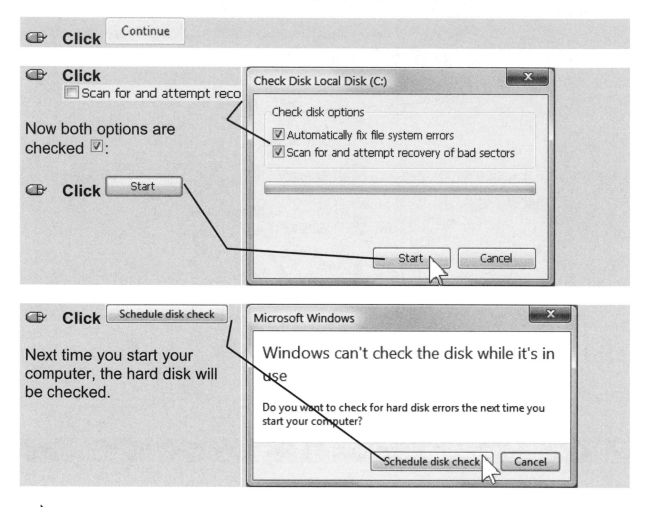

👆 **Click** | Continue |

👆 **Click**
  ☐ Scan for and attempt reco

Now both options are
checked ☑:

👆 **Click** | Start |

Check Disk Local Disk (C:)

Check disk options
☑ Automatically fix file system errors
☑ Scan for and attempt recovery of bad sectors

| Start | | Cancel |

👆 **Click** | Schedule disk check |

Next time you start your
computer, the hard disk will
be checked.

Microsoft Windows

Windows can't check the disk while it's in
use

Do you want to check for hard disk errors the next time you
start your computer?

| Schedule disk check | | Cancel |

⇨ **Please note:**

It is advisable to check your hard disk before continuing with the next steps. Shut
down your computer and start it again. After error checking you can continue with
the next section.

7.28 Defragmenting Your Hard Disk

Over time, the files on the hard disk become fragmented, and your computer slows
down as it has to look in many different places to find parts of a file. You can solve
this problem by defragmenting your hard disk. *Disk Defragmenter* is a tool that
rearranges the data on your hard disk and puts fragmented files back together so
your computer can run more efficiently. You start the disk defragmentation like this:

☞ **If necessary, open the window *Local Disc Properties* 𝒮𝒞⁴⁰**

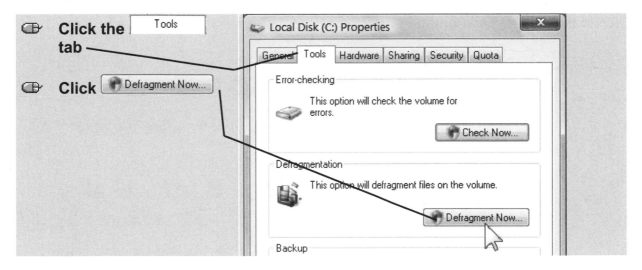

☞ **Click the** `Tools` **tab**

☞ **Click** `🛡 Defragment Now...`

Your screen goes dark and you need to give your permission to continue.

☞ **Click** `Continue` **in the window *User Account Control***

You see the window *Disk Defragmenter*:

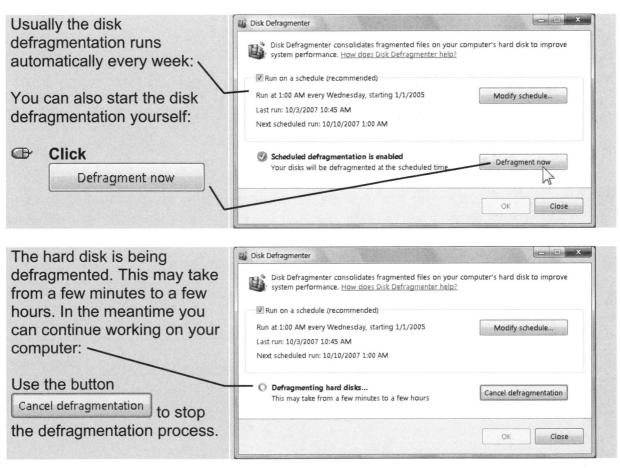

Usually the disk defragmentation runs automatically every week:

You can also start the disk defragmentation yourself:

☞ **Click** `Defragment now`

The hard disk is being defragmented. This may take from a few minutes to a few hours. In the meantime you can continue working on your computer:

Use the button `Cancel defragmentation` to stop the defragmentation process.

When the disk defragmentation has completed, you can close the window:

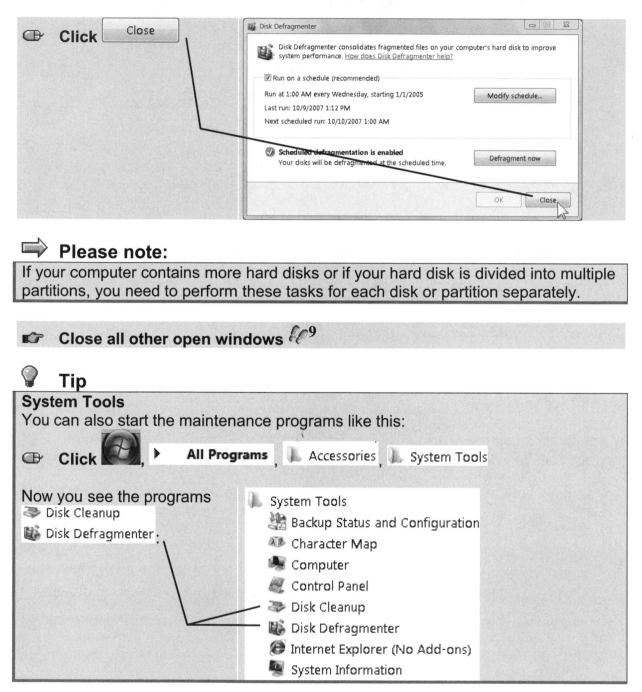

⇨ Please note:

If your computer contains more hard disks or if your hard disk is divided into multiple partitions, you need to perform these tasks for each disk or partition separately.

☞ **Close all other open windows** ℓℓ⁹

💡 Tip

System Tools

You can also start the maintenance programs like this:

⊞ **Click** , ▶ **All Programs** , 📁 Accessories , 📁 System Tools

7.29 Common Problems

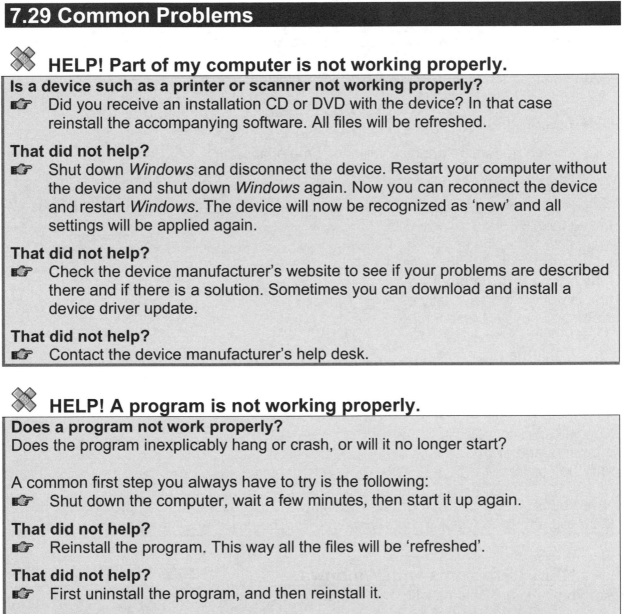

HELP! Part of my computer is not working properly.

Is a device such as a printer or scanner not working properly?

☞ Did you receive an installation CD or DVD with the device? In that case reinstall the accompanying software. All files will be refreshed.

That did not help?

☞ Shut down *Windows* and disconnect the device. Restart your computer without the device and shut down *Windows* again. Now you can reconnect the device and restart *Windows*. The device will now be recognized as 'new' and all settings will be applied again.

That did not help?

☞ Check the device manufacturer's website to see if your problems are described there and if there is a solution. Sometimes you can download and install a device driver update.

That did not help?

☞ Contact the device manufacturer's help desk.

HELP! A program is not working properly.

Does a program not work properly?
Does the program inexplicably hang or crash, or will it no longer start?

A common first step you always have to try is the following:
☞ Shut down the computer, wait a few minutes, then start it up again.

That did not help?

☞ Reinstall the program. This way all the files will be 'refreshed'.

That did not help?

☞ First uninstall the program, and then reinstall it.

That did not help?

☞ Check the software manufacturer's website to see if your problems are described there and if there is a solution. Sometimes you can download and install a software update or patch.

That did not help?

☞ Contact the software manufacturer's help desk (by telephone or e-mail). It is important that you can describe the specific problem. If you contact them by phone, make sure you are sitting at your computer and that the computer is on. That way you can immediately try out the solution while you have them on the line.

HELP! One of my programs hangs.

Does one of your programs suddenly stop working? Or does it run wild and no longer responds to your commands?
You can close it using the following 'emergency' procedure:

Simultaneously press the keys Ctrl , Alt **and** Delete

Your screen goes blue and you will see some options.

Click *Start Task Manager*

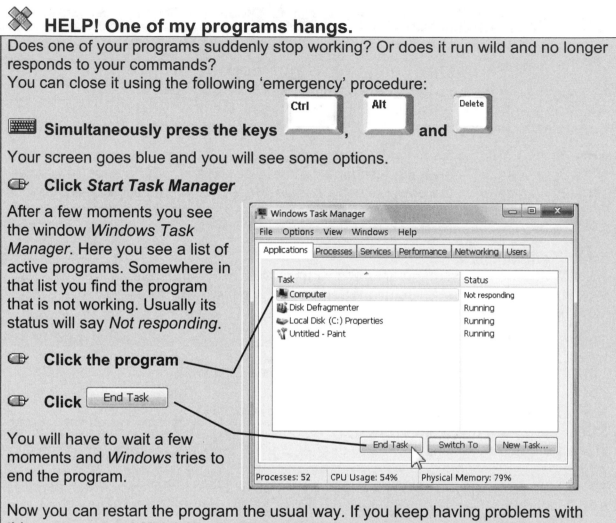

After a few moments you see the window *Windows Task Manager*. Here you see a list of active programs. Somewhere in that list you find the program that is not working. Usually its status will say *Not responding*.

Click the program

Click End Task

You will have to wait a few moments and *Windows* tries to end the program.

Now you can restart the program the usual way. If you keep having problems with this program, read *Help! A program is not working properly* on the previous page.

HELP! Problems with Windows.

Are you having problems with one or more components of Windows?

Take a look at the *Microsoft* website: www.microsoft.com This website contains an extensive support section.

You can search these pages in different ways to find a solution for your problems.

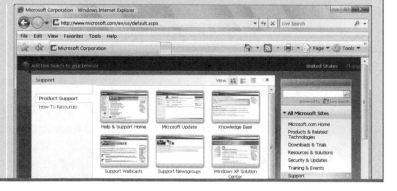

7.30 Background Information

Glossary

Administrator account	User account that lets you make changes that will affect other users. Administrators can change security settings, install software and hardware, and access all files on the computer. Administrators can also make changes to other user accounts.
Adobe Reader	Program you can use to view PDF files.
Antivirus program	Program you can use to scan your computer for viruses. Found viruses are removed if possible.
Backup	A backup is a copy of files, programs and/or settings. Preferably, a backup is stored in a separate location from the original. You can have multiple backups of a file if you want to keep track of changes.
Complete PC Backup	Backup image, which contains copies of your programs, system settings, and files. The backup image is stored in a separate location from the original programs, settings, and files. You can use this backup image to restore the contents of your computer if your hard disk or entire computer ever stops working. *Windows Complete PC Backup* is not included in *Windows Vista Home Basic* and *Windows Vista Home Premium*.
Complete scan	Option in antivirus or antispyware program to scan all files and folders on your computer.
Custom scan	Option in antivirus or antispyware program to scan only the folders you specify yourself.
Disk Cleanup	Tool you can use to clean up unnecessary files on the hard disk and free disk space.
Disk Defragmenter	Tool that rearranges the data on your hard disk and puts fragmented files back together so your computer can run more efficiently.

- Continue reading on the next page -

Firewall	Software or hardware that checks data traffic coming from the Internet or a network to your computer and vice versa, and then either blocks or allows it, depending on your firewall settings. A firewall is not an antivirus program since the contents of the data traffic are not checked for viruses.
Full backup	Backup of user files, like documents, images, music et cetera. Programs and *Windows Vista* files are not copied when a full backup is created. Also refer to: *Complete PC Backup*.
Guest account	An account for a user who does not have a permanent account on your computer. With a *Guest* account users can access the computer, but not your personal files. Users with a *Guest* account cannot install programs or hardware, change settings or create a password.
Incremental backup	Additional backup that only stores files that were added or changed since the last full or incremental backup.
Malware	Computer program designed to deliberately harm your computer. Viruses, worms and Trojan horses are examples of these harmful programs.
NTFS	A file system used by a computer to organize files on the hard disk. If you install a new hard disk, it must be partitioned and formatted using a file system before you can store files or data on this disk. In *Windows Vista* you can choose between the file systems NTFS and FAT32.
Partition	Part of a computer hard disk that functions like a separate disk. Separate, formatted partitions share your computer's memory and storage space. Partitions allow you to install and use more than one operating system on the computer.
Password	A secret string of characters that lets users log on to a computer and access files, programs, and other resources. Passwords help ensure that unauthorized users do not access the computer.
Password hint	Hint to help you remember your password that appears when you type the wrong password.
Password reset disk	Use this to set a new password when you have forgotten your old password. Although the name indicates otherwise, you can also create a password reset disk on a USB stick.

- Continue reading on the next page -

PDF file	The abbreviation PDF stands for *Portable Document File*. This file format is often used for information you can download from websites of businesses or institutions.
Quick scan	Option in antivirus or antispyware program to only scan those locations where malware is most likely to be found.
Restore point	A representation of a stored state of your computer's system files. Restore points are created by *System Restore* at specific intervals and when *System Restore* detects the beginning of a change to your computer. Also, you can create a restore point manually at any time.
Security Center	Here the current security status of your computer is displayed, and you are advised what actions you can take to protect your computer even better.
Setup program	Also called *installation program*: utility tool that installs a software program on your computer.
Spyware	Computer program that can display advertisements (such as pop-up ads), collect information about your surfing behavior and send the information to the software's creator.
Standard user account	This type of account lets you use most of the capabilities of the computer, but permission from an administrator is required if you want to make changes that affect other users or the security of the computer.
System Restore	*System Restore* helps you to restore your computer's system files to an earlier point in time using a restore point. It is a way to undo system changes to your computer without affecting your personal files, such as e-mail, documents, or photos.
System Tools	Collection of tools you can use to perform maintenance on your computer or to improve the performance of your computer.
Trojan horse	Unwanted software that comes with an innocent program installed by the user. The program itself appears to be harmless, but is actually harmful when executed.
User account	A user account is a collection of information that tells *Windows* what files and folders you can access, what changes you can make to the computer, and your personal preferences, such as your desktop background or color theme. User accounts make it possible that you can share a computer with several people, but still have your own files and settings.

- Continue reading on the next page-

User Account Control	Feature in *Windows* that can help prevent unauthorized changes to your computer. Before performing actions that could potentially affect your computer's operation or change settings that affect other users, you are asked for your permission or a password. The screen goes dark when that happens. You are asked for permission to continue (if you are logged in as administrator) or you are asked to enter the administrator password (if you are logged in as standard user).
Virus	A program that attempts to spread from computer to computer and either causes damage (by erasing or corrupting data) or annoys users (by displaying messages or changing the information displayed on the screen).
Windows Defender	Antispyware program that is packaged with *Windows Vista*.
Windows Live OneCare	*Microsoft* program you can use for the complete protection of your computer. The program not only protects your computer against viruses, but also contains a firewall and spyware protection.
Windows Update	System that checks if you are using the most recent version of *Windows Vista*. Available updates can be downloaded and installed automatically.
Worm	Malware in the form of a self-replication program. A typical worm sends out copies of itself to everyone in your *Contacts* folder and then does the same thing on the recipients' computers. This creates a domino effect that could cause your computer or a web or network server to stop responding.

Source: Windows Help and Support

Store your backups in a safe place
You can also lose your data as a result of fire or theft. Always keep one set of backup discs outside your own home or office when you keep important data on your computer. Keep in mind that insurance companies will most likely not compensate the loss of computer data if you keep the backups in the same building as the computer itself.
Remember it is also important to renew your backup files regularly.

Grandfather - father - son backups

Even if you create backups on a regular basis things can go wrong. You can end up being unable to use your original data as well as your backup. For example when a malfunction occurs during the backup process. Or when you infect the backup with a virus that has not yet been discovered on your computer. Then both your original files as well as the backup will be infected.

To warrant the reliability of your backups, you can save different generations of backups on rewritable discs. This is done as follows:

- You start by making a full backup you call the *grandfather*.

- Sometime later, for example a week or a month, you create another full backup on a new set of discs you call the *father*. You also keep the *grandfather*.

- The next time you create a new full backup you call the *son*. You also keep the *grandfather* and *father*.

- Then the next time you create a full backup on the *grandfather* discs, then on the *father* discs and finally on the *son* discs.

When something goes wrong during the backup process, or the backup contains an error or a virus, you can always go back two generations. This increases the chance of having a reliable backup. Do not make the interval between the generations too short, for example use intervals of a week or a month. In between these full backups you create the regular incremental backups.

Creating a backup or copying files yourself

You can secure your data by creating backups or by copying files to another disc yourself. What is best in your situation depends on the type of data and the things you want to do with the data:

- If you want to create a safety copy of (all) your data that you can restore to your computer if necessary, it is best to create a backup. A backup file is always compressed and takes up less space.
  A compressed backup CD or DVD is not always readable on another computer, especially when that computer works with another version of *Windows*.

- If you want to copy data so you can use it on another computer, it is best to copy it to a separate CD, DVD or external hard disk. Copied files can more easily be used by another PC.

- If you want to put a couple of files or folders on a disc, you need to collect these files yourself and copy them to a CD or DVD.

- It is best to copy data you want to keep for a longer time, like your bookkeeping or important documents, to a separate CD or DVD. That way these files are easily accessible on any computer you might want to use.

To summarize: you create backups for security reasons and to ensure the continuity of your work processes. After a crash you can use the backup file to quickly restore your files and settings and get back to work after that.

If you want to use the files for activities other than restoring your computer (share, show, archive, etcetera) it is better to burn a separate CD or DVD.

Best by date

Keep in mind that CDs and DVDs have a 'best by' date: they cannot be kept forever. It is advisable to transfer the data to another medium every four or five years. Also keep in mind that external hard disks do not last forever.

Backups, recovery CD or restore points?
Creating backups and creating recovery points are both methods to make sure you can keep working after something has gone wrong. In some cases you need the backup; in other cases you use *System Restore* or your recovery CD.

In the next summary you can read which one to use in different situations:

- In case you have lost (or are unable to use) part of your personal files (documents, photos, music, etcetera), you can restore these files using your (full or incremental) backup. During the restore process you can choose which files you want to restore.

- When a program does not work properly or no longer works properly, you have to reinstall the program from the original discs or download it again from the Internet. This is also a reason not to sell or give a program you bought to another person. It is best to remove the program completely using the *Control Panel* before you reinstall it.

- If your computer functions, but you get error messages from *Windows Vista*, then you can use *System Restore* to try to restore your system to a point in time when *Windows Vista* still worked properly. Usually, this will be right before the moment you installed a new program or device, or before a *Windows Vista* update. Also read the tip in *section 7.31 Tips* about going back to the *Last Known Good Configuration*.

- If your computer does not function at all, or shows very serious problems, you can restore your complete PC backup (recovery CD or image). If you do this, you will lose all your files and data and also the programs you installed. Then you need the original program discs to reinstall the programs and the full backup to restore your personal files. Very often you will need additional CDs with drivers or other programs to be able to install the devices you use with your computer, like a printer or a modem.

Make sure to keep your recovery CD, backups and original program discs in a safe place, so you can find them easily when you need them.

7.31 Tips

Tip

Last Known Good Configuration

Last Known Good Configuration is a *Windows Vista* startup option that uses the most recent system settings that worked correctly. Every time you turn your computer off and *Windows Vista* shuts down successfully, important system settings are saved in the registry. You can use those settings to start your computer if a problem occurs. For example, if a new driver for your graphics card is causing problems, or an incorrect registry setting is preventing *Windows Vista* from starting correctly, you can restart your computer using *Last Known Good Configuration*.

Follow these steps:

☞ **Remove all diskettes, CDs and DVDs from the computer**

☞ **Click**

☞ **Click** **next to** **and click** Restart **in the menu that appears**

Do one of the following:

1. If your computer has a single operating system installed, press the F8 key repeatedly as your computer restarts. You need to press F8 before the *Windows* logo appears. If the *Windows* logo appears, you will need to try again by waiting until the *Windows* logo prompt appears, and then shutting down and restarting your computer.
    In the *Advanced Boot Options* screen, use the arrow keys to highlight *Last Known Good Configuration*, and then press the Enter key.

2. If your computer has more than one operating system, use the arrow keys to highlight the operating system you want to start, and then press F8.
    In the *Advanced Boot Options* screen, use the arrow keys to highlight *Last Known Good Configuration*, and then press the Enter key.

Windows Vista will then resume starting normally.

Last Known Good Configuration only affects system settings. It does not change your e-mail, photos, or other personal data on your computer. It will not help you recover a deleted file or a corrupted driver. To do that, you need to have previously backed up the data, or you need to reinstall the driver from the original source.

Source: Windows Help and Support

Appendix A. Basic Tasks Excel

Here is a quick overview of how to perform various basic tasks in *Microsoft Excel*.

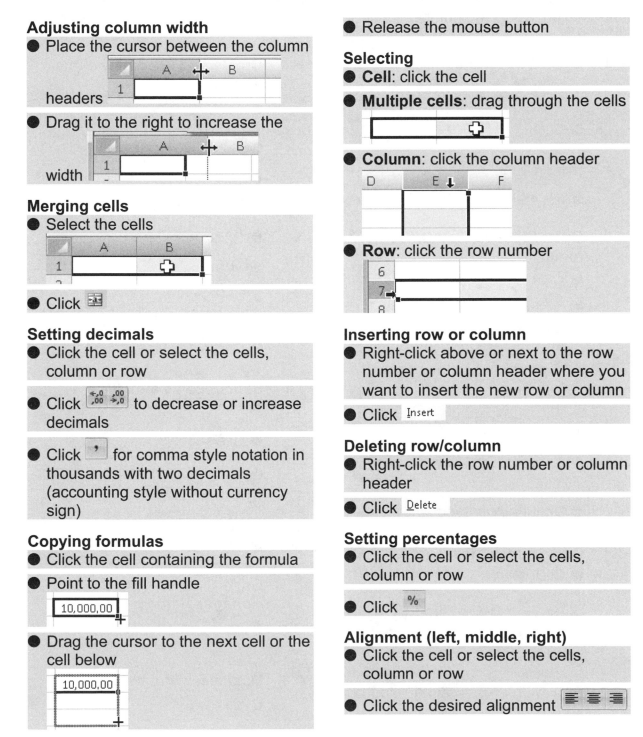

Adjusting column width
● Place the cursor between the column headers
● Drag it to the right to increase the width

Merging cells
● Select the cells
● Click ⊞

Setting decimals
● Click the cell or select the cells, column or row
● Click ⌐⌐ to decrease or increase decimals
● Click ⌐ for comma style notation in thousands with two decimals (accounting style without currency sign)

Copying formulas
● Click the cell containing the formula
● Point to the fill handle
  `10,000,00`
● Drag the cursor to the next cell or the cell below
  `10,000,00`

● Release the mouse button

Selecting
● **Cell**: click the cell
● **Multiple cells**: drag through the cells
● **Column**: click the column header
● **Row**: click the row number

Inserting row or column
● Right-click above or next to the row number or column header where you want to insert the new row or column
● Click Insert

Deleting row/column
● Right-click the row number or column header
● Click Delete

Setting percentages
● Click the cell or select the cells, column or row
● Click %

Alignment (left, middle, right)
● Click the cell or select the cells, column or row
● Click the desired alignment

Appendix B. How Do I Do That Again?

In this book some actions are marked with footsteps: 🐾 1
Find the corresponding number in the appendix below to see how to do something.

🐾 1 **Open a program**
- Click [start icon]
- Click ▶ All Programs
- Click Microsoft Office
- Click the program

🐾 2 **Open *Practice files Office 2007* folder**
- Click Documents
- Double-click
  Practice files Office 2007

🐾 3 **Add photo to business card**
- Click [photo icon]
- Go to the folder containing the image
- Double-click the image

🐾 4 **Close e-mail message**
- Click X
- Click Yes to save the message

Or:
- Click No to delete the message

🐾 5 **Create and send new e-mail message**
- Click ✉ Mail
- Click 🖃 New

Or:
- Click ▾ next to 🖃 New
- Click Mail Message

Send:
- Click [Send button]

🐾 6 **Send/receive e-mail**
- Click Tools
- Click Send/Receive
- Click Send/Receive All

Or:
- Press F9

🐾 7 **Go to the *Business Contact Manager Home* page**
- Click 🏠 Business Contact Manager Home

🐾 8 **Maximize window**
- Click [maximize icon]

9 Close window or program

Close program:
- Click `X`

Save changes:
- Click `Yes`

Do not save changes:
- Click `No`

Or:
- Click (Office button)

- Click `Close`

Save changes:
- Click `Yes`

Do not save changes:
- Click `No`

10 Save e-mail as a template

- Click (Office button)

- Click `Save As`

- Click `Save As`

- Type the file name next to `File name:`

- Click next to `Save as type:`

- Click `Outlook Template`

- Click `Save`

11 Open/close *Developer* tab

- Click (Office button)

- Click `Word Options`

- Click
  - ☐ Show Developer tab in the Ribbon

12 Open file from the *Practice files Office 2007* folder

- Click `Documents`

- Double-click
  - `Practice files Office 2007`

- Double-click the file

13 Select paragraph

- Click paragraph three times

14 Open existing template

- Click (Office button)

- Click `New`

- Click `My templates...`

- Double-click the template

15 Use drop-down list in templates

- Click the control

- Click `▼`

- Click your selection

16 Insert date in template

- Click the date control

- Click `▼`

- Click the date or `Today`

17 Save and close new document

- Click 🔲
- Click 📁 Close
- Click Yes
- Go to the folder where you want to save the file
- Type the name
- Click Save

18 Save new document and keep it opened

- Click 🔲
- Click 💾 Save
- Go to the folder where you want to save the file
- Type the name
- Click Save

19 Open new document

- Click 🔲
- Click 📄 New
- Click Create

20 Open Print Preview

- Click 🔲
- Click 🖨 Print

- Click Print Preview

21 Set decimals

- Select the cells, columns or rows
- Click to increase decimals

Or:

- Click to decrease decimals

22 Select cells, columns or rows

- Drag through the cells to select them

Or:

- Click the column header to select a column

Or:

- Click the row number to select a row

23 Switch to another worksheet

- Click the worksheet you want to open at the bottom of the page

Sheet1 / Sheet2 / Sheet3

24 Insert image

- Go to the folder that contains the image
- Double-click the file

25 Create text box

- Place the mouse pointer at the spot where an upper corner of the text box should appear

+

● Drag to the opposite lower

corner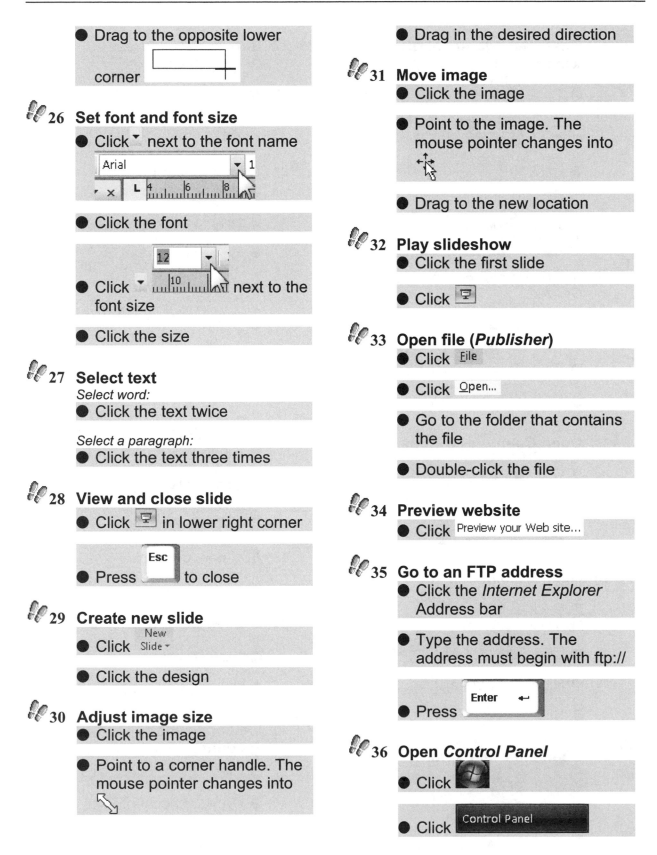

26 Set font and font size
● Click ˅ next to the font name

● Click the font

● Click ˅ next to the font size

● Click the size

27 Select text
Select word:
● Click the text twice

Select a paragraph:
● Click the text three times

28 View and close slide
● Click in lower right corner

● Press **Esc** to close

29 Create new slide
● Click **New Slide ˅**

● Click the design

30 Adjust image size
● Click the image

● Point to a corner handle. The mouse pointer changes into

● Drag in the desired direction

31 Move image
● Click the image

● Point to the image. The mouse pointer changes into

● Drag to the new location

32 Play slideshow
● Click the first slide

● Click

33 Open file (*Publisher*)
● Click **File**

● Click **Open...**

● Go to the folder that contains the file

● Double-click the file

34 Preview website
● Click **Preview your Web site...**

35 Go to an FTP address
● Click the *Internet Explorer* Address bar

● Type the address. The address must begin with ftp://

● Press **Enter ↵**

36 Open *Control Panel*
● Click

● Click **Control Panel**

𝄤 37 Open *Manage Accounts* window

● Click ⊞

● Click Control Panel

● Click
  🛡 Add or remove user accounts

● Click Continue

𝄤 38 Open *Backup and Restore Center*

● Click ⊞

● Click Control Panel

● Click Back up your computer

𝄤 39 Open *Computer* window

● Click ⊞

● Click Computer

𝄤 40 Open *Local Disk Properties*

● Click ⊞

● Click Computer

● Right-click the disk

● Click Properties

𝄤 41 Open *Internet Explorer*

● Click ⊞

● Click Internet
  Internet Explorer

𝄤 42 Surf to web address

● Click the Address bar

● Type the web address, for example: www.visualsteps.com

𝄤 43 Create a category

● Right-click a contact

● Click Categorize

● Click All Categories...

● Click a category

● Click Rename

● Type the name of the category

● Click OK

𝄤 44 Add contact to category

● Right-click the contact

● Click Categorize

● Click the category

𝄤 45 Add new contact
In the Contacts window:

● Click 🔖 Nieuw ▾

● Enter the information

● Click ✕

● Save the contact information

𝄤 46 Link opportunity or project to account

● Click Link To...

● Click the account

● Click Link To ->

● Click OK

47 Save a document with another name

● Click

● Click Save As

● Type the new file name next to File name:

● Click Save

48 Print document

● Click

● Click Print ▶

● Select the right printer settings

● Click OK

49 Save existing docment

● Click

50 Save website

● Click File

● Click Save

● Type the file name next to File name:

● Click Save

51 Open document in *Word*

● Click

● Click Open

● Select the file

● Click Open ▼

Appendix C. Index